H55 £17.50

Matthias Buschkühl

Great Britain
and the Holy See
1746-1870

MATTHIAS BUSCHKÜHL

Great Britain and the Holy See
1746-1870

IRISH ACADEMIC PRESS

621001

This book was typeset by
Datamove Limited,
31 Wicklow Street, Dublin 2 and
printed in the Republic of Ireland
for Irish Academic Press Limited,
Kill Lane, Blackrock, Co. Dublin.

© Matthias Buschkühl 1982

ISBN 0 7165 0290 9

 British Library Cataloguing in Publication Data

Buschkühl, Matthias
   Great Britain and the Holy See 1760-1870.
   1. Great Britain—Foreign relations—Papal States
   2. Papal States—Foreign relations—Great Britain
   I. Title
   327.41045'6   DA566.7

   ISBN 0-7165-0290-9

Printed by Merrion Printing Services

For
LUDWIG BORINSKI

CONTENTS

List of illustrations   8
Preface   9
Abbreviations   11
British and Papal Agents in London and at the
   Holy See   13
Introduction   15

I From Culloden to the French Revolution   17

II Facing the Common Enemy   25

III The Papal States and the Irish Veto   45
  1 The Napoleonic Years   45
  2 The Last Years of Pope Pius VII and Cardinal
     Consalvi 1815–1823   56

IV Catholic Emancipation and Repeal   64
  1 Leo XII and Pius VIII, 1823–1830   64
  2 Gregory XVI, 1831–1846   71

V 'The soothing influence of religion' and
     'papal aggression'   83
  1 The Minto mission   83
  2 The Years of Estrangement, 1850–1858   88

VI Odo Russell in Rome   96
  1 Rapproachement, 1858–1862   96
  2 The American Civil War; the *Syllabus*; and
     Quanta Cura: 1862–1865   99
  3 Manning, Archbishop of Westminster 1865   107

VII The Fenians and the Garibaldini   111
  1 Russell and Clarendon   111
  2 The Conservatives and Disraeli   112

VIII England and Papal Infallibility prior to
     Vatican I   126
  1 Manning and his friends   127
  2 Döllinger and Acton   133
  3 The Catholic Church in English Literature and
     the Press   146
  4 The Papal Decree condemning Fenianism 149

IX Britain and Vatican I   152
    1 The First Vatican Council   152
    2 The Aftermath   167
    Conclusion: A Survey of Anglo-Papal
        Relations 1870–1982   171
    Appendix: Documents   177
    Notes   214
    Bibliography   241
    Index   256

ILLUSTRATIONS

Illustrations

1. Pope Benedict XIV
2. Pope Clement XIV
3. Pope Pius VII
4. Cardinal Consalvi
5. Pope Leo XII
6. Pope Pius IX
7. Map of Italy in 1858
8. Cardinal Antonelli
9. Cardinal Wiseman
10. Cardinal Manning
11. Odo Russell, Baron Ampthill
12. Lord Acton
13. Ignaz von Dollinger

Preface

My first thanks are due to my friend Ciaran Ryan, who corrected the English of my manuscript and typed it, which was not an easy task as English is not my native language. Without his help this book could never have appeared, and it is in a way his as well as mine. I also thank my publisher Michael Adams for his care, patience and advice. Professor Ludwig Borinski of Hamburg University first suggested to me the subject and gave me valuable advice during my research; as a token of my gratitude for this and all I owe him I have dedicated this book to him. Miss Joan Gibbs, archivist and librarian (Palaeography Room) of the University of London Library always took an interest in my research, sent me photocopies and introduced me to sources and people.

Transcripts of Crown copyright records in the Public Record Office appear by permission of the Controller of H.M. Stationary Office. I thank the Duke of Norfolk for permission to quote from the Arundel papers; the late Earl Fitzwilliam as owner and the Northamptonshire Record Office as custodian, to quote from the Fitzwilliam (Milton) manuscripts; the Earl of Clarendon as owner and the Bodleian Library as custodian, to quote from the Clarendon papers; Lady Anne Bentinck as owner and the University of Nottingham as custodian, to quote from the Bentinck papers; Sir William Gladstone, Bt., to quote from the letters of W.E. Gladstone; and the Niedersächsisches Hauptstaatsarchiv and the British Library to quote from manuscripts in their possession and custody. I also thank the archivists and librarians of the following libraries for their kindness and help: Trinity College Library Dublin, University College Dublin Library, University of Vienna Library, Hamburg State and University Library, National Library of Ireland, Austrian National Library, Catholic Central Libraries of Dublin and London, Northelbian Church Library, Commerce Library of the Chamber of Commerce Hamburg, and State Library of Prussian Cultural Resources Berlin.

After five years of research I started to write this book in Cologne at the time of Pope John Paul II's visit; I continued it in Eichstätt and Dublin, where the Pope was in 1979 – and finished it in Edinburgh, where Pope John Paul will come in 1982.

Eichstätt (Bavaria), at the Catholic University,
March 1982

Matthias Buschkühl

Abbreviations

A	Lord Acton
AA	Auswärtiges Amt
A.D.B.	*Allgemeine Deutsche Biographie*
Add MSS	Additional Manuscripts
A.H.C.	Annuarium Historiae Conciliorum
A.H.P	*Archivum Historiae Pontificiae*
A.Mrh.KG.	*Archiv für mittelrheinische Kirchengeschichte*
A.Pps.	Ampthill Papers, P.R.O., Kew
Arch. Vat.	Archivio Vaticano
A.Z.	*Allgemeine Zeitung*
B	Lord Burghersh
BM	British Museum (British Library), London
BN	Bilbiothèque Nationale, Paris
B.Pps.	Bentinck Papers, University of Nottingham Library
Ch.H.	*Church History*
C.H.R.	*Catholic Historical Review*
Civ.Catt.	*Civilta cattolica*
Cl.	Lord Clarendon
Cl.Pps.	Clarendon Papers, Bodleian Library, Oxford
Coll.Lac.	Collectio Lacensis
D	Döllinger
D.A.B.	*Dictionary of American Biography*
D.B.F.	*Dictionnaire de biographie francaise*
D.B.I.	*Dizionario biografico degli Italiani*
D.D.A.	Dublin Diocesan Archives
D.H.G.E.	*Dictionnaire d'histoire et de géographie ecclésiastique*
D.N.B.	*Dictionary of National Biography*
D.R.	*Downside Review*
Dublin R.	*Dublin Review*
D.Z.A.	Deutsche Zentralarchiv II, Merseburg
f.	folio
F.MSS,N.	Fitzwilliam (Milton) Manuscripts, Northamptonshire Record Office
F.MSS,Sh.	Fitzwilliam Manuscripts, Sheffield City Libraries
F.O.	Foreign office
Gl.	Gladstone
Gl.Pps.	Gladstone Papers, British Library
H	Sir John Cox Hippisley

11

Abbreviations

H.Corr.	Hippisley Correspondence
H.H.St.A.	Haus-, Hof-und Staatsarchiv, Vienna
Hist.MSS	
Comm.	Historical Manuscripts Commission
H.J.	*Historisches Jahrbuch der Görresgesellschaft*
H.N.Z.	*Hamburgische Neue Zeitung*
H.O.	Home Office
H.P.Bl.	*Historisch-politische Blätter für das katholische Deutschland*
I.E.R.	*Irish Ecclesiastical Record*
I.H.S.	*Irish Historical Studies*
I.L.N.	*Illustrated London News*
Ing.	Inghilterra
J.E.H.	*Journal of Ecclesiastical History*
K.M.H.	Kestner Museum, Hanover
L.Th.K.	*Lexikon für Theologie und Kirche*
M.A.E.	Archivio storico del Ministerio degli Affari Esteri, Rome
M.E.	*Merry England*
M.H.P.	*Miscellanea historiae pontificiae*
M.Pps.	Minto Papers, N.L.S., Edinburgh
N.A.F.	Nouvelles acquisitions francaises
N.A.R.	*North American Review*
N.D.B.	*Neue Deutsche Biographie*
N.H.A.H.	Niedersächsisches Haupstaatsarchiv, Hanover
N.L.S.	National Library of Scotland
O.R.	Odo Russell
P	Lord Palmerston
P.A.	Politisches Archiv
P.Pps.	Palmerston Papers
priv.	private
P.R.O.	Public Record Office, Kew
Q.R.	*Quarterly Review*
R	Earl (John) Russell
R.Q.	*Römische Quartalschrift für christliche Altertumskunde und Kirchengeschichte*
Ser.Pol.	Serie Politica
St.G.Z.	*Staats-und Gelehrte Zeitung des Hamburgischen unpartheyischen Correspondenten*
W	William Windham
West.Pps.	Westmoreland Papers, Cuba
W.Pps.	Windham Papers, British Library

12

British and Papal Agents
in London and at the Holy See

AGENTS REPRESENTING BRITISH INTERESTS AT THE HOLY SEE

February 1772	William Duke of Gloucester (1743–1805), brother of George III
1792–96	Sir John Cox Hippisley (1748–1825): cf. *D.N.B.*, vol.9, p.904
1793	Augustus Frederick (1773–1843), in 1801 created Duke of Sussex, sixth son of George III
April/May 1795	Frederick North
1799 & April–October 1814	Robert Fagan, painter, consul at Naples
(1796–1806	Thomas Jackson, minister to the King of Sardinia)
1815	[while Pius VII was in Genoa] Lord William Cavendish Bentinck (1774–1839: *D.N.B.*, vol.2, pp.292–3)
15 April 1817–16 March 1819	Baron Friedrich von Ompteda (1772–1819), minister of the kingdom of Hanover in Rome
1 July 1819–1825	[in absence of Burghersh] Franz von Reden (1754–1831): *A.D.B.*, vol.17, pp.507–8; minister of the kingdom of Hanover in Rome
13 April 1825–1849	[in absence of British agent] August Kestner (1777–1853): *N.D.B.*, vol.11, pp.553–4; chargé d'affaires of the kingdom of Hanover in Rome
1823–30	John Fane Lord Burghersh (1784–1879), from 1841 earl of Westmoreland, since 1814 British minister to the grand duchy of Tuscany, residing in Florence
2 April–June 1831	Sir Brook Taylor (1776–1846)
Feb.–21 August 1832	George Hamilton Seymour (1797–1880) British minister to the grand duchy of Tuscany
22 August 1832–12 May 1844	Thomas Aubin (died 12 May 1844 in Rome), attached to legation in Florence
	At the same time contacts via *Vienna*: British Ambassador there Sir Robert Gordon (1791–1847: D.N.B., vol.7, pp.228–9), brother of foreign secretary 4th earl of Aberdeen (1784–1860); nuncio there Altieri (1805–67): *D.B.I.*, vol.2, pp.559–60; Weber, *Kardinäle*, vol.I, pp.277–8, vol.2, pp.768–9)
September 1844–1853	William Bernard 12th Baron Petre (1817–84), a Catholic (Artz, *Newman-Lexikon*, p.834), attached to legation in Florence

March 1847	via *Vienna*, British ambassador there Ponsonby (1770– 1855) (*D.N.B.*, vol.16, pp.86–7), Nuncio Viale Prelà (1798–1860) (*L.Th.K.*, 2nd ed., vol.10, p.761; Weber, *Kardinäle*, vol.2, pp.527–8)
4 November 1847 –3 February 1848	Gilbert Elliot earl of Minto (1782–1859) (cf. *D.N.B.* vol.6, pp.675–6), brother-in-law of Lord John Russell (1792–1878)
1852	Sir Henry Lytton Bulwer (1801–72), British minister to the grand duchy of Tuscany in Florence
1853–58	Richard Bickerton Lord Lyons (1817–87), became catholic on his deathbed; attached to legation in Florence
1858–70	Odo Russell (1829–84), later 1st Baron Ampthill, nephew of Lord Russell and son-in-law of the earl of Clarendon (1800–70)
1870–74	Sir Harry Samuel Cumming Clarke Jervoise (1813–1911)

PAPAL AGENTS IN LONDON

June 1772	Mgr Giovanni Battista Caprara–Montecuccoli (1733–1810), nuncio in Cologne (*D.B.I.*, vol.19, pp.180–86)
13 November 1793–12 December 1801	Mgr. (since 23 Feb. 1801 Cardinal) Charles Erskine (1739–1811): *D.H.G.E.*, vol.15, pp.819–20
9 June–7 July 1814	Cardinal Secretary of State Ercole Marchese Consalvi (1757–1824) (*L.Th.K.*, 2nd ed., vol.3, pp.42–3)
October 1830– September 1831	Mgr Capaccini (1784–1845) internuncio to the Low Countries (*D.B.I.*, vol.18, pp.372–4)

Introduction

POPE JOHN Paul's visit to Britain has brought Anglo-papal relations into the focus of interest, yet Britain's relations with the Holy See have not generally claimed such attention: for example, Odo Russell, British agent to the Holy See (1858-70), ordered that all his correspondence be destroyed after his death;[1] it was only in 1967 that copies of his letters came to light.[2] In Norbert Miko's article on diplomatic relations between England and the Vatican in the nineteenth century[3] there is a curious absence of detail during the pontificate of Pius IX. When Noël Blakiston, then principal assistant keeper of the Public Record Office, published extracts from Odo Russell's despatches in 1962, he selected only about a quarter of them for reasons he explained in his introduction: 'The selection has been made with a view primarily to the light that the despatches throw upon Italian history'.[4] The aspect for which they are sources in the first place — Britain's intentions in her relations with the Holy See — was not taken as his principle of selection; Blakiston himself points this out: '. . . much has been omitted even with regard to some subjects such as . . . Fenianism . . .'.[5] Those sections omitted from the despatches and indicated by ellipses in Blakiston's work are often very revealing: Victor Conzemius has published many of these excised passages in the footnotes of his edition of the correspondence of Lord Acton and Döllinger;[6] yet these very footnotes were criticised as being too voluminous. It is worth noting that Frederico Curato's *Gran Bretagna e Italia nei documenti della Missione Minto*,[7] in which the documents are printed in the original English, and Frederick Cwiekowski's *The English Bishops and the First Vatican Council*,[8] in which additional documents are printed, have been almost totally disregarded. Gary Mooney has recently written an article entitled 'British Diplomatic Relations with the Holy See, 1793-1830';[9] while Patrick O'Donoghue and John F. Broderick have studied Irish aspects of these relations in the late eighteenth and early nineteenth centuries.[10] Much is revealed about Anglo-papal relations at this time by Disraeli's novel *Lothair* in which it becomes apparent that the Vatican sought British help in maintaining its temporal power over the church states, while Britain required papal assistance to uphold her rule over Ireland.[11] In 1980 Massimo de Leonardis published a book on England and the Roman question 1859-1870, in which he translated into Italian all documents cited.[12] This present study is, however, the first comprehensive monograph on Anglo-papal relations from the final defeat of the catholic Stuarts in 1746 to the end of papal temporal power in 1870. Throughout this period Anglo-papal relations were maintained at an unofficial level. The act of 1563 (5 Eliz., C.1, sect. 2) could be interpreted as attempting to prohibit any formal communications with the Roman pontiff; official relations had in fact ceased in 1558. In 1621-3 a catholic named George Gage acted as Roman agent of James I, a move that was inspired by the marriage to a catholic of James's son, the future Charles I. In 1653 Sir Robert Douglas, a catholic scotsman, acted as Roman agent of Queen Henrietta Maria and to a certain extent (unofficially) of Charles I. On Douglas's suggestion the pope sent an agent, the Oratorian Gregorio Panzani, to London. As official agent to the queen Panzani was succeeded by a Scotsman, George Conn, in 1636. Conn in his turn was succeeded by another Scot, Sir William Hamilton. The puritan revolution brought these diplomatic relations to an end. After a brief interlude during the reign of James II when Lord Castlemain acted as the king's envoy to Rome in 1687, anglo-papal relations ceased for some considerable time due to the 1688 revolution.[13]

CHAPTER I

From Culloden to the French Revolution

THE DEFEAT of the Jacobites at Culloden removed any threat of the catholic Stuarts returning to power, just as the great famine a hundred years later ended any threat that the catholic Irish, together with the Oxford Movement converts, might bring about a catholic majority in the population of the United Kingdom. In the rising of 1745 Prince Charles Edward had attempted to assert his family's claim to the Scottish and English throne but it ended in disaster for the Stuarts and their followers. As a result the authorities in England could now afford a more relaxed attitude towards catholicism,[1] especially as Irish catholics had abstained from participating in the rising. When the Irish parliament, which was the representative body of the protestant ascendancy of the time, attempted to pass a new penal law against catholics it was prevented from doing so by the crown.[2]

Benedict XIV (1740-58), pope at this time, encouraged policies that favoured British interests: he expressed his approval of the Jansenist faction in the French parliament; recognised the Hohenzollerns as kings (a title they had assumed) in Prussia; lifted restrictions of trade in the papal states; authorised the translation of English literature into Italian; and banned Chinese rites (this was deemed to be against the interests of the French). British interests in the Mediterranean coincided with those of the papal states as illustrated by the fact that two frigates were purchased by Benedict XIV from the British.[3]

In August 1741, during the first year of his pontificate, Benedict addressed an encyclical to the Irish bishops — many of whom spent much of their time on the continent and were thus liable to French or Spanish influence — in which he reprimanded them for their abrogation of duty and demanded that they remain in their dioceses.[4] He later issued his directive *Apostolicum ministerium,* in May 1753, establishing the rules according to which the catholic church in England was to be governed, which remained in force till the nineteenth century.[5] In July 1747, Prince Henry Stuart, the duke of York, was elevated to the position of cardinal by the same pope: the latter had been offered £150,000 sterling by the duke of Hanover (George II) if this appointment were made. Benedict declined the offer of money, but he did in fact act in accordance with George's wishes. The size of the sum offered indicates the extent of the benefits likely to accrue in the king from such an appointment.[6] When Charles Edward died in

1788 and Cardinal York succeeded him as the last surviving male Stuart, this spelt the end for what remained of Jacobitism in Scotland. Scottish presbyterians would hardly accept a cardinal as their king and even the episcopalians now forsook the Stuart cause. The French cardinals were not completely happy about York entering their college, while Louis XV accepted the appointment as a *fait accompli.*[7]

Benedict confided all details of his policies to Cardinal Tencin (1680-1758), who was a member of the French privy council and apostolic legate and who was greatly influenced by his anglophile sister, Madame de Tencin.[8]

Although official sources are lacking, those sections of Samuel Richardson's novel *Sir Charles Grandison* (completed in 1754) which are set in Italy give ample evidence of this *rapprochement* between England and the Vatican. Ludwig Borinski has illustrated this fact with a brief outline of the story from the above-mentioned book: Grandison, resident in Italy for some time, associates with the della Poretta of Bologna, a family of high nobility in what was then still part of the papal states; Clementina della Poretta, a daughter of this family, falls in love with Grandison with whom she reads Shakespeare and Milton; they are prevented from marrying, however, because of their different denominations. Like the Porettas of the novel, Benedict XIV was of Bolognese nobility and had been cardinal-archbishop of Bologna before becoming pope. In the novel, the second son of the Porettas is archbishop of Bologna and it is expected that he will soon be made a cardinal. The first son is a Neapolitan general and the third a Sardinian colonel. Anti-catholic prejudices, which often abound in English literature, are noticeably absent from *Sir Charles Grandison*, where even veneration of our Lady is presented as acceptable; and Richardson shows himself to be well informed about conditions on the continent.[9]

Another English writer, Sir Horace Walpole (son of the powerful whig prime minister), displayed such sympathy for Benedict XIV in June 1757 when he learned that the pope was seriously ill, that he made him the subject of a eulogy to Benedict. In it he eloquently expresses his admiration for the pontiff:

> He restored the luster of the Tiara by those arts alone by which alone he attained it, his virtues.
>
> Beloved by Papists, esteemed by protestants: a Priest without insolence or interest; a Prince without nepotism; an Author without vanity; in short a Man whom neither Wit nor Power could spoil.
>
> The Son of a favourite Minister, but one who never courted a Prince nor worshipped a Churchman, offers in this free Country this deserved Incense to the Best of Roman Pontiffs.

Benedict thanked him in a personal letter in which he observed: 'We are like the statues on the facade of St Peter's, which appear better when seen from a distance.'[10]

Benedict XIV died on 3 May 1758; he was succeeded by Clement XIII, during whose pontificate Vatican policies underwent significant changes, although this was largely attributable to the secretary of state, Cardinal Torrigiani. While Benedict had stood for conciliation by any means, Torrigiani's priority was to uphold the rights of the papacy at all costs.[11] It was in Rome, during the pontificate of Clement XIII that King James III died in 1766, having spent his life in exile. Like his father before him James III had participated in the nomination of bishops to Irish sees.[12] Clement, however, did not recognise James's son, the young pretender, as the lawful heir to the throne of England, Scotland and Ireland. By acting in this way Clement and Torrigiani hoped that any obstacle to the resumption of Anglo-papal relations would thus be removed and that any pretext for maintaining the penal laws against catholics in England, Scotland and Ireland would be eliminated. (Cardinal York regarded this slighting of his brother as work of the Jesuits.[13]) From 1768 onwards, English and Irish catholics, who had already proved their loyalty in the Anglo-French war of 1756-63, prayed in church for George III as their legitimate sovereign.[14]

Clement XIII died in 1769 and was succeeded by Cardinal Ganganelli; the latter chose the same name as his predecessor yet set about overturning his policies. He acted in accordance with the wishes of the great powers who were anxious to see the dissolution of the Society of Jesus and made friendly overtures towards England. He confided to a British gentleman friend in 1748: 'I personally have a passion for your brave poets and philosophers.' He was especially fond of reading Newton and Berkeley and was well liked as pope in England.[15]

In 1772 the time seemed ideal for re-establishing contacts between the papacy and the court of St James. The pope issued a special invitation to the duke of Gloucester (1743-1805), younger brother of King George III, to visit Rome. All the papal domains through which the duke was to pass were ordered to extend a hearty welcome to the king's brother.[16] The duke arrived in Rome on 25 February 1772 and, as was the custom with all important visitors, he was presented with fifteen loads of foodstuffs by the *maggiordomo* on behalf of his holiness. The duke was lavishly entertained at the villa Martinez, where he watched the horse racing, and later at the theatre d'Aliberti, where he attended the opera as a guest of the *governatore* of Rome.[17] In the days that followed he spent his time being shown around the antiquities of Rome and in the evenings attended various festivities held in his honour, most notably those arranged by the French and Venetian ministers to the Holy See. When news of his mother's death reached him on 4 March he retired into complete seclusion until Ash

Wednesday when he and his entourage, still in deep mourning, attended mass and the ceremony of the ashes in the Sistine chapel. After mass the duke retired to the papal gardens where he and the pope held a private conversation in the pavilion. Their meeting lasted for some time and was completely private so there are no sources to divulge the contents of their conversation: the papers merely reported that they held each other in the highest esteem. According to Theiner, who is not always reliable, the duke visited the pope several times.[18] Clement XIV presented the duke with two paintings and a collection of prints by Piranesi of ancient and modern Rome, while the duke reciprocated this kindness by presenting the pontiff with a gold-embossed bible.[19]

On the following Sunday the duke was the guest of Cardinal Allessandro Albani (1692-1779); several cardinals, ambassadors and ministers of foreign courts were present and at the duke's behest the papal choir sang the *Miserere* followed by a passion oratorio. From the balcony of the Altieri palace the duke witnessed the great papal procession on the feast of Annunciation, 25 March. He spent the remainder of his days in Rome viewing the art treasures and ancient monuments of the famous city and being entertained by the Roman nobility, staying on until Easter to attend the ceremonies of holy week. He was so moved by the singing of the famous *Miserere* that the pope ordered it to be written down, ornately bound and then presented to the duke. He left Rome on Easter Tuesday in April 1772 having spent fifty-six days in the holy city at the palace of the Marchese Correa.[20] He arrived back in London on 18 May and proceeded immediately to Kew to meet his brother King George to report on his visit. He presented the king with three vases as a gift from the pope, and George III responded by asking, in a letter to Don Paolo Borghese,[21] that his appreciation be conveyed to the pontiff for the favourable attention bestowed on his brother during his stay.

Two days after the duke left Rome the young pretender, Prince Charles Edward Stuart, entered the city. The prince had been denied recognition as king of England by the French and Spanish monarchs, despite the fact that they were anxious to ensure that the Stuart line be continued; and it was as a result of this that the prince was induced to marry Princess Louise von Stolberg (1752-1824).[22] They were married on Good Friday (remarkably) at Macerata by Cardinal Marefaschi and immediately set out for Rome. They entered the city with two outriders announcing them as 'king' and 'queen'. It was widely believed that the pope, in unison with certain courts, would recognise the pretender as king of England. Accordingly, the Roman nobility went to pay their respects to the 'royal couple' who remained seated while receiving all their visitors. It was soon revealed, however, that Pope Clement was actually rather displeased by these pretensions. The prince had lived up to then as the unobtrusive Count Albany but now announced himself as king of England in an official message to the cardinal secretary of state and wanted to be received by the pope as such. Pope Clement reacted by expressing his pleasure at the arrival of 'Count Albany' and his honoured wife and would let this be known to them when he would receive them. The cardinal duke of York entreated his sister-in-law to exercise her influence on Charles and induce him to refrain from such ridiculous pretensions of royalty. Theiner saw this was an attempt by forces inimical to Pope Clement to sabotage his policy of *rapprochement* with England, which was aimed at obtaining toleration for the catholics living in Britain and Ireland, for this had been the purpose behind the secret negotiations between Pope Clement and the duke of Gloucester.[23] Theiner asserts that 'the exercise of the Catholic religion at this time was connived at in Ireland' and that 'the penal laws affecting the property of professors [of the catholic religion] were so frequently and rigorously executed, that several wealthy families were reduced to the sad alternative either to quit their native country or to starve in it'.[24] Those catholics without property, on the other hand, were treated like serfs by their landlords, while the tithe-proctors of the anglican church 'by process, citation and sequestration, dragged from them the little which the landlord had left them'.[25]

Pope Clement persisted in his attempts to procure relief for catholics living in the British Isles. To further this aim he sent Mgr Caprara, his nuncio in Cologne, to London to sound out the situation there. As Clement XIV explained to Cardinal Bernis, the French minister to the Holy See, the purpose of this mission was to try to free the catholics in Britain and Ireland from the oppression which they were forced to endure. He believed that the British court had already done much in their favour and he hoped that it would concede yet more relief.[27] Caprara had been archbishop of Iconia and nuncio in Cologne (1767-75) and later served in Lucerne, Vienna and in Paris during Napoleon's time; he became a cardinal soon afterwards. Caprara was regarded as easy-going in his dealings with the great powers.[28] He arrived in London in June 1772 and was introduced at the court by Count Belgiojoso, the Austrian ambassador to London and doyen of the diplomatic corps.

Caprara attended the court twice a week. He found George III to be well-disposed to the papacy, as he later reported to Rome. This was largely a result of the favourable reception accorded by the pope to the duke of Gloucester. Caprara reported that influential members of parliament had assured him of their desire to see catholics in England live in peace and security. He also observed that hatred of the Holy See had vanished among the educated classes and this too could be attributed to the visit by the duke of Gloucester to Rome.[29] George III had requested that some of the famous Roman gargle to be sent to him and the pope complied immediately. It seemed to be an ideal time to initiate negotiations. The English ambassador to Paris was instructed to negotiate with the nuncio there on the conditions of Scottish catholics. The pope had ordered his nuncio in Paris to approach the British ambassador and intervene on behalf of two hundred catholic families who had been persecuted by their landlord, a Mr MacDonald. On 24 June the pope instructed the nuncio to try to extend any relief he might procure for Scottish catholics to catholics in Ireland.[30]

Those opposed to Pope Clement's policy of *rapprochement* with Britain reacted by circulating papers in which they questioned his motives and described him as a half-protestant. On 23 September 1772 an article published in the *Staats- und Gelehrte Zeitung Des Hamburgischen unpartheyischen Correspondenten* (State and Learned Journal of the Hamburg Impartial Correspondent), which had been reprinted from a report originally emanating from London, dated 15 September 1772, stated that a courier had arrived in London from Rome two days before and that this resulted in speculation that the pope had become a protestant. This report alleged that some ministers had voiced this speculation from the pulpit the previous Sunday and had included his holiness in their prayers.[31]

In Ireland, a catholic committee of merchants and landlords, established in 1759, had continually campaigned for the relief of catholics there, and not without results:[32] in 1772 an act was passed by the Irish parliament which sought to encourage the reclamation of unprofitable bogs, and this allowed catholics, who were hitherto excluded from almost all lucrative occupations, to rent up to fifty acres of bog.[33] In 1774 another act was passed which enabled catholics to take an oath testifying their loyalty by declaring allegiance to the king and denying that the pope possessed any temporal authority in Ireland. Yet it was in Canada that catholicism was recognised for the first time by a British act of parliament. The Quebec Act, passed in 1774, guaranteed catholics free exercise of their faith and enabled the clergy to levy tithes. The British government allowed a diocese of Quebec to be set up and the bishop was officially referred to as 'Superintendant of the Romish Church', a position which held the exclusive right to select parish priests without interference from the governor. A precedent had been set.[34]

In 1775 there began a new pontificate, that of Pius VI (1775-99). The duke of Gloucester paid a second visit to Rome to meet the new pope. Elsewhere in 1775 the first confrontation in the American war of independence occurred; in 1778 the first Catholic Relief Act was passed in Britain and Ireland (17 & 18, Geo. III, C.49).[35] In 1779 John Cox Hippisley (1748-1825), member of parliament for Sudbury, was stationed in Rome for a year. There was now a strong case for further relief for catholics, and the anti-catholic Gordon riots in 1780 in London proved to be only a temporary setback, for it was just two years later that two more acts were passed granting further relief for the test oath (*Loyalty Asserted or the Test Oath Vindicated*).[39]

From Culloden to the French Revolution

Irish catholics: the first relaxed some of the burdens endured by those professing the catholic faith (21 & 22 Geo. III, C.24); and the second allowed catholics to teach in schools and to regulate the education of fellow catholics and repealed parts of certain laws relative to the guardianship of their children (21 & 22 Geo. III, C.52). The viceroy of Ireland at the time, the third duke of Portland, was instrumental in securing these reforms.[36]

In 1782 the anglican bishop of Meath held discussions with the rector of the Irish college in Paris, Dr Markey, and the catholic bishop of Meath in an attempt to evaluate the implications of these reforms: he planned to secure their co-operation with an offer of financial payment. O'Donoghue sees this in the context of universal attempts by secular authorities in eighteenth century Europe to subject the church to the authority of the state. Other methods in addition to financial grants were used to gain control of the clergy, the most notable being interference in the appointment of bishops. The British authorities were anxious to secure a right of veto in the nomination of bishops to vacant sees as was the case in continental countries.[37]

In 1784 the British secret service employed a Franciscan, Fr Arthur O'Leary (1729-1802), to spy on Irish catholics. Orde, the Irish secretary at the time, reported to the British authorities after an interview with O'Leary at Dublin castle on 24 September 1784: 'O'Leary has it in his power, *if we can depend on him,* to reveal to us the real designs of the Catholics, from which quarter, after all, the real mischief is to spring.'[38] It may be said in O'Leary's favour that when he undertook this mission he knew that there were no such designs at all. Thus he reported back that the Irish catholics were loyal subjects, but at the same time he exercised all his power to inspire in the Irish people an unquestioning loyalty to the crown. In his *Address to the Common People of Ireland,* published in Dublin in 1786, he denounced Whiteboyism, that desperate attempt by young Irishmen to overthrow oppression; he even went to such extremes as to defend the test oath (*Loyalty Asserted or the Test Oath Vindicated*).[39] Rome's soothing influence on Ireland was strengthened in 1786 by the elevation of two ecclesiastics, both of whom had been educated in Rome, to the primatial sees of Dublin and Armagh. Richard O'Reilly was appointed archbishop of Armagh, a position he held until 1818; he had left Ireland in 1762 at the age of sixteen to study in Rome at Propaganda. Dr John Thomas Troy was appointed archbishop of Dublin; he too had gone to Rome at an early age to study with the Dominicans; later he became rector of S. Clemente, the Irish Dominican convent in Rome. As bishop of Ossory in 1779 he was foremost among Irish bishops in interposing against Whiteboyism: he had obviously absorbed continental thinking of absolute obedience to the civil authorities, as a result of his many years in Rome.[40]

Patrick O'Donoghue has recently analysed the attitude of the papal authorities during these years: Ireland was subject to the authority of the prefect of the congregation for the propagation of the faith right up until the twentieth century. Cardinal Antonelli was prefect at this time and in 1778 he exhorted Dr Troy and his brother bishops to pay due respect to the British government and show themselves to be 'obedient subjects, zealous for the good of the state and the prosperity of the sovereign'. He replied to Dr Troy, when questioned on the issue, that he saw this as the only means of preventing the king from interfering in the nomination of Irish bishops. While deploring interference by the crown in nominations to vacant sees, he did not see how this could be avoided or how they could refuse to comply with royal wishes.[41]

CHAPTER II

Facing the Common Enemy

THE FRENCH revolution had served to strengthen this Roman attitude of obedience to the civil authority. Revolutionary France had invaded and annexed the papal territory of Avignon and Venaissin. Britain and the Vatican found a common enemy in revolutionary France and this inevitably drew them closer together. In June 1791 Cardinal Antonelli, in a lengthy address to the four archbishops of Ireland, outlined the religious duty of obedience to 'the legitimate government of George III' (by quoting 1 Peter 2:13ff and the fathers of the church); he recalled the advice of Benedict XIV to the English vicars apostolic when he urged that those who do not respect the institutions of the state be punished. The conduct of French Canadians in the American war of independence was held up to the bishops as an example worthy of emulation by catholics everywhere, particularly in Ireland. The thinking and policy of this Roman document was to be reflected continually in the pastorals of Irish bishops in subsequent years.[1] In December 1791 Antonelli continued this theme in letters to Dr Troy and Fr Charles O'Conor of Belanagare when he especially forbade 'any union of catholics and presbyterians against the secular authority'.[2] These letters unwittingly played into the hands of the British authorities when, in 1795, the conciliatory earl of Fitzwilliam was recalled and replaced as viceroy of Ireland by the earl of Camden, who received secret instructions to set the protestants in Ireland against the catholics. Acting on these instructions Camden sent secret agents and emissaries to the north, and especially to County Armagh, to revive religious strife. As many catholics had recently become tenants of land formerly rented by presbyterians this was no difficult task. After the battle of Diamond in 1795 the Orange order was founded and many catholics became victims of this organised sectarianism. The policy of playing two religious communities off against each other (each usually having an ethnic as well as a regional basis) was adopted by Britain in many parts of the empire — catholics and protestants in Ireland and Canada; anglican settlers of British origin and calvinist Boers in South Africa; hindus and moslems in India. This policy was chiefly employed by whigs to begin with (some tories still had ambitions of protestantising Ireland and Canada); in the nineteenth century it was applied by most British administrations somewhere or other.[3]

Catholics in England had been granted complete religious toleration in 1791. Some of the vicars apostolic were opposed to the oath of allegiance which catholics were compelled to take under the act; however, the British foreign secretary, George Canning, was in Rome at the time and, in conversation with him, Puis VI declared his satisfaction 'that the vicars apostolic were to *blame* and directed his disapprobation of their proceedings to be strongly expressed to them'.[4] In Ireland another Relief Act was passed in 1792: this aimed to remove certain restraints and disabilities to which catholics were still subject (32 Geo. III, C.21).[5]

In the first half of 1792 Sir John Cox Hippisley returned to Rome; he had acquired a large circle of contacts during his previous tour of duty there, and the fact that his sister was married to a Roman nobleman gave him an access to influential people that might otherwise have been denied to him. Cardinal Secretary of State Zelada (1717-1801) had a particularly favourable opinion of Hippisley.[6] On 27 June 1793 Hippisley wrote to the lord chancellor Alexander Wedderburn, Lord Loughborough (1733-1805) so that he should inform George III: 'In a conversation with my Brother-in-Law on that occasion, the Cardinal Secretary of State observed — "I am from my family a Spaniard, — by birth a Roman, — but my Heart is English".'[7] In a letter to his friend William Windham (1750-1810), a man of influence with the government, Hippisley repeated this and commented: 'He might have added almost his House too, as you see nothing but English Prints, etc. ...'. Another of Hippisley's main contacts was Cardinal Campanelli, as he informed Windham in the same letter:

> He is the great confidant of the Pope and it is considered from his influence with the College and the foreign States that He is the most likely to succeed on a Vacancy, to the Tiara — no other of the College, except [Giovanni] Albani [1727-1803], the Cardinal Dean (who is a very sensible Man and in fact made the Present Pope), has any influence with the Pope. — I made an early acquaintance with the Cardinal Campanelli thro' Monsignor Erskine who is his great favourite and who succeeded him in his office as Promotore della Fide.[8]

Erskine's father had emigrated to Rome to the court of King James III and had married a Roman princess, Agatha Gigli. He died while his son, Charles Erskine, was still very young, leaving him to be brought up and educated under the guardianship of Cardinal York; he was especially favoured by Pope Pius VI (1775-1799). Erskine was a subdeacon, not a priest, and was a famous and eloquent advocate. Hippisley's original mission was to establish trade relations between Britain and the papal states.

Late in 1792 Prince Augustus, second-youngest son of George III and later duke of Sussex, visited Rome. He was secretly married there in April 1793 by an English clergyman to Lady Augusta Murray, eldest daughter of the Scottish earl of Dunmore. The prince requested that a plan of defence for the papal states be drawn up by Captain Collier, an English artillery officer, who was also to endeavour to establish a papal army. During an audience with Prince Augustus the pope expressed 'great attachment to the British Interests and much obligation to His Royal Highness for suggesting the survey of Captain Collier as well as to the King himself for permitting the Captain to remain and complete his work'.[9] The prince also discussed with the pope the possibilities for setting up commercial links between Britain and the papal states, emphasising his country's needs for a reduction in the duties imposed on British manufactures. When questioned on the fate of Corsica the pope replied that he would restore his nominal supremacy over that island while Britain would receive a port there. Prince Augustus, who was 'well liked by Pius VI and the Roman people',[10] left for England in July 1793 accompanied by Count Münster, the future Hanoverian prime minister; the war between Britain and France delayed their return until September. From Bologna the prince asked Hippisley to procure the pope's 'specific ideas on the subject of a connection with England' as well as his ideas on Corsica etc. Pius VI answered Prince Augustus in a personal letter in which he again expressed his gratitude to the king and the British nation.[11] Hippisley meanwhile was trying to further British interests in the papal states when in June 1793 he received a letter from the British consul at Leghorn lamenting the fact that the British fleet could not obtain supplies there: he applied to Cardinal Secretary of State Zelada for permission to be granted for the British fleet to receive provisions in the papal states: his request was immediately granted and 500 oxen and 570 tons of grain were supplied.[12]

Pius VI won the esteem of Hippisley who reported to Windham: 'I have attempted to do justice to the Pope', and went on to denounce 'these disgraceful penal laws'.[13] He continued in his letter to Windham:

> At about this period I received a letter from Stanley [M.P. for Wootton Basset] detailing the proceedings of the Committees for the relief of the Emigrant priests, etc., of which I gave an extract to the Cardinal Secretary of State, subjoining a note (which the fact warranted) viz: that the annual proportion of allowance to the Emigrant priests in Britain and the Jersys *exceeded* the annual provision for the *whole Church* of the Kingdom of Scotland ... and that the number relieved exceeded the *whole number* of Ecclesiastics *regular* and *secular in Rome*.

In such a precarious situation the Roman authorities felt obliged to print an article by Hippisley in the Roman ecclesiastical gazette in which he depicted his native Britain in a highly praiseworthy manner.

When Mgr Jean Maury (1746-1817), Mirabeau's antagonist and defender of the rights of the Church, dared to comment that 'he should have regretted to have been obliged to eat the "Bread de la nation la plus orgueilleuse du monde"', Hippisley expressed his disgust at Maury's insolence to Cardinals Zelada and de Bernis, in an effort to silence this 'son of a miserable shoemaker ... who on all occasions scatters his diatribes against our Country which in his estimation is both "faithless and insolent"'. Hippisley was pleased to report to England that Maury's popularity was on the wane;[14] but in fact Maury was made a cardinal in 1794.

In 1793 the great Relief Act was passed 'for the Relief of His Majesty's Popish, or Roman Catholick Subjects of Ireland' (33 Geo. III, C.21). Catholic freeholders with land valued at over forty shillings were enfranchised by this act, and the penal laws which had prohibited catholic education of their children and imposed fines for not attending anglican services were repealed. The Irish hierarchy and the catholic committee sent notes of thanks to King George III. Pius VI expressed his thanks in a letter to de La Marche, bishop of St Pol de Leon, who had found refuge in England and organised relief for the *emigré* clergy, for the much-awaited relief of Irish catholics and for the kind treatment extended to the *emigrés*; the letter was subsequently published in British newspapers.[15] Hippisley strengthened this feeling of gratitude by supplying the pope with translations of parliamentary speeches, including Burke's speech on the Catholic Dissenters Bill of 1791 as well as a copy of Burke's *The Case of the Suffering Clergy of France*. The pope sent a personal note of thanks to Burke on 7 September 1793.[16]

At about the same time Hippisley received exaggerated reports of outrages by the Defenders, a group formed to defend catholics against atrocities by the Orange lodges. These reports came to his attention as a result of speeches made in the Irish house of lords by John Dawson (first earl of Portarlington), Charles Dillon Lee (twelfth Viscount Dillon) and Lord Fitzgibbon. These reports were confirmed by Brownslow North (1741-1820), bishop of Winchester, who was in Naples at the time.[17] Hippisley immediately approached the cardinal secretary of state, providing him with an extract of Lord Portarlington's speech and seeking his condemnation of the Defenders.[18] The result was another letter from Propaganda to the Irish bishops condemning the actions of those catholics 'led astray by democratic principles which flourished at the time to the detriment of church and state. The bishops ... are strongly exhorted to take the necessary measures to bring back to their duty those who had been deluded by mischievous people.'[19] Cardinal Zelada sent Hippisley a copy of this circular and in the accompanying letter assured him that the holy father was conscious of the favours which the king and the English nation had bestowed on the catholics in Ireland (by passing the Relief Act) and that he deplored the seditious acts perpetrated by the lower classes of catholics there.[20] Hippisley exclaimed to Windham: 'Examine the conduct of the *Pope and his Ministers* on the present subject of *Ireland* — Could the whole Bench of British Bishops have done *more* to support *our Government*.'[21] Rome was preoccupied with the revolutionary regime in France and allowed itself to heed the advice of Hippisley concerning the situation in Ireland — and Hippisley himself was misinformed about conditions there. Archbishop Troy was obliged to inform Propaganda on 'the reasons that gave rise to the very name Defenders'.[22] Meanwhile the papal states were in actual need of British assistance, since the French revolutionary forces had already annexed Avignon and it was not long before the *Patrimonium Petri*, the core of the papal states, was itself threatened. Furthermore, Britain had advanced sufficiently on the question of religious toleration to appease Vatican officials: the papal authorities could not afford to antagonise a much needed ally in their hour of crisis and so waived for the time being their moral and theological obligation to defend the rights of Irish catholics.

In letters and memoranda passed on to Pitt through Windham, Hippisley pointed out the advantages of securing a closer relationship with the papal states, laying particular emphasis on their need for British military assistance and the possibilities for expanding commercial links. Windham, who had been Irish secretary in 1783, replied to Hippisley in March 1793: 'I long to think that Rome, our common mother, should owe her safety, if danger must approach her, to the protecting justice of Great Britain.'[23] Like Edmund Burke he expressed himself in favour of resuming diplomatic relations with the Holy See. The foreign secretary, Lord Grenville (1759-1834), who had been Irish secretary under the duke of Portland, shared Burke's enthusiasm for this proposal.[24] Hippisley pointed out to Windham: 'The facts I have stated of the Pope's injunctions to the Irish prelates goes to prove the occasional advantages in a *civil* view, which may result from the *spiritual* interference of Rome.' He then asked Windham to advocate the resumption of Anglo-papal relations from the parliamentary floor remarking: 'Recollect how peculiarly the English Nation have been marked by the respect and esteem of the Romans from the time of Benedict XIV downwards.'[25] When Cardinal de Zelada addressed a letter to Grenville, the latter refrained from answering, fearing repercussions as a result of a penal law passed during Queen Elizabeth I's reign forbidding such intercourse. Hippisley, however, assured Zelada that 'any remaining penal laws on this subject ... would be repealed', quoting the bishop of Winchester and Lord Pelham as his sources.[26]

The pope now instructed Mgr Charles Erskine to travel to England; the move was objected to by Dr Douglas, the vicar apostolic for the London district, who had conferred with Grenville on the matter, on grounds that the appointment of a papal agent was disagreeable to the British government. He offered himself instead to act in the papal interest. Hippisley, who had long been a close friend of Erskine and had corresponded with him all the years he was absent from Rome, participated in arranging Erskine's mission, as he later reported to Burke:

I started a conversation between the Secretary of State ... and Mgr Erskine. The Cardinal's words were, 'I have been thinking for these six months of a connexion with England, as being within possibility, but who shall we send?' I must add that a *public* delegation was never on the speculation of *this* Government without the *approbation* of our own. The only question was, whether a private authority should be given to Dr Douglas (on his own recommendation); [or] to a Mr Hussey at the instance of the Spanish Minister here; or whether Mgr Erskine, who had long speculated on a visit to his family and friends in Britain, should have a private authority to communicate the wishes of this Government to the British Ministry. All the three were subjects of Great Britain, and therefore it was supposed by means of either, the object might be obtained without Eclat. The Court of Spain has strongly recommended to the Pope the appointment of some person at *this important Crisis*, for the exclusive management of his Interests in relation to Great Britain. This letter (of 27 June) I sent with a flying Seal to my Lord Chancellor so that Lord Loughborough might foward it to George III.[27]

As Hippisley stated in his letter, a Dr Hussey had been recommended for the mission by the Spanish minister in London, José Nicolas de Azara, a man of great influence at the Vatican as he had been Spanish minister to the Holy See before. Hussey was an Irish priest who had already been twice employed by the English government for diplomatic missions. In 1780 he had accompanied Richard Cumberland on a mission to Spain to conclude a treaty with the Spanish minister Del Campo. The Gordon riots in London sounded the death knell for this particular mission, but Del Campo (a descendant of an English catholic family named Field) became Spanish minister in London until he was succeeded by Azara. Hussey, originally a Carthusian monk, was chaplain to the Spanish embassy there. He attracted particular attention for his diplomatic efforts when in 1786 an English settlement in Sierra Leone 'was attacked by the French; Spain sided against England; Dr Hussey again repaired to Madrid, healed the rupture, and Sierra Leone [became] a bishopric. For these and other services Hussey enjoyed a pension from Pitt.'[28]

Erskine's mission to England was disguised as a private visit, as revealed by Hippisley in a letter to Windham:

Erskine ... has received ostensibly from the Pope permission to visit his *family in Britain.* As Erskine has long been speaking of such a visit, there seems to be no conjecture abroad beyond the ostensible reason. The Cardinal Secretary and Cardinal Datary are the only persons privy to his private Instructions: part of his Instructions, such as expressing the gratitude of this Government for the exertions of our Country in favour of the Emigrant priests etc. and the relief given to the Catholics have indeed been proposed in the Congregation of State (consisting of seven Cardinals) and highly approved by all the Cardinals — as has been also the Letter from the Pope to the Bishop of St Pol de Lon. Erskine's object is to proceed for a short time to Scotland to see his friends there and where he understands his particular friend Mr Andrew Stuart now is; with him he proposes to communicate and be directed. If the Penal Laws exist to the extent apprehended, his first object will be to state the hopes of this Government for their repeal that the Pope may, as a *Temporal Prince,* be at liberty occasionally to treat with Great Britain for the mutual advantage of their states.[29]

Cardinal Zelada attempted to advance the cause of the mission by making known the pope's recommendations to his clergy in Ireland in the hope that it would meet with a good reception in Whitehall. In October 1793 he transmitted to Erskine a copy of his letter to Archbishop Troy and in an accompanying letter he instructed him to communicate the thoughts contained therein to the ministers of the British government. Then, if he thought it opportune, he should pass the letter on to Archbishop Troy.[30] On Hippisley's suggestion it was decided that he should write in the pope's name to direct 'any *measures* to be adopted by the Irish Catholic Bishops as may be most agreeable to our Government.'[31]

On 7 September 1793 Hippisley announced Erskine's arrival to the prince of Wales stating that Erskine was sent to England by the pope, 'but without any public character, to express there fully the grateful sentiments of His Holiness'. Hippisley pleaded with the prince that it should mark the beginning of official diplomatic relations 'with the Pope as a Temporal Prince, for the advantage of both states'.[32] He then wrote to Grenville requesting a passport for Erskine, but was informed that he did not require one. Dr Douglas and the other vicars apostolic were not happy at the prospect of Erskine's arrival.[33] Erskine wrote to his friend Andrew Stuart regarding his forthcoming visit:

We had heard of the troubles excited in Ireland by some of the low class of Catholics. The Pope had ordered the Congregation of Propaganda to express to the Bishops there his *indignation of the ungrateful conduct* of these men, ordering them to use all means to recall the misled wretches to their duty, and has now ordered them to communicate with me whilst in England for that purpose, and has ordered me to second any measures which the Government may think proper to communicate to me.[34]

On 4 November 1793 Cardinal Antonelli informed Archbishop Troy of Erskine's mission.[35]

Erskine set out on his mission to England, travelling through Florence, Bologna, Verona, Innsbruck, Augsburg, Stuttgart, Aachen and Brussels to Ostend, where he caught the boat to Margate. British customs officials were ordered to receive him with all the honours due to a fully accredited diplomat. He was publicly announced at every hitching post on his journey to London as the 'Ambassador of the Pope'. He arrived in London on 13 November 1793.[36] Hippisley had lined up a list of dignatories, including radicals and 'Friends of the People', whom Erskine was to meet and stay with upon his arrival. Burke, whom Hippisley had asked to arrange for Erskine to meet members of the government, thought this to be unsuitable for a papal representative and informed Hippisley of his feelings on the matter. He even went so far as to rebuke Hippisley for seeking the pope's intervention in Ireland;[37] Hippisley defended his actions in a lengthy letter to Burke.[38] Windham, however, was more praising of Hippisley's behaviour and on 11 October 1793 wrote to Pitt: 'I most sincerely wish that the views which he has opened may be found capable of being realised; so as ... to place us in the situation of becoming the protectors of the Italian states and (odd as the idea may seem) the supporters, within certain limits, of the Papal power.'[39]

Many of the people to whom Erskine carried letters of introduction were out of town, but Windham (who had been entreated by Hippisley to seek a means whereby Erskine might meet Pitt),[40] on hearing of his arrival, went to meet him. After visiting the head of his family, the earl of Kellie, in Scotland, Erskine returned to London in January 1794. Erskine brought with him two letters from the pope, one for Prince Augustus and one for the king. Acting with great caution and diplomatic tact he knew he was not entitled to any special distinction and so judiciously sought to maintain his diplomatic character. On the occasion of his first appearance at court he was pleasantly surprised to find his coach being admitted into the courtyard reserved for the coaches of officially accredited diplomats. He avoided any conflict with court etiquette by taking the last place in the diplomatic corps. The government approved of this caution and King George rewarded him by granting him a lengthy audience, causing consternation and surprise among the assembled diplomats; in his first conversation with the king he entertained and fascinated the monarch and at the same time flattered his vanity. Erskine always appeared at court in black court dress with his sword worn on the left side; he stuck to this attire even on the king's birthday although no one was allowed to wear black on that day. When the master of ceremonies informed him that he could not enter the court on account of his black dress, Erskine explained that in his case black did not signify mourning but reflected the character of his office. The master of ceremonies went to seek the king's command on the matter; he gave full permission for Erskine to be admitted to the court in his black dress, thus openly recognising him as a Roman diplomat in front of the whole court.[41]

The first matter Erksine had to negotiate was the establishment of a seminary in Ireland for the education of young men for the priesthood. Karl Wöste has looked into this subject in great detail.[42] In 1782 the bishop of Leighlin had founded the first catholic college in Ireland since the Reformation, St Patrick's college, Carlow; it was officially opened in 1793. Two further colleges were subsequently founded — St Kieran's in Kilkenny and St Finian's in Navan. Many priests had previously received their education in the Irish colleges on the continent, but this was now impossible due to the revolution in France.

On 17 December 1793 the catholic bishops of Ireland presented Lord Lieutenant Westmorland with an address of loyalty to George III and in an accompanying letter they deplored the lawlessness of the lower class of catholics; the letter was well received by George III.[43] When approached by the Irish bishops on the matter of establishing a seminary, Burke referred them to his son, Richard, and to Dr Thomas Hussey. On 4 January 1794 Richard Burke and Dr Hussey informed the home secretary, Dundas, that they had been entrusted by the Irish hierarchy to negotiate with him to set up a seminary. Dundas was in favour of this proposal and requested Hussey to negotiate with the Irish hierarchy and the Irish administration.[44] On 14 January Archbishop Troy of Dublin addressed an official request to Lord Lieutenant Westmorland for permission to set up a seminary. He explained that under previously existing laws they had been forced to educate catholic theologians abroad, usually in France, and that this was no longer possible nor desirable. He felt that the university of Dublin was unsuitable for the training of Irishmen for the priesthood.[45] Lord Portland, soon to be home secretary, now came to favour this proposal and on 17 February Mgr Erskine was able to inform the cardinal secretary of state in a letter from London that the English government intended 'to erect and endow a seminary for Irish Catholic priests, at a cost of twenty-four thousand pounds sterling annually'.[46] Hussey at the same time continued his negotiations with the new lord lieutenant of Ireland, Earl Camden. On 23 April 1795 a bill was passed which provided £8,000 from the education fund for the building of the college. On 5 June the bill received royal consent (35 Geo. III, C.21). A college for the education of priests was established at Maynooth — St Patrick's college; eleven of the trustees were catholic (four catholic archbishops and six bishops) as well as Dr

Hussey, who became the first president of the new college.

At the same time as Pitt had informed Erskine of the government's intention to set up the college, he had also informed the cardinal secretary of state of Britain's intention to protect the church states as far as was possible.[47] Anglo-papal relations now hinged upon two issues — the question of Ireland and that of papal temporal power. Britain had tried to exercise control over Ireland through Rome and the catholic church, and in return the pope was promised protection by Britain of the papal states. William Pitt sought the pope's participation in a coalition against France and called for a general crusade against the activities of the revolution, claiming that revolutionary ideas could only be vanquished by religion. The French prelates exiled in England were used by Pitt as a means to convey these proposals to Cardinal Bernis, the former French minister to the Holy See.[48] Pius VI, however, declined the offer of limited security through the proposed coalition, largely because of the changing influences within parliament, and because he did not want to involve the papal states in a war which would fuel complaints against the Vatican; papal involvement in the wars of princes and peoples had damaged the image of the papacy and it was felt that another war would harm the pope's spiritual reputation.[49] Had Pius VI consented to Pitt's proposals it could have seriously impeded, if not prevented altogether, the return of religion to France.[50]

Prince Augustus returned to Italy in January 1794, accompanied by Count Münster; they remained there for almost five years and became acquainted with the future cardinal secretary of state, Consalvi. Hippisely had obtained an assurance from Cardinal Antonelli that in future no monk would receive an Irish diocese. In a letter to the vicars apostolic in England Antonelli exhorted them to preach obedience and loyalty to the monarch.[51] Meanwhile, offers continued to be made for the subvention of the clergy by Britain; and in April 1794 Antonelli congratulated the Irish hierarchy on their truly apostolic refusal to countenance such schemes.[52] Antonelli once again demonstrated his ignorance of realities in Ireland by condemning the oath by which Irish catholics obtained a vote in parliamentary elections. In a letter to the bishops and archbishops of Ireland in December 1794 he referred to certain parts of the oath, reproaching the hierarchy for not denouncing them; he objected mainly to that clause where catholics had to swear that papal infallibility was not a defined article of faith, that they would not obey an order from the pope or any other ecclesiastical authority that was of its nature immoral, and that they would not subvert or weaken the protestant establishment in church and state.[53] Archbishop Troy replied by a letter wherein he attempted to vindicate the hierarchy adopting both a theological and a diplomatic stance; it was also an attempt to instruct the Roman authorities on the reality of the catholic church's position in Ireland.[54] Antonelli continued his correspondence with the Irish bishops and the vicars apostolic in Britain in February 1795, persisting with his theme of obedience to George III.[55] Antonelli resigned from his position of prefect of Propaganda a short time afterwards on account of age.[56]

The English, Scottish and Irish colleges in Rome had been removed from Jesuit control sometime before and handed over to Italian rectors. James Macpherson, who was the Roman agent for the Scottish vicars apostolic and clergy and an associate of the Scots college there, had approached Hippisley and requested his intervention in order to secure native rectors for the three colleges.[57] Hippisley addressed a letter to Pius VI in January 1795 in which he entreated the pontiff to comply with this request by appointing rectors native to the relevant countries of the colleges.[58] Pius replied that the matter would be investigated.[59] Cardinal Livizzani, however, was not in favour of the idea; as Hippisley reported to Windham, he 'addressed a letter full of arrogance and false reasoning on the subject of the Irish College, of which he is Protector, declaring He would never remove the Italian Rector, who enjoys the Esteem of his Sovereign'.[60] Hippisley reacted by corresponding with the cardinal dean, Albani, on the matter.[61] The Scottish vicar apostolic Bishop Hoy wrote to Macpherson and the London vicar apostolic Bishop Douglas wrote to the agent of the English vicars apostolic, both gratefully acknowledging Hippisley's services in this matter.[62]

In October 1793 Hippisley had requested Windham to work on his behalf should there be an opening for a special envoy to the Holy See: 'My dear Windham ... I hope and trust ... that you will endeavour to *see* my Lord Grenville as well as my Lord Loughborough to keep the situation open for me'.[63] In spite of all Hippisley's efforts to further British interests in Rome, Grenville was not wholly satisfied with his conduct, as he reported to Portland: 'Although he [Hippisley] had been active and useful in a sort of volunteer negotiations, he has, I think, proceeded a little further than was necessary. Mr North's presence would set all this right.'[64] Grenville had commissioned Frederick North (1766-1827), who was to be secretary of state for Corsica, as he was informed by letter:

It may be very advantageous to His Majesty's Service that during your stay at Rome, on your way to Corsica, you should take every opportunity of informing yourself particularly of the Disposition and Means of the Government of the Ecclesiastical State with respect to any Assistance which would be given from thence to His Majesty's Efforts against the Common Enemy; and it would in particular be useful to ascertain whether if a permission could be obtained to raise recruits within those Territories. ...You will also endeavour to inform yourself what Supply of Provision might be procured from thence for His Majesty's Forces by Sea and Land, or for those of the Allies.[65]

North received a letter of recommendation from Cardinal Zelada. It was, of course, impossible for the pope to allow the British to recruit soldiers in the papal territories, as North reported back from Rome; he added that Hippisley was rather offended by his mission.[66] He had assured Cardinal Zelada that the cordial relations already existing between Britain and the Holy See would continue, and that in view of the existing circumstances in France and elsewhere, their two powers had been united against a common enemy for a common purpose; he urged that where their interests abroad were inseparable they should strive to unite their means of defence.[67] During an audience with the pope North urged that Britain be allowed to recruit soldiers in the papal territories, but his efforts proved fruitless. The pope expressed his hope that Britain would continue to wage war against the French revolution.[68] Despite the pope's apparent lack of commitment to the war effort, he did grant permission for British troops under Captain Gardner to march through his territory.[69] In 1796 a British merchant living in Rome was commissioned, on the initiative of Prince Augustus and with the support of Hippisley, to further British commercial interests there.[70] Hippisley left Rome soon afterwards and on his return to England was made a baronet. British interests in the papal states were now the concern of Thomas Jackson, minister to the king of Sardinia.[71]

On 1 September 1796 Lord Lieutenant Camden advised Lord Portland that under present circumstances it would be desirable to establish direct contacts with leading catholic clergy and laymen in Ireland. It was decided that the best person for the job would be the president of Maynooth, Dr Hussey.[72] Portland promised to talk with Hussey who would, in his opinion, readily return to Ireland to assist him[73] (in September of the same year the Irish administration had appointed Hussey as first chaplain to the Irish brigade, hoping that as a staunch anti-Jacobin he would strive to stamp out disaffection in the army: Hussey had long campaigned for the appointment of catholic military chaplains to the forces).[74] In February of the following year Hussey was consecrated bishop of Waterford and Lismore, while still retaining his presidency of Maynooth; his elevation to this see was largely through the influence of the British crown. To the dismay of Camden, however, he did not become the 'Castle bishop' he had hoped for; a short time after assuming the see of Waterford, Hussey issued a pastoral to his clergy in which he violently attacked that regulation which compelled catholic soldiers to attend protestant Sunday service. He asserted that insofar as they were subjects of the king they were duty-bound to obey their officers, but in matters which related to the King of kings the officers had no authority over them.[75] On 15 April 1797 Camden addressed a highly secret and confidential letter to Portland, urging him to suggest to the pope that 'such a dangerous man' be removed from Ireland.[76] Hussey was forced to resign as president of Maynooth and in January 1798 was replaced by Dr Peter Flood, formerly professor of moral theology at the Sorbonne.

Meanwhile, the catholic church was in an extraordinarily weak position; Rome was occupied by French revolutionary forces in 1797 and declared a republic on 20 February. Pius VI became a prisoner of the French at Valence and most cardinals were forced to flee from Rome. One of these was Cardinal York. In an address to the German bishops in November 1792 Pius VI had acknowledged the benevolence of George III and the British nation. Pius VI showed his sympathy for George III also by firmly acknowledging him as lawful King of Great Britain. Hippisely reported to London that 'the Cardinal d'York' had suggested to the pope that in the letter the words 'Princeps regnans' (implying that he was merely de facto prince) might be better substituted for 'Magnae Britt. Rex'. The pope, however, adhered to his original phrase and indemnified York by entrusting to him the 'spiritual kingdom' (or protectorship) of the Capuchins. In his report to London Hippisley wrote:

> I was present, with Monsignor Erskine, and congratulated the Cardinal on his address to the Friars, which was very long and well delivered. — He observed: *'I made it all myself.'* He has since sent me a Copy. The Cardinal seems to be wholly engrossed with his new Kingdom. He sleeps only one night in the year at Rome, and tho' on the death of his Brother he was persuaded to strike a medal privately with the Inscription of *'Hen. IX'* he now takes his old Title and in the printed address which he sent me he calls himself 'Serenissimus et Eminentissimus Cardinalis Dux Eboracensis nuncupatus Episcopus Tusculanus'.[77]

Although deprived of his revenues from France and his pension from Spain, York sold his family jewels in 1796 to help Pius VI raise the sum of money demanded of him by Napoleon. In 1798

> French revolutionary troops attacked his palace, plundered his valuable collection of manuscripts and antiquities, and compelled him to fly for his life. Infirm and almost destitute, the last male descendant of a long line of kings, fled ... first ... to Padua and subsequently to Venice. For a short time he supported himself and his household by the sale of a small quantity of silver plate, which he had saved from the wreck of his property; but this fund was soon exhausted and his condition at length became pitiable in the extreme.[78]

Cardinal Borgia wrote to Hippisely, asking him to help, and Hippisley sought the assistance of Pitt, Windham, Dundas and Andrew Stuart.

Pitt relayed Cardinal Borgia's letter to George III, along with some additional observations by Hippisley.[79] The British ambassador at Vienna, Lord Minto (1751-1814), was instructed by George III to offer the cardinal a pension of £4,000 per annum — the offer to be made as tactfully as possible.[80] Cardinal York gratefully accepted the offer and expressed his thanks in letters to those responsible. The newly installed Pope Pius VII also thanked Hippisley for his intercession.[81]

Mgr Erskine did not escape unscathed as a result of the French occupation: his source of income suddenly terminated until George III stepped in to offer him a sum of money. Erskine assumed a key position in church government during this period of destitution: he and Cardinal Borgia conducted the entire business affairs of Propaganda Fide. Erskine dealt with the nunciatures at Madrid (Nuncio Casoni), Lisbon (Pacca), Vienna (Ruffo), Cologne (Della Genga) and Holland (Brancadoro). These despatches were sometimes relayed through the Neapolitan minister in London and sometimes through Canning, who was then under-secretary of state. In the same way he managed to send letters to Rome and to the pope, who was exiled in France.[82]

The French revolution was responsible for unleashing an unprecedented reign of terror on the catholic church; many of the faithful and the clergy were massacred; prostitutes were placed on descrated altars and hailed as goddesses of reason. The British government offered refuge to persecuted French bishops and clergy and sustained them financially: it was not surprising, therefore, that Erskine expressed surprise and incredulity at the prospect — now very clear — of the Irish catholics rebelling against Britain and so making common cause with the French revolutionaries. In April 1798, on the eve of the rebellion, Erskine wrote to Archbishop Troy of Dublin reiterating the point that the people were duty-bound to obey the civil authority: he used even stronger terms than those employed by Antonelli in his frequent reminders to the Irish hierarchy of their obligations. Erskine asked whether it was possible that Irish catholics who

> for centuries have withstood all temptations and hardships not to forsake the religion of their forefathers and the duties inseparable from it, should now have given way to the deceitful insinuations of designing persons and think of joining hands with the declared enemies of religion? ... should wish to put their necks under the yoke of a people without religion, or faith, or honour, or mercy, that wherever they have gone have brought with them impiety, plunder and devastation? ... Make use of all the means that your situation affords you to open the eyes of that deluded people: sermons, exhortations, confessions, prayers.[83]

Erskine sent a copy of this letter together with Troy's reply to the home office in London, giving it complete freedom to use the correspondence in whatever way they saw fit. He promised to exercise all his influence on the Irish bishops so that they might inculcate in the people a loyalty and obedience to the government.[84] Erskine's efforts were not without effect; on 28 May the Irish hierarchy condemned the rebellion in a joint declaration and called on all catholics to refrain from participation. Two days later Lord Lieutenant Cornwallis received an address of loyalty signed by all the catholic bishops, by Dr Flood, the new president of Maynooth, and by other leading catholic clergy and laymen. A similar address of loyalty was sent the following July.[85] The bishops continued in this vein by issuing individual or joint pastorals condemning the rebellion; however, only Archbishop Troy went to the extreme of publicly excommunicating those who took part in the rebellion.[86]

Just as the kirk is one of the foundation-stones of the union of Scotland and England, so the catholic church in Ireland was planned by the British government to be part of the union of Great Britain and Ireland. It was decided that the state would subvent the catholic church in return for a veto by the government in episcopal nominations. In a long letter to Archbishop Troy in January 1799 Hippisley pointed to the example of the Scottish vicars apostolic who had accepted a state subsidy negotiated by Mgr Erskine.[87] When the ten catholic bishops on the board of Maynooth assembled in Dublin later that same month, Pitt used the opportunity to allow Lord Castlereagh to put his proposals before them. The bishops were assured by the government that 'on the acquiescence of the Irish hierarchy in these measures, the fate of that great national question, Catholic Emancipation, entirely depended'.[88] The bishops[89] feared the possible consequences of rejecting the proposals and having received no backing from Rome, since the pope was still being held prisoner in France, they eventually gave way and consented to the proposals

> that in the appointment of Roman Catholic prelates to vacant sees within the kingdom, such interference of the Government as may enable it to be satisfied of the loyalty of the persons appointed, is just, and ought to be agreed to [and] that a provision, through Government, for the Roman Catholic clergy of this kingdom, competent and secured, ought to be thankfully accepted.

It was stipulated, however, that these proposals could have no effect without the sanction of the Holy See.[90]

The bishop of Cork, Dr Moylan, pressed the government for an endowment in March 1799.[91] The vicar apostolic for London, Dr Douglas, wanted the same conditions for the English clergy.[92] Following enquiries made by Hippisley to Archbishop Troy on the subject, a detailed plan for the payment of Irish catholic prelates and clergy was prepared by the bishop of Meath and sent to Castlereagh, indicating the extent to which the government would be given control over church affairs. It was proposed that a positive selection of catholic bishops should be made by the government from a short-list of three candidates, nominated both by the bishops and the metropolitan of the province. Furthermore, there would be state control of all communications between Rome and the catholic clergy in Ireland, and only one general agent approved by the government would be allowed to reside in Rome on behalf of the catholic bishops.[93] The anglican bishop of Meath insisted that 'the whole of this business must be transacted by a direct negotiation with the court of Rome ... Mgr Erskine, if he were not so much in Hussey's hands, as I know him to be, might receive full power to settle all the points in London.'[94]

Dr Hussey had petitioned Rome in March 1798 for leave of absence from his diocese and for a coadjutor to be appointed, 'as he could not obtain the consent of the Court of Spain to leave its service'.[95] Suspicions were aroused in the home office that Hussey had secretly indicated to the Spanish government his distaste of the government's control over the clergy. Wickham, the under-secretary at the home office, revealed to Castlereagh that his suspicions on this matter had been strengthened as a result of his contacts with the Spanish chargé d'affaires in Hamburg and with Del Campo in Paris; Hussey, he believed, had reported to the Spanish government on the degree of state intervention in the affairs of the church and on the general temper of the catholics in Ireland.[96] Hussey was not granted the coadjutor but was allowed leave of absence, provided he was able to find a replacement.[97] He spent the whole of 1799 in London, where he busied himself with the affairs of the clergy. He was in favour of maintaining the union but was opposed to state endowment of the clergy. He pointed out to Fr J. Bernard Clinch, a Maynooth professor, that he had been consulted on the matter of salaries and pensions for the catholic clergy: he regarded this as completely at odds with the interests of religion and detrimental to the already slender relationship between the pastor and his flock:

> by turning the discipline and laws of the Church into a mercantile, political speculation, [it] must end in making the people unbelievers, and consequently, Jacobins — upon the French scale. Whether the prelates of Ireland have courage or energy enough to oppose any such project so hurtful to religion, I will not say. Indeed, the infernal Popery laws have lessened the courage of the clergy, as well as destroyed the honesty and morals of the people.[98]

Hussey exerted his influence on Mgr Erskine who came out against the scheme and prevented the Irish decisions of January 1799 from coming into effect. In a letter to Cardinal Borgia Erskine pointed out that 'the proposals for payment would put the clergy in the position of hired government servants and cause them to be despised by the people'.[99] Borgia then wrote to Troy in June 1799 condemning the bishops' acquiescence to the government measures as an infringement of the rights of the Holy See and reproaching him for not first referring the matter to the pope.[100] Erskine himself reproached Bishop Moylan of Cork while he was in London in 1799, pointing out to him that 'the Irish bishops had placed the Holy See in a most difficult position by putting on its shoulders all the odium of a negative to the proposals'. He also told Moylan that the bishops should consult together as soon as possible, to find a way of retracing their steps.[101] Erskine, meanwhile, successfully negotiated for a pension to be granted to the Scottish vicars apostolic who were ministering to a tiny minority of the population in Scotland;[102] he had gained a position of considerable influence in London and had been introduced to Mrs Fitzherbert. During the pope's captivity Erskine had public prayers said for him in all chapels of the three kingdoms, and when Pius VI died in French captivity, in August 1799, Erskine organised a solemn requiem mass for him in London.[103]

Robert Fagan, consul general for the two Sicilies, was sent to Rome in 1799 by Sir William Hamilton and Lord Nelson; there he received due recognition as a British agent and managed to recover all British property which had been confiscated by the revolutionary regime, particularly that which had been owned by catholic establishments such as monasteries and colleges.[104]

On 14 March 1800 the church received a new pope in the person of Pius VII. The French allowed him to return to Rome; the position of the church remained weak, however, and was under constant threat from Napoleon. As before, the Vatican was in need of every friend, and so Borgia adopted a cautious policy in his dealings with Britain; as regards Britain's treatment of the catholic church in Ireland his attitude was one of hopeful procrastination. Archbishop Troy's agent in Rome, Dr Concanen observed that Borgia was 'loth to offend or contradict Sir John Cox Hippisley'.[105] On 6 July 1800 Borgia wrote a 'most effusive letter to Hippisley', thanking him for the grant to the Scottish clergy.[106]

Bishop Hussey of Waterford died in 1803 and at the funeral soldiers tried to throw the coffin into the river Suir as a protest against his attitude to the government.[107] Bishop Moylan, on the other hand, had become an ally of the British government: 'This prelate — who had denounced the French when their fleet lay in Bantry Bay, for which he would have lost his head had they been able to land — became a great favourite with Pitt and Portland.'[108]

Hippisley sought an Irish peerage. On 4 August 1800 in a letter to Windham he gave the following account of his attempts to bring the catholic church and Britain together:

You will recollect that from 1792 to 1795 inclusively, I was occupied in Italy, in Services which are familiar to you. They were recognised by Lord Grenville, within whose Department they properly fell; — by Lord Minto, who urged me to many of them; — by the Duke of Portland and originally by yourself who afterwards founded upon them a successful application to your colleagues, in my favour. From that period to the present hour I have not been less occupied in objects of public utility. ... My communication with Lord Hobart [1760-1818; 1789-93 Chief Irish Secretary] and Lord Castlereagh has been exclusively on the Catholic subject of Ireland. They both considered that the view I had given of the subject was highly interesting. ... The Speaker communicated my Ideas to Mr Pitt, who as the Speaker told me, approved of my suggestions. The letters of Lord Castlereagh not only express his approbation of my correspondence, but assure me that he is about acting in conformity to it. ... (The proposed regulations are principally sketched in my letters to Ld Hobart, which he transmitted to Lord Castlereagh, of 12 January and 10 February 1799).

The duke of Portland was greatly interested in his scheme.[109] From this letter, in which Hippisley appears engrossed in his own merits, it would appear that he was the originator of the scheme to unite church and state in Ireland. In the same letter he reported to Windham that Bishop Moylan and Archbishop Troy had initiated a decision on his suggestion to insert a section into the Irish catechism stressing the duty of the faithful to obey the state authorities:

At a General Meeting of the Roman Catholic Prelacy, a few months since, a suggestion *from me* was brought forward, and unanimously approved, and a measure which would probably contribute much to the useful instruction of the lower classes of the Catholic Community in their Civil Duties. This I considered would be best accomplished by *addenda* interwoven with their *common Catechism,* and following the *Commandments* of *God* and their Church. ... In a letter under the joint Signatures of the Metropolitan Archbishop of Dublin, and the Catholic Bishop of Cork, (the latter was much at Balstrode last Summer) they inform me (on 1 March 1800): The Addenda you suggested have been inserted in a new edition of our Church Cathechism, now printing; which is to be taught in every Diocese in the Kingdom, and it shall be our study to continue to impress our People with a due Sense of the Social and Political Duties of good Citizens etc.[110]

In 1803 Archbishop Troy wrote to Hippisley: 'the old Calumnies against Catholics are revived, and daily urged since the late insurrection, altho' as religionists, they are as little connected with it, as with a rebellion against the Emperor of China'; he enclosed a brochure condemning the Irish rebellion of 1803, quoting the relevant section of the new catechism:

> Lesson XVII ...
> Q. What are the duties of subjects to the temporal powers?
> A. To be subject to them, and to honour and obey them not only for wrath, but also for conscience sake; for so is the will of God: 1 Peter 2; Romans 13.
> Q. Does the Scripture require any other duty of subjects?
> A. Yes, to pray for Kings, and for all who are in high station, that we may lead a quiet and peaceful life: 1 Timothy 2.
> Q. Is it sinful to resist or combine against the established authorities, or to speak with contempt or disregard of those who rule over us?
> A. Yes; St Paul says, let every soul be subject to higher powers; he that resisteth the power, resisteth the ordinances of God; and they that resist, purchase to themselves damnation: Romans 13.[111]

Sometime later the statutes of Maynooth laid down that it was the duty of the professor of moral theology to indicate to his students that no power or authority could release them from the duty to obey their king.[112] Here it again becomes apparent that Britain intended to govern Ireland through Rome.

Hippisley also concerned himself with the question of the national colleges in Rome. At the same meeting as decided on the addendum to the catechism, the bishops agreed to Hippisley's call for national superiors for the colleges in Rome as he reported to Windham: 'in conformity to a similar measure in which I succeeded after two years negotiation with Rome in favour of the English and Scotch Establishments for the Education of Priests'.[113] Lord Hobart expressed himself well satisfied with Hippisley's achievements and was subsequently informed by Lord Grenville that Mr Paget, the new appointee to Naples, would soon receive instructions regarding the national colleges in Rome.[114] In January 1801 Hippisley reported to Lord Castlereagh that the attempt to frustrate arrangements for the appointment of national superiors to British and Irish colleges in Rome had not succeeded and that Pius VII was favourably disposed towards the project.[115]

Important changes took place in 1801 from the British point of view: on 1 January the union of Great Britain and Ireland came into effect, and on 14 March Pitt delivered up the seals of office. The lord chancellor, Lord Loughborough, exerted pressure on George III not to grant catholic emancipation on the grounds that it was incompatible with the coronation oath.[116] Pitt resigned over this issue and catholics were denied the long-awaited emancipation; but it also meant that the proposed changes in the administration of the church were temporarily shelved.[117] In the autumn of 1800 Hippisley wrote to Bishop Moylan of Cork on the subject of a state provision for the prelacy and clergy, enclosing copies of letters he had received from the cardinal prefect of Propaganda and Cardinal Antonelli: these letters were interpreted by Hippisley as proof that the catholic clergy would soon express their approval for the proposed state subsidy of clergy.[118] When Cardinal Borgia received an explanation from the Irish bishops regarding their conduct at the meeting of January 1799, he appeared satisfied with it and conveyed his approval of their actions to them.[119] After Pitt's resignation, Propaganda advised the Irish bishops to 'show their gratitude and attachment to the British government by declining to accept the liberal bounty lately offered.'[120]

Hippisley informed Cardinal York of the change of government in London and of the events leading up to the change, at the same time expressing his hope that this would not be regarded as an act of hostility towards Rome; he requested York to communicate these facts to the cardinal secretary of state.[121] Mgr Erskine, the papal envoy in London, was elevated to the rank of cardinal in February 1801 but he had requested that his appointment be *in petto* while he remained in London. It was usual for former nuncios to the great catholic courts (Vienna, Paris, Madrid and Lisbon) only to be made cardinals on their recall to Rome.[122] This exceptional promotion was not only a favour for Erskine but a mark of distinction for London. Erskine's health had begun to suffer as a result of the damp English climate and at his own request he was recalled to Rome. He left England on 12 December 1801 and carried with him a recommendation from the British government as to who should be selected for a certain Irish bishopric that had become vacant.[123] He also carried a passport made out by the secretary of state, Lord Pelham, referring to him as 'Monsignor Erskine, late Legate from His Holiness at this Court'. In addition to his already considerable list of achievements Erskine had succeeded in obtaining for the papal authorities jurisdiction over British subjects who transgressed the law of the papal states; he had helped scotch a bill seeking the dissolution of all nuns' convents in England; he looked after the interests of the French bishops exiled in England who had to resign in accordance with the French concordat; he also asked the British cabinet to notify the Russian emperor of its wish to see the legations (Bologna, Ferrara, Romagna, Urbino, Ancona, Perugia and Spoleto) restored to the pope. Furthermore, in all treaties signed between Britain and France and particularly the treaty of Amiens, he ensured that the interests of the Holy See were protected. The papal states were explicitly named and recognised by a British diplomat in this treaty for the first time since the 1688 revolution. Erskine's devotion to the interests of Rome was absolute, even foregoing the usual luxury of a paid secretary while in London, so as to avoid being a financial drain on the Vatican.[124]

CHAPTER III

The Papal States and the Irish Veto

1. THE NAPOLEONIC YEARS

FOR THE first thirty years of the nineteenth century relations between Britain and the Holy See were dominated by the questions of veto, *placet* and catholic emancipation. The promise of emancipation had been held out to catholics if only they would accept the union: this promise had not been fulfilled when in 1805 Grattan initiated a new move to secure catholic emancipation. Hippisley proposed an amendment which would grant the government a right of veto in episcopal nominations, as well as a right of *placet* for all communications between the Holy See and the catholic church in Britain and Ireland; in return the government should concede emancipation for catholics. It was proposed that a special civil servant should be employed to scrutinize all communications, approving (*'placet'*) or disapproving (*'non placet'*) each message and if necessary, witholding permission for them to be passed on.[1]

The motion was not carried in parliament but it instigated a controversy among catholics; the majority of English and Scottish catholics were in favour of the motion, while most Irish catholics, supported by Dr Milner (vicar apostolic in the midland district in England, 1803-26, and London agent for the Irish bishops from 1807),[2] were against it. A small section of Irish catholic notables were in favour of the motion — among them Francis Mangan, the informer responsible for the betrayal of Lord Edward Fitzgerald; Lords Fingall, Trimleston, Kenmare, Gormanstown and Southwell; Wolfe (later chief baron), Shiel (later master of the Mint and minister at Florence), Bellew, Lynch, Donellan (who successfully campaigned for government pensions), Wyse (later a privy councillor and minister at Athens), Ball (later Mr Justice Ball) 'and others anxious to reach by a short cut the good things of the State'.[3] English catholics were apt to compromise, since they constituted a small minority of the population in England. Irish catholics, however, resented interference by England in the affairs of the church. Milner appealed to Rome for a decision regarding veto and *placet*; Propaganda answered in September 1805 that a positive nomination by a heterodox government was forbidden and that 'a mere negative power of objecting to episcopal candidates by an non-catholic sovereign admits of fewer difficulties', yet it pointed out that 'in case such a negative power should ever be granted, effective precautions would be requisitie to prevent this negative power from growing into a positive one'.[4] On 14 September 1808 the Irish bishops resolved not to consent to any alteration in the manner of nominating Irish catholic bishops but they would, however, only commend to his holiness such candidates for vacant bishoprics who were unquestionably loyal and peaceable.[5] At the same time a catholic board of English laymen, while conducting negotiations with Lord Grey and Lord Grenville, indicated their willingness to concede a right of veto in episcopal nominations to the British crown.[6] In Ireland, Daniel O'Connell began a popular agitation against the veto and in 1810 the Irish bishops reiterated their opposition to it.[7]

In 1809 Pius VII was imprisoned in the Palazzo Lansone in Savana on the Italian riviera. In 1812 Hippisley devised a plan to free the pope and deliver him to safety with the help of the British fleet. The government approved of the plan and it was decided that the idea would be communicated to the pope by Macpherson, a friend of Hippisley and rector of the Scots college in Rome. News of the plan reached Napoleon before it was implemented and the pope was moved to Fontainebleau.[8]

Charles Butler of the catholic committee meanwhile agreed with Canning on a form of veto and *placet* to be included in Grattan's emancipation bill. This 1813 bill would empower the king to nominate a committee, made up of protestants as well as catholics, whose purpose it was to decide on the candidates for vacant catholic bishoprics — the committee would be presided over by a government minister. Grattan's bill was withdrawn from parliament, however, before being put to the vote.[9] At a meeting of English and Scottish vicars apostolic, for which Milner received no invitation, a resolution in favour of the bill of 1813 was carried.[10] The catholic committee was not content with this and sought to obtain Rome's approval of veto and *placet* as laid down in the bill; Dr Macpherson acted on their behalf to procure this approval. The curia was at the time in an extremely weak position: Pius VII was still a prisoner at Fontainebleau, most cardinals were either imprisoned or banished from Rome, and Propaganda Fide was without a prefect (only the vice-prefect, Quarantotti, was in Rome). It seemed to be a good time to lean on that powerful enemy of France, England. Thus Quarantotti yielded to Macpherson's entreaties and in February 1814 issued a rescript approving of the emancipation bill of 1813 which included the clauses concerning veto and *placet*.[11]

Pius VII was released by Napoleon some time later. Rome was still in the hands of a Neapolitan provisional government, so the pope found refuge in Bologna. During this time the pope held several conferences with Lord William Bentinck (1774-1839), son of the duke of Portland and commander-in-chief of the British forces in Italy, who presented him with 50,000 zechino on behalf of the prince regent to cover the expense of his journey.[12] Pius VII sent Count Francesco Felippe Magauly Cerati to London with a letter for the prince regent in April 1814.[13] Macauly, an Irishman from King's County, was under orders to 'explain verbally the Pope's situation — his hopes of British assistance against Murat — his disposition to accede to any measures which may be deemed necessary to secure the allegiance of the Roman Catholics — and his hopes that he might have an English Resident at Rome, and be allowed to send a Minister to England'.[14] Before Macauly had reached England the papal nuncio in Lucerne, Mgr Testaferrata, reported to Pius VII that Lord Castlereagh had informed him of the British government's desire to see the pope at liberty with all his states restored to him. The catholics in Ireland, meanwhile, were not behaving well, and it was in the pope's power to appease them; Pius VII received this report on 29 April.[15] At the same time the British consul general at Naples, Mr Fagan, returned to Rome to await the pope's arrival. He was received there, as he reported to Lord William Bentinck, 'with the joy and expressions of all classes of people' with cries of 'Viva il re Georgio! Viva la nazione inglese!'.[16] While Fagan was still consul at Palermo, the vicars apostolic of England and Scotland, together with the bishops of Ireland, had appealed to him to seek the restoration of property belonging to the religious establishments of their respective nations in Rome which had been confiscated by the French in 1797 and partly sold. Fagan accordingly appealed to the Neapolitan provisional government in Rome to comply with this request.[17]

Fagan appointed Mr Richard Bartram, formerly a consul at the papal port of Civita Vecchia, to officiate *pro tempore* as vice consul in Rome; Italians were appointed to officiate as vice consuls at other ports so as to protect British trade. Fagan reported to Bentinck:

Monsignor Attanasio, who officiates for his Holiness, has just been here conveying his own request and that of the public that an English Regiment might be sent to Civita Vecchia, and come here for the Pope's arrival, for there is a general alarm, fearing a disturbance in Rome on his arrival this would be against the Neapolitans, and the French Party and might have the most serious consequences.

Fagan was of the opinion that his presence was more necessary in Rome than at Naples and sought Bentinck's approval: 'I presume that there will be no advantage at present at Naples in the Consular line.'[18] He forwarded copies of his correspondence and asked: 'May I request your Lordship to inform Government of my conduct if approved by you?'[19]

While still at Cesena Pius VII wrote to the prince regent requesting British assistance against Murat, then still 'King of Naples':

After a vigorous struggle we were despoiled of all our dominions; and it was announced to Europe, in a decree, that this spoilation was the consequence of the temporal Sovereign of Rome having constantly refused to make war upon the English ... we have ... nevertheless resolved to depute again to them a Nuncio Extraordinary, Monsignor Annibal della Genga, Archbishop of Tyre, in order to explain in person the various objects of our distress and the cogency of our arguments. He will have the honour of delivering the present respectful memorial for your Royal Highness, to Lord Castlereagh, your Minister. We earnestly intreat your Royal Highness's protection on behalf of our rights.[20]

A few days before he re-entered Rome Pius VII addressed another two letters to the prince regent from Foligno, in which he thanked the British nation for his liberation and requested British backing at the congress of Vienna to regain the church states.[21] On 23 May he spoke with Fagan 'at the Justiniani', seven miles from Rome (i.e. La Guistiana, today a suburb of Rome). On this occasion the pope dwelled for the most part on memories of his French captivity; Fagan reported: 'He praised extremely the English nation and particularly Lord W[illiam] B[entinck] saying that had it not been for us, affairs would have finished badly.' Pius VII did not extend his trust to the Austrians; he was well-disposed to the emperor but the Austrian cabinet was unreliable, as Fagan reported on his conversation with the pope. Napoleon had argued to the pope that he should declare war on England because it had a protestant government, to which the pope replied that as he was the 'Padre commune', he could wage war with no one.[22]

Robert Fagan became severely ill, his health and nervous system succumbing to the strain imposed on him by his unfaithful Italian wife in Palermo.[23] Having sufficiently convalesced, Fagan, accompanied by his friend Edward Dodwell (1767-1811), was granted an audience with Pius VII who had recently returned to Rome.[24] In a report to Bentinck on the audience he disguised the pope's identity by referring to him as 'the great Personage',[25] stating that it was he

who honoured me with a familiar conversation, making me sit down by him — He mentioned with every warmth of Gratitude, the particular attentions and Treatment your Lordship has held towards Him — and said — that he was fully sensible that the restitution of the Temporal power was entirely owing to the interference of England, and that our Country was the source of every obligation. He believed some little to Russia[sic], that the Austrian court was similar to that of Naples, full of intrigue and on which there could be little dependence — He also said that Bonaparte had frequently insisted on the declaration of war against England, — and that of the great Personage [= Pius VII] entering into the coalition, that B[onaparte] had promised should this His will be put into practice, he would agree to those adjustments desired on the subject of Religion — He was answered, 'What have we to do with coalitions', or with war; the convention you insist on is in direct opposition to the character of the church, Her principles being to contribute by every means to Peace, and to prevent as far as She can the destruction of human nature — It was further observed that if these insurmountable difficulties did not subsist, England had done this State no injury — and that if she had, that this Government did not possess a sufficient force to enable it to act — B[onaparte] replied that the English were the worst of Heretics — and that notwithstanding it was true they [the church states] had no force yet the declaration of war would have the best effect on the Public Opinion — He was answered that the principles of the Church, and the Great Man's [the pope's] conscience could not permit him to accede to the demand. B[onaparte] got into a violent passion and said — You must attribute to yourself alone the consequence that will result from this your Negative.[26]

Fagan was granted several more audiences by the pope, as he subsequently reported:

The Pontiff is frank in expressing his sentiments and seems to honour me with His confidence. . . . He is pleased to pay me on any public occasion a distinguished attention, and at every audience he favours me with, insists on my sitting close to him, and on leaving His room, takes my hand in His, generally accompanying me to the door — such humility from a person of His rank, and situation fully proves his benign disposition. . . . I am on the very best of footing with this Government and have the full confidence of the Ministers, for in any intricate business they do me the honour to consult me — and I freely advance those sentiments which candour imposes, or Circumstances permit; I have advantaged no *pretentions,* but have under the character of *consul* for *the two Sicilies,* proposed, in a friendly way, the adopting those Measures, which I conceived might be advantageous to our Interests: both Political and Commercial.[27]

Soon after Pius VII's return to Rome, the vicar apostolic of the midland district of England and London agent of the Irish bishops, Dr Milner, arrived to acquaint him with the arguments of those opposed to the veto. Irish catholics had rallied to oppose Quarantotti's rescript and his concession to the British government of a right of veto in episcopal nominations. At a meeting in Dublin on 12 May 1814 they denounced the rescript as non-obligatory. The Irish hierarchy convened at Maynooth on 27 June and endorsed this action; Dr Murray, the coadjutor-archbishop of Dublin, was sent to Rome to submit to the pope the opinions of the Irish bishops on the subject.[28]

Fagan met Milner in Rome and on discovering the purpose of his
mission cautioned the pope against conceding to his wishes, as he
reported soon after:

> In a conversation I had with his Holiness I made free to observe,
> that some points that are the object of Dr Milner's mission, might in
> the present state of affairs in England and Ireland, relative to
> Religion, merit His Holiness's consideration, before they were
> acceded to; the holy father answered, 'what you say is just. I shall
> desire the Bishops to give in writing every demand which I shall
> examine and give due consideration to.' I flatter myself that this
> prevention may merit your Lordship's approbation.[29]

During an audience with Milner the pope severely criticised
Quarantotti's action as being arbitrary but did not voice any opinion
on the matter. Milner was requested to submit his view on the matter
in writing to Cardinal Litta. On the eve of the feast of Saints Peter and
Paul, Milner was advised at an official audience 'that he had done his
duty, and ought to proceed on the track he had hitherto pursued; but
it was added that this ought to be done with moderation, and without
irritating the feelings of others'.[30] The catholic board which had
appealed to the pope in support of the veto received a similar reply in
which the pope was absolutely non-committal; this communication
arrived on 28 December 1814 but did indicate that a further rescript
would be issued on the matter.[31] Pius VII appeared to be buying time
in view of the British government's desire to secure a right of veto.

Fagan had an audience with Cardinal Pacca, the pro-secretary of
state, on 22 June 1814 during which it was revealed that Napoleon
appeared to be planning a come-back and that Murat intended to
make a sudden incursion into papal territory; these suspicions were
aroused by two letters intercepted from Elba.[32] Cardinal Pacca and
Pope Pius VII both expressed their hope that Fagan would remain in
Rome; Fagan himself was eager to stay. He sent his brother-in-law,
Luigi Ferra, to Palermo to deliver his letters to Lord Bentinck,
together with a present from the pope containing two gold medals,
each with a portrait of the pope, for Lord and Lady William. On his
return Ferra was to bring Fagan's family with him.[33]

In June 1814 Cardinal Consalvi came to London, where the
emperor of Russia and the king of Prussia were present to take part in
the allied victory consultations. Twelve years earlier Cardinal Erskine
had appeared at court in London dressed in the black robe
characteristic of his office while remaining *in petto* in deference to the
English court. Cardinal Consalvi, however, was the first Vatican
representative since Cardinal Pole to appear publicly in London 'by
the kind and generous permission of the government adorned with the
distinctive badge of his dignity, in the same way as if he had been in
this our city', as Pius VII was to gratefully acknowledge in his

allocation to the consistory on 4 September 1815:

> And further, when he proceeded to an audience of His Royal
> Highness, the Prince Regent of England, to present our brief, and
> to express the sentiments of admiration, friendship, and attachment
> which we entertain towards him, as well as towards that valiant and
> in so many ways illustrious nation, he was received at the palace
> with such marks of benevolence and of kindness for us whom he
> represented, as could with difficulty have been exceeded. On which
> account, professing ourselves deeply obliged to that Prince, and to
> the different orders that comprise that generous nation, towards
> which we always entertained great goodwill, we most gladly seize
> such an occasion to attest thus publicly our esteem, and our lively
> gratitude.[34]

On 23 June 1814 Consalvi wrote to Castlereagh requesting British
assistance in regaining the church states, including Avignon.[35]
Consalvi had an audience with the prince regent on 5 July, but only
after the Spanish ambassador had been received; the reason for this
was that the pope, whom Consalvi represented, was recognised merely
as prince of the church states and not as pope.[36] Consalvi reported to
Pacca on his meeting with Castlereagh on 4 July which had lasted for
one and a half hours. Consalvi was pleased to inform Pacca that
Britain favoured the restitution of the legations to the Holy See. In
return Britain wanted the pope to exert influence on those countries
still engaged in the slave trade, particularly Spain and Portugal, to
stop this evil practice. The main topic of their discussion, however,
was Ireland. Consalvi informed Pacca that it was impossible to relate
briefly all that Castlereagh had said to him on that subject; but in the
context of Quarantotti's rescript Castlereagh pointed out that it was
impossible to bring either parliament or cabinet to consent to a change
in the English constitution which would result in the much-desired
catholic emancipation as long as all the government would receive in
return was an assurance from the Irish hierarchy of their good
conduct and the innocent nature of their communications with
abroad. Consalvi replied that granting the exequatur or 'placet' right
was impossible; while the holy father tolerated some catholic states
practising the exequatur, he did *not approve* of their doing so. In
reference to Quarantotti's letter he believed that the bill referred to in
it had been rejected and therefore saw no need for the pope to
comment on it. Consalvi indicated to Pacca that the holy father
should indirectly refer to the matter, lest his silence be mistaken for
approval of Quarantotti's opinions. Consalvi went on to inform
Castlereagh that the pontiff would make his opinions known through
Propaganda Fide to the bishops of the three kingdoms, and his
opinions would be those contained in the new letter and not those
expressed in Quarantotti's. Castlereagh stuck to his demands for an

oath of allegiance to be taken by catholics and for a right of veto in episcopal nominations as well as the right of exequatur for all communications between the bishops and Rome. However, he did not foresee any difficulty in admitting a chargé d'affaires from the Holy See to London and, notwithstanding impeding laws, an appointee from London to the Holy See: all impeding laws would be repealed as soon as they came to an agreement and the proposals were put before the new session of parliament. Castlereagh was willing to receive an ecclesiastic but Consalvi commented that as he would have to assume an unofficial character he would first have to operate under the title 'ambassador', as did Mgr Arezzo at St Petersburg. Consalvi concluded his report by informing Pacca that a certain Signor Bonelli from Rome, a convert from Judaism, was apparently destined to become 'Agent of the Holy Father in London' as this was the express wish of the prince regent, and it merely required the sanction of Pius VII before becoming a reality. Castlereagh, however, did not mention anything about Bonelli during their conference.[37] Consalvi's report was brought to Rome by Crown Prince Ludwig of Bavaria.[38]

On the evening of 6 July Consalvi was accompanied in London by Mgr Della Genga, the future Pope Leo XII, and Mgr Raffael Mazio (1765-1832), since 1814 secretary of Latin letters and later actively involved in dealings between Hanover and the Holy See; in 1830 he became Cardinal.[39] (The secretary for Latin letters was responsible for those letters penned neither by the more important secretaria brevium — responsible for papal letters, like that establishing the English hierarchy — nor by the secretaria brevium ad principes — responsible for letters to princes.) On 9 July Castlereagh wrote to Consalvi again urging the pope's intervention to procure the total abolition of slavery.[40] From Paris Consalvi addressed further reports on his stay in London to Cardinal Pacca: he observed that catholics had polarised into two distinct groups: English and Scots catholics on the one hand and Dr Milner and the Irish on the other. Consalvi described Milner as being of the best intentions and greatly attached to the Holy See, but also a hothead who engaged in intrigue and who was inimical to the government. The Irish were attached to the Holy See to the extent of martyrdom but were natural enemies of the English and apt to see everything English as 'being coloured black'. He regarded the Irish bishops and clergy as being dominated by the Irish catholic lords and their clubs; his suspicions deepened when the clergy who had signed a document which would have secured a government pension for them now regarded the whole proposal contrary to religion. Consalvi had spoken with Bishop Moylan of Cork while he was in London and deduced from the situation in Ireland that opposition to the proposed veto and government pension was in fact attributable to the enmity that existed between Ireland and England, and to the political power of the catholic nobility which resulted in their exercising considerable influence over the hierarchy; it could also be attributed to ignorance of the actual position of religion in all other states. The English and Scottish catholics, however, while being attached to the Holy See were drawn to the government. Consequently Milner found himself totally isolated in that he had become a serious obstacle to good relations between Rome and the English government.[41] Consalvi requested a decision from Propaganda Fide on the three British demands: a special oath, a voice in the nominations of bishops and deans in England, Scotland and Ireland and the right of exequatur.[42] On 13 August Cardinal Pacca addressed a letter to the cardinals of the congregation for the propagation of the faith, offering his opinions on the subject: with regard to the special oath which assured the government of the allegiance and submission of her catholic subjects, he declared it ought not to be contrary to the principles of their religion; regarding the nomination of bishops and deans the government could reject a candidate if he was an enemy of that government, and instruct the electors to choose a new candidate; the right of exequatur should not be granted. The congregation together with Cardinal Pacca were to devise a formula for implementing the oath that would satisfy the government yet was not contrary to religious principles, and decide on terms for the election of bishops and deans; they had also to decide on the wording for a refusal on the right of exequatur.[43]

Meanwhile Lord William Bentinck, commander of the British fleet in the Mediterranean, had received his gift from the pope, delivered by Ferra, and thanked him in a warm-hearted letter dated 14 July 1814.[44] During his stay in Rome Fagan had been received by Pius VII and by Cardinal Alessandro Mattei,[45] and on 7 September of the same year he reported to Bentinck on his final days in Rome.

I had the honour of addressing a letter to your Lordship which I am informed by Mr Webb, arrived at Genoa after your Lordship had left that city — this however I am informed was forwarded to you, there was inclosed a duplicate of an official paper from the Roman Government to ours, requesting a Loan of three hundred thousand pounds, and proposing to give any security that Government could offer, till the Capital and Interest was paid. The hopes of receiving a letter from your Lordship relative to some Instructions I requested to have, united to the desire His Holiness expressed that I should remain in Rome till He received an answer to the letter he had desired me to forward to you, caused my stay in that City till the 10th of August. During which period I procured this Government annulling the duty on Tonnage, the lessening other duty on commerce, the restitution of the funds belonging to the Catholic Establishments, and the assent of His Holiness to permit those I had appointed to act pro tempore as Vice Consuls under the provisionary Government, to continue to officiate till the approbation of our Government might be received relative to such appointments. Being disappointed in my hopes of receiving a letter, my health having meliorated considerably I determined to quit Rome for Naples.[46]

Fagan, who was disgusted with Sicily for personal reasons, beseeched William Bentinck:

Permit met at present to supplicate your Lordship's kind Influence towards obtaining a confirmation to the situation I at present fill, ..., either this or a diplomatic appointment at Rome with a competent salary would be the ne plus ultra of my wishes; His Holiness has expressed to many his ardent wish, that Government would honour me with an appointment at his Court.[47]

Forced to return to London on account of his daughter's illness, Fagan received a letter from Cardinal Pacca assuring him 'that the Holy Father is very much satisfied with the conduct you held during your stay at Rome, where it will give him much pleasure to see you again, and if possible, officially established'.[48] Fagan forwarded a copy of the letter to Bentinck, expressing his hope 'by your Lordship's kind influence that I might at least get that appointment which in fact I have every claim to ... Mr Dodwell by desire of the Pope presents all the English and does every other little business at Rome that should any of your Lordship's friends go there he will render them every service, indeed he begged me to tell you so.'[49] Fagan, however, was disappointed. In a last letter from Lyons in France on 15 November 1814 he sent an estimate of Murat's force to Bentinck and commented:

and to these may possibly be added, as I am informed by good authority, the greatest part of the military of the Venetian and Milanese states who, disgusted with the oppressive conduct of the Austrians, have offered themselves to Murat, and he is only expecting the determination of our Government relative to himself either to accept, or reject, their offer and it may be expected should he despair that we may soon see the Emperor of Elba at the head of Murat's army, which in the existing state of Europe, may probably fling it in a new revolution ... as the Northern part of Italy are all dissatisfied and in France almost all the military and those who were employed express openly their sentiments in their favour.[50]

Fagan's apprehensions proved to be only too well founded. Napoleon returned from Elba, and Murat at the head of 90,000 men invaded the church states. During the previous weeks the foreign secretary, Lord Castlereagh, had taken steps to enter into regular diplomatic communications with the papal states. The under-secretary of the foreign office, Edward Cooke, who was due to visit Italy, was given instructions to include Rome in his itinerary and sound out the possibilities for an exchange of accredited agents without, if possible, a public character. On 18 March 1815 Cooke had been able to report to Castlereagh that Cardinal Pacca had expressed to him the delight of Pius VII at this English overture, and that his holiness was willing to accomodate himself to whatever was most suitable and convenient to the British Government.[51] The pope fled from Murat's troops to Genoa and placed himself under the protection of England, the British fleet being at anchor there. The commander of the British fleet and garrison at Genoa was Lord William Bentinck, and it was he who incurred the ultimate responsibility for the pope's safety and maintenance.[52]

This provided the British government with an ideal opportunity to press for the right of interference in episcopal nominations in Ireland as desired by Castlereagh and other British politicians. On 26 April 1815 Cardinal Litta, the prefect of Propaganda Fide, issued a rescript in the name of the pope to Doctors Poynter (1762-1827; since 1812 vicar apostolic of the London district), Milner and Troy permitting such interference: 'The agency employed in procuring this official paper, was even at that period far from being a mystery. Lord Bentinck ... frankly acknowledged to have used all his influence on this occasion, while it is equally certain that Dr Poynter had contributed to advance the measure.'[53] However, Cardinal Litta, whose signature the letter bears, was no supporter of the scheme. He later observed to the representative of the Irish catholics in Rome, Fr Hayes: 'In Genoa I said and repeated to the pope, and to his advisers, and to all, do not execute this letter, meddle not in any shape with this matter; but my admonition was fruitless; and against my own decided private opinion I affixed my signature thereto.'[54] It was in fact Cardinal Consalvi and Fontana, the pope's private theologian, who were in favour of the scheme. The rescript was 'penned and executed by Fontana, but it had, in the first instance, been obtained from the pontiff at the urgent persuasive suggestions' of Consalvi.[55] At the congress of Vienna England was decidedly in favour of the restoration of the church states. For this reason and in the hope that it would eventually lead to catholic emancipation, Consalvi sought to cultivate good understanding between the Holy See and London. In Vienna he negotiated with Castlereagh; the historian Brenan states that Consalvi applied to Rome for full power to reach an agreement with Castlereagh on the mode of government interference in the selection of catholic bishops. Rome, however granted powers only *ad referendum,* i.e. that he might confer with Castlereagh on the matter 'but should come to no definite arrangement without first referring it to his holiness'.[56]

It is now necessary to outline the content of Cardinal Litta's rescript. It comprised three clauses: the third clause rejected the proposal that the British government should be granted a right of exequatur, i.e. the right of government to supervise all correspondence between catholics in the British Isles and the Holy See. In the first two clauses he outlined the two concessions that the Holy See was willing to make once catholic emancipation had been granted: firstly, the holy father would allow catholics to take an oath of loyalty to the king and his lawful authority, and secondly, a right of veto in episcopal nominations would be granted to the government in accordance with the following mode: those entitled to vote would be required to submit their list of candidates to government ministers who could then eliminate from the list those whom they considered disloyal but leaving a sufficient number of candidates from which to make a selection. Popular resistance prevented this. This mode of government interference, the so-called 'Irish Veto', was prevented in Ireland; however, it was adopted in certain German states, e.g. Baden and Hanover.[57]

2. THE LAST YEARS OF POPE PIUS VII AND CARDINAL CONSALVI, 1815 – 1823

Napoleon and Murat were finally defeated in 1815 and Pius VII was able to return to Rome. During the campaign against Murat the British minister at Florence, Lord Burghersh, the future earl of Westmoreland, had his first meeting with the Roman authorities and in particular Cardinal della Somaglia (1744-1830).[1]

At the end of July 1815 it was leaked in Ireland that 'vetoism had obtained a triumph,' and on 2 August the *Cork Mercantile Chronicle* printed this extract of a letter from Rome: 'The Pope in Genoa consented to the veto — Dr Poynter was for it; Dr Milner against it; but the number of English Catholics who came here last winter persuaded his Holiness; so Dr Poynter went contented from the Pope.'[2] This announcement created a public outcry: the independent papers agitated against the measure and the clergy and laity appealed to the Irish hierarchy, who were assembled in Dublin, not to acquiesce to the government veto. The vetoists, on the other hand, resorted, for the first time, to stressing papal infallibility as a means of silencing those who opposed the wishes of the government. As we shall see, this idea was taken up by the British government in the 1860s.[3] On 23 August 1815 the Irish catholic bishops who were assembled in Dublin for a national synod 'pronounced every, the least, interference of the crown, direct or indirect, in the appointment of bishops for the Catholic Church in Ireland, essentially injurious, and eventually destructive to the Roman Catholic religion in this country; declaring themselves bound, by all canonical constitutional means in their power, for ever to deprecate and oppose it'.[4] They sent a deputation to Rome comprising Dr Murray, the coadjutor for the archbishop of Dublin, Dr Murphy, bishop of Cork, and Dr Blake, archdeacon of Dublin, to protest against the decision of the pope. The Irish catholic laity likewise appointed a deputation: Sir Thomas Esmonde and Owen O'Conor declined to go, so it became the responsibility of one man, the Rev. Richard Hayes.

Hayes was born in Wexford on 20 January 1788 and had become well acquainted with the language and customs of the Roman court, as he had previously spent eight years in Rome studying scripture, church history, canon law, Italian and Hebrew. He had returned to Ireland in August 1811. He now departed from Ireland charged with representing the case of Irish catholics and arrived in Rome on 25 October 1815 after a long and difficult journey. The two episcopal deputies had arrived the day before; they had their first audience with the cardinal secretary of state, Cardinal Consalvi, and afterwards met Pius VII, to whom they submitted the resolutions and remonstrances of the Irish hierarchy. Against normal procedure they were directed to refer these to Consalvi for further consideration. Thus the matter was taken out of the hands of Propaganda, where it would have had better prospects of success. On 9 November Fr Hayes received his first audience with the pope; knowing that Propaganda was the legitimate body for investigating ecclesiastical matters with regard to Ireland and Britain, he was determined not to let the issue pass through any other channel. Pius VII assured him that the prefect of Propaganda would be consulted on the matter but still referred it to the congregation for extraordinary ecclesiastical affairs, which was dominated by Consalvi. Meanwhile, the vetoists together with Hippisley were exerting their influence: numerous pro-government Irish papers such as the *Carrick Morning Post* were sent to Rome for circulation. They contained articles depicting the delegation and remonstrances of the Irish laity as emanating from a few Dublin hotheads who were not representative of the nation. In this way they sought to discredit Hayes, but Cardinal Litta, the prefect of Propaganda Fidei, gave these assertions little credence. (Authentic documents subsequently discovered at Propaganda have shown how false in fact they were.) It was unfortunate for the Irish delegation that he was appointed an ambassador extraordinary at this time, charged with greeting the Austrian emperor, Francis I, who was arriving at Milan. During his long absence the efforts of the Irish deputies to obtain a favourable hearing proved fruitless. The British government, meanwhile, stumbled upon yet another reason as to why the pope should be grateful to them: under the second treaty of Paris France had to return all works of art stolen during the revolutionary wars; the British government decided to cover the expense of returning these art treasures to Rome. The famous sculptor, Canova, travelled with them, bringing letters from the prince regent and Castlereagh to the pope and Cardinal Consalvi.[5] On 26 October 1815 Pius VII sent letters of profuse thanks to the prince regent and Castlereagh;[6] the prince acknowledge the pope's letter with a personal and friendly reply on 4 December.[7] The pope responded to this exceptional gesture in February 1816 by expressing his hope that there might follow an exchange of diplomatic agents: 'We anxiously look forward to the moment when the relations of good understanding and intimate amity with your Royal Court and the great and generous English nation shall be established upon an uninterrupted firm footing.'[8]

Against this background it hardly seems surprising that the efforts of the Irish deputies were in vain. On 5 January 1816 they demanded their passports. The following day they received a document allegedly drawn up by Mgr Mazio. The document confirmed the Genoese rescript granting a right of veto in episcopal nominations to the British government; it even went so far as to censure the Irish prelates. The Irish prelates refused to receive the document and in their final audience with Pius VII they complained about the letter and left. Hayes was the only Irish representative remaining in Rome and he was granted a third audience with the pope the following day. During the forty-five minute audience Hayes elaborated on his argument while the pope expressed his fear that if they did not concede on the question of veto, Irish catholics might once again suffer persecution at the hands of the British government. Hayes replied: 'Holy father, we dread no persecution; but we dread your holiness's sanction of a measure which we must resist, as we would be thereby deprived of those sympathies of the Holy See, which have ever consoled us under the fierce trials we have endured for our attachment to the centre of unity.'[9]

Pius VII, however, felt it more important for the well-being of the catholic church to remain on friendly terms with the greatest power of the time, England. He also believed that he could silence Irish opposition to the veto by exerting his papal authority. In February 1816 he addressed a letter to Archbishop Troy of Dublin in which he attempted to vindicate his concession to the British government on the question of veto by pointing out that it was not a right of nomination, and even the right of veto was restricted insofar as the government had to leave a sufficient number of candidates on the list for the pope to make a selection. His ignorance of the Irish way of thinking became apparent when he referred to the precedent set by St Leo the great, who sought the people's approval before choosing a bishop so as to ensure that the new incumbent did not meet with opposition. The fact that approval of the people and approval of the British government were so irreconcilably opposed in Ireland did not even enter his mind. This attitude was once again reflected in a letter to the Irish prelates in which he attempted to palliate their apprehensions that the British government would use its right of veto to let only weak and servile men become bishops: he said that it seemed inconceivable that the British cabinet, which only a short time ago had repealed many penal laws and had assisted the Holy See in regaining the church states, would want to injure or ruin the catholic church. He concluded his letter by asking the Irish bishops to preach submission to the Irish catholics so that a climate might be created where emancipation would be granted.[10]

This papal rescript met with determined and unanimous resistance in Ireland.[11] This reaction should have served to indicate to the British government that the pope had only limited influence over catholics in political matters and that it was illusory to believe that Irish catholics could be governed through Rome without paying heed to their rights and interests.

The Irish delegate in Rome, Richard Hayes, sought to obtain papal sanction for the domestic nomination of candidates for bishoprics. He formulated a plan according to which 'the parish priests, including the members of chapters, were to elect three candidates; the metropolitan and his suffragans should then record their opinions with respect to the merits of each, and Propaganda should then institute upon their joint testimony'.[12] Propaganda Fide looked favourably on the plan and it seemed at first to have a good chance of success.

Britain, however, was not content to leave the matter there. A British consul, Mr Parke, was appointed to the Roman states in 1816 and placed under Lord Burghersh, the British minister at Florence. Burghersh was in Rome often during his time at Florence and he corresponded with Cardinal Consalvi whenever circumstances required.[13] Yet the existence of old laws prevented the opening of official relations between England and the Holy See. However, the English sovereign at this time was also king of Hanover, so steps were taken to establish official relations between *Hanover* and the Holy See (Pius VII meanwhile continued to make friendly gestures towards Britain by sending to the prince regent copies of those art treasures which had been restored to Rome with English assistance.)[14] Since the Hanoverian succession in 1714 there existed a German chancery in London; since 1727 it was headed by a 'Minister to the Highest Person' who was senior (though not in rank) to other ministers of the Hanoverian government as he alone had the right to be in personal attendance to the king (the 'Highest Person'). Count Münster was minister at the time and had, as previously mentioned, been in Rome with Prince Augustus in 1794 and was personally acquainted with Cardinal Consalvi. The prince regent and Münster chose Baron Friedrich von Ompteda (1772-1819) as the first Hanoverian minister to Rome. Ompteda, a notorious gambler in his youth, had previously been sent to Italy in 1814 on a secret mission to spy on Princess Caroline of Wales.[15] On 9 July 1816 Münster asked Ompteda if he was willing to take up the post.[16] He agreed and on 11 October he was appointed minister to the Holy See. As he was not well acquainted with canon law, Justus Leist (1770-1858), who had been professor of canon law at Göttingen university, was appointed counsellor for the mission, and August Kestner (1777-1853), who was fluent in Italian and knew the country well, was appointed secretary.[17]

In September 1816 Pius VII addressed a letter of thanks to the prince regent for the liberation by the British fleet of Christian slaves at Algiers. The prince regent replied to the pope in December thanking him for the replica statuary he had sent.[18] On 10 January 1817 the pope was officially informed by the prince regent of the establishment of a Hanoverian mission in Rome.[19] On his way to Rome Ompteda sought the advice and information of Prince Metternich.[20] The Hanoverian secretary, Kestner, arrived in Rome on 20 March; in his first letter home to his sister he declared himself struck with the great number of Englishmen in Rome, estimating their number as being about 1,800.[21] The Hanoverian counsellor, Leist, reported to London that English prestige in Rome was so great that in order to effect something it was sufficient to say that the prince regent required it and it would be granted, as the pope could not refuse him anything.[22] Baron Ompteda arrived in Rome on 15 April and was received the next day by Cardinal Consalvi and two days later had his first audience with the pope. Ompteda's instructions were issued in London and the secretary of the legation had to copy the correspondence in duplicate, sending one copy to London and the other to Hanover.[23] Ompteda's first request was that the Irish delegate, Hayes, be banished from Rome. The British consul, Parke, and especially Ompteda used every means possible to remove Hayes; Ompteda had long and repeated interviews with Consalvi during which he urged the necessity of Hayes's banishment; Consalvi replied that he was unable to get the consent of his holiness the pope on the matter. Ompteda then approached the general of the Franciscan order, to which Hayes belonged, and the guardian of his monastery, S. Isidore, in Rome. Both refused Ompteda's request as no charge of immorality could be brought against Hayes and he was in Rome as a delegate of a nation and therefore beyond their jurisdiction. Hayes was informed of Ompteda's intrigues by some priests who were associated with the cardinal secretary of state; he continued undeterred to solicit support in Propaganda for his plan for domestic nomination in Ireland. The plan had been printed by Propaganda at the end of April and on 19 May 1817 the cardinals of Propaganda Fide took a vote on the issue: all but Cardinal Fontana, the co-author of the Genoese rescript, voted in favour of the plan. Fontana then proposed an amendment that Cardinal Litta should refer the plan to the court of ecclesiastical affairs, to which Litta conceded. Ompteda and Parke went immediately to Castel Gandolfo and presented their arguments so forcefully that this time they succeeded in obtaining an order of banishment for Hayes. Two days after the meeting at Propaganda, where only the procrastination of Cardinal Fontana had prevented the immediate success of Hayes's plan for domestic nomination of bishops for Ireland, he received an order of banishment from the Roman states, and the plan, for the moment, was shelved. Hayes was suffering from a malignant fever when he was arrested in the convent of S. Isidore and placed in custody while he lay in bed. On 16 July he was led out of the Roman states by a junior officer; after a four-day journey he was issued with a passport of banishment. He reached Ireland on 24 September in poor health.

News of Fr Hayes's mission and subsequent banishment became known in Ireland through a letter from Dr Dromgoole in Rome which was printed in the July issue of the *Orthodox Journal or Catholic Monthly Intelligencer*. At a general meeting in Dublin on 19 July 1817 the catholic board addressed a remonstrance to Pius VII complaining that no answer had been received following their previous communication, and their disappointment had been heightened on hearing of Fr Hayes's banishment. A letter bearing the signature of Pius VII was issued from Rome on 21 February 1818 in answer to this remonstrance. Two reasons were given as to why the original remonstrance had not been replied to: firstly that a sufficient answer had already been given to the episcopal delegation and secondly that the tone of the laity's remonstrance was disrespectful. It denied any foreign interference in the decision to banish Fr Hayes, insisting that he had brought this action on himself through ill-conduct; his writings were regarded as intemperate and his language to the pope as offensive; his distrust of Consalvi and incessant aspersions on the Roman government were cited as evidence of this. This document was read at a meeting of catholics in Dublin on 1 June 1818 and might have provoked anti-papal feeling among Irish catholics. Yet it was Fr Hayes himself who stepped in to defuse the potentially dangerous situation triggered by this ill-advised document by solemnly declaring that he would choose death rather than allow any private or personal feeling betray him into the slightest contest with the authority or dignity of the head of the catholic church. Soon after this he received an invitation to form a schismatical church of the United States, its originators in South Carolina obviously playing on his maltreatment by the Roman authorities. It was also suggested that he allow himself to be consecrated bishop by the Jansenist archbishop of Utrecht and then proceed to North America to consecrate other bishops for the new national church. Fr Hayes again proved his loyalty to the catholic church by denouncing the schism to Dr Troy and sending an Italian translation of the denunciation to Rome for which he was highly lauded by Fontana, now prefect of Propaganda. (This was not the last attempt in the United States to form a national church.)[24]

Many of the papers and correspondence of the Hanoverian mission in Rome were destroyed by bombs in World War II, so it is difficult to determine which areas of anglo-papal relations were dealt with by the mission and which by Lord Burghersh. However, certain matters were dealt with by direct correspondence. In January 1817 Castlereagh wrote to Consalvi: 'Your Eminence is aware that in the present state of our Laws there are delicacies to be observed, but I trust that nothing will impede the mutual desire between the two states to render each other genuine and reciprocal acts of kindness.'[25] This act of kindness which Castlereagh was hinting at was a thinly-disguised invitation to select his nominess as vicars apostolic of the new vicariates of Canada; these nominess were Dr MacDonell for Upper Canada, Burke for Nova Scotia and MacEachern for Prince Edward Island. Four months later Consalvi replied that MacDonell and Burke had been appointed but they wanted to inform themselves on MacEachern before deciding on his appointment.[26] Britain would in return recognise Mgr Plessis as bishop of Quebec, a position he had held since 1806.

Pius VII and the prince regent also exchanged letters: in April 1817, against normal procedure, the pope sent a letter to the prince regent thanking him for his letter announcing the establishment of a mission in Rome.[27] On 30 March the pope congratulated the prince regent on his escape from an assassination attempt; the prince regent acknowledged this letter and some months later wrote a letter of thanks for the Stuart papers which had been handed over to him. In November 1817 Pius VII sympathised with the prince regent on the death of Princess Charlotte, for which he was sent a letter of thanks in January 1818.[28]

In the aftermath of Hayes's banishment from the Roman states Hippisley returned to Rome where he received an audience at the Quirinal; he used the occasion to instruct Rome on what in his opinion were Irish misrepresentations.[29] During the negotiations for a Hanoverian concordat the Roman negotiator, Mgr Mazio, proposed to Baron Ompteda that the English monarch, as king of Hanover, should content himself with the right of veto he had been granted in the Genoese rescript of 1815 as sovereign of Ireland and which he had accepted as such.[30]

The British government was in fact exercising its influence on Irish episcopal nominations in a very surreptitious manner: on the death of an Irish bishop the foreign secretary instructed Lord Burghersh to communicate with Consalvi on who he regarded as the most suitable successor and who he regarded as unsuitable to succeed to the vacant bishoprics. As a rule Rome complied with British wishes, not always by appointing the British candidate but usually by not appointing those deemed to be unsuitable. It was in this way that Patrick Curtis became archbishop of Armagh and primate of all Ireland in 1819.[31]

Dr Curtis had been head of the Irish college in Salamanca for fifty years. It was reported that he

> had communicated very valuable information to the Duke of Wellington while Soult held his headquarters at Salamanca. His connection with the Duke was suspected ... had not the English arrived ... he would have been executed as a spy. It may be added that the mysterious reference in Wellington's despatch of May 8, 1811 is to Curtis. ... The Duke of Wellington maintained for many years a constant and cordial correspondence with the Primate.[32]

In 1823 Propaganda Fide, which continued to supervise the affairs of Ireland throughout the nineteenth century, it is true, refused to appoint an Englishman as archbishop of Cashel; however, the pope saw to it that of those three nominated by the Cashel clergy the man most favoured by the British government was appointed.[33]

All negotiations for a concordat between Hanover and Rome were dealt with by Counsellor Leist because of his familiarity with canon law, while all matters of importance to England such as Irish affairs or the supervision of the princess of Wales were the concern of Baron Ompteda who acted in unison with the British minister at Florence, Lord Burghersh. When Ompteda died in March 1819 Burghersh wrote to Castlereagh: 'I believe no man can be more regretted and that as a servant of the Crown's, or as a private friend (to those as to like myself who were intimate with him) there cannot have been a greater loss.'[34] Counsellor Leist was recalled soon after.

The new Hanoverian minister, Franz von Reden (1754-1831), arrived in Rome on 1 July 1819; Kestner, who was now made counsellor of the mission, had already established good relations with a number of influential monsignori of the Roman curia: he was especially friendly with Mgr Francisco Capacini (1784-1845), who had served as secretary to Consalvi since 1815.[35]

In 1820 Pius VII congratulated George IV on his accession to the throne in a personal letter for which he received a cordial letter of thanks from the king in his own handwriting; the British government was so alarmed at this that it tried to get the letter recalled. Consalvi also sent a letter to George IV and likewise received a reply. Later in the year Consalvi gave Castlereagh details of an insurrection that had occured in the Roman states and 'expressed his regret at the non-appointment of a British minister to Rome'.[36] Some weeks later Castlereagh was succeeded by George Canning as foreign secretary. Canning wrote a very friendly letter to Rome informing Consalvi of his appointment.[37]

CHAPTER IV

Catholic Emancipation and Repeal

1. LEO XII AND PIUS VIII, 1823-1830

GEORGE IV was informed of Pius VII's death by the college of cardinals on 21 August 1823.[1] Lord Burghersh told Canning of his intention to travel to Rome for the coronation of the new pope.[2] Canning then instructed him to go with great haste to Rome and reside there during the conclave and keep him regularly informed. He pointed out to Burghersh that the candidate who had the support of Cardinal Consalvi was considered the most desirable choice by the British government.[3] This letter did not arrive before 5 October. Burghersh in fact arrived in Rome just as the conclave was breaking up, too late to exert any influence. On 28 September Burghersh informed Canning of 'the election of Cardinal della Genga to the Chair of St Peter' under the name of Leo XII;[4] he followed this in a few days with a detailed account of his discoveries concerning the conclave: he had learned that one of 'the leading principles by which the majority of the Cardinals was directed in the Conclave was hostility to Cardinal Consalvi'.[5] He alleged that the new pope himself bore a grudge against Consalvi. He then went on to give an account of his audiences with the new secretary of state, Cardinal della Somaglia, whom he had been acquainted with since 1815, and with the new pope, Leo XII.[6] He expressed his satisfaction with the new pontiff and with the secretary of state, as he believed both entertained friendly feelings towards England. In two further reports Burghersh answered queries by Canning concerning commercial regulations in the Roman states; he was forced to investigate these matters himself as Consul Parke had been living in Bologna for the last five months without giving notice and without leaving a vice-consul.[7] He also provided Canning with further details on the conclave, referring him to the report of the Hanoverian minister for further details: 'The Hanoverian Minister to whom I am endebted for a great deal of information has himself detailed to His Majesty the line he adopted (during the conclave).' Although Burghersh lamented 'the total exclusion of Cardinal Consalvi from any share in the government' he regarded the choice of della Genga for pope as 'consolatory'.[8]

Leo XII's most notable feature was his patronage of art and science. The works of Galileo and others of a similar nature were removed from the index during his pontificate.[9] Together with his secretary of state, della Somaglia, he continued the policy of friendly relations towards Britain established by Pius VII and Consalvi; the situation, however, was different: Castlereagh and Consalvi were personal friends and when Consalvi died some months after his replacement as secretary of state, he bequeathed some of his belongings to Castlereagh's family; however, the new incumbents, Somaglia and Canning, were unacquainted with each other. On 28 September 1823 Leo XII had announced his election to George IV while Somaglia gave similar notice of his appointment to Canning: but neither of these letters was answered. Before venturing to answer Canning referred the matter to the attorney-general and the solicitor-general: they were of the opinion that any answer to these letters violated statute 5 Eliz. C.1, sect. 2, and therefore incurred penalties. Canning also ordered a search to be made in the archives for relevant precedents; the report of the search, which covered the period 1558-1775, was negative. Lord Chancellor Eldon, an ultra-protestant, prevented the letter from Leo XII from even being submitted to the king.[10] Thus the correspondence between the pope and George IV and between the two secretaries ceased. It was only when Mr Planta at the foreign office was informed in a letter from Rome that Consalvi, then still alive, was offended at London's silence that Canning sent letters to Consalvi and della Somaglia in a personal capacity, excusing himself from any official correspondence because of the Elizabethan statute.[11]

In 1825 the Hanoverian minister, Reden, was recalled from Rome and Kestner promoted to the position of *chargé d'affaires*. Kestner had established a particularly friendly relationship with Somaglia;[12] Mgr Capacini, now substitute (i.e. second in command) in the secretariate of letters (secretaria brevium) and an influential prelate, had become a close personal friend of Kestner on the day when he introduced him to Somaglia in 1825, after which he embraced him and promised him that he could always rely on him; it was a promise that Capacini had kept.[13]

Meanwhile, Daniel O'Connell had formed the 'Catholic Association' to pressurise the English government into granting emancipation. A bill to grant emancipation to Irish catholics had passed through the house of commons in 1821 but was blocked by the lords. In 1825 a select committee of both houses on the state of Ireland heard evidence from the archbishops of Armagh, Dublin and Tuam, the bishop of Ardagh and Dr Doyle, bishop of Kildare and Leighlin, as well as O'Connell and various other laymen; it questioned them on various points of the catholic faith (points which they could have learnt from any catechism) and on their opinions on payment of the clergy. Dr Doyle, by then a leading figure in the Irish hierarchy, made his stand on this point quite clear: 'I would beg the Committee to understand that I would not, for any consideration whatever, receive a stipend or a means of support, which it would be in the power of His Majesty's government to give or withold.'[14] At the same time Burghersh negotiated with the Roman authorities: on condition that catholic emancipation was granted and that there would be no statute restricting direct communications between Rome and the catholics of the United Kingdom, Rome was willing to meet British wishes, as Burghersh reported:

> The Court of Rome see with dissatisfaction the unruly spirit at various times shown even against itself by the Catholic Clergy of Ireland: it would be anxious to reduce it to a more orderly conduct, both as regards the British Government and its own authority: to do this it would receive with gratitude any proposition for the payment of that Church,...granting to the Government a power in the election of bishops and other of the Church dignitaries, such as has been secured to other Protestant Governments. These arrangements, when completed, would be promulgated by a Bull which would put down all opposition. The Court of Rome believe that such a settlement of a difficult position must be of service to the British Government: it would lead to a connection between it and the Catholic Clergy, which, by degrees, would bring about a feeling of dependence which the Court of Rome is far from objecting to: it would lead the Catholic priest to look to the approbation of the Government as a means of advancement, and the Court of Rome would encourage this feeling.[15]

This letter was then submitted by Canning to the cabinet. It was received by Lord Liverpool, the Duke of Wellington and Burghersh's father, Lord Westmoreland, as 'the mode by which Catholic claims might be settled whenever it became possible to do so..., but when the Question was brought forward by the Duke of Wellington and Sir Robert Peel, the opposition was so strong against the measure that they did not venture to undertake the details which the Pope's Government had proposed'.[16]

Canning had employed Burghersh on other missions to Rome regarding British commercial interests there,[17] but then on 20 April 1826 Burghersh was officially instructed to 'abstain from all communication and correspondence with the Vatican', while his previous correspondence was submitted to the law officers to determine its legality.[18] Burghersh did not heed this instruction.

Following Canning's death in 1827 he wrote to the new foreign secretary, Lord Dudley, 'asking leave to go to Rome, and telling him that in accordance with instructions from Mr Canning he had come to some satisfactory arrangements with the papal Government in case a measure of Relief was granted to the Catholics of the United Kingdom', thus reminding him of the outcome of his negotiations with Rome in 1825.[19] To this Dudley replied that his hands were tied.[20]

The Hanoverian chargé d'affaires in Rome, Kestner, was preoccupied with the day-to-day business of caring for the needs of English visitors, accompanying them to audiences with the pope and the secretary of state, etc.,[21] and in April 1828 he forwarded a message from the Camerlengo, the papal minister of the interior, to Count Münster in London, requesting permission that a papal consulate be set up in England. There had been a vast increase in the number of trading vessels carrying goods from the church states to England and it would be the duty of the papal consul in England to look after the interests of the church states in England and see to the needs of papal subjects living there; and Camerlengo had pointed to the fact that England had a vice-consul residing in Rome. Münster gave a copy of this letter to Lord Dudley but no answer was ever received from the government.[22]

Some months later the papal nuncio in Paris deduced from a remark by the British ambassador there that the British government was seeking to establish a concordat with Rome; the papal nuncio sought the guidance of Cardinal Bernetti who had just succeeded the ageing Somaglia as secretary of state.[23] Bernetti provided the nuncio in Paris, Lambruschini (1776-1854), with a comprehensive account of the British government's conduct up to that time; he did this with a certain amount of trepidation so as not to antagonise the English ambassador in Paris. He reported that this was not the first time that the English cabinet had tried to determine the attitude of the Holy See towards a possible concordat and that London was perfectly well aware that before anything could take place, those laws prohibiting correspondence with the Holy See had to be repealed.[24] There had been contacts between the British ambassador in Brazil and the papal delegate there at various times but these too had arrived at nothing.[25] Bernetti had obviously lost patience with Britain's procrastination on the matter and the obsequious nature of Rome's offer of 1825 was now evaporated in a mood of self-assertiveness.

Soon afterwards Daniel O'Connell learned that the British government was tentatively examining the prospects of a concordat with Rome and he made this public in an address to the Catholic Association in Dublin on 19 November 1828; he mistakenly presented the Hanoverian ambassador at Rome, rather than the British ambassador at Paris, as the instigator of these advances. O'Connell's speech was printed in *The Times* on 22 November 1828.[26]

The British government immediately set about locating the source from which O'Connell had received his information and whether in fact the Hanoverian chargé d'affaires at Rome had carried out negotiations on behalf of London, and if he had, from whom did he receive his instructions. Even before Wellington's demand for 'a distinct statement from the Hanoverian Minister Plenipotentiary at Rome'[27] had been received by Kestner, Count Münster had demanded that he supply information of the matter. Kestner had already investigated on his own behalf. In a third despatch on 27 December 1828 he summed up the results of his investigation stating that he himself had never given the slightest cause for O'Connell's statement. He also cleared those English or Irish catholics who were resident in Rome at the time: Lord Arundel, Lord Shrewsbury, his theologian Dr Rock, Lord Meath, Lord Kenmare, Mr Canning, Mr Philips, Mr Petre, Bishop Baines and Dr Wiseman (the future cardinal), with whom Kestner had often conversed on the catholic question; they were all regarded as being above suspicion, although it was noted that Baines held O'Connell in high esteem.[28] Münster forwarded a copy of Kestner's despatch to Wellington and added: 'I have not found in my official or private correspondence with the Hanoverian Mission any allusion to any communication whatsoever having been made on the subject of the Catholic Question in this Country.'[29]

Bishop Baines, mentioned by Kestner as being well-liked by Leo XII, was the coadjutor of the vicar apostolic of the western district of England. He had been residing in Rome since the winter of 1826 on account of ill-health. Pope Leo XII had expressed his wish to create an English cardinal and thought of elevating Baines to the purple.[30] Lord Arundel, however, recommended Bishop Weld, who then lived at Hammersmith having resigned his coadjutorship of Upper Canada due to failing health, as a more suitable candidate and one that would have a more beneficial effect on the cause of catholic emancipation.[31] Leo XII died on 10 February 1829 before any of these plans could be advanced.

In 1829 the strength of O'Connell's agitation forced the British government to concede on the question of catholic emancipation or face an uprising in Ireland. On 5 March Peel introduced a bill for catholic emancipation in the house of commons and supported it in a speech lasting four hours. He declared that the proposed inspection of correspondence with Rome (exequatur) and the veto in episcopal nominations were unnecessary: 'On the one hand, it [the veto] would merely give to the Crown a nominal but ineffectual control, and, on the other, it ... might, after what has passed, detract from the grace and favour of the measures of relief.' Wellington echoed these sentiments in the house of lords.[32] It was realised by the government that by *officially* exercising its right of veto, the effect would be counter-productive; it still intended to influence events in Ireland by *secretly* exercising its influence in episcopal nominations but without the knowledge of Irish catholics.

As in 1823, Burghersh was ordered to Rome for the sitting of the conclave to elect a new pope in 1829. The new foreign secretary, Lord Aberdeen, instructed him: 'Your Lordship will communicate to me, for the information of His Majesty's Government, all such occurrences during the sitting of the Conclave, as you may deem to be of sufficient interest, and which may serve to develope the views and motives of the different Parties concerned.'[33] Burghersh fulfilled these instructions, reporting on every detail of the conclave as well as on the behaviour of the French and Austrian ambassadors etc. He reported that the French ambassador, Chateaubriand, was in favour of Cardinal de Gregorio, who was strongly opposed by the Austrian ambassador, Lützow; however, the Netherlands ambassador together with the Prussian minister and the Hanoverian chargé d'affaires, Kestner, supported Cardinal Capellari (the future Gregory XVI).[34] On 31 March 1829 Burghersh announced to Aberdeen the election of Cardinal Castiglione as Pope Pius VIII.[35] He added that the new pope 'was the person supposed to have been designated by Pius the 7th as successor; he was the friend of Cardinal Consalvi, and as such he was supported in the Conclave of 1823 by the influence of all the Governments of Europe and by all the Cardinals who were … anxious for the continuation in the office of Secretary of State of Cardinal Consalvi'.[36] With the help of the new secretary of state, Guiseppi Albani, Burghersh was granted an audience with Pius VIII soon after his election. Pius VIII expressed profuse thanks to Burghersh for the granting of catholic emancipation and declared great enthusiasm for England. He expressed his opinion 'that obedience to their Sovereign was the first duty of true Catholics … that even under Pagan Sovereigns the duty was obedience, that it was due to a Nero, how much more so then to a Christian King, such as the present Sovereign of the British Empire'.[37] This statement supports the opinion that Pius VIII's attitudes were the product of the *ancien regime* of pre-revolutionary Europe and his reference to George IV as 'Sovereign of the British Empire' implies recognition of George IV as head of the empire of which Irish catholics only constituted a very small part.

Before leaving Rome Burghersh conferred with Albani, who requested him to 'rely upon his anxiety on all occasions to be of service to the British Government'.[38]

While Burghersh had been making his way to Rome for the sitting of the conclave he had asked Aberdeen for instructions should the Roman authorities enquire as to whether an official announcement of the pope's election could be made in England: he reminded Aberdeen that at the previous election Mr Canning had been obliged to decline an official announcement from the cardinal secretary of state.[39] When Cardinal Albani announced the election to Aberdeen, and Pius VIII to George IV, no official reply was received. Aberdeen did, however, ask Count Münster to pass on his instructions to the Hanoverian minister at Rome 'to explain the cause of this silence'.[40] The message was passed on and on 4 May Kestner offered an explanation to Albani as to why no official reply had been received from Aberdeen.[41] Münster then informed Aberdeen that he had fulfilled his instructions but at the same time expressed discontent with Aberdeen's decision not to send a reply by remarking: 'You must recollect Cardinal Albani when Nuntius apostolicus at Vienna in the year 1815.'[42] Albani answered Kestner on 6 May, acknowledging Aberdeen's explanation but expressing his wish that the difficulties prohibiting direct communication between the British government and Rome would soon be removed; a copy of this letter was sent to Aberdeen by Count Münster.[43] Some days later Kestner received an audience with Pius VIII during which the pope echoed Albani's wish and asked repeatedly that Kestner convey to King George his gratitude for the granting of catholic emancipation and his sincere wish that the monarch's catholic subjects would prove themselves to be as loyal and obedient as the others; he regarded it as his responsibility to remind them of this their duty. Kestner then sent a report of this audience to George IV.[44] King George responded to the pope's kind sentiments with a handwritten letter in his capacity as king of Hanover.[45]

Since catholic emancipation had been granted without any concession on the question of veto, Propaganda Fide was able to issue a decree on 1 June 1829 laying down the mode of election of Irish bishops in accordance with the plan for domestic nomination. As before, when a vacancy arises the parish priests and canons of the diocese are to assemble and vote; after this a *terna* is made up, i.e. a list of the three candidates who scored the highest number of votes; then the bishops in the province of the vacant diocese assemble to record their views as to the merits of the three candidates on the *terna* and this is then sent to Rome. The decree of 1829 established that if the judgments of the bishops on the three candidates was not favourable then the pope had the option of appointing someone not on the *terna*.[46] Until 1910 — when this practice was forbidden by Pius X — it was possible for outsiders to know whether the candidate selected was one of the three on the *terna* or not, as parish priests informed press reporters as to whose names were included on the list.[47]

In 1829 the see of Waterford became vacant; the vicar capitular of the diocese, Foran, received the highest number of votes, and so was placed highest on the *terna*. The English government, however, had received unfavourable intelligence reports on Foran and the duke of Wellington instructed Burghersh to prevent his appointment and to use all his influence to have Bishop Weld appointed instead.[48] Despite the fact that Pius VIII and Albani were always eager to please the British government, they realised that they could not ignore the decree of 1829 by appointing an Englishman who was not on the *terna* instead of someone who was: in so doing suspicions would be aroused that the pope was subservient to British influence. The Holy See decided on a compromise by appointing Dr Abraham, who was on the *terna* although lower down on the list and who was more favourably disposed to the British. Cardinal Albani explained this in a letter to Burghersh.[49] As it turned out, their choice was fortuitous, as Dr Abraham did indeed become what is known in Ireland as 'Castle bishop'. Bishop Weld was also rewarded for being the preferred choice of the British government by being called to Rome from London and made a cardinal[50] (Weld had once served in the British army as a colonel under Wellington, having entered the priesthood on the death of his wife.) George IV congratulated him on his elevation to cardinal, remarking that it gave him no small pleasure to see an English colonel wearing the purple robe of a Roman cardinal.[51]

Pius VIII's brief pontificate had resulted in an Englishman being appointed cardinal for the first time in over a century (Cardinals Stuart and Erskine were Scotsmen), and in the presence of a nuncio in London. Mgr Capacini, the papal representative at the Hague since 1827, was raised to the position of internuncio in 1829. When the catholic south of the United Low Countries rebelled against Holland, Capacini maintained close contact with the catholic Belgian revolutionaries, and in October 1830 he went to London where the future of Belgium was to be decided. He intended to gain influence in the affairs of Belgium for the Holy See and supported Belgian independence from Holland; he found the atmosphere in London favourable for pursuing these objectives. On 18 January 1831 he had a meeting with Lord Palmerston which served to prevent the prince of Orange from assuming the Belgian throne. He left London in February 1831. Pius VIII died on 1 December 1830.

2. GREGORY XVI, 1831 – 1846

Following the death of Pius VIII the conclave convened in the traditional manner to elect a new pope. One of the candidates, Cardinal Giustiniani, whose mother was English, was prevented from being elected by a Spanish cardinal exercising the Spanish veto. Cardinal Albani refrained from exercising his veto on the candidature of Cardinal Capellari, so as to frustrate the election of his great enemy, de Gregorio — and so it was that Capellari succeeded as the new pope, Gregory XVI.[52] Gregory, a Benedictine of impeccable character, had been prefect of Propaganda Fide and as such had lacked the diplomatic training of his predecessors; he was therefore more inclined to place the interests of the church and the faithful above the wishes of governments. His secretary of state was Cardinal Bernetti who had previously filled that post in 1828-9. Bernetti was now in poor health and this necessitated his leaving Rome quite frequently in order to convalesce. The reactionary elements in the college of cardinals availed of these frequent absences to indulge in intrigue. On Capaccini's return from London he was appointed Bernetti's substitute. Capaccini was widely regarded as being a learned man with great *esprit,* elegance and subtlety.

Gregory's election had coincided with the outbreak of revolution in the papal states. The revolt was quickly crushed with the help of Austrian troops called in by Cardinal Bernetti. Bernetti's Austrian connections served him well, and the Austrian commander, Sabregondi, proved to be an obliging ally.[53] When the rising had been crushed the great powers sent representatives to Rome to confer on the question of the church states. Britain's envoy was Sir Brook Taylor who arrived in Rome on 2 April 1831. The representatives from Austria, France, Britain, Prussia, Russia and Sardinia issued a circular in which they demanded that the pope make certain changes in the administration of the papal states. Two of these demands, namely the introduction of a privy council of laymen separate from or, rather, in opposition to the council of cardinals, and popular elections for local and provincial councils were unacceptable to the pope. The French ambassador, St Aulair, was the main force behind this circular; the irony of this action was heightened by the fact that it was the French government which had only quite recently, i.e. well after the 1830 revolution, allowed the mob to devastate and desecrate churches and cathedrals such as Notre Dame in Paris; Russia, too, was pointing an accusing finger, although the majority of its citizens endured abject poverty under a vicious and repressive system. Negotiations between the Roman authorities and the British for a loan of three million scudi from Britain came to nothing, as Rome had refused to mortgage its land and properties as the British had demanded.[54] Taylor left Rome in June 1831.

In March 1832 the representatives of the great powers in Rome met again to confer on the administration of the church states. They were joined by the British minister at Florence, Mr George Seymour, accompanied by his attaché, Mr Aubin. They arrived in Rome on 10 March 1832. Seymour wrote in his diary: 'I am supposed to be sent here merely to back up St Aulair and to bully the Pope.'[55] On 13 March Seymour met with the cardinal secretary of state, Bernetti, whom he tried to 'poultice and soften'.[56] Following long conversations with the French, Austrian and Prussian ministers, as well as with the English Cardinal Weld, Seymour was granted an audience with Gregory XVI. He afterwards noted in his diary: 'He talking in Italian and I in French the conversation was not of a very interesting nature.'[57] Seymour tried to mediate between St Aulair on the one hand and Bernetti and Capaccini on the other, but with the express intention of trying to influence events in Britain's favour; however, he reported that he 'found him quite deaf to the power of the charmer'.[58] Seymour cultivated the friendship of Cardinal Weld and also became acquainted with Cardinal de Gregorio, with whom

Seymour shared a house.[59] On 15 July Seymour and Aubin left Rome and returned to Florence.

Meanwhile in Ireland the see of Armagh had become vacant with the death of Curtis; the British government, unaware of Dr Kelly, the bishop of Dromore, being coadjutor with right of succession to the vacant see, feared the succession might pass to Dr Doyle, the bishop of Kildare and Leighlin, who was a leading figure in the Irish hierarchy and a staunch supporter of repeal of the act of union. The foreign office therefore instructed Seymour to prevent Doyle's appointment, Seymour dutifully returning to Rome to see Bernetti and reporting that he found the cardinal 'fearfully ignorant of everything relating to the affairs of the Irish Catholics'. He added that he found Mgr Capaccini, 'who entered the room during the conversation', to be more approachable. Seymour insisted during this meeting that the wishes of the British government be carried into effect. He emphasised the pro-catholic conduct of his government, which 'fully entitled it to all the co-operation and assistance which the Papal Government had in its capacity to bestow'.[60] In compliance with Seymour's wishes the matter was immediately submitted to the pope. The next day Bernetti informed Seymour that Gregory XVI, whom he had visited that morning, had asserted that Dr Kelly, as coadjutor, had the right of succession and therefore Doyle's promotion was never even a possibility.[61] Being instructed not to conduct any part of his negotiations in writing, Seymour visited Bernetti and personally thanked him for complying so readily with the wishes of the British government. He also expressed his hope that 'if at any future time, when no English agent might happen to be at Rome, it might be proposed to promote to any high dignity in the Catholic Church in Ireland any person of the same dangerous political principles as Dr Doyle, the Papal Government would refuse to sanction [the] nomination'. Bernetti assured him that he was 'quite disposed to act in this manner and begged me that if the case should arise while [Seymour] was in Italy, [he] should transmit to him the name of any person whose appointment might be displeasing to the English Government undertaking at the same time to use his best endeavour to prevent the confirmation of such a choice.[62]

The British foreign secretary, Palmerston, now instigated enquiries as to whether, 'as the law now stands, it would be legal for the King to accredit a Diplomatic Agent to reside at the Court of Rome in the character of Minster or Chargé d'affaires'.[63] The law officers subsequently deemed it legal.[64] On 22 August 1832 Thomas Aubin was ordered to reside at Rome permanently, while officially still being attached to Florence.[65] In September Seymour himself arrived in Rome and during an audience with Gregory XVI he urged that various reforms be carried out for Britain's advantage.[66]

When, towards the end of 1832, the see of Cloyne and Ross became vacant, the British government was determined to prevent the nomination of J. O'Connell, who had received the highest number of votes from the diocesan clergy. The foreign office declared themselves in favour of the second candidate on the list, Bartholomew Crotty, president of Maynooth college, as he had abstained from any political involvement. The bishops of the province of Munster were likewise in favour of Crotty.[67] Seymour once again communicated to Bernetti the wishes of the British government.[68] Bernetti 'immediately spoke to the Pope who ordered the case to be forwarded to the Prefect of the Congregation of Propaganda, under whose administration the matter belonged'.[69] Bernetti advised Propaganda to observe secrecy.[70] Mgr Capaccini assured Seymour of his help,[71] while Cardinal de Gregorio promised Aubin, who was handling the matter in Rome, that he would 'exert all his influence to meet the wishes of Britain when the case was laid before the Congregation of Propaganda, of which he was a member'.[72] Capaccini regarded this as a great asset because Propaganda generally disliked pressure from the secretaries of state and it was better that such matters were advanced by someone within Propaganda.[73] Bernetti's attitude cooled somewhat towards Britain as he began to resent so much interference by a foreign government in ecclesiastical affairs. Cardinal de Gregorio, however, assured Aubin: 'But be tranquil about Mr O'Connell. I will boldly pledge myself that he shall not be appointed.'[74] Gregory XVI had meanwhile taken the matter into his own hands, as he too resented Britain's heavy-handedness; but at the same time wanted to promote tranquility. He ordered the *terna* coming from Ireland to be forwarded to him immediately; when it arrived he quietly nominated Crotty without informing Capaccini or Bernetti. Aubin only learned of the appointment a year later when he discovered it in the Roman almanac.[75]

Anglo-papal relations were severely strained following the publication of Seymour's notes on his Roman mission in which he denounced the Roman government in the strongest possible terms for its domestic policy.[76] The British government therefore decided it would be wiser to use the Hanoverian chargé d'affaires in Rome, Kestner, for the next mission. On 23 March 1833 King William ordered Baron Ludwig von Ompteda to present Kestner with a gift in return for undertaking a mission 'on the point of the Irish Catholic Clergy'.[77] Ompteda had been the Hanoverian minister in personal attendance to the king in London since 1831; he sent instructions to Kestner, in the form of a ciphered letter, to enlist the support of the pope and urge him to exert all possible influence on the Irish catholic clergy so as to dissuade them from participating in anti-British political agitation; they should instead be encouraged to preach obedience to their flocks. Kestner was instructed to act unofficially and in secrecy. Ompteda trusted that Kestner, who had been in Rome for a long time, would operate through the best possible channels to attain this end.[78] Having received and deciphered Ompteda's letter, Kestner immediately sought a meeting with Bernetti. Bernetti declared himself ignorant of the extent of political agitation engaged in by the Irish clergy but agreed to submit the matter to the pope and observe secrecy. He did, however, ask for the names of the priests involved and for details of their misdoings, using the opportunity to point out that it would be much easier to deal with the matter if a nuncio or agent were allowed to reside in London acting on the pope's behalf. While Bernetti expressed his opinion that the pope would never side with the people acting against their sovereign,[79] Gregory in fact flatly refused the British demand. He was still very bitter over the publication of Seymour's negotiations with the Holy See, which he regarded as a breach of confidence. He referred the British government to his encyclical letter of 1832 in which he exhorted the faithful to be law-abiding subjects and recommended that the British make use of this pronouncement themselves. In so doing he had reminded Britain that they could not ask him to put his authority at their disposal when they did not recognise him officially. He also refused to reprimand the Irish clergy indiscriminately when even the British government could not themselves deny that the majority of Irish people were law-abiding. He requested the names of offending priests and details of their conduct.[80] In his reply to Kestner's despatches Ompteda evaded the issue, to such an extent as to give the impression that the British government was either unwilling or unable to supply the names and details requested. Regarding the publication of Seymour's negotiations with the Holy See, the British government placed the blame on some subordinate office.[81]

Acting on Ompteda's instructions Kestner once again called on Cardinal Bernetti to urge the pope to reprimand those Irish priests involved in political agitation. Despite the fact that Capaccini had been trying to influence Bernetti in Britain's favour, the British demand fell on unreceptive ears: Gregory XVI was adamant in his refusal to reprimand the Irish clergy and once again asked for names and details. Bernetti understood the reason for this refusal was Gregory's fear of a repetition of events in Poland, when similar action was demanded by the Russian tsar to discourage priests in Poland from participating in the Polish revolution against Russian rule; Gregory had complied by addressing a letter to the tsar disapproving of their actions only to have this letter used by the Russian authorities to compromise the position of the Polish clergy. Gregory feared a similar course of events would expose the Holy See, should he fulfill the British government's request.[82] Britain therefore relented, albeit temporarily, in its attempts to enlist papal support against the Irish catholic clergy.

The following year, in 1834, the English agent in Rome, Mr Aubin, was chosen to communicate London's wishes to the Holy See. In April of that year the archbishop of Tuam had died; and before the diocesan clergy had assembled to elect three candidates from which a successor would be chosen, the foreign secretary, Palmerston, had sent a messenger to Florence and Rome 'to try to get the Pope not to appoint an agitating prelate'.[83] The British government had asserted that, since the previous incumbent had died while in the papal states, the pope was no longer bound by the list of three candidates submitted by the diocesan clergy and was free to select whom he desired. Aubin was instructed to prevent the appointment of Bishop Browne or Bishop MacHale to the archbishopric. Seymour, the British minister at Florence, observed in his instruction to Aubin: 'His Holiness has on former occasions listened to representations similar to that which you will now have to address to the Cardinal Secretary. I cannot doubt that in the present instance He will be equally disposed to act in a manner which will prove their desire to promote the interests of good government.'[84] The government need not have had any fears regarding Browne since his name did not even appear on the list of candidates submitted to Rome — first on the list was a Dr Burke, second Bishop MacHale and third Rev. Nolan.[85] Aubin's mission was hampered by the ill-wind created by the publication of Seymour's notes, as Aubin informed Seymour: 'Nothing can remove from the mind of this Government the persuasion that they were made public out of keen hostility to them.'[86] Having conferred with Bernetti and Capaccini on the matter, Aubin reported a month later on 21 June 1834: 'His Eminence acquainted me that the Pope ... shewed such a disposition to meet the wishes of the King's Ministers, that unless some unforeseen event occurred, he considered their object as attained.'[87] When Aubin received the names of the three candidates selected by the Tuam clergy he asked Bernetti to have Burke appointed. Seymour was already confident of victory.[88] This confidence, however, rested solely on the good-will of Bernetti and Capaccini, who had hoped for British assistance in Portugal against an anti-catholic régime. Gregory XVI, however, would not be swerved from his adopted stance, so much so that Mgr Capaccini exclaimed to Aubin in exasperation: 'To talk of true policy to the Pope is like addressing a discourse to a stone.'[89] Palmerston then ordered Seymour to enlist the support of the English cardinal, Weld.[90] Weld, however, was engaged in caring for the children of his daughter, Lady Clifford, and had little to do with Roman affairs and even less influence.[91]

The bishops of the province of Tuam had judged MacHale as the only person worthy of being archbishop. The cardinals of Propaganda Fide voted to postpone their decision until they had received accurate information on MacHale, since they had only the word of the British government on his involvement in political agitation. To the dismay of Capaccini the pope regarded it as a matter of conscience. He had become personally acquainted with MacHale when the young bishop had visited Rome two years previously and suitably impressed the pontiff. Concerning Britain's preference for Burke as the new archbishop of Tuam, Gregory remarked: 'I have seen recommendations arrive from other parts of the world prejudicial to worthy individuals.'[92] Gregory had resented Britain's interference in every nomination of bishops to Irish sees since catholic emancipation and feared that they were gradually acquiring a right to do so each and every time a vacancy arose.[93] On 1 August 1834 Aubin was informed that MacHale was the new archbishop of Tuam. Bernetti reported the pope's words regarding his decision to Aubin: 'I had received so many applications in his behalf from Ireland, and from an immense number of Irish Bishops, that had I appointed anyone else, it would have been evident that I had been entirely swayed by the British Government, and that feeling could not but have produced an increase in hostility.' Bernetti added that even newspapers praising MacHale had been sent to the pope and one of them cited the following discourse: '. . . wherein he draws a comparison between the condition of the lower classes in the Papal States and the lower classes in Ireland, proving the condition of the former as happy and enviable when compared with the latter'.[94] Aubin and Seymour lamented the failure of their efforts.[95] In Ireland the reaction was enthusiastic: when news broke of the British government's efforts to prevent MacHale's nomination, bonfires were lit and a huge procession marched to greet him as he entered his new diocese.[96] MacHale (1791-1881), who as a young boy of six had witnessed the brutal execution of Fr Conroy on a false charge of high treason, was indeed the Irish patriot the English government had feared; he became known as the 'Lion of Judah' and proved to be their most formidable adversary during his time as archbishop of Tuam.[97]

MacHale's reception as he entered Tuam was reported in the Roman newspaper *Notizie del Giorno;* to avoid any erroneous impressions created by the article, the *Diario di Roma* in its next issue, and on the instigation of Mgr Capaccini, printed a report on the resolutions adopted by the Irish hierarchy to discourage the holding of political meetings and the making of political speeches in chapels. Both Aubin and Kestner sent copies of the report to London.[98]

In 1834 Seymour suggested changing the manner of dealing with the court of Rome 'so that England could count with more certainty upon the good offices of the Holy See in cases of need'.[99] In 1835 plans were made for effecting this change, as Wiseman reports:

It was, if I remember aright, on the 27th of March, 1835, that his Holiness summoned me to attend on him without delay. On my coming into his presence he graciously informed me that an English nobleman, well known in the diplomatic world, had come to Rome, and had solicited an audience through his Eminence Cardinal Weld, with the intention to speak on the subject of renewing official relations between the Holy See and the British Empire. After asking me such questions as he thought fit, his Holiness concluded the subject by words to this effect: 'It is the duty of the English Government to take the first step. We have no laws to repeal on this subject, but could enter on such intercourse tomorrow. But England has a law ... It must begin by repealing that'.[100]

Wiseman's date is most probably wrong as there is a record extant from 1837 of Fox Strangway of the foreign office requesting the law officers to record their opinion on the lawfulness of relations with the Holy See.[101] Nothing, however, became of this request and the situation remained as before.[102]

In the following years nothing of interest arises in the despatches of Aubin except that in 1837 he reported that Gregory XVI was inimical to the payment of the Irish catholic clergy by the British government as he thought it would 'be hurtful to the cause of religion and to what influence He may have in that quarter'.[103]

In 1839 Cardinal Fransoni, head of Propaganda Fide, advised Archbishop MacHale to abstain from engaging in political controversies when speaking at meetings or assemblies so that he would not provide anyone with the opportunity to calumniate him. He also sent a similar letter to Archbishop Crolly of Armagh, the primate of Ireland since 1835, asking him to take care that his brother bishops do not busy themselves with political controversies.[104] Both MacHale and Crolly then enlightened Fransoni on the reality of the situation in Ireland, where a powerful protestant faction was intent on restoring penal laws for catholics and was eager to proselytise them 'or else to despoil them of civil liberties'. The primate warned: 'The greatest prudence is necessary lest we offend a faithful people by an unexpected separation from them.'[105]

Prince Metternich, in the meantime, had succeeded in having Cardinal Bernetti replaced by Lambruschini, now a cardinal,[106] as secretary of state, in return for withdrawing Austrian troops from the church states. Metternich's influence at the Vatican was powerful, and it is not surprising that the English government co-operated by exerting pressure on the pope to use his influence in Ireland for its own ends. Metternich thought O'Connell to be the devil and classed the Irish, as well as the Belgian and Polish catholics, as radicals: he was intent on stamping radicalism out of existence, as he wrote to Prince Wittgenstein in 1837.[107] In the course of conversation with the nuncio at Vienna he accused some Irish priests of being pure liberals.[108] He also urged Palmerston to make the pope speak authoritatively against the repeal movement.[109] A few weeks later the nuncio at Vienna, Altieri, again reported to Rome that Metternich would impress upon the English government that 'authoritative intervention of the Supreme Pontiff would be indispensable and useful'.[110]

The British agent in Rome, Mr Aubin, was more concerned with other matters, in particular the system of public education in Ireland. In January 1840 he reported to Florence that MacHale and Archbishop Murray of Dublin had sent representatives to Rome with the purpose of objecting to the system of public education in Ireland. Murray approved of the government measures, while MacHale asserted that the books that were to be issued were anti-catholic. Aubin spoke with Capaccini and attempted to influence him against MacHale.[111] A year later Propaganda Fide decided that each bishop in Ireland 'should be free to determine in his own diocese as to the fitness of the books to be used'.[112]

Metternich was not prepared to let matters lie there; as chancellor of a multi-national empire he was strongly opposed to Irish nationalism and the repeal movement, and was determined to crush it. On 13 June Sir Robert Gordon informed Lord Aberdeen, the foreign secretary, that Metternich had written to Rome urging the pope to intervene in Ireland. On 17 June 1843 the Austrian chargé d'affaires in Rome, von Ohms, received Metternich's letter and immediately sought a meeting with Cardinal Lambruschini, who assured him that the Vatican strongly disapproved of Irish bishops appearing at O'Connell's repeal meetings and of Irish clergy participating in these popular meetings.[113] On 12 July Gordon wrote more precisely on the matter to Aberdeen, giving details of Metternich's manoeuvre: 'Prince Metternich has written to the Court of Rome in order to suggest that the Pope should exert his influence with the Roman Catholic Priests in Ireland, and dissuade them from joining O'Connell in the cry for Repeal.'[114] The lord lieutenant of Ireland, Lord Grey, had similarly suggested that the pope should be used to exert influence on Irish priests and thereby on the common people; the idea was subsequently taken up by the home secretary, Graham, and the prime minister, Peel, himself.[115]

The British ambassador to Vienna, Sir Robert Gordon, now set to work. In discussions with the nuncio there, Mgr Altieri, he adopted quite a menacing stance and even resorted to blackmail: 'Unless the Pope realized his duty to repress the rebellion of the Irish, Gordon threatened that England need not consider herself bound to withold assistance to the insurgents at Bologna when they sought it.' The Vatican, on the other hand, had requested that the British government suppress the publication of seditious and revolutionary pamphlets that were then being printed in Malta — a British colony — and being disseminated in the papal states, since they had largely contributed to the recent disturbances there. Gordon replied that there was no possibility of compliance on the matter unless the pope first agreed to the British request.[116] 'In vain, Metternich had tried to persuade Sir

Robert Gordon that not all the fault lay on the side of the Irish, whom the Government antagonized by failing to grant what was in justice due to them. To this observation the Ambassador coldly answered that this Government could do no more for the Irish.'[117] Peel was highly pleased with Gordon and ordered that a dossier be drawn up by Earl Grey of acts, speeches, and writings of Irish priests against the British authorities.[118] This dossier was to be handed personally to the pope by Metternich. On 30 December the dossier was sent by Aberdeen to Gordon with an instruction approved by Peel:[119]

> Your Excellency will request Prince Metternich to bring this Collection of Treason and Sedition to the notice of the Papal Court, and you will engage His Highness to endeavour to persuade that Government to take the necessary measures for the suppression of such a flagrant abuse of their sacred functions by the Roman Catholick Priesthood in Ireland. This will scarcely be effected by the private circulation of Pastoral letters, ...demand the publick and unequivocal reprobation of the Holy See.[120]

Two days later, on 1 January 1844, Aberdeen repeated his instruction in response to the papal request through the Austrian minister in London, Baron Neumann, that Britain take some action in Malta and watch the Carbonari, one of the Italian secret societies, in England.[121]

Among the extracts of supposed incitals to sedition by Irish priests were summaries of nine sermons (the British authorities had planted agents at masses to take down details of sermons). None of these extracts, however, was accredited with the name of the priest alleged to have made the remarks. Only a brief selection of this material was forwarded to Cardinal Fransoni, the head of Propaganda, by Cardinal Lambruschini.[122] Aubin was to have reported on the Vatican's reaction to the communication but was absent from Rome at the time, so Lambruschini replied in the form of a *promemoria* to the Austrian ambassador in Rome and also sent a copy to the nuncio in Vienna. Lambruschini was of a different nature to Bernetti and Capaccini: he refused to have a solemn disapproval of the Irish clergy issued and was not impressed with the material submitted by the British authorities; he declared that he could not accept their portrayal of the disturbances in Ireland and Malta as identical. In Malta there were anarchists at the root of the disturbances; in Ireland there were people campaigning within the laws of the parliamentary system. He denied that the Irish clergy as such was responsible, nor even a majority of them. Lambruschini again expressed his amazement that 'numerous political refugees in the security of the British possession at Malta were free to hatch plots against all the thrones of Italy'.[123] It is not surprising that Metternich and Gordon were dissatisfied with this answer.[124] To do justice to Lambruschini it is necessary to point out that the British authorities were not against Irish priests being involved in political agitation as such, except for those who did not agree with the government viewpoint. They often bestowed favours on those who had supported the government stance (e.g. a priest who had 'supported the Government candidate very zealously in some election'[125] was recommended to the pope by Melbourne for some form of preferment). It was only on 15 October 1844 that Cardinal Fransoni of Propaganda Fide issued a letter to Archbishop Crolly of Armagh in response to the *promemoria* handed to him earlier that year by Lambruschini; in this letter he advised that the priests and bishops of Ireland should in future act more prudently and take care not to get involved in political strife: 'Singular prudence and moderation of soul were the fitting marks of their conduct.' Fransoni's rescript was worded in such a way that the Irish priests and bishops need not consider themselves reprimanded.[126]

Meanwhile Aubin, the British agent in Rome, had died on 12 May 1844; he was succeeded by William Bernard Petre, later twelfth Baron Petre (1817-84), who was a member of a well-known English catholic family. Some months after Petre's arrival in Rome in October 1844 Aberdeen commented in a letter to Peel: 'I apprehend that William Petre is a man we may trust politically, just because he is so little of a Catholick in reality. His being one nominally, and according to outward appearance, has certainly made his nomination very agreeable to the Court of Rome.'[127]

Soon after arriving in Rome Petre was instructed to negotiate with the Vatican on the Charitable Bequests Act (Ireland). He was requested by Canning to 'communicate immediately with the Roman Government respecting the opposition of the Roman Catholic Bishops in Ireland to the act'.[128] Petre was to support Bishop Healy, who was in favour of the act, against Dr MacHale, who opposed it, and to seek the assistance of the English Cardinal Acton (1803-47).[129] On 19 October 1844 Petre met Lambruschini to discuss the matter; during the course of the audience Lambruschini reverted to the question of papal interference in Ireland:

> I know from an authentic and friendly source that the Conte di Aberdeen desires that the Court of Rome should come forward in a more public manner, . . . but we have long and anxiously considered the question, and we fear that if we were to act differently from what we have done, we should imbitter instead of soften the animosities of parties, and in the end perhaps produce a schism.[130]

Petre continued in his efforts regarding the Charitable Bequests Act and enlisted the support of Cardinal Acton, who was opposed to O'Connell and the repealers; on 2 December 1844 Petre obtained his first audience with Gregory XVI. He presented the Charitable Bequests Act as ultimately leading to 'the endowment of the Catholic Church in Ireland'.[131] Aberdeen was eager to obtain a 'public declaration of papal approval of those prelates who supported the Bequests Act', yet all Petre obtained was a memorandum making slight objections to some provisions in the act but otherwise making no other judgment[132] (the memorandum was drawn up by Lambruschini). Whenever Petre raised with Lambruschini the subject of the Irish clergy's support for O'Connell and the repeal movement, the latter always turned the conversation to Archbishop Murray of Dublin whose conduct he regarded as highly praiseworthy.[133] Pope Gregory XVI died on 9 June 1846, and so began a new pontificate.

CHAPTER V

'The soothing influence of religion' and 'papal aggression'

1. THE MINTO MISSION

O N 2 June 1846 the college of cardinals informed Queen Victoria of the death of Gregory XVI; on 17 June Pius IX announced his election as pope to Victoria.[1] Pius IX's predecessor, Gregory XVI, was generally regarded as a conservative who had been tireless in his efforts to resist intrusions by Britain into the affairs of the papacy. The election of Pius IX to the chair of St Peter seemed to offer fresh opportunities to the British government who were keen to enlist the support of Rome against France and Russia.

Pius IX was a pious and venerable man whose winning ways captivated all who became personally acquainted with him; yet he lacked several qualities suitable to a leader of the catholic church: his nervous, fidgety temperament caused him to be impulsive in his decisions and he tended to oscillate between high-mindedness and utter dejection.[2] Furthermore, his education was fragmentary, as he lacked any real grounding in the fields of history and law. Nevertheless, what was written by the anglican Hitchman, a confidant of Disraeli, remains true: 'The impartial observer is forced to the conclusion that whatever may have been the mistakes of the Pope's political career, they were mistakes from the intellectual point of view alone, and that in all points of moral criticism his life has been well nigh irreproachable.'[3]

In 1847 Lord John Russell (who became prime minister in Britain in the same month that Pius IX was elected as pope) sent his father-in-law, Gilbert Eliot, Earl of Minto (1782-1859), to Italy. Minto was also a cousin of Palmerston. The British government at the time was anxious to thwart the plans of Louis Philippe, the king of France, who was eager to establish a union between France and Spain, a plan originally conceived by Louis XIV.[4] In October 1846 Maria Louisa, the sister of the childless Spanish Queen Isabella, married the duke of Montpensier, the son of Louis Philippe.[5] The British government was looking for allies to side against France and Russia and for this reason backed the radical revolutionary movements in Switzerland and Italy. Palmerston had indeed been successful in winning from France the influence she had gained in Italy as a result of her stance in the revolution of 1830 and her policy of liberalism.[6] Minto's mission to Italy and especially his stay in Rome (4 November 1847 to 3 February 1848) must be seen in this context. He had been sent to Rome to give backing to Pius IX in his course of reforms. Pius IX was immensely popular in Italy,[7] but was opposed by Austria and he had enemies even within his own states. He therefore instructed Bishop Wiseman (who became pro-vicar apostolic of the London district in 1847 on the death of Bishop Griffiths) to approach Palmerston in London and ask him what assistance England was willing to give to the pope in his policy of reform. The British Ambassador in Paris, Lord Normanby, was similarly approached by the Parisian nuncio, Fornari.[8]

With regard to Minto's mission to Rome, however, the British authorities were primarily concerned with their rule in Ireland.[9] The British prime minister, Russell, declared to a visitor: 'We have tried to govern it by conciliation, and have failed also. No other means are now open to us except those we are resolved on using, namely, to govern Ireland through Rome.'[10] The foreign secretary, Palmerston, explained the object of Minto's mission to Queen Victoria:

> While on the one hand he holds out to the Pope the support and protection which the countenance and good offices of the British government will afford, Lord Minto would endeavour to obtain from the Pope the exertion of his spiritual authority over the Catholic priesthood of Ireland to induce them to abstain from repeal agitation, and to urge them not to embarass but rather to assist your Majesty's government in the measures they may plea for ... Ireland.[11]

As regards British rule in Ireland, the viceroy of Ireland, the earl of Clarendon, observed on 1 October 1847 in a 'Memorandum upon the Exercise of the Pope's Spiritual Authority in Ireland': 'At no period of Irish History has the soothing influence of religion been more required ... than at the present moment.'[12] He was referring to the great hunger in Ireland: in 1847 the famine reached its climax.[13] While hundreds of thousands of people were dying from starvation, grain was still being exported from Ireland to England, despite the fact that the wheat harvest in England in 1847 was especially plentiful and had led to a sharp drop in wheat prices.[14] It is therefore understandable that the terrible plight of the people had resulted in agrarian crime.[15] Yet when the protectionists around Lord Bentinck and Disraeli proposed the building of railways in Ireland with the assistance of government credit so as to provide work and at the same time improve the country's infrastructure, the motion was defeated in its first reading by a majority of 214.[16] The whig government, 'the most purely aristocratic since the days of Henry Pelham' (i.e. 1762),[17] instead of improving the condition of the people and thereby

removing the causes of agrarian crime, decided to avail of the opportunity presented by Ireland's tragic plight and strengthen its hold over
those Irish who could not be got rid of through starvation or emigration. For this they needed 'the soothing influence of religion'. In his
'Memorandum' the earl of Clarendon offered his ideas on the subject:

> Among the social influences ... may be placed foremost the strong
> religious feeling which exists in the Roman Catholic people
> generally for Ecclesiastical authority and which would beyond
> doubt make them as a mass shrink from opposing any decided act
> of authority on the part of the Pope, as if they were committing
> sacrilege; an order however which should come from Rome merely
> as a feeler and not manifestly with an intention to compel obedience
> would provoke far more opposition.[18]

That section of the Irish clergy upon whom the British government
could most confidently count (e.g. Archbishop Crolly of Armagh and
Archbishop Murray of Dublin) had little influence over the Irish
people without backing from Rome. Clarendon therefore proposed
the following:

> Instructions [should] be issued by His Holiness to the Archbishops
> and Bishops of Ireland to prohibit the Clergy under certain pains
> and penalties from attending political meetings or joining political
> movements either by becoming subscribers or members or otherwise
> and that the restrictions should of course extend to the prelates
> themselves ... That any Archbishop or Bishop resisting the order,
> and setting the authority from which it emanates at defiance, should
> be suspended or removed from his see as may be thought expedient.
> A *lentum fulmen* would be worse than no interference.[19]

Lord Temple, the British consul at Naples and brother of Lord
Palmerston, paid a visit to Pius IX and so prepared the way for Minto
on his mission to Rome.[20] Minto noted on his arrival: 'The influence
of the English name is now so great in Italy that they [Pius IX and the
cardinal secretary of state, Feretti] look as much for my assistance in
tempering the views of their own public as in averting danger from
without.'[21] British influence remained strong until 1850. When Minto
raised the subject of political activity among the Irish clergy and urged
the pope to use his influence to prevent this, he found a receptive ear,
as he reported to Palmerston: 'On this subject I found no difficulty
with him [Pius IX] ... He admitted that they should confine themselves to their spiritual duties, and that we were entitled to expect from
him the assistance of his authority if needful to restrain them.'[22]
Early in 1848 Pius IX issued a call to the Irish clergy[23] and bishops[24]
to abstain from political activity; having achieved the aim of the
British government Minto, who had already left Rome for Naples,
instructed the resident English agent in Rome, Petre, to thank the

pope in its name.[25] Petre seized the opportunity to criticise Padre Ventura (1792-1861), a famous preacher in Rome and Paris, who had delivered an eloquent funeral oration for O'Connell in Rome, advocating repeal in an outspokenly anti-British address. Pius IX's reply was revealing: he remarked that Ventura 'was of that class of people who are sure to hurt by their advocacy the cause they undertake to defend'.[26] Pius IX had not in fact voiced any criticism of Ventura's cause, that of Irish rights, but had merely regarded his manner of advocating it as imprudent and even hurtful. The pope had also remarked during the same audience that a restoration of the church lands once belonging to the catholic church would be desirable.

The British prime minister, Russell, had intended to open official diplomatic relations with the Holy See but his efforts were frustrated. For this to take place it was first necessary to pass a law legalising such relations; the bill was passed by both houses in August 1848, but only after an amendment, introduced by Lord Eglinton, had been made prohibiting the pope from having a priest as his representative. This condition was unacceptable, as Pius IX had already informed Minto in November 1847.[27] The act therefore remained indefinitely shelved.

Another issue which required Earl Minto's intervention at the Holy See was that of the establishment of an Irish university. Ireland with her predominantly catholic population had only an anglican university, Trinity College Dublin. In 1845 Peel had founded three 'undenominational' colleges, one each in Cork, Galway and Belfast — these were known as the Queen's colleges, and in fact 'undenominational' meant that in Galway and Cork catholic students were to be educated by members of the established anglican church of Ireland.[28] The Irish catholic hierarchy had already rejected the bill which proposed the establishment of such colleges — on 23 May 1845 at the time of the first reading. Lord John Manners, a friend of Disraeli, had suggested that a catholic university be founded beside the existing anglican one, but there was no response.[29] These colleges which the M.P. for the university of Oxford, Inglis, had appropriately called 'godless colleges', became law on 31 July 1845. The Irish hierarchy met again on 18 November 1845 to discuss the matter; the majority, led by Archbishop MacHale of Tuam, reaffirmed their opposition to the idea of the Queen's colleges which in their opinion were intended to anglicise and anglicanise the young of Ireland, while a minority, including the two primates in Ireland, Archbishops Crolly of Armagh and Murray of Dublin, declared themselves in favour of the government measure. Because of this dissension they appealed to Propaganda Fide for a decision. On 25 November the British government instructed Petre to exert his influence in the matter,[30] while the rector of the Irish college in Rome determined to counter-act Petre's efforts.[31] On 9 October 1847 the prefect of Propaganda Fide, Cardinal Fransoni, issued the rescript *Mirum fortasse,* which was confirmed by Pius IX. In this rescript the 'godless colleges' were condemned and demands made for the setting up of a catholic university along the lines of Louvain in Belgium.[32]

The British government was quite annoyed at this rescript: Earl Minto now tried to exert his influence on the pope to have the decision retracted. Pius IX, however, wanted first to check whether Minto's claim, that the decision leading to the rescript of 9 October 1845 was based on wrong information, was in fact true.[33] Rome then sent an ecclesiastic to Ireland to examine the situation, in accordance with the wishes of the then viceroy of Ireland, Lord Clarendon.[34] Archbishop-coadjutor Nicholson of Corfu (at that time a British protectorate) was briefed in Dublin by Clarendon and Murray on the state of Ireland and seemed wholly sympathetic to the British cause.[35] However, those who supported MacHale did not remain indifferent on the matter; on 29 March 1848 MacHale addressed a letter to Pius IX in which he rejected all British accusations and implored him: *Time igitur, Beatissime Pater, time Anglos et dona ferentes!*[36] Propaganda Fide did indeed issue a new rescript, on 11 October 1848, in which it reaffirmed its decision of 9 October to oppose the idea of the Queen's colleges and support the establishment of a catholic university.[37]

Yet another of Russell's plans was to fail: in 1848 he favoured the idea of winning support for British rule in Ireland among the Irish clergy by means of state endowment. Lord Temple proposed the idea to the pope; Pius IX had no objections himself but insisted on consulting the Irish bishops before reaching any decision.[38] The Irish bishops once again rejected the idea of state endowment,[39] thereby frustrating Russell's plan.

Around the same time Paul Cullen became the new Irish primate. Born in 1803, he went to Rome at an early age and became rector of the Irish college in 1832. His appointment to the see of Armagh was supported by Russell's government, but not by Clarendon,[40] as asserted by the editor of the *Tablet*, Frederick Lucas (1812-55, M.P. for Meath), who in response to the pope's wish kept him informed regarding British politics:[41]

> While Dr MacHale was supporting him in Rome as a man who could be absolutely depended upon to make things safe for the Church against the Whig Ministers and any English politicians whatever — these same Whig ministers were supporting him in Rome, and were urging, directly and powerfully, his appointment to the See of Armagh, as a man whom they knew to be safe for their own purposes.[42]

Lucas's statement has since been rejected. It is interesting therefore to note what Disraeli writes about Cullen in his novel *Lothair*. In this novel Cullen appears under the name 'Churchill':

We want a statesman in Ireland. We have never been able to find one; we want a man like the Cardinal [Manning]. But the Irish will have a native for their chief. We caught Churchill young, and educated him in the Propaganda, but he has disappointed us. At first all seemed well; he was reserved and austere; and we heard with satisfaction that he was unpopular. But now [1868] that critical times are arriving, his peasant blood cannot resist the contagion.[43]

This would support Lucas's statement that Russell was in favour of Cullen's appointment as primate of Ireland since he would be out of touch with the mood of Irish people as a result of his long years in Rome and because of his opposition to revolution and secret societies. Cullen did favour the whigs but was always first and foremost a man of the church.

2. THE YEARS OF ESTRANGEMENT, 1850-1858

On 25 November 1848 the lay prime minister of the papal states, Count Pelegrino Rossi, was assassinated by freemasons[44] and Pius IX was forced to flee Rome for Gaeta. A revolutionary triumvirate was established. The cardinals were also forced to flee, while defenceless priests were being massacred and churches desecrated. Petre, the British agent in Rome, and John Freeborn, the British consul in Rome, were still resident in the city at the time; Moore, the British consul in Ancona, remained there. The latter was powerless to prevent the murder of Fr O'Kelleher, an Irish Carmelite, during the reign of terror in Ancona in June 1849. It was only when Captain Symonds landed at Ancona with the British warship *Spartan* that the revolutionary leaders could be made to stop the killing.[45] On 3 July 1849 Rome was occupied by French troops, and under their protection Pius IX was able to return to Rome. His temporal power now depended on the French troops stationed in his states and this made French influence at the Vatican decisive.

Soon afterwards, in 1850, there occurred what papal authorities could with reason regard as a case of deception of the pope by the British government. The pope intended to re-establish a catholic hierarchy for England and in March 1847 instructed the nuncio in Vienna, Viale Prelà, to negotiate with the British ambassador there, Ponsonby. On 14 March 1847 Prelà informed the secretariate of state in Rome that the British had no objections to the establishment of a catholic hierarchy.[46] In return Ponsonby demanded that the pope issue a *breve* (a brief, i.e. a papal letter of slightly less formality than a bull) to the Irish bishops urging loyalty to British rule in Ireland.[47] Pius IX agreed and issued the brief on 25 March 1847.[48]

In September 1847 the *Salisbury Herald* reported that Wiseman would soon return from Rome and establish a hierarchy of archbishops and bishops who would assume names of towns that were not already being used by the sees of anglican bishops. The paper listed some of the names of the new dioceses: Westminster, Birmingham, Derby, Nottingham, Liverpool.[53] Similarly, the conservative *Quaterly Review* printed a report on the project in December 1847, naming the future archdiocese of Westminster and the diocese of Birmingham;[54] the article was written by John Wilson Croker (1780-1857), for many years the secretary to the admiralty.[55]

On 1 November 1847 the brief establishing the catholic hierarchy was ready. A short time later Minto arrived in Rome and during an audience with the pope he was shown the document and invited to read it. Minto did not do this, as he wanted to be able to say later that he was unaware of any plan to establish a catholic hierarchy while in fact he was perfectly well aware of these proposals, as he admitted in private.[50] On 16 January 1848 he wrote to Palmerston on the subject of 'Dr Wiseman's advancement to the Roman Catholic Archbishopric of Westminster'.[51] Wiseman's advancement was indeed of interest to England, as Lord Shrewsbury pointed out in a letter which was forwarded to Minto:

> Dr Wiseman's appointment to the Metropolitan See of Westminster will be the struggle and the trial. He is presumed to be anti-Irish, and as such will be assailed ... I am convinced more and more every day of the *necessity* of Bishop Wiseman's appointment to the seat of government: it is the *only* means we have of effectually counter-acting Irish influence at Rome, and of rightly informing the Pope.[52]

The hierarchy project was reported in detail in the catholic *Tablet* and was mentioned several times in parliament.[56] On 17 August 1848 Lord John Russell, in answer to a question from Inglis, M.P. for Oxford University, who objected to Wiseman calling himself the archbishop of Westminster, declared that he himself was not opposed to the idea.[57] Russell reiterated this stance in 1849 to the earl of Shrewsbury, then leader of the catholic English nobility, saying that he had no objections to catholic bishops taking the names of English towns.[58]

There being strong opposition among English catholics to Wiseman, Pius IX first thought of making him a curial cardinal. However, the friends of Wiseman among English catholics opposed this idea so it was decided to make him a cardinal *and* archbishop of Westminster.[59] On 16 August 1850 Wiseman departed for Rome; before leaving he conferred with Russell, informing him that he would be made a cardinal. Russell raised no objections,[60] on the contrary he charged Wiseman with a special mission to obtain something from the pope on behalf of the British government.[61] Furthermore, in June 1850, the whigs expressed their pro-catholic leanings by increasing the grant for St Patrick's College, Maynooth.[62] Pius IX trusted

Wiseman's assurances that 'the Hierarchy would pass quietly and unobserved in England and would raise no opposition — had they known the result they would have followed another course'.[63] Wiseman had disregarded the tension created by the 'Gorham case'. In March 1850 the judicial committee of the privy council had directed the dean of Arches to have a certain Gorham instituted as anglican minister, despite the fact that Gorham did not believe in regeneration by baptism. As a consequence many clergymen left the church of England to become catholics (including Henry Edward Manning, the future cardinal), and at a meeting of tractarians royal supremacy was challenged.[65]

On 29 September 1850 a papal bull was issued proclaiming the establishment of a catholic hierarchy for England and Wales; the following day Wiseman was elevated to the purple and subsequently made archbishop of Westminster and *The Times* reported on the festivities in every detail, showering Wiseman with praise and flattery with the apparent intention of creating a false sense of security and acceptance over this new development. This may have led Wiseman to issue a rather imprudent letter *Ex Porta Flaminia* on 7 October, in which he announced the re-establishment of the catholic hierarchy to the English faithful in a somewhat histrionic and vain-glorious tone.[64] *The Times* printed the letter on 14 October, and in the leader column of the same issue the tone was set for the anti-catholic storm that was to follow. Shortly before this Russell had entertained the idea of sending the former repealer, R.L. Sheil, as a special envoy to Rome. However, on 4 November 1850 *The Times* printed another leading article, which reported on the deliberations of the bishop of London trying to soothe the passion created by the Gorham case, the catholicising tractarians in the anglican church, and then went on to dwell on Wiseman and the establishment of the catholic hierarchy. *The Times* leader stated:

> No doubt these external departures [of the tractarians]from the habits and the worship of our forefathers have materially contributed to embolden the Romish priesthood, ...all the experience, from the first statute of Elizabeth down to Cardinal WISEMAN's last pastoral, shows that if this country is to maintain the church of England and the Protestantism of England as the palladium of freedom of thought, of action, and of government, we cannot render a worse service to that sacred cause than to mimic the histrionic ceremonies of Rome. The arrival of a levy of bishops in all the pomp of their Romish attire may seasonably remind some of our clergy that these performances are the badges of foreign allegiance ... The re-establishment of an entire hierarchy by Papal authority, *without* the assent of the existing Government of this nation, ... is an act of sovereignty.

The leader ended with an emotional reminder of the gunpowder plot.[66]

Russell now feigned surprise and indignation at the prospect of the catholic hierarchy being re-established and on the same day wrote an open letter to the bishop of Durham calling the re-establishment 'Papal Aggression'. The English agent in Rome, Petre, as a catholic was not trusted by the British government, so it became the duty of John T. Lowe, since 18 March 1845 the unpaid British vice-consul at Civita Vecchia, to demand a retraction of the papal bull which established the hierarchy.[67] On Guy Fawkes day (5 November) that same year effigies of Pius IX and Cardinal Wiseman were burned, and many catholic churches were desecrated.[68]

Previous to this, in 1847, Russell had found himself in a precarious political situation with the Don Pacifico affair: Don Pacifico was a merchant from Gibraltar but living in Athens whose house was burnt by a mob infuriated by his practice of usury. The British government had demanded compensation from Greece and had enforced this demand by threat of using the royal navy; this had resulted in considerable anti-British feeling in the Mediterranean. As a result of his action over the papal bull, Russell's popularity enjoyed a tremendous upturn, and he exploited the opportunity to push through parliament a bill entitled the 'Ecclesiastical Titles Act' which imposed heavy fines on catholic ecclesiastics if they assumed the titles of English towns. Russell's majorities grew even larger in parliament as a result of these clauses.[69] While enjoying a resurgence in support for his policies Russell, like *The Times,* wanted to repress and intimidate the tractarians.[70] Even contemporary observers were able to identify the real target in his 'papal aggression' agitation.[71]

The British government believed that while conducting an anti-catholic crusade they could at the same time prepare for a concordat with Rome. On 12 December 1850 British ambassadors abroad were asked to transmit to the foreign office 'with as little delay as possible, a copy of any concordat or equivalent arrangement between [the respective] Government and the Court of Rome' and to report on the course pursued in that respective country 'with regard to the appointment of Roman Catholic Bishops, with regard to the publication of Papal Bulls and Rescripts, and whether such Bulls and Rescripts may be published without the previous knowledge and sanction of the Government, and, if not, in what way the consent or sanction of the Government is obtained'.[72] Needless to say nothing was to come of this advance.

The British government soon realised that it had earned itself a bad name as a result of its anti-catholic agitation. Since France was now the protector of the papal states and therefore all-powerful in Rome, the British government resorted to presenting its wishes to the pope via Paris. An Irish synod had condemned the 'godless [Queen's] colleges' and Petre had tried in vain to have the decision of the synod reversed by the cardinal secretary of state, Antonelli. Antonelli stood firmly and resolutely by the decision as he himself was hostile to the idea of the colleges. Mr Sheil therefore advised Palmerston to instruct the ambassador in Paris to impress upon the nuncio there, Mgr Garibaldi, 'that a decision in favour of the Irish Synod would greatly exasperate the English'. The British government was once again resorting to the use of threat in order to bend Rome to its wishes. Sheil continued by maliciously remarking: 'It is obviously in the interest of the Court of Rome that the public feeling recently created in England should be allayed.'[73] Palmerston ordered that the ambassador in Paris be instructed accordingly.[74] The ambassador, Lord Cowley, then met with his counterpart, Nuncio Garibaldi, but to no avail. The publication of confidential conversations between Cowley and Garibaldi's predecessor, Fornari, had made Garibaldi reluctant to commit himself to any utterance on Irish affairs.[75]

In May 1852 Peter O'Toole, vice-president of Queen's college, Galway, (a priest suspended by his bishop for taking up that position), arrived in Rome but despite Petre's exertions on his behalf his mission was a complete failure. O'Toole's suspension was not lifted and Rome would not change its policy with regard to the Queen's colleges.[76]

Meanwhile in England the whig government was replaced by a tory one. The new prime minister, the earl of Derby, sent Sir Henry Lytton Bulwer, the British minister at Florence, on a special mission to Rome. Derby instructed Bulwer in a lengthy private letter that the purpose of his mission was to exert all possible influence on the pope to issue a condemnation of political involvement by Irish catholic priests. What had actually prompted the mission was the influence exercised by the clergy on the people to elect only those candidates who declared themselves against the interests of the landlords and committed to changing the right of property of land in favour of the tenants; they were also urging the disestablishment of the church of Ireland. Bulwer was also instructed to sound out the possibilities for, and conditions of, an arrangement with Rome.[77] Since parliament had just passed a law prohibiting catholic religious processions, and a committee on Maynooth had recently been formed which posed the threat that the state grant might be taken away from the college, it is hardly surprising that Rome was less than favourably disposed towards the British government. The path had been cleared for Bulwer's mission by the French ambassador in Rome, de Ragneval, who approached Antonelli on Britain's behalf, conveying their wish to have the pope admonish 'the Roman Catholics in Ireland to pay greater respect to the law'. Cardinal Antonelli refused to take the initiative; Rome would only act if prompted by an Irish bishop.[78] The American minister to the Holy See, Lewis Cass, provided the most lucid and truthful account of the objects and results of Bulwer's mission:

Bulwer was to 'soothe the ruffled temper of the Vatican' by offering some concessions and 'obtain, in return, some respite from the clerical anathema wherewith the administration is assailed from all parts of Ireland'. Cass, who received his information from Bulwer himself, reported on another object of the mission of which there is no mention in the letters extant: 'In his interviews with the Cardinal Secretary Sir Henry proposed, first, that a representative of the Queen, with the style and title of Minister Plentipotentiary should be accredited to the Holy See ... The Cardinal ... is said to have signified, in the plainest terms, that under existing circumstances the presence of a British Minister must be useless, and was felt to be undesirable.'[79]

Cardinal Antonelli did, however, express to Bulwer his strong disapproval of those Irish clergy who had engaged in political agitation and of Archbishop MacHale's open letter to Lord Derby.[80] Antonelli went further than this and deplored the conduct of the Irish clergy in the recent elections and that of those priests who had actively promoted the aims of the Tenants Rights League; he described their conduct as detestable.[81] Antonelli even declared himself against the disestablishment of the church of Ireland. In a remark to Bulwer and Petre, Antonelli indicated the underlying motives which guided his actions when he expressed approval of the British government's policy towards the catholic church in the colonies (where catholic missions were preferred to anglican ones so that Christianised natives might be of a different denomination to their anglican rulers); this remark seemed to reflect his concern for the church's position in the entire British empire, of which Ireland was only a very small part.[82] Antonelli had nothing else to offer Bulwer but his opinions; it did not escape Bulwer's attention that Antonelli was alone in expressing pro-British opinions, while the congregation of Propaganda Fide, which directed the affairs of the catholic church all over the empire including England and Ireland, was unfavourably disposed to the British government at the time and believed that mass conversions would bring a return of catholicism to England.[83]

In April 1853 Petre was replaced as British agent in Rome by Lord Lyons.[84] Lyons was instructed by the government to use the occasion of his introduction to Antonelli (by Petre) to express once again his government's desire to establish official relations between England and the Holy See. Again Antonelli flatly refused so long as England did not repeal the Eglinton clause prohibiting the pope from sending an ecclesiastic as his representative to London. As regards political activity among the Irish clergy Antonelli was now better informed and replied to Lyon's remarks that, although he did not approve of their behaviour, they had acted within the framework of British law.[85]

In September 1853 the British government received information that the pope intended to establish a catholic hierarchy in Scotland; Lyons was instructed by the earl of Clarendon, now foreign secretary, to protest against the measure in the name of the British government.[86] Antonelli declared that he 'had not heard a word about such a measure' and having made some enquiries he authorised Lyons to 'state positively to Her Majesty's Government that there does not exist, and has never existed any intention, on the part of the Holy See, to erect a Roman Catholic Hierarchy in Scotland'.[87] This gave the British government a great deal of satisfaction.[88]

At about the same time Cardinal Cullen came to Rome for his *ad limina* visit. Antonelli informed Lyons that Cullen had recently issued a letter to the Irish clergy 'entirely in conformity with the sentiments which he had himself expressed to Sir Henry Bulwer'.[89] A copy of Lyons's dispatch which included this report was forwarded to Palmerston on Clarendon's request.[90] In January 1854 Antonelli once again gave praise to Cullen and expressed his hope to Lyons that the former would exert his influence on the Irish clergy. Lyons then requested that a change of course be adopted following the disastrous chain of events triggered by the erection of the hierarchy in 1850.[91] Wiseman was duly admonished by Rome and advised to act more prudently and discreetly in future.[92]

Cullen and MacHale were among the bishops called to Rome to confer on the doctrine of the immaculate conception. In a subsequent report Lyons took the opportunity to dwell on Roman attitudes towards Ireland; he correctly analysed that what deterred Rome from taking any public measure against Irish clergy involved in political activities was, as MacHale had argued, that 'attachment and submission to the Holy See, both of Clergy and People might be weakened by any attempt to interfere authoritatively with such conduct and language'.[93] In the same month Frederick Lucas, M.P., from the Tenants Rights League declared that he would proceed to Rome with a delegation to solicit the church's ultimate decision as to whether catholic priests were forbidden to voice any political opinions. Lyons immediately sought a meeting with Antonelli to influence him against Lucas's mission. Antonelli rebuked him with the following words:

> We have not hesitated to express in general terms our disapprobation of such proceedings, and our desire that the Clergy should devote themselves to their spiritual duties. And this is all we can do. We have neither the means nor the right, to interfere with the conduct of the Clergy, as Citizens. Our Principle is to preach obedience to the existing Government and laws in all Countries: but it appears that the law in Ireland permits the strong language and proceedings adopted by some of the Clergy in Ireland.[94]

The British government reacted by instructing Lyons to seek an intimation from the pope directed towards the Irish bishops 'that violent language and active participation in political strife on the part of the clergy was displeasing to His Holiness (and) that such intimation, in order to be useful, should appear to be spontaneous, as it would be set nought by the Irish Priests if they had reason to suspect that it was given at the instance of Her Majesty's Government'.[95]

Lucas arrived in Rome in January 1855 and was granted an audience with Pius IX. His arrival did indeed cause a new discussion on the question of Irish priests involving themselves in political activity. An Irish synod at Drogheda had enacted a canon 'prohibiting the Clergy from interfering in political matters in any Parish without the consent of the Parish Priest'. In the catholic church in Ireland there were two parties: Cardinal Cullen was at the head of the moderate party and possessed the power of an apostolic legate; he was opposed by Lucas and his party, who were anxious to prevent any sanctioning of the Drogheda canon by Propaganda Fide (Lucas wanted no restrictions whatever). Even the moderate party, however, was in favour of parish priests discreetly exercising their own personal influence in their own parishes at the time of elections. Lyons meanwhile was trying to exert his influence prudently and discreetly on the discussion. Lucas departed from Rome in May and Cullen left a month later; Lyons was, however, 'unable to procure any definite information on the issue of the struggle'.[96]

Another topic which was prevalent in Lyons's despatches was that of the administration of the papal states. The living conditions of the lower classes in the papal states at the time were considerably better than those of the lower classes in Ireland and even in London; they had experienced no great hunger, there were no children in mines or 'dark satanic mills', no crowbar brigades, no Dotheboys Halls, yet the same earl of Clarendon who had been viceroy of Ireland at the time of the great hunger and who now occupied the post of British foreign secretary thought fit to instruct the pope on how to govern his states. Lyons's despatches during this pontificate were all printed as parliamentary papers in 1860 and therefore need not be reported here.[97]

CHAPTER VI

Odo Russell in Rome

1. RAPPROCHEMENT, 1858-1862

NAPOLEON III's alliance with Piedmont in 1858 considerably altered the *status quo;* the Roman authorities now believed that Napoleon III could no longer be trusted, and this prompted a steep decline in France's level of influence at the Vatican, which was soon to be replaced by Britain. In the same year Lyons was transferred to Paris and was succeeded as British agent in Rome by Odo Russell.

Odo Russell (1829-84) was a nephew of the foreign secretary, Lord John Russell, and had spent the greater part of his childhood and youth in Vienna and Carlsbad. His mother, Elizabeth ('Bessy'), née Rawdon, was the famous beauty alluded to in Byron's *Beppo.* She was exceptionally intelligent and well-read, and it was under her influence that Odo Russell received his broadly based education.[1] Not only was he industrious and reliable in fulfilling his tasks, he was also a virtuoso, especially at music. He was fluent in French, German and Italian, but more important than any of these, however, was his great personal charm: all these talents ideally qualified him for his post in Rome. While most of his predecessors had merely succeeded in winning favourable hearings from one or other of the cardinals, Odo Russell was able to secure the friendship of Pope Pius IX himself and consequently became the most influential foreign diplomat in Rome. Odo Russell possessed a beautiful tenor voice largely as a result of his training in Vienna, which had been inspired by his mother.[2] The British critic, Blumenthal, was of the opinion that only the famous tenor Mario had a finer voice than Russell at the time. Russell used to spend the summer at Ariccia in a villa owned by his friend, Prince Chigi; this villa was not far from the papal summer residence, Castel Gandolfo. From there Pius IX would call Russell when he was tired and have him sing Italian folk songs.[3] Russell not only won the confidence of the pope but also that of the cardinal secretary of state, Antonelli, who enjoyed considerably more power than any of his predecessors.[4] After 1862 no cardinal was admitted to an audience with the pope without previously submitting to Antonelli the reason for the audience.[5] After two years in Rome Odo Russell wrote to his uncle, the foreign secretary, Lord John Russell: 'I also know many influential Priests and Dignitaries of the Church who are not generally accessible to foreigners. I have endeavoured to know as many English and Irish Priests as possible.'[6]

One of these was George Talbot de Malahide; after Russell it was largely due to the efforts of this man that English influence at the Vatican was so great. When Pius IX returned from exile at Gaeta in 1850, he decided to end his predecessor's policy of appointing only Italians to important posts by calling a number of non-Italian chamberlains to Rome — among them, George Talbot, from England. Talbot was descended from an old catholic family which had migrated to Ireland in the middle ages. His grandmother received a peerage in 1831, while his father and uncle had joined the church of Ireland. His father, James Talbot, later moved to England to live on his wife's estate at Evercreech, Somerset, where their twelve children were brought up. George was the fifth son and was born in 1816; after Eton he studied at Oriel college, Oxford, where in 1841 he was awarded his M.A. He spent some time as a country parson in Evercreech, and on 10 June 1843 Wiseman received him into the catholic church. Talbot travelled to Italy where he studied Italian and theology and in 1846 was ordained a priest. He was recommended to Pius IX by Cardinal Wiseman; even before Talbot became chamberlain to the pontiff in 1851, the pope had become personally acquainted with him.[7] As chamberlain he was required to live at close quarters with the pope at all times, and a trusting and personal friendship was soon established.[8] Talbot became consultor of Propaganda Fide and in this congregation he was responsible for the affairs of England, Ireland and the West Indies. He was also a canon of St Peter's at the same time and Dom Butler wrote of Talbot's childish 'love of managing things and persons, from the Pope downwards'.[9] Talbot's influence cannot be underestimated: not only did all matters concerning England and Ireland pass through his hands but he could, because of his personal friendship with Pius IX, also discuss with him the affairs of these countries in complete frankness. Odo Russell established close contacts with Talbot at an early stage.[10] Talbot, however, degenerated over the years as his egotism and self-indulgent behaviour completely consumed him in his capacity as *éminence grise*.[11] His unbalanced temperament eventually led to madness.[12] The Talbots of Malahide were whigs: George Talbot's brother, James, for example, was the liberal M.P. for Athlone from 1832-5; he had been an Irish peer up till then, in 1856 English peerage, a barony (Talbot de Malahide) was created for him; this can be regarded as a reward for the political services rendered by all the family. From 1863-6 he served as lord-in-waiting and became a member of the senate of the royal university of Ireland which comprised all the Queen's colleges.

Although Pius IX was influenced by Odo Russell and Mgr George Talbot, he was nevertheless aware of the true designs of the English whigs; Lord Palmerston's speeches especially made a very unfavourable impression on him.[13] When in July 1859 the tory government of Derby and Disraeli had once again handed over the seals of office to the whigs after only a short term of office, Pius IX declared to Odo Russell: 'I often wonder at the language your statesmen hold about us in the Houses of Parliament. I always read their speeches. Lord Palmerston, Lord John Russell and Mr Gladstone do not know us . . . Mr Disraeli was my friend, I regret him.'[14] However, because of the precarious situation in the church states, the pope depended on British support and backing; he therefore beseeched Odo Russell at the end of the same audience: 'Be our friend in the hour of need.'[15] Despite his plea for assistance Pius IX made it plain to Russell that he saw through the politics of the whigs, who constantly spoke of freedom while ruthlessly pursuing their own national goals. Thus in 1866 Pius IX ironically remarked to Odo Russell that 'he admired the power and energy of the English in the suppression of revolutions, such as the Ionian Islands, India, and lately in Jamaica, where they hung 2000 negroes and met with universal approval, while he could not hang one single man in the Papal States without incurring universal blame'. Odo Russell significantly answered that this proved the practical advantage of the British system.

In 1859 Odo Russell reported to Rome that 'Antonelli and the "Papalini" dwell fondly on the invasion of England by the Emperor'.[16] Wiseman pointed out to Russell that should a war ensue between England and France the catholic church would, in the case of an English victory, be rid of Napoleon III and, in the case of a French victory, obtain a catholic government for England. He reported to Russell that 'Emperor Napoleon had sounded the Roman Catholics of England and had held out promises and prospects of Catholic supremacy to them, to ensure their co-operation when he should deem the moment propitious for the invasion of Great Britain.'[17] Wiseman advised him that the church had access to sources of information which normal diplomacy did not command.

At the same time, however, Russell's position and influence in Rome was ever on the increase. In the autumn of 1859 he wrote to his mother: 'Antonelli is more amiable than ever to me.'[18] In 1859 France and Piedmont defeated Austria at Solferino, and this was followed some months later by the loss of the legations (the outlying papal states) which left the pope with the 'patrimony of St Peter', i.e. Rome and the surrounding province. Even here his security depended on the protection of French troops, and the long-term future of the state became even more precarious after Napoleon had taken sides with the enemies of the church states. Thus in January 1860 Cardinal Antonelli asked Odo Russell if England 'had any ships near Civita Vecchia', the harbour of the papal states, and whether 'Her Majesty's Government would afford the Pope personal protection should he require it', to which Russell answered in the affirmative. It became apparent that

England was the country that the pope was now looking to, in case of danger, as a place of exile.[19]

Odo Russell meanwhile was thriving in his official capacity in Rome, improving his ecclesiastical connections and sending home analyses of the Roman situation, hoping to make a career of it.[20] In May 1861 his uncle, the duke of Bedford, died leaving Odo enough money to become financially independent. His position was further enhanced when in 1862 his mother became a catholic. In October 1862 Russell conveyed an offer from his uncle, Lord John Russell, to accommodate the pope in Malta in the event of an Italian invasion of Rome;[21] this was a propitious manoeuvre on Britain's part since the pope would have been under complete control on the island. There were also thoughts of an 'Avignon' in England or Ireland circulating at the time.[22]

2. THE AMERICAN CIVIL WAR; THE SYLLABUS AND QUANTA CURA: 1862-1865

For the duration of the American civil war Pope Pius IX and Cardinal Antonelli stood firmly by the union and in November 1862 Pius IX acknowledged his gratitude to the American minister in Rome, Richard Blatchford, for 'the liberality shown to the Catholic Religion' in the United States, remarking that the affairs of the union 'had always interested him greatly' and that he always prayed for its welfare, especially then during the war. Antonelli openly declared: 'If I had the honour to be an American Citizen I would do everything in my power to preserve the strength of the Nation undivided.'[23] In sharp contrast to Odo Russell's unveiled duplicity in calling the pope 'Nine Pins' and a 'Fool' and Antonelli a 'Knave' in his private letters while remaining extremely cordial during audiences and even singing for the pope, Blatchford was scrupulously honest in his reporting of Roman affairs. He wrote to the secretary of state, Seward: 'Everybody is ready to ascribe to the Pope benevolence of heart and rectitude in all he says and does — his popularity is great, and is equalled only by the admitted ability and statesmanship of Cardinal Antonelli.'[24] On 4 April 1863 Blatchford again reported to Washington: 'Here, His Holiness, as well as the Secretary of State, are decided friends of the Union and ardently desire that its integrity may be preserved. The latter was strong in the expression of his hopes that the North would speedily subdue the Rebellion.'[25] Fr John Bannon, the confederate agent in Ireland, tried in vain to induce the pope to recognise the confederate states, and Bishop Lynch of Charleston, South Carolina, was sent to Rome as their minister to the Holy See but was not recognised by the pope as such. Pius IX declared to the new U.S. minister to the Holy See, Rufus King, that 'he could never lend any sanction to the system of African slavery'.[26]

Against this background of harmony between the United States and the Holy See there was one single event which, more than anything else, served to inflame anti-catholic polemics: in December 1864 Pius IX issued an encyclical titled *Quanta Cura,* to which was attached a list of eighty condemned errors of the time, the *Syllabus.*[27] From the catholic church's point of view it was perfectly justifiable and even useful to issue such an encyclical, for it aimed to elucidate certain points which were the cause of some confusion to the faithful; but due to its form it did in fact cause more irritation than enlightenment. Giacomo Martina S.J. pointed out these defects in the 1960s in his studies of the *Syllabus.*[28] He referred to the disastrous reception of this document in Belgium[29] and mentioned in passing that it met a similar response in another, more important country, the United States.[30] Josiah Strong, secretary general of the Evangelical Alliance in the United States, devoted a whole chapter in his book *Our Country* (1885) to the 'Peril Romanism'.[31] By 1916 this book had sold 175,000 copies and in terms of success can only be compared to *Uncle Tom's Cabin.* Extracts were printed in countless American newspapers and magazines;[32] In this chapter Strong contrasts clauses from the *Syllabus* and *Quanta Cura* with the American constitution and arrives at the conclusion that the *Syllabus* condemned principles of the American constitution: for example, condemned error 42 of the *Syllabus* decreeing that 'In case of conflicting laws between the two powers, the civil ought to prevail'[33] was against Article VI, paragraph 2 of the American constitution which stipulated that: 'This Constitution and the laws of the United States which shall be made in persuance thereof ... shall be the supreme law of the land.'[34] Error 15 condemned in the *Syllabus,* 'Every man is free to embrace and profess the religion he shall believe true, guided by the light of reason', was, according to Strong, in conflict with the freedom of conscience as laid down in the first amendment: 'Congress shall make no law respecting an establishment of religion, or prohibiting the free exercise thereof.' This fundamental right was also in conflict with a clause in *Quanta Cura:* 'Contrary to the teaching the Holy Scriptures, of the Church, and of the Holy Fathers, these persons do not hesitate to assert that the best condition of human society is that wherein no duty is recognised by the government of correcting by enacted penalties the violators of the Catholic Religion, except when the maintenance of public peace requires it.'[35] In the first edition of his work (p.47) Strong added another paragraph from *Quanta Cura* according to which all those 'who assert the liberty of conscience and of religious worship' were excommunicated. Furthermore, the first amendment established that 'Congress shall make no law abridging the freedom of speech or of the press', while Strong points out in the first edition of his book (p.48) that as a result of *Quanta Cura,* all 'who maintain the liberty of the press (and) all advocates of the liberty of speech' would be excommunicated. He stressed that Pius IX termed this the 'liberty of perdition' (*ibid.*). Strong also saw a direct conflict between the first amendment and error 55 of the *Syllabus*, which stipulated that 'The Church ought to be separated from the State and the State from the Church.' He wrote: 'None of our fundamental principles is more distinctly American than that of the complete Separation of Church and State.'[36] Strong then expands this theme by examining error 24 of the *Syllabus:* 'The Church has not the power of availing herself of force, or any direct or indirect temporal power' (*ibid.*). He then examines the position of public schools in the United States which are not controlled by the catholic church; the church's attitude is defined in error 45 of the *Syllabus:* 'The entire direction of public schools ... may and must appertain to the civil power and belong to it so far that no other authority whatsoever shall be recognised as having any right to interfere in the discipline of the schools, the arrangement of the studies ... or the choice and approval of the teachers' (*ibid.*): this, together with error 47, was tantamount to a condemnation of the American system of public schools. The same could be said of error 48 of the *Syllabus:* 'This system of instructing youth, which consists in separating it from the Catholic faith and from the power of the church may be approved by Catholics.'[37] In the first edition of his work Strong, rather than quote the relevant condemned error, gave its *positive* opposite; he then cited two further clauses from the *Syllabus* (p.50): clause 19 which stipulated that the 'Romish church has a right to exercise its authority without any limits set to it by the civil power', and clause 30, 'The Romish church and her ecclesiastics have a right to immunity from civil law.'

Strong's interpretation of the *Syllabus* was certainly malevolent.[38] The ill-advised form of the *Syllabus,* which allowed such a interpretation to be made, compelled the American bishops repeatedly to vindication. The third plenary council of Baltimore of 1884 felt obliged to declare that there was no contradiction between the law, institutions and spirit of the catholic church and those of the United States.[39] Bishop Kain of Wheeling, W.Va., devoted his lenten pastoral in 1889 to refuting Strong's thesis.[40] Bishop Spalding of Peoria in 1894 voiced his opinions in the *North American Review:* 'We accept with frank sincerity, with cheerful acquiescence, the principle involved in the rule of the people, by the people, and for the people, and are content to abide the issue.' He continued that the United States was 'a country in which all have agreed to make freedom of conscience and liberty of worship inalienable rights'.[41] Even Cardinal Gibbons felt obliged to calm the storm aroused by Strong's book with an article entitled 'Patriotism and Politics' in the *North American Review.*[42] A catholic layman, George Parsons Lathrop (1851-98), Hawthorne's son-in-law, entered the foray: 'The

Papacy neither exerts nor claims any power to dictate the political actions of Catholics, here or elsewhere.'[43]

It is significant that the text of the *Syllabus* used by Josiah Strong was part of a book which comprised a series of articles, all bound together in one volume, and which included Gladstone's *The Vatican Decrees in Their Bearing on Civil Allegiance,* Philip Schaff's *A History of the Vatican Council* inspired by Döllinger,[44] and the Latin and English texts of *The Papal Syllabus* and *The Vatican Decrees.*[45] Strong included a quotation from Gladstone's article in the context of his citations from the *Syllabus* and *Quanta Cura:* ·'The Pope demands for himself the right to determine the province of his own rights, and has so defined it in formal documents to warrant any and every invasion of the civil sphere.'[46] *Punch*, a much-read publication in the United States, set the tone for the ensuing tempest in its issue of 7 January 1865. Page one consisted of a parody with 'Punch's Encyclical Letter' which was followed up by a squib; it read: 'That Encyclical so contrary to reason/ .../ Insisting on priestly domination/ o'er civil power ... and public education;/ .../ Denying people's right to choose their rulers by election,/ .../ Condemning free press, conscience free, and liberal constitution.' Pages six to nine followed with another squib: 'Mr Punch's Non Possumus (Being a respectful Comment on the Pope's Encyclical and its Appendix)'. A cartoon depicting the encyclical as 'The Pope's Mad Bull!' occupied one page, showing the papal crest as the brand on the bull and a fool's cap on its horns. The bull is seen running into a wall on which were blazoned the words 'Science, Common Sense, Toleration, Civil and Religious Liberty, Progress' and then collapsing on to its knees. The American minister in Rome, King, immediately sent a copy of *Quanta Cura* and *Syllabus* to Washington.[47]

Odo Russell had previously been stationed in Washington before being posted to Rome; he wrote to his mother: 'I am reading all I can on America and I take an unusual interest in it.'[48] When Russell sent 'a short précis' of *Quanta Cura* and *Syllabus* to his uncle, Lord John, he selected the very clauses which were later used by Josiah Strong for his anti-catholic onslaught:

> Those are condemned who assere non dubitant optimam esse conditiones in qua Imperio non agnoscitur officium coercendi sanctis poenis violatores Catholicae religionis, nisi quatenus pax publica postulet, and erroneam illam opinionem libertatem conscientiae et cultum esse proprium cuiuscumque hominis ius, quod lege proclamari et asseri debet in omni recte constitua societate, et ius civibus inesse ad omnimodam libertatem nulla vel ecclesiastica vel civili auctoritate coarctandam, quo suos conceptus quoscumque sive voce, sive typis, sive alia ratione palam publiceque mainfestare ac declarare valeant.

Of the eighty condemned errors of the *Syllabus* Russell selected clause 55, which condemned the separation of church and state, as a frontispiece; this was totally irrelevant to England, where to this day there is no separation of church and state. Russell can only have been directing his thoughts at America: 'The appendix contains *LXXX praecipuos nostrae aetatis errores* which the Bishops are ordered to combat by all the means in their power. Among these 'heresies' is the principle *quod vocant de non interventu,* and also that church and state may be separated.'[49]

Here the political background becomes apparent. At the outbreak of the civil war the whigs had supported the south and set their hopes on the split of the Union. After the decisive battle of Gettysburg (1-3 July 1863) their hopes had been dashed, so they seized the new situation to foment anglophile agitation within the Union: this included fighting those forces in the Union opposed to Britain. At the forefront of these forces was the catholic church in the United States with her many Irish and anti-British members. Disraeli stressed the importance of the catholic church in the U.S. in his novel *Lothair,* where a papal legate is heard to say: 'We have lost provinces, but we have also gained them. We have twelve millions of subjects in the United States of America, and they will increase like the sands of the sea.'[50] The importance of the catholic church in the U.S. and her anticipated growth in membership and influence is also apparent in Strong's work: 'There surely can be no question on that point since the open declaration of the Pope that "America is the hope of Rome." Half a century ago, Gregory XVI, who held that "the salvation of the church would come from America", said: "Out of the Roman States there is no country where I am Pope, except the United States."' On account of the church-state regulations elsewhere this was only too true, yet the 'salvation of the church' in the U.S. rested upon a constitutional separation of church and state, and such was condemned in the *Syllabus.*

The *Syllabus* proved extremely useful to British policy towards the U.S.: in 1869, for example, the cardinal secretary of state, Antonelli, informed Odo Russell that news had reached him from the West Indies (an area where British and American interests clashed) of

> secret agents sent from Washington by President Grant at work enlisting the co-operation of the clergy to bring about the annexation of those Islands to the United States by universal suffrage. The priests had all behaved well in declaring that it would be their duty to oppose the intrigues they were asked to assist, because the principle of universal suffrage had been condemned by the Pope in his Syllabus.[51]

This was a reference to the clause in *Quanta Cura* which condemned the idea that public opinion, as the highest law in the land, was independent of all divine or human law. As in Strong's case the interpretation of these priests was fallacious, yet the very form of *Quanta Cura* and *Syllabus* rendered themselves vulnerable to such erroneous or malevolent interpretation.

Giacomo Martina in his investigation of the *Syllabus* came to the conclusion that in the course of compiling this document several different versions were constructed. Regarding the final version of the *Syllabus* Martina wrote that the cardinals of the Holy Office on 6 August 1864 declared that a new constitution, based on a pastoral letter of a French bishop, listing a series of errors (for such was the document before them), was inopportune; they suggested that the pope should merely issue an allocution referring to previous condemnations by popes; this is what was in fact done. This final version published in December was compiled between August and December 1864; during the same period *Quanta Cura* was constructed.[52]

We have seen how the wording of the final version of the *Syllabus* made it possible for Strong and others to interpret it as a condemnation of the American constitution. If the different versions of the *Syllabus* are compared the picture becomes even clearer. All those clauses of the *Syllabus* which Strong deems are in conflict with the American constitution, i.e. 30,[53] 55, 15, 19, 24, 27, 42, 45, 47 and 48 do not appear in the previous versions of the *Syllabus*.[54]

While clause 55 of the final version had crudely condemned the separation of church and state, a previous version had merely condemned the opinion: 'That connection of state and church is essentially contrary to a good constitution of human society.'[55] While this statement had remained an opinion it could not have been construed as a condemnation of the American constitution. Not a word was mentioned in the previous versions of the *Syllabus* of freedom of conscience, press and speech as defined in the American constitution and on which Strong lays so much stress.[56] These clauses which were seen to have a direct bearing on the American constitution were only included in the final version of the *Syllabus* which was made up between August and December 1864, i.e. after Gettysburg. Those clauses in *Quanta Cura* which were likewise referred to by Strong were also compiled in this same period.[57] Martina wrote in 1968 that apart from the time of its construction the only thing of which we can be certain was that the future Cardinal Bilio (1826-84)[58] had participated; who else took part in the construction of the final version is as yet unclear.[59]

One of the participants in the construction of the previous versions has since come to light: Fr Bernard Smith, OSB (1812-92). In the autumn of 1859 he had participated in the consultations which had resulted in the first version[60] and since 1861 had been a member of the commission responsible for the drawing up of the *Syllabus*.[61] It was in this capacity that he participated in the devising of the second last of the versions to be published. He was closely associated with Mgr Talbot and was an arch-enemy of John Henry Newman. Manning so trusted Smith that in 1865 he sought his advice as to whether he should re-publish his anglican sermons.[62] Smith and Talbot sent Newman's sermon 'The Pope and the Revolution' (delivered on 7 October 1866) to the *Index*.[63] Smith was also connected with William George Ward of the *Dublin Review*, to which he sometimes contributed himself. His position in Rome was far from insignificant: from 1850-5 he was the vice-rector of the Irish college in Rome and at the same time became professor at the Collegio Urbano of Propaganda Fide; later he became a teacher of Hebrew,[64] and protector of the Collegio Urbano.[65] He was a Benedictine and since 1857 a member of St Paul-Outside-the-Walls, but was permitted to live in the monastery of San Callisto in Trastevere. Since 1858 he was procurator general of the English Benedictine congregation in Rome, and since 1862 he was consultor of the new congregation for oriental rites. Smith also acted as a guide for prominent English-speaking visitors to Rome, especially non-catholics such as the prince of Wales who visited Rome in February 1859 and November 1862, Gladstone who was in Rome in November 1866,[66] the American president Franklin K. Pierce (democrat, 1853-7), and the writer Nathaniel Hawthorne who visited Rome in 1859. Next to Mgr Angelo Trullet (1813-79), a conventual of French origin,[67] Fr Smith was Odo Russell's closest ecclesiastical confidant and informant in Rome: in a letter to his mother in 1859 Russell referred to Smith as 'my friend the Irish Benedictine'.[68] Smith was not always able to furnish Russell with the necessary information,[69] but it was not for want of effort on Smith's part. Smith preferred the whigs as a political party[70] and it appears that it was he who in 1864 was described as a 'priest of high standing who does not wish to be named' when supplying Russell with information of 'an extensive conspiracy against British Rule organized all over Ireland by Irish Agents sent from the U.S.'.[71]

Smith specialised in American-Roman affairs and served as the first head of the American college in Rome from December 1859 to March 1860. He often conducted business on behalf of American and Canadian ecclesiastics from various dioceses, such as those of New York, Buffalo, Newark, Philadelphia, Louisville, Baltimore, St Louis, Cincinnati, Cleveland, Indianapolis, St Augustine, Savannah, Mobile, Pittsburgh, Boston, Hartford, Richmond, Dubuque, Leavenworth, St Cloud and San Francisco.[72] Smith was a member of that circle of intransigent ultras of which Talbot and Manning were at the forefront and which proved so useful to the whigs in the pursuance of their policies. When these fragments of information are pieced together it seems to lend credence to the assumption that Smith was involved in the drawing up of the final version of the *Syllabus* from

August to December 1864.

It was already apparent in 1862, at an assembly of bishops in Rome, that Manning and his circle were aiming to procure a condemnation of modern liberty, as was later enacted in the *Syllabus*. Manning occupied a position of considerable power and influence even before he succeeded Wiseman: 'The reign of Manning began in 1860, as Wiseman, an invalid, gradually slipped the helm into his rigid hands.'[73] In 1862 the bishops had assembled on the occasion of the canonisation of the Japanese martyrs and at the end of the meeting an unusual address was to be published by the bishops. A commission of eighteen bishops was appointed for the purpose of drafting this address: Wiseman set himself up as the head of a group of intransigents within the commission[74] and proposed a text which was a condemnation of modern liberties[75] — this was described: 'en termes très vifs et dans l'esprit le plus intransigent'.[76] Wiseman's proposition was rejected by the commission and the idea had to be shelved until, in 1864, the *Syllabus* gave vent to this much-desired condemnation of modern liberties.

It is certain that Bilio was involved in the drawing up of the final version of the *Syllabus* in the autumn of 1864. He was then only thirty-eight years of age and had just been appointed consultor of the Holy Office by Pius IX on the recommendation of the cardinal archbishop of Naples, Sisto Riario Sforza (1810-77),[77] who had become acquainted with Bilio in Naples. It seems highly unlikely that a man still largely unknown in Vatican circles would be set to drafting a document of such importance on his own: all previous versions of the *Syllabus* had been drawn up by commissions of several people, and each commission comprised members of earlier commissions as well as new members. This would seem to support the theory that Fr Smith was a participant in the drafting of the final version of the *Syllabus* since he had been a member of previous commissions. Bilio's biographer, Pica, asserts that Bilio merely selected clauses from previous encyclical letters and transposed them into the *Syllabus* as errors to be condemned.[78] According to Pica, Bilio can be held responsible only for clause 55 which, because of its unfortunate wording, was isolated by Strong for attack. The fact that freedom of conscience, press and speech were referred to in the *Syllabus*, which was not the case in previous versions of this document, was not Bilio's responsibility, according to Pica.

It is a fact, however, that Bilio was a friend of Manning:[79] on the death of Pius IX in 1878 Bilio was anxious for Manning to become his successor;[82] it was agreed, however, in one of the preliminary meetings of the cardinals to elect an Italian.[83] It was Manning with his extreme notions who provided Strong with so much ammunition in presenting the catholic church as a threat to American liberties. Manning was opposed to the American system and on 22 September

1867 he wrote to Gladstone: 'The American Irish are practically without religion, except a burning hatred of England.'[85] On 11 February 1868 he again wrote to Gladstone on the dangers he saw being transported from America to Ireland: 'Ireland is becoming Republican: not red but American republicanism, a calm and reasonable preference for the civil and religious equality of America rather than the irritating and impoverished inequalities of the United Kingdom's spreading.'[86] On 11 March 1868 he again wrote to Gladstone: 'Catholic education is the only hope I know, of keeping Ireland from American anarchy.'[87] Manning's preference was for an 'Imperial Federation'.[88] Strong wrote in the first edition of his bestseller: 'Cardinal Manning advises Romanists throughout the world to enter politics as Romanists and to do this especially in England and the United States.'[89] Strong continued: 'In a sermon, preached when he was Archbishop, Cardinal Manning put the following sentence in the mouth of the Pope: "I acknowledge no civil power . . . I claim to be supreme judge and director of the conscience of men . . . I am the sole, last, supreme judge of what is right and wrong.'[90] In the enlarged second edition of *Our Country* there are even more references to Manning, the most important of which is 'In *Essays on Religion and Literature*, edited by Archbishop Manning, 1867, we read, p.416: "Moreover, the right of the deposing kings is inherent in the supreme sovereignty which the Popes, as vice regents of Christ, exercise over all Christian nations".'[91]

3. MANNING, ARCHBISHOP OF WESTMINSTER, 1865

In 1864 anglo-papal relations attained a degree of cordiality which superseded anything before, as evidenced in a letter written by Russell to his mother after a long audience with Pius IX: 'Our relations were never interrupted and this year they are much *more* civil to me than *ever* before.'[92] The extent of English influence at the Vatican became apparent in 1865 when a successor to the late Cardinal Wiseman was to be chosen as archbishop of Westminster and English primate.

Earl Russell instructed his nephew Odo on 20 February 1865 to induce Cardinal Antonelli to have the archdiocese of Westminster suppressed and merged with the diocese of Southwark, failing which he should endeavour to secure the appointment of Dr Grant or Dr Clifford to the archbishopric of Westminster.[93] Grant had served as secretary to Cardinal Acton from 1841-3. Since 1851 he had been bishop of Southwark and also acted as mediator between the English hierarchy and the British government. He had secured the confidence of the whig government and 'was sought by Downing Street for information on Catholic affairs'.[94] Dr Clifford was Lord Clifford's brother. The Cliffords were among those of the English catholic nobility, who were intent upon imposing English practices on Ireland in the political, religious and intellectual spheres, against the wishes of the Irish clergy. The seventh Baron Clifford had tried in 1840 to counter the attempts of Irish bishops to effect a condemnation by Rome of the Irish state school system.[95] Odo Russell was instructed to prevent an appointment to Westminster being bestowed on Dr Ullathorne, then bishop of Birmingham, who had been instrumental in the establishment of the catholic hierarchy in Australia in 1842 and who had proved himself to be no willing servant of the British government and whom Earl Russell therefore regarded as 'very injudicious, capable of putting forward claims which would rouse resistance and indignation'.[96] On 28 February Odo Russell informed Antonelli of the British government's wishes, stressing that it was strongly opposed to any appointment being bestowed on Dr Ullathorne. Manning's name was incidentally mentioned in the course of their meeting, but Antonelli replied 'that he would not be suited for a post like that held by Cardinal Wiseman'.[97] In order to find a successor to Wiseman a *terna* was submitted to the pope listing the three most popular candidates as Errington, Grant and Clifford. Grant and Clifford both declined. Archbishop Errington, once coadjutor of Westminster, had come into conflict with Wiseman and Manning and, maligned by Mgr Talbot, had earned Pius IX's disapproval to such an extent that Pius IX had him removed as coadjutor in 1860.[98] That Errington was nevertheless first preference on the *terna* and that the other two candidates had declined the appointment angered the pope so much that he decided to set the *terna* aside.[99] Mgr Talbot, who was constantly around the pope, now suggested Manning as a possibility — in such a subtle and clever manner that Pius IX believed it to be an inspiration from heaven. Manning was supported by two other friends, Fr Robert Aston Coffin (1819-85) who was not without influence in Rome and who then occupied the post of provincial of the English province of the Redemptorists and who was a fierce enemy and detractor of Newman, and Cardinal Reisach (1800-1869), once bishop of Eichstätt, now an influential member of the curia.[100] Propaganda Fide supported the appointment of Ullathorne. The choice was now limited to Manning, who had made himself unpopular with the chapter of Westminster and the English hierarchy, and Ullathorne.

Odo Russell supported Manning. He informed his uncle, the foreign secretary, on 5 May 1865 on his reasons for doing so:

> His appointment would displease the English Catholicks, he was not popular among them and did not inspire them with confidence ..., but he ... was personally known to Her Majesty's Government ... and I felt sure his appointment would better please H.M. Govt. than that of Dr Ullathorne ... I am personally very well

acquainted with Dr Manning and think H.M. Govt. would like him better than many others the Pope might inflict upon us. As the matter now stands the infliction will probably be on the Roman Catholick Priesthood of England who detest Dr Manning.[101]

Russell had anticipated the appointment correctly: Pius IX succumbed to the persistence of Talbot and Russell, and Manning, not Ullathorne, became the new English primate. The foreign secretary sent the following message to his nephew Odo: 'I am by no means dissatisfied with Dr Manning's nomination.'[102] This tactic of *Divide et impera!* had once again produced the desired result, as Odo Russell pointed out to his uncle, the foreign secretary:

> Dr Manning will give the Roman Catholics far more trouble and annoyance than he can ever give Her Majesty's Government ... I cannot but think that division in the camp, differences of opinion and purpose between English Papists ... will prove favourable to the great cause of freedom in the future. The violent deep rooted irritation of the English Roman Catholic clergy in Rome proves that they foresee the dangers ... and the consequences of Dr Manning's appointment will be detrimental to popery in England.[103]

Henry Edward Manning (1808-92) came from a wealthy family; his father was a merchant who later became an M.P. for a period and also served as governor of the bank of England. Manning's uncle had been lord mayor of London. Manning went to Harrow for four years and later studied at Balliol college, Oxford. He had intended to enter politics until his father's bankruptcy forced him to enter the church. He had achieved the position of archdeacon of Chichester in 1840 and would no doubt have gone further, when in 1851 he converted to catholicism. G.W.E. Russell offered the following judgment on Manning: 'His subsequent career, though, of course, it superadded certain characteristics of its own, never obliterated or even concealed the marks left by those earlier phases, and the octogenerian Cardinal..., but for his dress, might have passed for a Cabinet Minister.'[104] During his twenty-one visits to Rome (often for rather long periods) he resolutely sought the acquaintance of those in positions of influence; as a student at the Academy for Noble Ecclesiastics in Rome (1851-4) Manning had won favour with Pius IX and the friendship of Mgr Talbot,[105] and by the end of the 1850s he knew all the influential cardinals in Rome. In 1857 he became the provost of the chapter of Westminster and in 1860 received the title protonotary apostolic (an honorary title bestowed on eminent canons). He was described thus: 'Manning's genius was not in the field of intellect. The limitations of his mind rarely permitted him to grasp more than the surface of the issue at hand. And as a man of action, Manning pursued issues with a zeal that outran precision or discretion' yet he took 'the line he had taken with an intransigence that made him incapable of seeing even the possibility of another position. Anyone who differed from his views was a low type of Catholic, antiRoman, antipapal, disloyal; and these charges came not from a burst of temper, but from the fullest conviction.'[106] Manning believed in his own mission to such an extent that 'all forces which opposed him were in effect opposing the Divine Will'. This was the underlying basis for the animosity he bore towards the English Jesuits and towards Newman: 'A power independent of, or hostile to his authority was inimical to religion, and must, as a religious duty, be checked, and, if possible, destroyed.'[107]

No sketch of Manning should ignore, however, the considerable social work he did in favour of the poor in England, especially the Irish poor; undoubtedly his *forte* lay in this direction, not in that of theology.

CHAPTER VII

The Fenians and the Garibaldini

1. RUSSELL AND CLARENDON

A FTER THE decisive battle of Gettysburg in the American civil war Disraeli referred to the 'increasing influence of the United States upon the political fortunes of Europe'[1] and identified the two greatest dangers which he saw emanating from the U.S. and threatening Britain — anglophobia and Fenianism.[2] The Fenian Republican Brotherhood (IRB) was founded in the U.S. and Ireland in 1858-9 and recruited soldiers who had been discharged after the American civil war to oust the British from Ireland. An insurrection had been planned as early as 1865, and in October of that year John O'Mahony was elected 'president' of the Irish Republic by a Fenian congress in Philadelphia. During the civil war the whig government in Britain had supported the southern states by building the war-ship *Alabama* which subsequently sank seventy Union ships and this led to the '*Alabama* crisis' in Anglo-American relations. The Fenians had some reason to hope for American assistance when they turned on Canada before attacking British rule in Ireland itself.[3] The American minister in Rome, King, reported Pius IX's opinion on the matter to Washington:

> His Holiness remarked ... Ireland was restless and discontented and Fenianism uttered an ominous threat. He had no idea, he said, that this movement would affect British rule of Ireland; for the ocean which rolled between the U.S. and G.B. forbade the idea of invasion. But Canada, with its extensive and exposed frontier, offered an easier prize, and thither, he thought, the Fenians might turn their arms. It would be for the advantage of all parties, the Holy Father remarked, that the U.S. should take Canada and incorporate it into the American Union, rather than allow the Fenians to possess themselves of it'.[4]

The Fenian threat meant that Britain was ever more reliant on the papacy in order to uphold her rule over Ireland, while the Vatican became increasingly dependent on Britain after the September convention of 1864 between France and Italy and the consequent evacuation of the papal states by the French protection forces in December 1866.

When Archbishop Cullen was appointed as Ireland's first ever cardinal in 1866, Clarendon did not interfere.[5] In April 1866, however, Odo Russell launched a tirade against the Irish clergy while speaking about Fenianism, accusing them of having been 'active Apostles of disaffection' and of having 'taught the people that all the misfortunes they brought upon themselves by their own idle Celtic habits were attributable to the government'.[6] Although Antonelli protested against these general accusations, Odo Russell did not relent and believed that his words would not be 'lost on His Eminence and would slowly and gradually bear fruit'.[7] A month later he again called on Antonelli complaining about priests who had joined the Fenians.[8] This time Russell was even more confident and privately wrote to Lord Clarendon asking him to supply the names of Irish priests who were addicted to Fenianism; he had little doubt that he would succeed in 'getting them Pontifically blown up'.[9] Pius IX did indeed act in the intended manner, if only in one or two cases.[10]

Shortly before the fall of the whig government in June 1866 the foreign secretary, Clarendon, instructed Russell to concern himself unobtrusively with the succession to the archbishopric of Armagh and primacy of all Ireland, following the death of Dr Dixon. Russell took care not to give the impression that the British government was interested in the succession.[11]

2. THE CONSERVATIVES AND DISRAELI

Disraeli, since June 1866 chancellor of the exchequer and from January 1868 prime minister, differed from his predecessors in his attitude to the papacy. John Pope Hennessy (1834-91), a catholic who was tory M.P. for King's county from 1859-65, reported Disraeli's words to Pius IX and his attitude to whig policy:

> The Minto system of trying to get at Irish Catholic votes and control Irish bishops through Rome was a wretched system: it was a double hypocrisy. The agents engaged in it would drive your countrymen from their country and also destroy in Italy the temporalities of the head of your Church. You rightly interpret my views; I object to see Ireland depopulated; I think the independence of the Pope should be maintained.[12]

Granted that here Disraeli was castigating his political opponents; however, he did accurately characterise whig policy regarding Ireland and Rome. For the pope to be of any use to them it was necessary that he be kept independent from other powers, including Italy. Yet, for the whigs this did not mean that the church states were to be preserved within their frontiers of 1858.[13] Lord John Russell wrote to Odo on 12 December 1859: 'I have great respect for the virtues of Pius IX and hope that he may be left undisturbed at Rome, but he must not seek to govern three millions of people for their perpetual misery, even though the pride of the Church may require it. In fact Italy has outgrown the Papacy. The Pope would be a saint at Madrid, Valencia or Majorca. In Italy he is only an anachronism.'[14] On 4 June 1866 Lord John (now Earl) Russell wrote: 'We cannot guarantee the temporal power of the Pope.... I hope he may rest quiet at Rome for the rest of his life and enjoy a *libera chiesa* while Italy possesses a *libero stato*.'[15]

With regard to Ireland the whig panacea was emigration. Those Irish who remained in Ireland were not to be assimilated but should by their catholic religion remain separate from the anglican English and, thus isolated, should be politically dependent on the whigs.[16] Furthermore, the whigs were anxious to prevent the establishment of a catholic university since they wanted the Irish to be dependent on whig leadership.

Disraeli differed in outlook from his fellow tories whose avowed aim was to decatholicise and assimilate the Irish. In contrast to the whigs, Disraeli did not want to use the pope for political ends but rather to co-operate with him. He regarded it as one of his life-tasks to bring about a catholic-conservative alliance,[17] to which end he relied on the tory predilictions of Cardinal Wiseman and the catholic tory M.P. George Bowyer (1811-83, M.P. 1852-68 for Dundalk). Despite the efforts of Bowyer and Wiseman, tory success in the election of 1859 was not altogether complete, largely because of the opposition to their campaign of Archbishop MacHale, the 'Lion of the West'.[18] Disraeli, however, was not easily deterred. On 7 January 1860 Odo Russell reported to London:

> Mr Bowyer, M.P. (has been very active at the Vatican and constantly with the Pope and Antonelli) leaves for London tomorrow. His judgment is highly thought of at the Vatican. ... Both he and Cardinal Wiseman ... say that ... the Pope's prospects would improve ... could the Irish Members bring about a complete change in government as the Conservatives will be found more favourable ... to the restoration of the status quo in Italy'.[19]

Bowyer and Pope Hennessy became president and vice-president respectively of the 'Peter's Pence Association' founded by Wiseman, and both were strong supporters of the pope in parliament, as was Disraeli.[20] Disraeli also lent his support to the law which provided catholic chaplains for prisons.[21] Following the elections of 1865 he explained to his future biographer, Kebbel, that during Palmerston's entire term of office he had sought an alliance with the catholic party, which had become very discontented with the whig policy towards Rome. But then a thoughtless speech by Lord Derby dashed all his hopes.[22] Disraeli was also a supporter of the pope's temporal power. When Garibaldi came to London in 1864 Disraeli refused categorically to meet him. He despised those drawing-room supporters of nationalism whose hypocrisy compelled them to condemn nationalism only when it occurred in Ireland: they became the subject of much ridicule in *Lothair*. Disraeli's anti-Italian and pro-papal feelings were well known to both the Italian government and to Pius IX, who regarded him as an ally.[23]

Disraeli's attitude towards catholicism has been repeatedly studied.[24] Since the anti-catholic 'No Popery!' outburst of the 'papal aggression' agitation of 1850, he was cautious not to reveal his pro-catholic sympathies publicly, and this pretence lasted right to the very end, while he maintained the outward appearance of anglicanism. In the later years of his life he secretly attended mass at Farm Street chapel and on his death-bed called for one of the priests from the chapel who was unable to arrive, however, because of adverse circumstances:[25] this fact has continually been suppressed by official tory historiography. He pointed to the importance of the catholic church in *Lothair*: 'If the Church were to be destroyed, Europe would be divided between the Atheist and the Communist. ... They will not rest until they have extirpated the religious principle from the soul of man, and until they have reduced him to the condition of wild beasts.' He goes on: 'The Church as witness, teacher, and judge, contradicts and offends. ... This is why it is hated; this is why it is to be destroyed, and why they are preparing a future of rebellion, tyranny, falsehood, and degrading debauchery. The Church alone can save us.'[26] When Disraeli died on 20 April 1881 he was praised in the obituary of the catholic daily *Le Monde* as the only statesman who had realised the danger of secret societies and who had elevated British foreign policy above Palmerston's complicity with revolution.

In *Lothair,* which depicted actual events and people in a fictional guise, Disraeli was able to describe and articulate certain contemporary episodes which normal political writing prohibited him from doing. The reviewer of the *Saturday Review,* like that of the German *Allgemeine Zeitung,* realised this:

> The confidential agent of the Holy See discusses in a secret interview with the French Ambassador in London the interest of the English Government in securing the support of the Pope against the Fenians. If he had mentioned the names of the Ministers whose judgment he hoped to convince he would have spoken of Lord Derby, Lord Stanley, and of Mr Disraeli himself.[27]

This was a reference to chapter 50 of the novel in which the papal legate, Mgr Berwick, meets the French ambassador in London. Berwick is thus described: 'Mgr Berwick was a young man, but looking younger from a countenance almost of childhood; fair, with light blue eyes, and flaxen hair and delicate features:'[28] this description coincides exactly with the appearance of Cardinal Howard (1829-92). He had a 'smooth and inexpressive, almost childlike face, with ... innocent blue eyes'.[29] Edward Henry Howard was born in Lincolnshire. His grandfather was the youngest brother of the twelfth duke of Norfolk and had engaged in chemical research, inventing a device for sugar refining by which he made his fortune.[30] Howard studied at St Mary's college, Oscott, from 1841-7 and later at the university of Edinburgh. In Edinburgh he stayed at the house of the Rev. J. Rigg, whom Cardinal Howard was later to consecrate as bishop of Dunkeld. On 18 January 1850 Howard joined the second regiment of the Life Guards in which his father had served. 'For a brief time the handsome young guardsman was the spoiled favourite of society.'[31] He had already become acquainted with Cardinal Wiseman by this time, and following a serious illness he journeyed to Rome in 1851 but was persuaded to return by his close friends. On 18 November 1852 he led the duke of Wellington's funeral procession in his capacity as an officer of the Life Guards. A year later he sold his officer's patent, left the army and returned to Rome to study theology.[32] At the Academy of Noble Ecclesiastics he used to serve Manning's early mass.[33] There is some confusion as to the exact date of his ordination: the *Tablet* stated in his obituary in 1892 that he was ordained by Cardinal Wiseman on 8 December 1854, while the *Oscotian* stated (when he was still alive) that he was ordained by Cardinal Patrizi (1798-1876) in 1856, which seems more likely.[34] 'The official service of the Papacy offered many opportunities to a young, eager, and well-connected ecclesiastic.'[35] Howard enjoyed a rapid rise through the ranks of the Vatican and in 1857 became papal chamberlain. He was fluent in Italian and French and also learned Arabic, Coptic, Armenian, Hindustani and Russian. He served in Propaganda Fide and in 1862 was appointed secretary of the papal commission sent to India to settle the conflict between Portugal and England over the church government in the province of Goa and to reach a concordat with Portugal.[36] Howard accomplished his task so admirably that on his return from India a year later he was made a prelate. In 1867, as was perhaps alluded to in *Lothair,* Howard was appointed vicar (or deputy archpriest) of St Peter's.[37] He had been sent to England on numerous occasions to deal with ecclesiastical and political matters, for example in May 1861,[38] in July 1864,[39] in August 1879 and in October 1880. He often conferred with Manning on matters of particular relevance to England.[40] Following Talbot's confinement to a lunatic asylum in 1868, Howard occupied his position to a certain extent as adviser to the pope. In 1872 he became auxiliary bishop of Frascati and titular bishop of Neocaesarea and in 1877, a cardinal priest. While normally resident in Rome he often visited England where he liked to stay at Arundel. He was also a keen socialite. Howard's mother was a Heneage and an anglican; therefore his four sisters were raised as anglicans. Since the earl and countess of Carnavon were both grandchildren of Howard's mother's brother, Sir

Henry Molyneux, Howard was often a guest at Highclere castle, a favourite meeting place of the English aristocracy of the day.[41]

Howard was well liked by Pius IX and after his death he continued to serve his successor, Leo XIII. In 1878 he became protector of the English college and in 1881 he was appointed archpriest of St Peter's and later, in 1884, he became cardinal bishop of Frascati (each of the latter two posts had been held by Cardinal York).[42] Howard was a member of five Roman congregations, and as a member of Propaganda Fide he was responsible for the affairs of England, Malta and Ireland. What Disraeli had described in chapter 50 of *Lothair* was accurate. On Howard's death the *Illustrated London News* wrote of him in its obituary column: 'He laboured unceasingly to establish the somewhat fitful relations between the Vatican and the British Government'.[43] It was to this end that he journeyed to England in July 1883.[44] In the negotiations between Britain and the Vatican on the Irish home rule movement Howard presented the Vatican's case and England was represented by Errington.[45] At the same time Howard was labouring for the establishment of a catholic university at Washington D.C. and a Canadian college at Rome.[46] He became an invalid in 1887 and returned to England, where he died in Brighton in 1892. The close attachment between himself and Manning, which was described by Disraeli in *Lothair,* was evidenced by Howard's bequests of his chalices and other liturgical objects to Manning.[47]

Howard's mysterious visitor described in chapter 50 of *Lothair* was in fact the French ambassador to London, La Tour d'Auvergne. Prince La Tour d'Auvergne-Lauragais (1823-71) had been the French ambassador to Rome in 1862-63; his term of duty there was characterised by his conservative and reserved nature and his enmity towards Odo Russell.[48] He became the French ambassador to London in 1863.

The meeting took place, according to Disraeli in *Lothair*, when 'The month of September was considerably advanced.'[49] The meeting occurs in the evening of the same day that news of Garibaldi's arrest reaches London.[50] The news of Garibaldi's arrest by the Italian government at Sinalunga did indeed reach London on the evening of 24 September 1867.

It is doubtful whether the meeting took place exactly as described by Disraeli in *Lothair* since the French ambassador is recorded as saying: 'I am engaged to dine with the Prussian Ambassador, who has been obliged to come to town to receive a prince of blood who is visiting the dockyards here.'[51] The Prussian ambassador, Count Bernstorff, was in fact still on holiday then and Prussia was represented by the chargé d'affaires, Katte.[52] Furthermore, the *Allgemeine Zeitung* reported from London on 25 September 1867 that the frigate *Kronprinz* was about to sail for Kiel, yet there was no mention of a prince.[53] It must be remembered, however, that Disraeli was writing a novel, not his memoirs. The French ambassador's other engagement with the

Prussian ambassador adds tension and importance to the meeting; Disraeli's reference to a ship called 'crown prince' as a 'prince of blood' is typical of his humour. The reviewer in the *Revue des deux mondes* presented the meeting as fictional: 'Monsieur Disraeli n'est pas homme à trahir les secrets de la diplomatie, il les a prudemment remplacés par les fictions.'[54] The semi-official connection between this periodical and the Napoleon III régime, and the tendentious nature of the denial, would seem to point rather strongly to the meeting being non-fictitious. The views expressed during the meeting coincide exactly with the actual standpoints adopted by the British and French governments and, just as Disraeli relates here,[55] La Tour d'Auvergne was sceptical about the possibility of a new French expedition to Rome in case of unrest there.[56]

One now has to examine the content of the conversation at the meeting described in *Lothair*. The position of the church states became critical in September 1867, and Howard ('Berwick' in *Lothair*) expressed his fear that the pope would once again be forced into exile: significantly he suggests Paris as a possible sanctuary. On 4 November 1866 the French foreign minister had asked Odo Russell, who was then in Paris, not to renew the Malta offer;[57] the request was duly carried out by the new conservative government.[58] At an earlier stage in the book Howard, in response to the question 'Is the Malta scheme again on the carpet?', answers 'Our Holy Church is built upon a rock ... but not upon the rock of Malta.'[59]

The papal legate had already approached everybody in Paris and now asks the French ambassador La Tour d'Auvergne to contact the British government: 'A word from you to the English Minister would have great weight at this juncture. Queen Victoria is interested in the maintenance of the Papal throne. Her Catholic subjects are counted by millions. The influence of his Holiness has been hitherto exercised against the Fenians. France would interfere if she was sure the step would not be disapproved by England.'[60] This is the focal point of what is said at the meeting. Disraeli attributes to Howard (Berwick) the statement that the most important man in the tory government (i.e. Disraeli) is anxious for the maintenance of the pope's temporal power. The conservative governments of France and England should therefore co-operate with the pope. This policy of co-operation between the pope and the conservative governments of the world as set forth here by Disraeli was later to become the policy of Leo XIII.[61]

The foreign secretary in Lord Derby's cabinet was his son, Lord Stanley, who possessed considerable financial interests in the Anglo-Italian Bank and was therefore committed to the pursuance of peace and stability in Italy; consequently he applauded the arrest of Garibaldi in 1867.[62] While he did not share Disraeli's pro-papal and anti-Italian views he did not protest when the French returned to Rome to assist the papal troops who had secured a victory over

Garibaldi's red shirts in the battle of Mentana on 3 November 1867.[63]
Stanley merely sought to prevent a Franco-Italian war over the Roman
question. Thus Stanley declared to the Italian minister d'Azeglio on 29
October 1867 that it was too late now to prevent a French return to
Rome but that England would do all in her power to ensure that an
invasion of papal territory by *regular* Italian troops (as opposed to
Garibaldi's red shirts) would not be regarded as a *casus belli* by
France.[64] Italy had since lost English sympathy after allowing
Garibaldi to escape.[65] Stanley opposed Napoleon's projected
conference on the Roman question for fear of exposing England by
adopting a stand which might displease the Irish catholics.[66] Stanley
tried to exert a moderating influence on France. He had little
knowledge of the realities of Italian nationalism, as he confessed to
the Italian chargé d'affaires Maffei that he could not understand why
Italy was so keen on possessing Rome which could only bring them
internal and external difficulties.[67] By and large Stanley assumed a
non-committal stance as foreign secretary, the preservation of peace
being uppermost in his thoughts. Judging from his remark to Maffei,
it becomes clear that he had no idea of the importance of Rome as the
symbol of Italian nationalism.

Disraeli finally realised that an annexation of Rome to the new
kingdom of Italy could not be prevented for very much longer and
eventually came round to accepting a proposal made by Lord Russell
in 1862,[68] as he indicates in *Lothair*: 'His Holiness should content
himself with the ancient city, and, in possession of St Peter's and the
Vatican, leave the rest of Rome to the vulgar cares and mundane
anxieties of the transient generation.'[69] Here Disraeli anticipated the
Lateran treaty of 1929. Stanley was also in favour of the proposal
which was still being encouraged by Russell and which in July 1866
seemed to be acceptable to d'Azeglio.[70]

While maintaining a cautious stand on the Roman question the
conservative government saw no need to exert pressure on the pope to
intervene in Ireland; they had also become distrustful of the whig,
Odo Russell. Disraeli had still thought highly of him in 1860 but by
1870 had become sufficiently familiar with his ways to refer to him as
the *'ambiguous* minister of the British Crown'.[71] Disraeli and the
conservatives thought it unnecessary to call on Rome to intervene in
Ireland since both Rome and the catholic hierarchy in Ireland were
strongly opposed to secret societies such as the Fenians. Such was the
feeling of security at the time that during a debate on Ireland in the
house of commons on 30 April 1869 Lord Stanley declared that the
Irish catholic clergy were in no way entertaining revolutionary
opinions and were men of 'exemplary personal conduct'.[72] Cardinal
Cullen in particular was singled out for his irreproachable behaviour.
In 1883, against the background of the negotiations then in progress,
Propaganda Fide compiled a collection of pastorals condemning

Fenianism, with the following prelude:

> The ... extracts ... are published with a view to show the attitude
> adopted by the Holy See towards Fenianism and all illegal associa-
> tions hostile to the established authorities. They prove that for a
> period of thirty years the efforts of the Irish Catholic Bishops were
> constantly and urgently directed to suppress sedition and check all
> attempts at illegal agitation.[73]

Cullen's pastorals against secret societies in general and the Fenians in
particular were numerous. He had hardly assumed the primacy of
Ireland when, still in Rome, he warned the Irish against joining secret
societies; during the 1860s he intensified his efforts. In April 1861 he
called on the clergy of the Dublin archdiocese to warn the faithful
against secret societies. Pastorals condemning these societies were
issued on 23 April 1861, 27 November 1861 and in May 1862; and on
St Patrick's day 1864 he warned the faithful in another pastoral
against the Fenian periodical *The Irish People*.[74] On 10 October 1865
in a letter to his clergy he again warned them against the Fenians and
the Orange lodges of the protestants: he branded the Fenians as 'a
compound of folly and wickedness, wearing the mask of patriotism to
make dupes of the unwary'.[75] In an address to the Irish clergy on 25
January 1866 he pointed to the evil consequences of Fenianism which
gave 'a pretext to the Orange lodges'. On 5 February 1866 he again
preached against *The Irish People* in his lenten pastoral. He adopted a
similar vein in his pastorals of 5 December 1866, May 1867, his lenten
pastoral of 1867 and finally in a letter to the Irish clergy in April
1868.[76] Cullen was not, however, pro-British; Britain was for him
'this wicked empire'. In the tradition of O'Connell he favoured
fighting within the limits of the parliamentary system and was
opposed to revolution.[77] In his pastoral of October 1865 he had
beseeched the Irish: 'Whilst we are weak and poor, and unarmed ...
it is sheer madness to talk of revolutions, or to pretend to assail such a
power as England.'[78] In his private correspondence he pointed to the
bloody reprisals meted out in the Indian rising and in the negro rising
in Jamaica in 1865, and feared that the protestants of Northern
Ireland might be set on the catholics in the south.[79]

Cullen was not alone in fighting the Fenians, Archbishop Leahy of
Cashel was able to report to Propaganda on 10 August 1865:
'Episcopi Hibernici ... monuerunt adversus hanc societatem pericu-
losam et perniciosam.' ['The Irish bishops have warned against this
dangerous and evil society'.][80] Most extreme in his pronouncements
against Fenianism was Bishop Moriarty of Kerry: he declared that hell
was not hot enough and eternity not long enough to punish the
Fenians.[81] This constant castigation of the Fenians by the hierarchy
was not without effect on the clergy, as reflected in a *Guardian* report

119

on 28 February 1866: 'The Priests are denouncing Fenianism on every side and warning their flocks against it.'[82]

However, this support for the fight against the Fenians began to wane among the lower clergy because of the government's failure to remedy long-standing grievances. This rapidly growing Irish discontent manifested itself among the clergy in their support for the Fenian prisoners. Even in the heart of Cullen's own archdiocese Fenians could have their confessions heard by the Jesuits in Gardiner Street, where no political questions would be asked and absolution would not be withheld because of their allegiance to the Fenian oath. Episcopal condemnations of the Fenians were countered by anonymous letters in the papers signed by 'an Irish priest', 'a Tipperary priest' or 'a country priest'.[83] Many Fenians were in fact practising catholics, disenchanted with and alienated by the policies of successive whig governments; some even became priests or missionaries in later life.[84] The Irish nationalists among the clergy, particularly Archbishop MacHale of Tuam and Father Lavelle (vice-president of the St Patrick's Brotherhood) enjoyed an increased following. The latter had preached in the Dublin Rotunda in 1862 on 'the Catholic doctrine of the right of revolution'.[85]

Disraeli, who was not the enemy of Ireland he is generally regarded to be, realised that remedial measures had to be taken. He had planned to grant the catholic university in Dublin a charter as early as 1858/9 during the previous tory term of office but the premature downfall of this government prevented any action being taken.[86] Shortly before his return to power Disraeli commented to Pope Hennessey: 'Ireland requires to have her population restored and not diminished. Many things in Ireland need reconstruction — almost everything — except religious acerbity, which should be destroyed.' He saw the catholic church and her bishops as spearheading this reconstruction, since they were most familiar with the country,[87] and planned to appoint a catholic bishop to the privy council.[88]

As Disraeli was eager to assist the catholic Irish it is understandable that he did not want his plans hampered by a repetition of the anti-catholic outburst following the establishment of the English catholic hierarchy in 1850; this time he anticipated a similar possible outburst in response to the imminent establishment of a Scottish hierarchy. Disraeli commented on this in *Lothair:* when Mgr Berwick (i.e. Howard) leaves Cardinal Grandison (i.e. Manning) the latter comments: 'All that I can do is ... to get it postponed until I go to Rome, and even then I must not delay my visit ... to prevent incalculable mischief. The publication of the Scotch hierarchy at this moment will destroy the labours of years ... yet they will not see it! I cannot conceive who is urging them, for I am sure they must have some authority from home.'[89] At another stage in the novel Berwick (Howard) comments: 'This Scotch business plagues me. So far as

Scotland is concerned it is quite ripe; but the Cardinal counsels delay on account of this country, and he has such a consummate knowledge of England.'[90] It was indeed true that a plan existed to re-establish a catholic hierarchy for Scotland.

At the time there was a concomitant conflict within the catholic church in Scotland between the Irish and the Scottish parties. Native Scottish catholicism had been uprooted during the highland clearances following Culloden, but catholicism did survive on the islands of Barra, South Uist, Eigg and Canny, and near Lochaber and Loch Morar as well as some parts of the highlands, and from these communities came the Scottish catholic clergy who were educated mainly in the Scots colleges on the continent. As the living conditions for the catholic Irish were worse in Ireland than in Scotland, thousands emigrated from there, mainly to Glasgow. In the nineteenth century by far the greater proportion of catholics in Scotland were of Irish origin, and Scottish catholics were fearful of being overwhelmed by the Irish immigrants.[91] Scottish and Irish catholicism differed considerably: the Scots loved an austere liturgy, the Irish a more emotional ritual. Since 1800 the relationship between the Scottish vicars apostolic, who were responsible for administering the affairs of the catholic church in Scotland, and the British government had been cordial. The Scottish priests favoured peace with the British government, while the Irish were avowedly anti-British.[92] Two parties were formed among laity and clergy in Scotland, one Scottish and one Irish. In 1851 the Irish founded the *Free Press* in Glasgow as a nationalist Irish paper in Scotland.[93] The *Free Press* indulged in continuous polemics against the vicar apostolic of the western district, Dr John Murdoch (who was of highland origin), and this campaign undoubtedly contributed to his early death in December 1865. He was succeeded by his coadjutor, Dr John Gray (1817-72), another highlander.[94] To appease the Irish Rome suggested to Gray that an Irish coadjutor be appointed; the suggestion was flatly refused by Gray, who had the backing of the other vicars apostolic, all of them Scots. At Cardinal Cullen's instigation, however, Rome did appoint an Irish coadjutor for Gray in the person of James Lynch, rector of the Irish college in Paris: this institutionalised the split among Glasgow catholics as the Scots rallied around Gray and the Irish around Lynch.[95] The *Free Press* sympathised with the Fenian movement and in 1867 asked the pro-Fenian Fr Lavelle to Glasgow 'to conduct missions on behalf of the Irish cause'.[96] As the conflict between the Scots and Irish catholics reached its climax, the *Free Press* called for the re-establishment of a hierarchy for Scotland to put an end to what were in its opinion the arbitrary measures of the Scottish vicars apostolic. This was in 1864 when both Wiseman and Manning still favoured the project of the hierarchy.[97]

In September 1867 the English primate archbishop, Manning

(Grandison in *Lothair*), was named apostolic visitator of Scotland. As indicated in *Lothair,* Manning now favoured a postponment of the re-establishment of a Scottish hierarchy until peace and quiet had returned. To accomplish this he was in favour of transferring both Gray and Lynch, after which an archdiocese and six suffragan dioceses were to be established. Apart from this his sympathies lay with the Scots and he was responsible for having the *Free Press* suppressed.[98]

The reason given for the postponment in *Lothair* was not Manning's but Disraeli's. In January 1868 Disraeli instructed the English agent in Rome to advise Cardinal Antonelli against the re-establishment of the hierarchy at that particular moment: Russell told Antonelli that it

> could not fail to excite in Scotland, and among the English also, a bitter anti-Catholic feeling. The present ... was the worst possible time, to set about such a feeling, inasmuch as there was among all classes a sincere desire to conciliate the Catholic Irish, and the Fenian danger made everyone anxious to give the Irish clergy, who could do so much to encourage or repress it, fair play and whatever they could reasonably ask.[99]

Gray and Lynch both resigned in 1869; Gray became chaplain to Lord Bute (the title hero of *Lothair*) for a time, while Lynch became coadjutor and later bishop of Kildare and Leighlin.[100] Manning proposed to appoint Dr Errington as the primate archbishop of the new hierarchy in compensation to him for the loss of the Westminster archdiocese, but when Errington learned of the British government's intervention to postpone the re-establishment of the Scottish hierarchy he declined the offer.[101] In the autumn of 1868 the project was leaked to the press. On 9 December 1868 the *North British Daily Mail* opined that the hierarchy would probably be established before the next consistory.[102] When the whigs returned to power in December 1868 the foreign secretary, Clarendon, instructed Russell to warn Antonelli again not to establish a Scottish hierarchy.[103] Antonelli had no knowledge of the project[104] and Manning likewise disclaimed the *North British Daily Mail* report. Manning 'admitted that a Hierarchy for Scotland had been under discussion at the Propaganda, but on mature reflection had been given up for various reasons'.[105] Eyre, then vicar general of Hexham and Newcastle, now became Manning's preferred choice to occupy the new Scottish primacy[106] and in preparation for this he was elevated to titular bishop and vicar apostolic for the time being, as Manning informed Rusell.[107]

As Disraeli hinted in *Lothair* it was Cardinal Howard (Cardinal Berwick in *Lothair*) who laboured for the re-establishment of the Scottish hierarchy.[108] Howard had discussed the matter on numerous occasions with Pius IX. On the pope's death in 1878 the project had advanced to such a stage that his successor Leo XIII was able to complete the work already started and establish the Scottish hierarchy as the first act of his pontificate.[109]

That the Scottish hierarchy was postponed in 1868 was only a slight relief for Disraeli and his plans of Irish reforms. His reform bill of 1867 which extended the right of vote to that of a democratic level had tried the patience of the tories to the utmost; in the house of lords signs of discontent began to emerge. When Disraeli became prime minister in March 1868 he could not have entertained thoughts of introducing similarly far-reaching reforms for the time being without endangering his leadership of the conservatives.[110] Even within the cabinet his views on the solution to the Irish problem were only shared by the earl of Mayo.[111] As leader of the party representing landed interest and the established church Disraeli judiciously sought to avoid conflict with the rank and file of his party by opting, not for the land, nor for the church question as a means of resolving the Irish problem, but for the university question. For decades the Irish had been demanding their rights as regards university education and at the same time there was no state-recognised university education for catholics. The 'catholic university' founded in 1854 was a private institution whose degrees were not recognised by the state. Since May 1867 Disraeli had been negotiating with Cardinal Manning on a state charter for the catholic university in Dublin. Had he succeeded in his plans a new Irish élite might have emerged who were not hostile to Britain; however, the prospect of a distinctly catholic Irish intelligentsia pumped fear into the hearts of the inner circle of the British ruling class and their political representatives in the liberal party under Gladstone.[112] They were willing to hand over the property of the established church in Ireland (whose members were voting conservative anyway) to the Irish poor, but the latter should in their opinion remain uneducated or else absorb English attitudes and ways of thinking through the state universities.

Disraeli wrote *Lothair* to take literary revenge on Cardinal Manning for having jilted him and caused the downfall of his government. Time and again there have been attempts to foist the blame on to the Irish bishops for the failure of the negotiations to establish a catholic university: this view, however, rests solely on Manning's version of the story. He would have us believe that the bishops pushed him aside and took matters into their own hands.[113] Norman, who did not rely solely on Manning's notes but also on Roman and Irish archives, has recently discovered the true story.[114] While Manning was negotiating with Disraeli he at the same time maintained contact with Gladstone. Manning's intimate relationship with Gladstone was interrupted when the former became a catholic in 1851, but it was resumed again in 1861.[115] Cardinal Cullen realised that as regards a catholic university nothing would be gained from Gladstone and the liberals,[116] so he was anxious for the negotiations with the Disraeli administration to succeed: an agreement seemed possible and near.[117] Having discussed the matter on 20 November 1867 the cabinet unanimously agreed to Mayo's plan for the catholic university on 2 March 1868.[118] On 10 March the Irish secretary, Mayo, presented his plan to the house of commons with a vague announcement that the government favoured 'concurrent endowment' for all three denominations in Ireland.[119] In Rome Pius IX 'said with great warmth that he hoped Mr Disraeli would employ the genius God had given him and the power the Queen had invested him with to improve the condition of Ireland'.[120] Yet when Mayo made his announcement there were already signs of resistance in the tory camp, even within the cabinet.[121] Gladstone seized the opportunity and on 16 March 1868 announced in the house of commons that he was in favour of disestablishing the church of Ireland.[122] Cullen was in favour of this but 'made no public declaration at this time'[123] as he was anxious to reach agreement with Disraeli on the university charter before Disraeli's possible downfall. Manning, however, ceased contact with Disraeli on the same day that Gladstone had made his announcement: he had deserted Disraeli for Gladstone.[124]

In *Lothair* Disraeli hints at his intended solution of the church question had he remained in power long enough. In the novel Berwick makes the following comment on Churchill (i.e. Cullen): 'In his eagerness he cannot see that the Anglicans have only a lease of our property, a lease which is rapidly expiring.'[125] Disraeli wanted to distribute the property evenly among the denominations, giving the catholic church the same status as its anglican counterpart. In contemporary debate this form of granting equality by elevating the status of the catholic church to that of the established church was referred to as 'concurrent endowment' or 'levelling up' as opposed to Gladstone's 'levelling down', i.e. lowering the status of the anglican church to that of the catholic church. This matter of 'concurrent endowment' had also entered into the negotiations between Manning and Disraeli;[126] both Disraeli and Mayo had expressed their general approval of the scheme in the house of commons. However, Disraeli was unwilling to reduce priests to being paid servants of the state; he preferred the idea of a lump sum being paid to the catholic church in Ireland as a whole.[127] In a memorandum to the queen Gladstone spoke deprecatingly of this proposal as 'endowment of the Roman Church but waiving all control over it by the state'.[128]

The general elections of 1868 were won by Gladstone on the Irish church issue. Disraeli resigned and Gladstone became prime minister. On 1 March 1869 he introduced his bill disestablishing and disendowing the Irish church; on 31 May 1869 it passed the house of commons, on 18 June the house of lords, and on 26 July it was signed by Queen Victoria and on 1 January 1871 it became law. 'In some respects it is not unfair to regard the Irish Church Act as a rescue operation on their behalf.'[129] When introducing the bill in parliament Gladstone had promised that of the property of the established church in Ireland, which was valued at sixteen million pounds, seven million would be given to the Irish poor. In actual fact only three million pounds were eventually given. This must be attributed to the 'negligence' of the commission set up by the Gladstone government to assess the claims of the anglican clergy; numerous double compensations and compensations to vicars ordained *en masse* while the bill was still being debated were paid out. This meant extra compensation of around £747,000.[130]

It can be argued that the difference between Disraeli's intended chartered catholic university and Gladstone's disestablishment and 'disendowment' was that the former would have cost the English taxpayer money while the latter did not. Cardinal Cullen wrote to Gladstone that the disendowment law as was *de facto* put into practice would only please the Fenians: 'It will give them an opportunity of proclaiming that Ireland can expect nothing good from British legislation.'[131] The fact that the same liberals who had opposed disestablishment of the Irish church in 1865 and 1866 had now reversed their decisions, particularly after the Fenian bombings of 1867 in Manchester and London, would lead the impartial observer to infer that the whigs would only redress grievances in response to violence.[132]

Fenian activities must be seen as playing a prominent role in the politics of the English government at the time. There were Fenians as far afield as Rome, where some of them attempted to enlist in the papal army but were refused because of unruly behaviour. Odo Russell was instructed to find out their names, along with particulars as to further destinations, and to contact two informers.[133]

CHAPTER VIII

Britain and Papal Infallibility prior to Vatican I

THE SINGLE most important event for this period concerning anglo-papal relations is the first Vatican council. In convening this council Pius IX sought to put an end to contemporary trends and errors which had begun to undermine the foundation of the catholic faith.[1] Other reasons for convening the council have been advanced: Norbert Miko postulated that Pius IX had doubted the continued survival of the church states ever since his days as bishop of Imola. By the convention concluded between France and Italy on 15 September 1864, French troops were to evacuate the church states within two years; and on 6 December that same year it was announced to the cardinals that a general council was being called. The pope had reason to fear that after the annexation of Rome to the new kingdom of Italy his status would be reduced to that of an Italian bishop, unless his position as pope was stressed free from all doubt by an ecumenical council.[2] This was achieved by the mere fact that a council had been called, as Disraeli pointed out in *Lothair*:

> The very assembly of the Fathers of the Church will astound the Freemasons, and the Secret Societies, and the Atheists. That alone will be a demonstration of power on the part of the Holy Father.
> ... It was only the bishops of Europe that assembled at Trent. ...
> But now the bishops of the whole world will assemble round the chair of St Peter, and prove by their presence the catholic character of the Church.[3]

A new situation now prevailed in the catholic church: the catholic states in the course of the nineteenth century had discarded their Christian foundations, while their princes and governments had become a burden for the catholic church. The states had rid themselves of their bondage to the church yet were still anxious to maintain control over her. In this situation the papacy became increasingly aware of its position as the central power of the church.[4] This fresh alignment became apparent when the governments of the catholic states were not invited to attend the council. Disraeli comments on this in *Lothair*:

126

It [the council] will exhibit to the Christian powers the inevitable future they are now preparing for themselves. ... At the Council of Trent the Christian powers were represented, and properly so. Their seats will be empty at the Council of the Vatican. What does that mean? The separation between Church and State. ... Society is no longer consecrated. The civil governments of the world no longer profess to be Catholic ... the civil powers have separated themselves from the Church either by royal edict, or legislative enactment, or revolutionary changes, they have abolished the legal status of the Catholic Church within their territory. ... The coming anarchy is called progress, because it advances along the line of departure from the old Christian order of the world. Christendom was the offspring of the Christian family, and the foundation of the Christian family is the sacrament of matrimony, the spring of all domestic and public morals. ... When they have destroyed the hearth, the morality of society will perish. A settlement in the foundation may be slow in sinking, but it brings all down at last. The next step in de-Christianising the political life of nations is to establish national education without Christianity. ... Some think this bodes ill for the Church; no, it is the state that will suffer ... monarchies and law and civil order will ultimately fall and perish together.[5]

Throughout his life Disraeli defended the union of church and state.[6] He regarded the church as the only bulwark against moral anarchy, the only secure foundation on which the state could rest. He wrote in *Lothair:* 'Atheism may be consistent with fine taste, and fine taste under certain conditions may for a time regulate a polished society; but ethics and atheism are impossible; and without ethics no human order can be strong or permanent.'[7] While Disraeli regretted the movement towards separation of church and state and, had he stayed in power, would have sought the co-operation of an invigorated papacy, the actual developments were quite different.

1. MANNING AND HIS FRIENDS

Any reader of *Lothair* will observe the great influence Cardinal Grandison seems to have exerted on the affairs of the catholic church. When someone asks as to the whereabouts of Mgr Catesby in *Lothair* the following answer is given: 'He is in Ireland, arranging about the Oecumenical Council ... his Holiness, by the Cardinal's advice, has sent the Monsignore to put things right.'[8]

Disraeli modelled the character of Grandison on the English primate, Cardinal Manning, who did in reality possess this influence in the Vatican. While Cardinal Lambruschini had first suggested to

Pius IX in 1849 that a council be convened,[9] it was Manning who urged the pope to act on the proposal.[10] Manning travelled to Rome regularly and as early as 1863 had acquired a degree of influence with the pope and some of the cardinals.[11] As mentioned earlier he at first exerted his influence directly through Mgr Talbot; after the latter's breakdown[12] Manning occupied his position to a certain extent, assuming with it much of the influence and manipulative authority previously enjoyed by Talbot.[13]

On the eve of the first Vatican council a controversy arose in the church over papal infallibility. As Brandmüller has recently proven, the majority of ultramontane theologians were moderates,[14] yet the extremists on both sides continually strove to outbid each other. In England the controversy over papal infallibility had begun in 1863, before the matter had come into the centre of debate in other countries.[15] Manning was the chief polemicist on the side of the ultras, usually referred to as 'neo-ultramontane'.

W.G. Ward (1812-82) in the *Dublin Review* spearheaded the crusade of neo-ultramontanism in England on behalf of Manning. Ward's father was for many years M.P. for the city of London and governor of the bank of England. Ward was married and had become a catholic in September 1845. He had inherited a huge fortune from an uncle. In 1853 he became professor of dogmatics at Old Hall College.[16] Manning had taken over the *Dublin Review* in 1862 and appointed Ward as its editor. The review was subject to a threefold censorship: theologically, philosophically and for ecclesiastical opportunism; in all respects Manning exercised complete control. Ward became Manning's willing instrument and obedient servant in every respect. Ward's fiery temperament and narrow-mindedness led inevitably to his espousal of extreme opinions on the question of papal infallibility, and for those catholics who thought differently he had only personal attacks and polemics. Newman wrote of Ward: 'controversy is his meat and drink'.[17] Brandmüller has come to the conclusion that Ward's concept of papal infallibility was so inclusive that he regarded practically every papal statement as an infallible *ex cathedra* pronouncement.[18] A number of Ward's articles in the *Dublin Review* on the subject of papal infallibility were published in 1866 as a book: *The authority of doctrinal decisions which are not definitions of faith considered in a short series of essays reprinted from the Dublin Review*. This book was reviewed in Germany by Döllinger[19] in the *Theologisches Literaturblatt* under the title 'Theologische Extravaganzen' (theological extravagances) in which a German summary of the most important passage in the book was provided; Ward especially stressed the infallibility of the encyclical *Quanta cura* and the *Syllabus* and even went further than this in his assertion that all doctrinal teaching of papal allocations, encyclicals and even letters to individual pastors from which they were collected

1.
Benedict XIV
(1675-1758)

2.
Clement XIV
(1705-1774)

3.
Pius VII
(1740-1823)

4.
Cardinal Consalvi
(1757-1824)

5.
Leo XII
(1760-1829)

6.
Pius IX
(1792-1878)

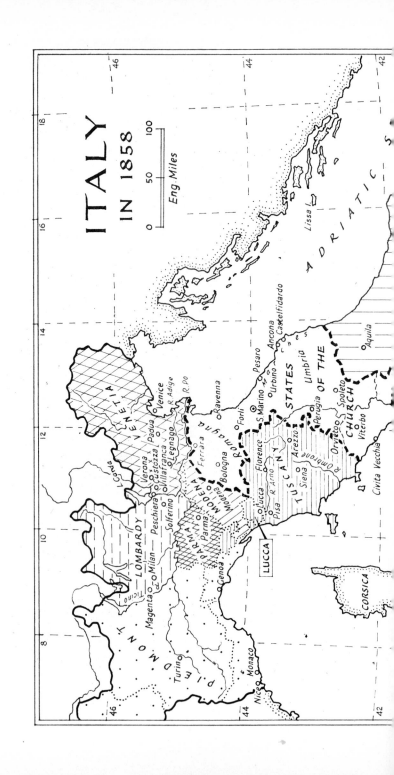

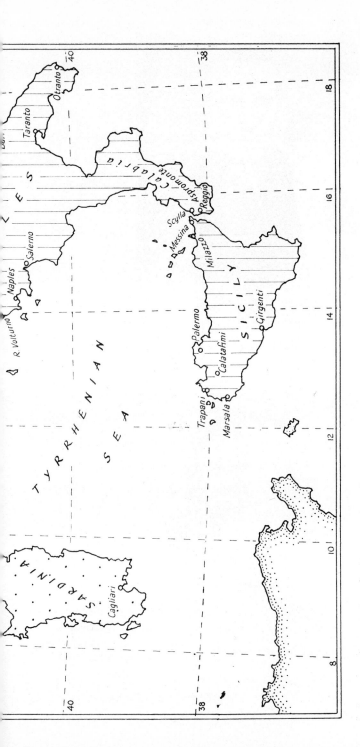

7.

**Map of Italy, reproduced with permission, from *The Roman Question*
(ed. Noel Blakiston), Chapman & Hall, London 1962.**

8.
Cardinal Antonelli
(1806-1876)

9.
Cardinal Wiseman,
Archbishop of
Westminster
(1802-1865)

10.
Cardinal Manning,
Archbishop of
Westminster
(1808-1892)

11.
Odo Russell, first Baron Ampthill (1829-1881)

12.
Lord Acton (1834-1902)

13.
Ignaz von Dollinger (1799-1890)

were infallible.[20] To do justice to Ward it should be pointed out that the German Summary presented his opinion of infallibility as being more unconditional than it actually was. In 1867 a controversy arose between Ward and H.J.D Ryder (1837-1907), who rejected Ward's assertions in a pamphlet entitled *Idealism in Theology*.[21] The most salient feature of Ward's writing was that he assigned infallibility not only to theological but also to political pronouncements by the pope.[22] In Germany only Scheeben supported Ward, in the periodical *Der Katholik*.[23] The *Tablet*, having previously supported Disraeli in the political arena and maintained a middle-of-the-road stance in theological matters, was now acquired by Herbert Vaughan (1832-1903), then under Manning's influence (later he became Manning's successor as archbishop of Westminster).

Manning gradually acquired influence over the Jesuits in Rome, who were responsible for editing the *Civiltà cattolica,* despite his hostility towards the English Jesuits because of their independence from his control.[24] Bishop Ullathorne of Birmingham reported to Newman in March 1867 that, according to Neve, the rector of the English college in Rome, the Roman Jesuits were hostile to Newman's project to erect a catholic college in Oxford;[25] in other words they were taking Manning's side in matters of solely English interest which were of little concern to them. In 1867 Manning received the support of one of these Roman Jesuits, Fr Liberatore, (1810-92), in his fight for the dogmatisation of papal infallibility.

Liberatore contributed to the publication of *Civiltà cattolica* and was later engaged by Manning as his theological adviser at the Vatican council; from June 1867 onwards in a series of articles in *Civiltà cattolica* he propounded the same ideas as Manning had been propagating in the *Dublin Review* since 1863.[26] Odo Russell immediately reported this to London,[27] indicating the negative reaction of the native and positive reaction of the foreign clergy.[28] Manning profited from the accession in 1868 of Fr Valerian Cardella, SJ (1820-91) to the post of rector of the Jesuits' house in Rome which was responsible for *Civiltà cattolica*. Cardella had been professor at St Benno's college in North Wales from 1848-52. In 1852 he became professor at the Collegio Romano 'but kept up his English connections':[29] he occupied this post until 1876 when he became provincial of the Roman province of the Jesuit order, a post he held until 1879. After this he became professor for canon law in Woodstock in the U.S., where he was to play an important role at the third plenary council of Baltimore in 1884.[30]

Manning believed it was his mission to pursue the dogmatisation of papal infallibility. In 1867 the bishops assembled in Rome for the 1800th anniversary of the martyrdom of Saints Peter and Paul in Rome. On 28 June that year Manning and the bishop of Regensburg, Ignatius von Senestréy (1818-1906), swore an oath at the grave of St

Peter, with words composed by Fr Liberatore, to do all in their power to have the doctrine of papal infallibility defined.[31] By so doing Manning had established a connection with the bishop of Regensburg who was later to become his closest ally at the Vatican council.

At this assembly of the bishops a controversy arose over the final address: Manning wanted it to take the form of a declaration in favour of papal infallibility, as he had told Odo Russell.[32] Bishop Dupanloup of Orleans, however, was against the word 'infallible' being used in this address; Manning resisted and saw to it that the passage promulgated by the Council of Florence which stressed the divine teaching office of the pope would at least be inserted.[33] On the same occasion Manning issued a pastoral to his clergy (8 September 1867), which was subsequently published as a pamphlet in English, Italian and German,[34] in which he elaborated on the evils of Gallicanism and proposed the dogmatisation of papal infallibility as a possible cure.

To prepare for the council, five commissions were formed in 1867 for dogma, discipline, orders, eastern churches and questions of ecclesiastical policy. Priests were called to Rome as consultors to enlighten the curia on the position and needs of the church in their own countries.[35] Manning used the occasion to press for the dogmatisation of infallibility — hitherto it had not featured prominently in discussions. Some light is thrown on this matter by the letters of one consultor, Moufang. He was a member of the commission on matters of church policy which was headed by Cardinal Reisach. Moufang was regent of the seminary of priests at Mainz and a confidant of Bishop Ketteler of Mainz. On 6 January 1869 he wrote to Ketteler that Manning was exerting his influence in Rome.[36] From his diary it would appear that Moufang had ten different meetings with Manning: on 27 December 1868, on 2 January 1869, on 15, 20, 25 and 29 January, on 9, 17, 21 February and on 1 March 1869.[37] Manning, who became acquainted with Moufang in London in 1862,[38] approached him in Rome to propose the formation of a philosophic-theological alliance.[39] Shortly afterwards Cardinal Reisach relayed to Moufang a message that Manning wanted to see him again. In the course of their subsequent meeting Manning was more precise and outlined his plan to form a 'corpe des Zuaves' (papal army) of twelve theologians from France, Italy, Germany and England, and referred Moufang to the passage in his pastoral of 1867 relating to papal infallibility.[40] He also gave Moufang some literature advocating the dogmatisation of infallibility,[41] as well as Ward's recently published *De infallibilitatis extensione*.[42] Moufang, however, regarded the dogmatisation as inopportune and presented Manning with a written statement of twelve points as to why he thought so.[43] These points were to form the basis of the arguments of the 'inopportunists' during the council. Manning replied with fifteen *rationes* which were promptly confuted by fifteen *responsiones* from Moufang.[44] Moufang reported to Ketteler on 29 January 1869 that Manning was labouring to promote the dogmatisation of infallibility when, as he had heard, not even the opinion of Roman theologians was settled on the matter.[45]

Before Manning's return to England on 1 March 1869,[46] the *Civiltà cattolica* on 6 February 1869 published a 'French correspondence' which purported to reflect the wishes of 'catholics *in the real sense'* (as opposed to catholics differing from the Civiltà who were stigmatised as no true catholics) that the council should promulgate the teachings of the *Syllabus* and that it would be especially pleasing to catholics if the council dogmatised papal infallibility.[47] The 'correspondence' which originated from the editor-in-chief of *Civiltà cattolica,* Fr Piccirillo, SJ struck with devastating effect. Piccirillo wanted to report on the attitudes of people in the different countries on the eve of the council and asked Antonelli to contribute some material: Antonelli obliged him with some reports from France; among them was the one published.[48] The nuncio in Paris, Flavio Chigi,[49] later one of Leo XIII's opponents in the conclave of 1878, had been responsible for sending the 'correspondence' to Rome. He was in contact with Veuillot and was well acquainted with Odo Russell.[50] The 'correspondence' had been written by two priest friends of Louis Veuillot (1813-83).[51] The *Civiltà cattolica* printed the article without comment. Now that the horse had bolted people were anxious to shut the stable doors: the general of the Jesuits expressed his strong disapproval of the 'correspondence'.[52] The pope, who was friendly with Piccirillo and saw him every week, asked him if he really believed that he was doing the church a service by such actions.[53] Cardinal Sacconi, a leading opponent of Antonelli,[54] went as far as to say that the ink must have gone to Piccirillo's head while Antonelli himself and his supporter Berardi[55], another curial cardinal, were also unhappy at the way the article had been published unaltered.[56] Piccirillo defended himself in a private letter by stating that Cardinal Caterini (1795-1881)[57] had seen and approved the 'correspondence' before it went to press.[58] The wave of indignation triggered by the article rose to such a level that Pius IX felt it necessary publicly to present the periodical with some gifts to show, as Piccirillo said, that he bore no grudge against the fathers editing the *Civiltà cattolica.* However, to bear no grudge against someone is not the same as approving of their conduct. When Pius IX discussed the 'correspondence' issue with Piccirillo a year later, he said that they had been thoughtless in their advocacy of papal infallibility.[59] The tendentious presentation of the story by the *Civiltà* editors of 1870 (i.e. a year after the event), which has been used time and again in an attempt to foist the blame for the 'correspondence' on Pius IX himself, has little bearing on our discussion. The decree of the second plenary council of Baltimore (cited by Giacomo Martina, SJ attempting to represent Pius IX as a protagonist in the campaign for papal infallibility being defined as a dogma) — to quote Cardinal Cullen — 'admits infallibility but does not define it'.[60] The fact that the discussion on papal infallibility started before the publication of the 'correspondence' and that in the autumn of 1868 the pope perhaps approved of or even instigated the *Civiltà's* defence, against French accusations, of the view on infallibility of St Antoninus of Florence has no importance when judging the 'correspondence'. It was not the decrees of provincial synods or the *Civiltà* defending the opinions of St Antoninus of Florence, but the 'correspondence' itself that created the storm between the two camps supporting and opposing the dogmatisation of infallibility. Indeed, if the pope himself had thoroughly read and approved of the 'correspondence' Piccirillo would surely have mentioned this rather than Cardinal Caterini's approval of the article in his letter to Le Grelle of 4 May 1869.[61] The fact is that the Jesuits editing the *Civiltà* were more intransigent than the pope himself as regards infallibility. Pius IX was moved to restrain the passionate *Civiltà* on numerous occasions. It seems that in fact Piccirillo, who was the pope's confessor, brought his influence to bear on the pope rather than the other way round.[62]

In France agitation on behalf of the neo-ultramontanes was conducted by Louis Veuillot in his review *Univers*. From 1860-7 Veuillot's *Univers* was banned by Napoleon III. Veuillot was a convert who in 1838 reverted from agnosticism to catholicism; he was an intractable who hated all compromise, and after 1850 this was to earn him the enmity of all liberal catholics among whom were counted most of the French bishops. By attacking these bishops he won the support of the rural clergy, who felt they were being governed autocratically. Veuillot's pen, full of venom and zest, set about destroying his enemies with all the biting sarcasm of his Gallic wit, and this deepened the rift between catholics in France. His opponents, the liberal catholics, accepted the challenge and leaped into the fray: the fight was conducted by both sides with the aim of proving that the others were traitors of the church.[63] Veuillot became so excessive in his vituperation that in 1872 Pius IX sent him a personal brief admonishing him for making such bitter judgments on his enemies in a style that was uncharacteristic of the charity of a true catholic.[64]

Manning maintained contact with Veuillot who printed his writings in the *Univers;* Manning's sermon delivered in Sant' Andrea della Valle in Rome in January 1853 was also printed in *Univers*.[65] The English convert, Frederick William Faber (1814-63), who came from a calvinist family and whose uncle George Stanley Faber (1773-1854) had in 1851 published an anti-catholic pamphlet entitled *Papal Infallibility,* wrote a book with the title *Devotion to the Pope* which adopted such an extreme standpoint that it bordered on blasphemy. The book was immediately translated into French.[66] Not only did

Veuillot, like Ward, extend the normal interpretation of infallibility to include practically all papal pronouncements, but he went to the extreme of blasphemy in *Univers* of having hymns which were dedicated to the Holy Spirit re-dedicated to the pope.

The power of the pope in the catholic church is often over estimated by non-catholics.[67] As it has become clear by now the agitation of the ultras on the issue of papal infallibility had not been instigated by the pope and this is supported by a remark made by the pope to Piccirillo in 1870. At the end of the centenary celebrations of St Peter in 1867 Pius IX declared to Piccirillo that he had anticipated dissension over the question of infallibility in view of the conflict over the form of the final address, but not that there would be fierce fighting: had he known this he would not have called a council. This would seem to prove the assertion that a council would not have been called given a climate of fierce conflict and enmity.[68] There is no evidence to prove Hasler's accusation that Pius IX was insincere when he said to the Belgian minister in Rome in June 1869: 'They want to bestow infallibility on me. I do not need it',[69] and when he said to the Austrian ambassador in November 1869: 'They are talking of papal infallibility. I believe in it, but in my proposals there is no word of it. I do not know what the outcome is likely to be.'[70] In actual fact, the pope was exercising the infallible teaching office of the church — as in 1854 when he promulgated the dogma of our Lady being conceived without original sin. This time the bishops were consulted beforehand; the pope himself saw no need to *dogmatise* papal infallibility. He was quite happy to maintain the *status quo* until provoked by the opponents of infallibility.

2. DÖLLINGER AND ACTON

The excesses of the neo-ultramontanes contributed to a swelling in the ranks of their opponents, the liberal catholics; both sides went to such extremes that the unity of the church seemed in danger.[71] The leader of the liberal catholics was Professor Döllinger (1799-1890), of Munich, who had been ordained priest in 1822 and had started his career as an ultramontane. Brandmüller has recently published a critical evaluation of Döllinger which contrasts with the Döllinger apologetics of recent decades. With regard to Döllinger's conduct he came across some paradoxical problems.[72] Here the English influence on Döllinger offers an explanation; only Christoph Weber has mentioned this influence in passing when dealing with Döllinger's book *Kirche und Kirchen. Papsttum und Krichenstaat. Historisch-politische Betrachtungen.*[73] (Church and Churches. Papacy and Church State. Historico-political observations.) Very early in his career Döllinger became acquainted with some English catholics. In

1836 he stayed in England for six weeks and was invited to several aristocratic country houses. Oxford made a lasting impression on him. From now on Döllinger's foreign sympathies lay with the English and he was therefore, for example, opposed to O'Connell's repeal movement.[74]

Since 1845 he had been in contact with Gladstone. Gladstone wrote to his wife on 30 September 1845 of his first meeting with Döllinger: 'He surprises me by the extent of his information and the way in which he knows the details of what takes place in England.'[75] This lifelong interest in England was not limited to religious questions but included politics too: Döllinger commented in a letter to Acton in January 1868 that he feared the Fenian problem might entangle England in a war with the United States.[76] He was kept up to date on matters of English interest through his confidant, Acton, and through the *Allgemeine Zeitung,* which provided detailed reports on England. These reports were particularly comprehensive when Manning was the subject: it even gave details of his travel arrangements to and from Rome, the nature of his mission there and on 24 September 1869, for example, it printed a translation of a letter from Pius IX to Manning which had originally appeared in *The Times.*

On the occasion of their very first meeting Döllinger and Gladstone became engaged in a lively conversation that lasted till the early hours of the morning; a lifelong friendship was struck that day, concurrent with the incipient transformation of Döllinger from being an ultramontane to being an enemy of the papacy. In the letter cited above of 30 September 1845 Gladstone wrote: 'He seemed to me one of the most liberal and catholic in mind of all the persons of his communion I have known.'[77] On 2 October he added:

> What I like perhaps most, or what crowns other causes of liking towards him, is that he ... seems to take hearty interest in the progress of religion in the Church of England ... and to have a mind to appreciate good wherever he can find it. ... He is a great admirer of England and English character, and he does not at all slur over the mischief with which religion has to content in Germany. Lastly, I may be wrong, but I am persuaded he in his mind abhors a great deal that is too frequently taught in the Church of Rome.[78]

Gladstone also discussed the eucharist with Döllinger, especially the question of the real presence of Christ.[79] He further noted: 'He had read my article on Ward, and said certainly Ward could not complain of it. He had read Manning on the Unity of the Church.'[80] Döllinger wrote an article in 1844 approving of Manning's writings (Manning was still an anglican) while at the same time criticising the anglo-catholics, a view that would seem to indicate his pro-anglican leanings.[81] This shows that Döllinger had read Ward's writings shortly after the latter became a catholic and Manning's before Manning had left the church of England. In 1847 Manning visited Döllinger on his way to Rome.[82]

Döllinger's friend and pupil, John Acton (1834-1902), had even closer connections with the whig government than Döllinger himself had. Acton's father had died young: his mother was a daughter of the duke von Dalberg; her second marriage was to Earl Granville, who became colonial secretary in Gladstone's government in 1868. Since visiting Rome together in 1866, Gladstone and Acton became good friends.[83] Much of the excessive criticism of Gertrude Himmelfarb's book on Acton[84] — E.D. Watt accused her of 'intemperate prose'[85] — originated from the fact that she draws a more realistic picture of the otherwise glorified Acton, who has even been described as 'Freedom's Advocate'.[86] Himmelfarb took Acton's assessment of the American civil war as her starting-point and presented him as what he really was — a period whig. Acton had told Döllinger in February 1861 that events in America had produced a very welcome impairment of the democratic element in Germany[87] and in June 1862 he declared that he was convinced of the justice of the confederates' cause.[88] Himmelfarb pointed to Acton's review of Samuel Sugenheim's *Geschichte der Aufhebung der Leibeigenschaft und Hörigkeit in Europa* (History of the abolition of serfdom in Europe),[89] in which Acton wrote in 1863: 'Just as a Christian subject is often called upon to obey an arbitrary monarch, so the slave must obey his master, for both are part of the "divine economy"'.[90] In the same year Acton wrote in a review of E.H. Hudson's *Second War of Independence:* 'Indeed in some stages of history, slavery was not only permissible, it was prescribed as a necessary experience in discipline and probation, always provided, however, that the society administering the discipline was Christian.'[91] In judging Acton's essay 'Political Causes of the American Revolution'[92] Himmelfarb wrote: 'It betrays an occasional hint of sophistry suggesting a lack of feeling for the moral problems that agitated the abolitionists.'[93] In his essay Acton had written of the abolitionists: 'Their democratic system poisons everything it touches.'[94] On the question of slavery he wrote: 'If the Americans were to admit the Indians, the Chinese, the Negroes, to the rights to which they are justly jealous of admitting European emigrants, the country would be thrown into disorder, and if not, would be degraded to the level of the barbarous races.'[95]

Acton displayed an equally callous indifference to the plight of the Irish. In 1858 an Irish Archdeacon Fitzgerald (Rathkeale) proposed to an assembly of catholic clergy and laity in Paris that pressure be brought to bear on the British government with the help of Napoleon III to put an end to the cruel and barbarous treatment of Irish tenants by their landlords, who had pulled down 400,000 cottages occupied by the poor and expelled them from their homes. In reply to an attack on his proposal by Count Montalembert, Fitzgerald very aptly replied: 'I was born under a free constitution, free at least for the high classes.' This remark led Acton, 'Freedom's Advocate', to write to Döllinger from Castle Aldenham that Fitzgerald had defended despotism against Montalembert.[96] The fact is that Fitzgerald's remark was uncomfortably true. Lord Acton's concept of freedom was not drawn from that natural law around which the American declaration of independence and bill of rights were shaped.

While Acton and Döllinger glorified the unwritten constitution of England, southern German liberals of the 'Vormärz' (i.e. the period before 1848) saw it quite differently.[97] In the first edition of the *Staatslexikon* of 1841, which was the all-important encyclopaedia of 'Vormärz' liberalism, W.H. Murhard contrasted the North American constitution with that of the English. The following is an English translation:

> In England one often hears the opinion that the English nation is the freest in the world. In actual fact the citizens of the United States can boast of more freedom than the English. For, in England the principle of individual freedom is limited by the double aristocracy of the noble and the rich, who hold the greatest part of the people — the farm labourers and the industrial workers — in a state of unfreedom and the great mass of the population screwed down to dependency and subjection, while all wealth of land and capital is in the hands of a minority. English freedom, especially political freedom, is merely for the aristocracy and the rich — the landowners and the capitalists — and the upper middle class. According to the terms which have developed in America of true freedom the English cannot truly claim to be really free.[98]

Carl von Rotteck, editor of the *Staatslexikon* and one of the leading figures of pre-1848 German liberalism, preferred the American way of life. The house of commons, in his opinion, did not represent the people: the bulk of wealth and property was concentrated in the hands of two million people in contrast to the seven million agricultural and industrial workers who possessed virtually nothing.[99] These comments made in 1841, of which Döllinger and Acton could quite possibly have been aware, were to a large extent still justifiable in the 1860s. In *Lothair* Princess Borghese ('Tivoli' in the novel) says this of England: 'In your constitution, if the father sits in the upper chamber, the son sits in the lower house.'[100] In actual fact there were 165 sons or near relatives of peers in 1865 sitting in the house of commons; in 1880 the number was still 155.[101]

In 1860 Döllinger in the first edition of *Christentum und Kirche in der Zeit der Grundlegung* (Christianity and the Church at the time of foundation) devoted paragraphs 54 to 58 (pp. 30-2) to the precedency of St Peter. Here he presented the office of St Peter in clear and unequivocal terms with an explicit discourse on apostolic succession. In 1868, in the second edition of the book, he changed all this: he gave the other apostles equal status and merely implied the succession of the popes. As regards the papacy Döllinger's tendency was towards the episcopalian system of the anglicans. From having been a governing head Peter becomes a mere 'good shepherd': the pope is even reminded not to act as a hired man. Furthermore in 1860 Döllinger still presents the church as being made up of living human beings with Peter and his successors as actual governors. In 1868 however he writes of preservation — his image of the church has become static.[101a]

Between 1860 and 1868 Döllinger reached a crisis point which brought to the surface all those tendencies observed and remarked upon by Gladstone. In 1863 Döllinger wrote of Pope Honorius (who was condemned by a council, a condemnation which Döllinger was later to exploit to the fullest): 'And yet it is certain that he was not heretical in the real sense'.[102] Theology which did not coincide with Döllinger's own ideas was no longer worthy of his attention; by 1862 he had only a haughty scorn for the Roman theology of Mainz,[103] and this became even more evident after his speech to the congress of theologians in Munich, 1863.[104] The historian Janssen tried to divert Döllinger's pugnacious spirit to a more deserving cause, i.e. to attack the national liberal Berlin historians.[105] Those tendencies in Döllinger detected by Gladstone began to assert themselves ever more vigorously as the contempt with which he was met in Rome grew correspondingly stronger. His visit to Rome in 1857 must have been a traumatic experience for him.[106] His only defence against this hostile reception was to think maliciously of those who held him in contempt, and this attitude let him to absorb only negative impulses. Through his favourite pupil and confidant, Acton, he learned of the notions of the Manning circle and of their influence in Rome; Acton informed Döllinger on every detail of Manning's policy with the *Dublin Review*.[107] Citing Newman, Acton wrote of the 'dull tyranny of Manning and Ward'.[108] Furthermore, Henry Nutcombe Oxenham (1829-88)[109] stayed with Döllinger in Munich in 1863-4; in 1863 the controversy on infallibilty had started in England and before Oxenham's arrival Acton informed Döllinger that his guest would keep him informed of the situation there.[110] Having studied at Harrow and Balliol, Oxenham became an anglican minister in 1854 and in 1857 converted to catholicism. In the *Rambler,* with which Acton was connected, he had attacked seminary education; Ward denounced his attitude and Wiseman consequently refused to ordain him.[111] Thus Oxenham felt a bitter personal enmity towards Ward.

In a non-extant letter Döllinger commented to Acton in mid-February on a recently published book by Ward, as is indicated from Acton's reply.[112] The only book Ward had published at this time was

The Relation of intellectual power to Man's true perfection;[113] in a subsequent edition a revealing sub-title was added: *On the dangers to be apprehended from intellect when not spiritually regulated and controlled.* It is also important to note that in his fight against anything which did not strictly conform to the Roman line, Ward attacked Döllinger as well, criticising the first edition of his *Christentum und Kirche* in the *Dublin Review* and condemning his speech to the Munich congress in 1863.[114]

Döllinger read the *Chronicle,* to which Acton contributed articles in 1866-7, and on occasion *The Times, Daily News* and the *Pall Mall Gazette.*[115] Furthermore Döllinger was friendly with the anglican bishop Forbes (1817-75) of Brechin and Dundee, who was a friend of Gladstone's and who later established contacts with the 'Old Catholics'.[116] In May 1863 Forbes visited Döllinger in Munich. When on his return Forbes delivered a copy of Döllinger's *Papstfabeln* to Acton, the latter commented that it could be inferred from the preface that Döllinger was going to write a complete history of the papacy; he suggested that anything which was not a strictly dogmatic controversy could thus be dealt with in the book, i.e. infallibility etc.[117] This would seem to indicate that as early as 1863 he was already preoccupied with the question of infallibility, long before it became the cause of such controversy in Germany, while in England the discussion was well under way.

Döllinger also got to know of Manning's *Essays on Religion and Literature* of 1867, and an essay entitled 'On Church and State' by Manning's protégé and future biographer, Purcell, in which he asserts that the right to depose kings belonged to papal sovereignty: Josiah Strong would later make much capital out of this in his campaign against the catholic church in the U.S., as we have seen. Regarding Manning's pastoral, *The centenary of St Peter and the general council,* of 1867 Döllinger was visited in the summer of 1868 by the auxiliary bishop in Paris, Maret, who was also dean of the theological faculty at the Sorbonne and one of the leading opponents of infallibility in France, and advised that he regarded Manning as their most dangerous opponent.[118]

Döllinger believed that the distorted image of infallibility presented by neo-ultramontane propaganda *was* infallibility. He thus wrote to Acton on 1 October 1868 that the council was, according to all indications, squaring up for a fight between Ormuzd on the one hand and Ahriman on the other, with Ahriman and his forces of evil better armed and prepared and *viribus unitis.* From the United Kingdom he expected Manning and Cullen 'and their band of kindred or character-less and fearful spirits' to fight under Ahriman's banner. Because of information received from the lord chancellor of Ireland, O'Hagan (1812-85), he expected no better from the Irish than from the English hierarchy.[119] On 8 February 1869 Döllinger wrote to Acton that the bishop of Augsburg had received news that the plan to dogmatise papal infallibility had been given up. Döllinger regarded this as a heavy blow for Manning.[120]

The concept of infallibility advocated by both Manning and Ward was indeed a contradiction of catholic faith and tradition, yet in his fight against it Döllinger adopted positions that increasingly favoured the direction of independent national churches. In 1849, at a meeting of the catholic clubs of Germany, Döllinger proposed a toast in favour of a national church.[121]

Döllinger's anti-Roman tendencies surged forth with unrestrained passion when, unlike many other German theologians, he was not invited to participate in the preparatory commission for the council; he was deeply hurt by this.[122] The man responsible for Döllinger's omission was his bitter enemy since 1850,[123] Cardinal Reisach (1800-69) of the curia. Bellesheim, who was well acquainted with both men, relates that Reisach and Manning were in close contact: 'Among the men with whom Manning was in closest contact in Rome, I name the late Cardinal Carl August Count Reisach, a man who was fluent at English and deeply understanding and sympathetic towards Manning and his work. He included all the works of the "Abbate Manning" as he called him ... in his private library and [these] were always at the disposal of anyone wanting to consult them.'[124] His feelings for Manning are indicated by the manner in which he treated Newman, in accordance with Manning's wishes, when Newman proposed the establishment of a catholic college in Oxford. On 30 July 1866 Manning introduced Reisach to Gladstone, whom Reisach would render assistance to when he visited Rome later the same year. Acton informed Döllinger of the close relationship between Manning and Reisach.[125]

While Döllinger had originally planned to write a scholarly book on the papacy and the question of infallibility, he changed his mind following the uproar caused by the publication of the 'correspondence' by *Civiltà cattolica* in February 1869.[126] Döllinger now intended to influence events within the catholic church through journalism, and to fight his ultramontane opponents, whom he regarded as the forces of evil, with the help of the liberal press. One has to bear in mind the fact that Döllinger regarded public opinion as the queen before which everything, willingly or unwillingly, has to bow.[127] He believed that public opinion should be managed, and as far as the church was concerned those managers should be the professors of theology; he regarded the common people of the church as a mindless mass ('gedankenloser Haufen') who were incapable of independent judgment.[128] It is significant that he selected the *Allgemeine Zeitung,* published in Augsburg, to print his articles: this paper reported in minute detail on matters of English interest. In a long series of articles on Earl Russell the paper commented that the world would be a better place if there were more aristocrats like him.[129] In March 1865 August Jos. A. Altenhöfer (1804-76) became editor of the paper; since November 1833 he had been responsible for articles on England and America. In his capacity as editor he adopted a pro-Prussian stance.[130] In March 1869 he handed over the editorship of the paper to Otto Braun (1824-1900)[131] but continued to contribute articles on England. Otto Braun was decidedly anti-catholic. As was the case with the English liberal press, he looked on catholicism with detached irony and a feeling of cultural superiority. His readers were mostly bourgeois, addicted to the pursuit of progress with little or no contact with the church.[132] The readers of the *Allgemeine Zeitung* had a contemptuous regard for Roman catholics and did not see the council as presenting any threat or danger, because of their belief that the church would not last very much longer anyway. What the average reader knew about catholicism amounted to a litany of clichés inherited from protestant polemics and reinforced by popular and nationalist journalism: they saw the church as a strictly hierarchical organisation based on magic rites to govern primitive minds and under-educated people.[133]

Döllinger embarked on his campaign against the forthcoming council with a series of anonymous articles entitled 'Das Concilium und die Civiltà' (The council and the *Civiltà*) printed consecutively over a period of six days from 10 to 15 March 1869 in the *Allgemeine Zeitung*.[134] His pro-English leanings became apparent in the second instalment of 11 March 1869 when he singled out the Magna Carta, as the antithesis of ultramontanism, as 'the revered ancestor of European constitutions'; 'while Pope Innocent immediately had the Magna Carta declared null and void and excommunicated its authors'. Döllinger went on to remark: 'Let us therefore do justice to Pius IX and his advisors, the Jesuits, who are as everybody knows the intellectual authors of the encyclical letter and the syllabus, and admit that they merely did in 1864 what Innocent had done in 1215.'[135] Brandmüller has pointed out that at the time of writing (in 1869) Döllinger was not up-to-date with the historical research of his time. Ranke had written in 1859 that Innocent was compelled to act as he did as lord paramount of King John.[136] Ranke also realised that the revolt against King John was not popular, but was confined to the city of London and the wealthy barons, while among the common people there was a party siding with John which was soon crushed by the powerful barons and the wealthy of the city.[137] Döllinger knew Ranke, as he often mentioned his name in his correspondence: on 22 January 1867, for example, he drew Acton's attention to the publication of the sixth volume of Ranke's *Englische Geschichte* (English history).[138] Brandmüller justly remarked that Döllinger's judgment was ill informed since he disregarded the feudal system and even falsely attributed democratic processes to the Magna Carta. (This was already exposed by Hergenröther in 1872.)[139] The fact that Döllinger, who always took pride in being an historian, was capable of such uncritical judgment can largely be attributed to his being consumed by English ways and attitudes. The whig concept of history derived its foundation from the Magna Carta: English history was seen as a glorious movement towards freedom despite the fact that the act of settlement (14 Ch.II, c.12) introduced villeinage, and that living conditions for the common people of France under Louis XIV and XV were indisputably better than those in England.[140] In contrast with the English constitution which stressed its saxon-germanic character, was the absolutist nature of that of the Romance peoples, for which they were decried. To this was added the cry of 'no popery' by those who had acquired their wealth through the expropriation of English church property after 1535, and which they jealously defended. Since the sixteenth century Italy has been disparaged by anti-catholics in clichés which have remained unchanged: while ancient Rome is acknowledged, modern Italians are depicted as the degenerated descendants of their ancient past, a degeneration which is born out of their acceptance of a priest-ridden society.[141]

Döllinger's writings are infested with such stereotypes: England is seen as the mother country of the bills of rights.[142] Döllinger plagiarised these whigs clichés and used them to assail Italy, the papacy and the Romance peoples. He wrote that in his opinion distrust and discrimination had been the fate of Germans for centuries, long before the reformation, so long as the Romance oligarchy was governing in Rome. He went on to say that it seemed to be in heaven as it was on earth: Spain, Italy, Southern America and France were providing the papal congregation with numerous candidates for canonisation while the Germans here, as well, were relegated to a last place among the nations. Döllinger referred to the forthcoming council as an assembly comprising two-third Romance people. Finally he concluded that a deep-seated resentment and loathing for the ubiquitous Italian priesthood was bound to flourish in people's minds.[143] That a catholic theologian who had once been ultramontane was capable of writing this can only be attributed to his having absorbed the stereotypes propagated by the whig concept of history.

Döllinger's English orientation also became apparent when he focussed on Manning, whom he believed to be working in unison with Cardinal Reisach, Döllinger's arch-enemy.[144]

In August 1869 Döllinger's *Der Papst und das Council* (pope and council) was published under the pseudonym 'Janus'. His Munich colleague Johann Nepomuk Huber (1830-79), a professor of philosophy, had assisted in the composition of the book. It was not merely a revised edition of his anonymous articles published in March, for those sections on papal infallibility (pp.40-448) were for the most part new.[145] Here again he presents a clerical Italian frame of mind as typical of ultramontane thinking.[146] Before the German edition had actually been published, H.N. Oxenham had begun translating the book into English; it was published by Rivingtons, Ward's publisher. There were also translations in Italian, French and Hungarian[147] and in 1873 the English translation reached its fourth edition. In October 1869 Gladstone wrote a long letter to Döllinger praising him for 'Janus'.[148]

The Munich theological faculty published a paper in September 1869 on the possible consequences to be expected from the dogmas of the council; it was drafted by Döllinger at the request of the Bavarian prime minister, Hohenlohe. In it Döllinger affirmed that the council would make dogmas of positive opposites of the errors condemned in the *Syllabus*: thus for example, where the *Syllabus* had condemned separation of church and state, the council would dogmatise in favour of the union of church and state. Döllinger also stated that there could be no doubt that if infallibility was dogmatised, so too would papal power over the secular sphere become a dogma.[149] This meant that papal pronouncements on Ireland would have been infallible. It is therefore not surprising that *The Times* printed a translation of the treatise on 20 September 1869 and devoted its leader column to the treatise which in turn was translated into German for publication in the *Allgemeine Zeitung* on 25 September.[150]

Many of Döllinger's co-thinkers were similarly prone to English influences: Count Montalembert, who was of part-British ancestry and the leading layman among liberal catholics in France, worshipped England and the English system with romantic enthusiasm. In 1856 a German review wrote that Montalembert placed England alongside France and then, like an ill-tempered husband, found everything amiable and attractive in the other woman while seeing his own wife as disgusting and repellent.[151] His aim was to import English institutions and conditions to France. In the 1840s, when catholics in France fought for independent schools, he pointed to the English example: 'Pour Montalembert, les écoles et les universités anglaises étaient la vivante incarnation de son idéal éducatif.'[152] He condemned the continental countries which, unlike Britain, provided school education for every citizen, as he believed that by educating the masses they became estranged from the class to which they belonged. In his writings he indulged in an 'éloge sans restriction de l'Angleterre'.[153] He felt that French catholics should no longer call for 'la liberté comme en Belgique' but for 'la liberté comme en Angleterre'.[154] He travelled to Britain many times, where he met Gladstone, Lord Aberdeen and Macaulay. Montalembert only saw the free institutions of England while remaining oblivious to the plight of those people who had not right to vote, in particular the Irish poor.[155]

Early in May 1869 a Baden judge, Franz August Beck, who initiated the 'Old Catholic' movement in Baden in 1865, issued a call to the

the catholics of Baden *(Aufruf an die Katholiken Badens)* in which he depicted the catholic church as having fallen under the sway of absolutism, against which he contrasted the 'Glorious Revolution'.[156] Calls were continually made for an independent German national catholic church. The catholic professor Peter Volkmuth, for example, in his work *Petrus and Paulus auf dem Konzil von Jerusalem* (Peter and Paul at the Council of Jerusalem) (published in 1869), cited Paul as his example, who in his opinion had stood against the uniform church system of the catholic church and for the principle of free national churches.[157] This call partly sprang from German traditions,[158] but it also coincided with the aim of Lord Clarendon and other English circles. The *Allgemeine Zeitung* was especially engaged in promoting a German national catholic church. In a report from Rome on 2 January 1869 the correspondent spoke of the feeling that when the council dispersed, some dormant differences in the catholic church would develop to bring about a great schism.[159] A review of Franz von Baader's *Grundzüge der Staatsphilosophie: Ideen über Recht, Staat, Gesellschaft und Kirche* (Basics of State philosophy) of 1865, concluded that the schism between catholicism and the papacy should be allowed to develop itself freely.[160] On 3 and 4 October of the same year the *Allgemeine Zeitung* printed a review of *Janus* by a suspended priest, Jacob Frohschammer (1821-93), then professor of philosophy at Munich university. Frohschammer concluded that it would be of help to the church if the crude papal system were replaced by the episcopalian system.[161] On the burial of Bishop Lipp of Rottenburg the paper reported that good catholics had given the signal for the founding of a German national church and separation from Rome.[162] On 5 August it printed an article on the bull *Unam Sanctam* by Dr Doergens of Heidelberg university, who suggested that perhaps matters would not have arrived at their present state with the impending threat of absolutism in faith had the council of Constance (1414-18) envisaged national churches or at least racial churches.[163]

As was happening in England, those who merely regarded infallibility as inopportune came in for strong attack.

In his March articles Döllinger had aroused the interest of the readers of *Allgemeine Zeitung* by stating, for example, that (as stated in Manning's 'Essays on Religion and Literature') all catholics would from now on have to believe, and all teachers of law and theology would be obliged to teach, that even today the pope had it in his power to depose kings at will.[164] Now, in a further series of anonymous articles, Döllinger set about inculcating in them the idea that the council represented a threat to the state. In the first of further anonymous articles he stated that from the next year (when papal infallibility was to have been promulgated) the complete dominance of the church over the state would become a principle and article of faith and a factor with which any community or state with catholic inhabitants would have to reckon. No government would then, so long as it did not receive papal consent for its actions, be able to count on the loyalty and obedience of its catholic subjects.[165] By including Pius IX and Gregory VII in the same sentence any reader with historical knowledge was reminded of the medieval extravagances of papal power.[166] Brandmüller came to the conclusion that papal infallibility would have passed as quietly and unobserved as the dogma of the immaculate conception of 1854 had Döllinger not made a political controversy out of a theological issue.[167]

Döllinger's histrionics also made the Bavarian prime minister issue a circular to the European governments urging common action over the council: Döllinger drafted the text of the circular. Here it was stated that by dogmatising papal infallibility the power of the sovereign pope would be raised above all princes and people, even in secular matters.[168] On 29 October Döllinger published anonymous *Erwägungen für die Bischöfe des Conciliums über die Frage der päpstlichen Unfehlbarkeit* (Thoughts for the bishops of the Council on the question of papal infallibility); French and English translations were published simultaneously with the latter addressing itself to the American bishops by virtue of its subtitle. Döllinger had it distributed to the bishops arriving to the council.[169] Still prior to the sitting of the council, on 19 and 20 November 1869, Döllinger had a final anonymous article published in *Allgemeine Zeitung* entitled 'Die Bischöfe und das Council' (The bishops and the council), in which he assailed the inopportunists who merely regarded the moment as inopportune for the dogmatisation of papal infallibility:[170] both Döllinger and Acton saw the inopportunists as a great danger.

Döllinger also maintained contact with the French opponents of infallibility. When Maret visited him in July 1868 Döllinger undertook to supervise the translation of Maret's anti-infalliblist *Du Concile génerale et de la paix religieuse* even before the French original had been published.[171] In September 1869 Maret's work was published in two volumes. On 4 and 5 September Döllinger, Acton, Countess Leyden (the future Lady Blennerhasset) and Bishop Dupanloup of Orléans met in Acton's castle, Herrnsheim near Worms, to discuss the council.[172] On 3 October Manning published his 150-page pastoral *The Oecumenical Council and the Infallibility of the Roman Pontiff* which was divided into four chapters, the second of which was dedicated to papal infallibility; in this he seized the opportunity to attack the paper of the Munich theological faculty on the consequences of the dogmas expected from the council.[173] The text of Manning's pastoral was toned down by Bishop Ullathorne prior to publication; at the last minute, however, Manning added a *Post scriptum* which was a sharp reply to Maret's work: 'The doctrine maintained by me ... is that the judgements ex cathedra are, in their essence, judgements of the Pontiff, apart from the episcopal body, whether congregated or dispersed. The concurrence of the episcopal body may or may not be united to the act of the Pontiff, which is perfect and complete in itself.'[174] Manning's *Post scriptum* was immediately translated into French and printed in Veuillot's *Univers:* through translation, however, the statement acquired an extremist slant, e.g. 'apart from the episcopal body' was translated as 'séperement des évêques'.[175] Dupanloup answered with a pastoral entitled *Observations sur la controverse soulevée relativement à la définition de l'infallibilité au prochain concile,* published on 11 November 1869, in which he opposed both Manning and Ward.[176] Countess Leyden immediately translated it into German. Döllinger himself did the proof-reading and the German translation, published by Manz, went into two editions.[177] Veuillot not only translated Manning's *Post scriptum* but also initiated a vigorous campaign for the dogmatisation of papal infallibility through *Univers,* in co-ordination with Manning's *Dublin Review* and *Tablet.* Manning also had his deliberations on papal infallibility translated into Italian and published in Naples.[178] It was here that Salesius Mayer, who was to be Cardinal Schwarzenberg's theological adviser during the council, had his work *De Summi Pontificis infallibilitate personali* published at the instigation of Cardinal Rauscher of Vienna, in which he singled out Manning as one of the main advocates of papal infallibility.[179]

In America the editor of the New York *Freeman's Journal,* James E. MacMaster, an admirer of Veuillot, propagated the works of Manning, Ward and Veuillot.[180]

Having met Veuillot in Paris on 22 November 1869 Manning asked him to publish his pastoral on infallibility in the *Univers* in full and stated: 'Nous sommes voici bien entrés dans le combat. Mais le dernier coup est providentiel.'[181] Dupanloup reacted with a scathing *Advertisement* in which he presented Veuillot as a villain of the piece within the church, as well as a slanderer.[182] At the end of November 1869 Louis Veuillot went to Rome as correspondent of his paper. Manning immediately arranged an audience for him with the pope — which was extraordinary as there were no audiences during the council. On 5 December Manning and Veuillot discussed their future course of action.[183] Manning saw to it that Eugène Veuillot, who edited the *Univers* in his brother's absence, translated and printed a letter by himself in which he scolded Dupanloup for his theses against Manning.[184] Veuillot continued to let Manning use the *Univers* despite the fact that he gradually came to be disgusted by Manning's methods.[185]

3. THE CATHOLIC CHURCH IN ENGLISH LITERATURE
AND THE PRESS

The extremist position adopted by Manning and his party on papal infallibility played into the hands of the whigs led by Clarendon[186] whose major interest in the affair was to pursue the old strategy of governing Ireland with the help of the pope's authority, and to do this more effectively, the pope's authority had to be strengthened. It was also therefore in their interests not merely to have infallibility dogmatised but to have it dogmatised in the extreme form as advocated by Manning and Ward, who even regarded papal pronouncements on political issues as infallible. This would have meant that papal pronouncements on Ireland were infallible. In order to lull the catholic church into the right frame of mind, the pope, the catholic church and the catholic Irish were all curiously presented in a positive light in English literature and the press. This contrasted strikingly with the prevailing prejudices of former times[187] and seems to point to political motivations.[188] The wooing of the catholic church started in the mid-1860's. When Cardinal Wiseman had died Lord Campbell, the son of the lord chancellor who had been at the forefront of the anti-catholic agitation following Cardinal Wiseman's appointment as cardinal archbishop of Westminster, attended the funeral service; *The Times* printed an extensive report on the funeral proceedings and praised him in its obituary.[189] Manning reported to Talbot in Rome that the English press, especially the *Pall Mall Gazette* and the *Saturday Review*, were now in favour of the pope and his temporal power, adding: 'It is wonderful what a change has come over England about the Holy Father. It is the chief subject, and, except *The Times* and *Standard*, which are vile, even the political papers wish him well'.[190] Yet, when Garibaldi made his famous anti-papal speech at the conference of Geneva in 1867, even *The Times* ridiculed him.[191]

When the whigs returned to power late in 1868 this strategy of wooing the catholic church was intensified. The whig writer, Anthony Trollope, in his novel *Phineas Finn* of 1869, presented a catholic Irishman as the title hero and wrote of the 'dear old Pope'.[192] The poet Robert Browning in his *The Ring and the Book,* also published in 1869, glorified Pope Innocent XII (1691-1700), the pope who had ostracised nepotism in his bull *Romanum decet Pontificem* of 1692.[193]

Matthew Arnold, in his major work *Culture and Anarchy,* also published in 1869, displays similar sympathy for the Irish and catholicism.[194] Arnold expresses indignation at the fanatic Murphy, who in 1868 toured all over England inciting people with anti-catholic speeches which led to attacks on catholic Irish people living in Britain. Arnold declared that Murphy had employed words to describe the catholic population that were fit only for thieves and murderers.[195]

Arnold treated the normal English attitude towards Fenians with irony:

> We can have no scruple at all about abridging, if necessary, a non-Englishman's assertion of personal liberty. The British Constitution, its checks, and its prime virtues, are for Englishmen. We may extend them to others out of love and kindness; but we find no real divine law written on our hearts constraining us to extend them. And then the difference between an Irish Fenian and an English rogue is so immense, and the case, in dealing with the Fenian, so much more clear! He is so evidently desperate and dangerous, a man of a conquered race, a Papist, with centuries of ill-usage to inflame him against us, with an alien religion established in his country by us at his expense, with no admiration for our institutions, no love of our virtues, no talents for our business, no turn for our comfort! ... Evidently, if we deal tenderly with a sentimentalist like this, it is out of pure philanthropy.[196]

In his criticism of the establishment of the church of Ireland Arnold already implies what he states explicitly elsewhere in the book: 'For Ireland the ends of human perfection might be best served by establishing, — that is, by bringing into contact with the main current of national life, — the Roman Catholic and the Presbyterian Churches along with the Anglican Church ... because we should be making Roman Catholics better citizens, and both Protestants and Roman Catholics larger-minded.'[197] Here Arnold adopted the same stand as Disraeli on concurrent endowment and levelling up. The property of the established church was to be redistributed to give the other communities a fairer share.[198] He opposed Gladstone's policy of levelling down, for he believed it was instigated, not by public opinion, but by English nonconformists and the free kirk. Gladstone's policy would in his opinion fail to win the affections of the Irish people.[199]

In the October 1869 issue of the *Edinburgh Review,* to which Gladstone contributed articles, there appeared an anonymous article by Dean Stanley of Westminster, the leader of the liberals in the Church of England, on 'The Oecumenical Council'. Here it became apparent precisely what intentions lay behind 'concurrent endowment'. Stanley wrote: 'In France, in Austria, in Spain, in Portugal ... the bishops are named by the Crown or the first Minister of the Crown, the Pope having the right only of objection on special canonical grounds. And this right exists even where the Prime Minister is not a Roman Catholic.' Stanley quoted the French protestant prime minister, Guizot, as an example. He then turned his attention to Prussia: 'In Prussia the same right is exercised though under a different form, by the Protestant King. The Pope selects, but the King approves, and by witholding his approval virtually appoints.'[200] In Ireland the catholic church was to be endowed so that the English government could appoint the Irish bishops either directly, or indirectly as in Prussia. This is the very same policy as pursued at the turn of the century during the veto controversy. Stanely's hopes were now directed towards the Vatican council. The *Syllabus* had condemned the separation of church and state, and it was anticipated by Manning and Ward, as well as by their opponents Döllinger and Acton, that the *Syllabus* would be dogmatised in an assertive form. Stanley wrote: 'Let us hope that the Council at least will determine for them whether the doctrine which has hitherto prevailed in the R.C. Church throughout Europe as to the lawfulness and advantage of endowment is the correct one, or whether for the future it is to adopt that which is the offspring of ancient Irish barbarism and of Scottish Puritanism'[216] — a reference to the resistance offered by the Irish catholics and the free kirk to his plan. In reality Cardinal Antonelli was against the catholic clergy being salaried by a non-catholic government, as Odo Russell reported in 1868 to foreign secretary Clarendon. At the same time Antonelli rejected Gladstone's disendowment scheme as he opposed any separation of church and state in any country, a policy which he later retracted, however, following consultations with Manning.[218]

As already mentioned, for the British government to solve the Irish problem through Rome it was not only necessary that the *Syllabus* be dogmatised, as advocated by Manning and Ward, but also that infallibility be dogmatised, again as advocated by Manning and Ward, since it included political pronouncements by the pope. It is therefore not surprising that liberal catholics such as Dupanloup became the targets of virulent attacks in the English press. Manning's reply to Dupanloup's *Advertisement* was lauded and supported by *The Times* and the *Pall Mall Gazette*. The *Pall Mall Gazette,* on 12 October 1869, carried a leader on the first two pages on 'The Position of Liberal Catholics' where it stated: 'It is impossible entirely to reconcile any form of systematic Christian theology with what we call civilization and progress ... perhaps of all the absurd devices which have been invented for the purpose none is so absurd as the device which French Liberal Catholics usually adopt of dividing the provinces of the State and the Church.'[219] Furthermore, it declared this article that liberal catholics were advancing towards a mild 'High Church Anglicanism'. Their absorption into the anglican church was anticipated.

An article entitled 'The Political Aspects of the Oecumenical Council' by Walter Bagehot in the *Economist* also welcomed the fact that the 'supreme power of legislation' was to be passed from the council to the pope.[220]

4. THE PAPAL DECREE CONDEMNING FENIANISM

Together with this journalistic and literary support of the papacy the whigs commenced action in Rome. Odo Russell informed Clarendon on the usefulness of Archbishop Manning: 'His strongly expressed Gladstonian predilections are said by many to have alarmed ('spaventato') the Vatican, but I do not believe it, for the Pope has implicit faith and confidence in him'.[221] Russell wrote that, apart from Cullen, Manning was the only one who could influence the Vatican on the Irish church and not only did he favour Gladstone but he also preferred Clarendon to his predecessor Lord Stanley.[222] On 10 February 1869 Russell again wrote to Clarendon concerning Manning: 'You will ... find him useful'.[223] In accordance with Clarendon's wishes Russell asked Antonelli and Manning to bring their influence to bear on Ireland. By 24 February Russell reported to Clarendon that he had had a favourable effect on Cullen.[224] Odo Russell also reported on the favourable impression left by Gladstone's disestablishment policy in Rome: 'My despatch No. 11 will shew you that Mr Gladstone's Irish Church speech has found favour at the Vatican, which is important'.[225] 'The Irish Priests in Rome are delighted with Mr Gladstone's policy and very angry with anyone who is not'.[226] At that time there was a wave of agrarian crime in Ireland and the government believed that a great number of catholic priests were involved. In accordance with Clarendon's demand of 19 April 1869[227] Odo Russell called on Antonelli and asked that the pope himself should directly exert his influence in Ireland. Antonelli's reply proved that he was responsive to such demands at the time: 'Cardinal Antonelli replied that the state of Ireland filled him with horror and distress and that the Irish character was incomprehensible to him. He knew no nationality so difficult, so hopeless, so disagreeable to deal with.'[228] Following this second intervention Rome acted, and Archbishop Leahy of Cashel consequently issued a pastoral, for which Russell thanked Antonelli at Clarendon's request.[229] Clarendon, however, was outraged at the behaviour of the Irish priests: 'The fact is that priests have with such continuous pertinacity educated their flocks in disloyalty to the Crown, and defiance of England that they find themselves powerless now if they attempted to preach or warn in a different sense.'[230] Clarendon completely distrusted Cardinal Cullen. He asked Odo Russell to contact Bishop Moriarty of Kerry who had arrived in Rome for the council. Moriarty's true sympathies became apparent in a letter written in 1868, which was forwarded to Gladstone; here he imagines the positive developments following the disestablishment of the church of Ireland:

> I do believe that there is in the British constitution that which will attach to it the Irish priests and Irish people if this barrier is

removed. . . . They will begin to admire the magnificent combination of freedom, of power, and of right, which permeates your whole system and especially the administration of justice . . . the day will come when the Irish priest will cry 'Civis Romanus sum' with as much sense of its value as St Paul or Lord Palmerston.[231]

Russell was to propose to Moriarty that the Irish priests should be told to preach against uproar. As Clarendon had requested, Acton engineered a meeting between Russell and Moriarty.[232] Russell also contacted Bishop Butler of Limerick and MacEvily of Galway, both of whom he described as 'well-disposed and ready to talk, but it takes time to gain their confidence'.[233] Russell complained to Antonelli about Fathers Lavelle and Ryan (who had spoken in favour of the actions taken against landlords) and asked for their suspension.

Russell now demanded an *ex cathedra* condemnation of the Fenians by the pope and Antonelli promised to direct the holy father's attention to the matter.[234] The use of the term *ex cathedra* makes it clear why Clarendon and Russell, in accordance with Clarendon's instructions, were anxious to have the most extreme form of infallibility dogmatised: thus it was envisaged that an *ex cathedra* condemnation of the Fenians by the pope would become infallible. Russell reported everything Antonelli had said to him to Moriarty and the other Irish bishops with whom he was acquainted, Butler of Limerick and MacEvily of Galway. They promptly called for a meeting of the Irish hierarchy. At the meeting all the Irish bishops assembled in Rome, except Archbishop MacHale of Tuam and Bishop John Derry of Clonfert, signed an appeal to the pope 'to get the Fenians condemned *nominatim*'.[235] Morarity informed Russell of this appeal on 7 January 1870.[236] Clarendon wanted to push the matter and instructed the Irish viceroy to compile a dossier of incitements to Fenianism and uproar by Irish priests, which was subsequently sent to Russell to use in Rome.[237] On 13 January 1870 Russell had a private audience with Pius IX and repeated his request for a papal condemnation of the Fenians; he stated that the Irish bishops were supportive of such action but that the lower clergy did not follow them.[238] This new English intervention may not, however, have been necessary: prior to Russell's request to the pope Cullen had informed his secretary in Dublin: 'The Fenians will certainly be condemned *nominatim*'.[239] On 20 January 1870 the Irish primate, Cullen, was handed the papal document dated 12 January 1870 condemning the Fenians by name.[240] On 23 January Manning and Moriarty informed Russell of the decree.[241] The decree was published by the vicar generals at the end of February 1870 and was read from all pulpits in Ireland; in many places in Ireland there was an outcry against it.

The decree against the Fenians applied not only to Ireland but also to the U.S. The American bishops, among them MacClosky of New

York, feared that the decree would have a devastating effect on the catholic church in the U.S. Cullen reported to his secretary: 'The American bishops (at least some of them) are displeased with the Irish bishops for getting the Holy Office to act in this case. Dr Spalding [archbishop of Baltimore] says we have done a great mischief.'[242] As a special thank you *The Times* on 17 February 1870 referred to the decree as a 'piece of toadyism to the British Government'.[243]

Foreign Secretary Clarendon thanked Odo Russell: 'Your handling of the Irish Bishops has been admirable and will I hope be productive of good results, i.e. if a good result of any kind is possible in that land of demons.'[244] The effect of the decree was negligible.[245]

CHAPTER IX

Britain and Vatican I

1. THE FIRST VATICAN COUNCIL

FROM THE British government's point of view everything had been conditioned in the best possible way so as to influence the approaching council according to its wishes. Nevertheless Clarendon wrote to Gladstone on 31 August 1869: 'You may be sure of the pleasure I shall have in taking every opportunity, legitimate or reverse, of throwing dirt on the Council.'[1] At first he thought of threatening the pope and his Jesuits through Napoleon III, but having consulted his son-in-law Odo Russell[2] Clarendon decided on a different procedure.

Victor Conzemius, while investigating Prussian policy towards the Vatican council, pointed to the similarity of policies pursued by both Bismarck and Clarendon: both men appreciated the importance of the press in their anti-conciliar policies, and both had refrained from direct confrontation with the curia, electing instead to operate behind the scenes.[3]

The British government began by analysing the forces most likely to command influence at the council and whether any of these presented an opportunity to it. The divide and govern method was used again. Manning was one of the leaders of the ultras, whose agitation for an extreme form of papal infallibility offered one possibility. It was also anticipated that among the supporters of dogmatisation of infallibility at the council Manning seemed likely to assume a leading role.[4] Disraeli indicated this in *Lothair* when he wrote: 'England also will send her prelates to the Council, and some of them will take no ordinary share in (the) transactions.'[5] Acton on the other hand, at Gladstone's recommendation, was made a baron on 11 December 1869, a move that was designed to secure his services for the liberal party in the future.[6] When the colonial secretary, Granville, wrote to Queen Victoria to quieten her over the fact that this was the first time a catholic had been elevated to the peerage since James II, his main point was that if Manning had a say in the matter, Acton would not have been made a peer.[7] It seems that when Acton was raised to the peerage, Granville, who always closely co-operated with Clarendon, was anxious to foment rivalry between Manning and Acton. After his arrival in Rome Acton was instructed by telegram to act against

Manning.[8] Unlike the other whigs Gladstone, encouraged by Döllinger and Acton, was in favour of intervention by the powers against the dogmatisation of infallibility. Gladstone feared that his reform legislation might be defeated in parliament as a result of an aggressively ultramontane decision by the council, since there were many members of his own party who were extremely anti-catholic and nonconformist.[9] Clarendon, however, was strongly opposed to any English intervention, a view which was supported by the majority of the cabinet. It is still widely today believed that Cardinal Manning was able to manipulate Odo Russell and through him had prevented any intervention by England, thus saving the council.

This idea that Russell had fallen under Manning's sway was merely a figment of Manning's own imagination. His biographer, Purcell, cast him in a very negative light,[10] while Lytton Strachey even depicted him as an arch-villain,[11] yet they both inadvertently fell victim to Manning's megalomania. Manning realised that a strengthening of the pope's power would be useful to uphold English rule in Ireland, as he indicated in a letter to Gladstone.[12] Russell needed no persuasion of this fact since he was already well aware of it. Russell, however, was not nearly as pro-catholic as Manning had imagined. Unlike Manning, Archbishop Darboy of Paris did not allow himself to be deceived by Odo Russell as he remarked on him in his diary: 'Toute fois je crois remarquer que c'est un sceptique et que le concile l'amuse.'[13] Russell had successfully secured the confidence of the pope and in order to preserve this confidence he sometimes had to conceal his true feelings. In his private correspondence, however, he referred to Pius IX (up to 1863 invariably, thereafter rarely) as 'Nine Pins', 'Fool', 'Kegelkönig' and once as the 'great Mumbo Jumbo Nine Pins'. Elsewhere he wrote: 'I thank God with all my heart that we at home have broken forever with this infernal papacy' and even referred to our Lady as 'the immaculate goddess he invented'.[14]

Odo Russell was indeed the reliable diplomat whom Randall described as 'faithfully yet tactfully carrying out his instructions'.[15] These instructions were issued by his father-in-law, Clarendon, and it was he, not Gladstone, who decided English policy towards the Vatican council.[16] Clarendon was an extremely able politican, who employed his substantial talents for flattery and deception in order to achieve his aims.[17] He opposed any direct intervention by England in the council because of the effect it might have on Ireland; he had been viceroy of Ireland from 1847-52 and Ireland still played an important role in his deliberations.[18] The cynical Clarendon expressed only sarcasm for Gladstone's Irish policy and wrote to him: 'You have a fervent imagination and a yearning for benevolent action towards your fellow creatures. ... I am sorry to go between you and your dream, for a dream it will prove that justice will make the Irish happy or content.'[19] He believed that the only way to control Ireland, if that was at all possible, was through Rome. For this reason he opposed any overt anti-papal action and decided that any intervention would not only be fruitless but would harm England: it would turn the pope and the Irish bishops against the British government. On 23 February 1870 Clarendon wrote to Gladstone: 'I do not wish that we should be regarded as enemies by the Papal Court whose goodwill may be more or less useful to us in Ireland.'[20]

Antonelli realised that the British government, if it hoped to use the pope's authority in Ireland, had to be in favour of this authority being strengthened through the dogmatisation of papal infallibility; this so surprised Russell that when he reported the fact to London he added an exclamation mark behind it. He did not, however, reveal his surprise to Antonelli.[21] Clarendon wrote to Odo Russell: 'Such interferences as we could resort to ... might do harm in the matters concerning which we want Papal assistance and which to us are of far more importance than defined or undefined infallibility.'[22] To Gladstone he wrote: 'Charity begins at home ... as we have need of the Pope and he has done us some service in Ireland it would be unwise in my opinion to indispose him.'[23] The colonial secretary, Granville, who was Clarendon's closest co-operator and later his successor, as well as being Acton's stepfather, agreed completely with Clarendon and wrote to Gladstone: 'Our immediate and selfish object seems to be to cultivate good relations with whoever has influence over the Irish Bishops and Priests.'[24]

While Clarendon believed that an intervention by Britain would only harm British interests, this did not mean that he was against other powers intervening at the Holy See. This was likely to widen the rift within the catholic church outside Ireland, while the intervening powers would make themselves unpopular with the pope, and with England abstaining from any intervention she would thereby endear herself to the Holy See. Finally, Clarendon could thus ease his position in the cabinet, since Gladstone was so much in favour of an intervention. On 15 January 1870 Clarendon instructed Lord Lyons, the British ambassador in Paris, to have Daru, the French foreign minister between January and April 1870, order his ambassador in Rome to call on Antonelli and threaten an irreparable rupture between church and state should infallibility and the *Syllabus* be dogmatised.[25] On 24 January, when Daru asked for English assistance, Clarendon sent a further instruction to Lyons 'in order to encourage Daru to speak stiffly to the Pope'.[26]

On 21 January the *schema de ecclesia*[27] was handed out to the bishops; by early February its contents were known to all important diplomats in Rome. The last six of the fifteen chapters and the appended twenty-one canons raised fears that the council would vote for a new syllabus. Chapters thirteen to fifteen as well as the last five canons dealt with church and state together with the primacy of the pope.[28] In France the foreign minister, Daru, now decided to intervene at the council: on 20 February 1870 he sent a note to Rome the first 'Daru note' which, after re-wording, was passed on to the Holy See in early March.[29] However, the French prime minister, Ollivier, was opposed to the intervention policy of Daru, and this fact was transmitted in confidence to Antonelli through Archbishop Lavigerie on 9 February; Lavigerie was also to plead on behalf of Ollivier for a moderate definition of papal infallibility. This fact remained a secret and was therefore unknown to Odo Russell.[30] Following Daru's intervention Clarendon wrote to Odo Russell: 'You might discuss them [Daru's opinions] as an *amicus curiae* with Antonelli.'[31] Clarendon opposed any real, active support for Daru's note; Acton requested the British government to intervene but Gladstone, however, was unable to secure majority support in the cabinet for such action.[32]

Clarendon also called on Austria and Prussia to intervene and on 16 February 1870 he informed Gladstone: 'I have privately but strongly suggested to Berlin and Vienna a common action with Bavaria in support of the German Bishops at Rome.'[33] On 6 March a chapter on papal infallibility was added to the *schema de ecclesia*. On 9 March Clarendon expressed his disappointment to the Prussian ambassador in London, Count Bernstorff, that Prussia did not act in unison with Austria and Bavaria against the power-mongering tendencies of the curia. Bismarck did break with his previous reserve and on 12 and 13 March tried to bring about a common action of the powers.[34] He also had his own reasons for doing so, but it cannot be denied that he may have acted on Clarendon's remark.[35] Conzemius wrote in 1962 that, considering Clarendon's repeated calls to Prussia to abandon her reserved attitude, this seems a plausible assumption.[36] Bismarck, however, failed in his attempts to bring about a common intervention by Austria, France and Bavaria.[37] On 23 March Clarendon again wrote to the English ambassador in Paris: 'I hope there will be a discussion in the corps legislatif and that Daru ... may not be reticent in expounding the inevitable evils of infallibility and the Syllabus. It will be the best mode of preventing these dogmas from being hereafter converted into political weapons.'[38] This remark was intended for the ears of Daru. Five days later, on 28 March, Clarendon instructed Odo Russell in Rome: 'My great desire is that we should not be hooked into French remonstrances.'[39]

In April 1870 a French memorandum, the second Daru note,[40] was presented in Rome against the *schema de ecclesia*. Clarendon had received the note on 5 April[41] and on 7 April he sent an *official* instruction to Odo Russell by normal post to support the Daru note to Antonelli.[42] On the same day, however, Clarendon sent a *private* letter to Russell with completely different instructions:

We don't want to assume an attitude unnecessarily hostile to the Pope and still less to impair the influence you have established at Rome which we would reserve for Irish objects, but we cannot altogether refuse the support that the French Govt. desire us to give ... the minimum of meddling is wanted. ... I think you might in a friendly and unofficial manner tell the Cardinal how much we are alarmed. ... State such arguments and others that will occur to you to the Cardinal with the assurance that we have no wish to meddle in ecclesiastical affairs.[43]

Meanwhile, the French foreign secretary, Daru, was forced to resign because of his opposition to Napoleon's plan for a referendum; his duties as foreign secretary were assumed for a time by the prime minister, Ollivier, who as a protestant quickly put an end to the catholic Daru's intervention policy.[44] Napoleon III needed the catholic vote in the referendum on his general policy (he governed by referendum rather than by elections). During an audience with Antonelli on 26 April 1870 Russell merely said that England shared French fears over the possible negative consequences that might follow the *schema de ecclesia* and would therefore prefer a re-wording of the *schema* in accordance with French wishes. Odo Russell, however, stressed in his report of the audience: 'I desired at the same time to remind him that Her Majesty's Government, full of respect for the liberty of the Church ... in no way pretended to interfere with the Synodical deliberations on spiritual matters.'[45]

Russell resisted pressure from his foreign counterparts, the Prussian minister Arnim for example, to present a written letter of support for the second Daru note to Antonelli. In Paris Clarendon successfully concealed the true extent of Britain's support for the note.[46] Gladstone wanted to support the Daru note in written form, whereas Clarendon did not: the matter was submitted to the cabinet for consideration and Clarendon's view was upheld. Clarendon's victory over Gladstone regarding the policy of intervention was later used by Manning to lend credence to the story that he himself had prevented any English intervention by bringing his influence to bear on Russell. On 28 April 1870 Clarendon defended his position in a private letter to Gladstone:

It must be remembered that although we undertook to support the French note we gave no promise as to the mode of doing so. ... Six months ago M. de Banneville as Doyen of the Corps diplomatique took upon himself to exclude Odo from the opening ceremony of the Council as an unaccredited Person, a nobody, and one devoid of diplomatic attributes. As such therefore I think he might decline the French Ambassador.[47]

In other words Odo Russell could now avenge himself on the French ambassador Banneville, for having excluded him from the opening ceremony, an exclusion which infuriated Russell.[48]

Ireland was the most important, but not the only consideration determining Clarendon's policy towards the Vatican council. The authority of the pope was, as stated above, to be strengthened by a definition of papal infallibility which included political decisions of the pope: this would serve Britain's interests in Ireland. With regard to the other countries, particularly in France and Germany, there were strong anti-curial, liberal currents in the catholic church whose reaction to the passing of such a dogma proved counter-productive. It was hoped that a great many of these people would lapse from catholicism. This view becomes apparent in an article printed in the *Spectator* on 16 July 1870, i.e. two days before the decision on papal infallibility was made. The author was most probably Russell's friend, W.C. Cartwright (1826-1915), M.P. for Oxford and a frequent visitor to Rome. The article referred to the impending dogma:

It replaces the vast, formless, mystical entity, the Church, which is like the universe in its aggregate invisibility, by an individual Italian who eats his dinner, and will be watched by a million eyes eager to convict him of an error. The substitution ... will compel them to criticize and consider, and give reasons to themselves for believing in verbal inspiration. ... The masses ... will be more and more tempted to ask for proof that this man, whom they see described by a thousand pens as a man considering, scheming, arguing, perhaps plotting, is indeed the exponent of unerring truth. ... Silently ... the people will retire from its pale ... until some event ... reveals to themselves the depth of their unbelief. The event may be the proclamation of some new dogma by the Pope's own authority, or some demand of extreme inconvenience, or the consecration of some old idea which the world has given up ... Some such blunder, some such patent proof that the oracle can err, is sooner or later certain, for the Pope after this decree is under a temptation to use his new power. ... Now [16 July 1870] he is restrained from blundering by a necessity, more or less felt, of consulting the episcopate; then he will be alone, uncontrolled. ... Whenever such an incident occurs, the Catholic community ... will throw off ... the chain of its ancient creed. This process is going on everywhere in all Catholic countries, except Ireland — where it has been prevented by Protestant social persecution.[49]

Already on 28 June 1869 Clarendon had written to Russell: 'For my own part I hope that the dogmas and doctrines to be pronounced will be to the last degree extravagant.'[49a] The key to Lord Clarendon's strategy is indicated in a report from the north German ambassador in London to Bismarck on 12 January 1870: 'Lord Clarendon, by the way, holds it to be desirable that the Council makes extreme decisions, because he regards the reaction that would follow among the people, the governments and in the Church itself as the best corrective against the evil.'[50] On the basis of this it can be argued that Clarendon wanted as extreme a definition of infallibility as possible, not only to blacken the catholic church in the eyes of the world, but also to split it. Bismarck also seems to have taken up his hint as is suggested by a report by the imperial ambassador in Berlin to Vienna concerning Bismarck: 'If Rome does not give way in any point, which he hopes for and believes most, he anticipated from the difficulties, rifts and splits in the Catholic Church only gains.'[51] The Bavarian minister in Berlin also reported on 25 March 1870 that Prussia was anxious to create a rift in the catholic church and that extreme decisions by the council would therefore serve Prussian interests.[52] In the grand-duchy of Baden there were also plans to further schismatical tendencies within the catholic church.[53]

According to Clarendon's wishes schismatical national churches should be founded in the U.S., Germany and France by those who opposed the extreme definition of infallibility, and these churches, it was anticipated, would soon fall under the sway of the anglican church as later happened the 'Old Catholics'. This objective was not as unrealistic was it may seem. In the spring of 1869 Victor de Buck, the future theological adviser to the general of the Jesuits at the council, had written to Acton concerning Bishop Dupanloup of Orléans: 'Il travaille avec une ardeur infatigable l'épiscopat allemand et francais pour les rendre indulgante envers les orientaux et les anglicans.'[54] On 11 December 1869 he was able to report to Clarendon: 'To judge from the present language of the opposition led by the bishop of Orléans the definition of the dogma would lead to schism.'[55] Gregorovius, who was acquainted with Russell, noted in his diary: 'I was told yesterday that Dupanloup ... is on the verge of separating from the Church and the same is said about Darboy. They will drag a swarm of others with them. They are intriguing with France to bring about the great thing.'[56] On 19 January 1870 Granville wrote to Gladstone: 'I never thought it was an object for Protestantism ... to prevent the council erring by extreme views, which will by reaction probably loosen the hold of Rome on the National Hierarchies.'[57] During the council the anglican bishop of Lincoln, Wordsworth, was in close contact with Archbishop Darboy of Paris (this was the same Wordsworth who established contacts with the 'Old Catholics' after 1870).[58] When Odo Russell wrote 'humanity will gain more in the end by the dogmatic definition of Papal Infallibility than by the contrary',[59] he meant, as Aubert and Cwiekowski have pointed out, that not only would an extreme decision discredit the papacy,[60] but also that it would split the church by driving the anti-infallibilists out of the church, although Russell already realised in February 1870 that a schism was unlikely.[61] On

25 March Gladstone wrote to Döllinger of the ideas of Clarendon, Granville and Russell regarding the catholic church: 'Treating this body as a sort of incarnation of an evil principle, [they] assume that the worse it behaves, the greater will be the reaction and recoil of mankind, which reaction and recoil they treat as so much of accession on the side of good and truth. The whole of this theory, I need not say, I regard as radically false, but it prevails.'[62] Döllinger, however, failed to acknowledge his part in intensifying this reaction against the catholic church through his portrayal of the papacy. He merely believed that he had been proved right and twice wrote to Acton of Gladstone's letter.[63]

Clarendon's most important aide in pursuing his objectives was Russell, who had prepared for the council with his usual thoroughness, informing himself on every detail and problem to be discussed at it. He read all the relevant literature, sought the information of experts in their respective fields and saw to it that he was sufficiently informed on all aspects;[64] and still he was not satisfied with his preparation.[65] Manning's biographer, Shane Leslie, realised that Russell was playing a double game.[66]

On the one hand he befriended Manning and regularly went for walks with him and managed to fool Manning into believing that he was a co-infallibilist by a subtle ridiculing of the anti-infallibilists.[67] In this way Russell was able to obtain the latest information from the council through Manning, who, as the only bishop to be granted access to the private chambers of the pope during the council,[68] was relieved from the oath of secrecy in the council: this allowed him to inform Russell of the proceedings. Manning was also to counteract Acton's influence on Gladstone.

At the same time Russell maintained contact with Manning's adversary Lord Acton and showed sympathy for his fight against the dogmatisation of papal infallibility.[69] In his private correspondence during the sitting of the council, Russell disguised Acton's identity with the pseudonym 'Becdelievre'. This supports the view that they had hoped for a split in the catholic church: Becdelievre was a major in the papal army who had distinguished himself at Castel Fidardo in 1860, but following a dispute with the papal minister of war, de Merode, he left the papal army and all the officers from Savoy followed him.[70] When Clarendon enquired whether Acton had received a bad name in Rome because of his usefulness to the British government, Russell replied on 22 Deember 1869: 'I see a great deal of him, and he is most kind and useful to me.'[71] Archbishop Darboy of Paris observed Russell's technique: 'Il questionne plus qu'il ne répond.'[72]

Manning was leader of the infallibilists at the council: this has been confirmed as a result of Schatz's publication of the diary of Manning's ally, Bishop Senestréy of Regensburg. The great majority (about 80 per cent) of the bishops at the council favoured some definition of papal infallibility but for Manning and his circle to make this the single most important issue facing the council required a determined political will.[73] Senestréy in his diary noted that 'the leader is the Archbishop of Westminster. This father of the council, whom I with justice call a postulator and promoter of the cause, who was appointed by God himself, worked day and night with unbroken spirit and never tiring zeal to bring the cause to a good ending.'[74]

Manning and his party met in the villa Caserta which was the residence of the superior general of the Redemptorists where Bishop Adames of Luxemburg was staying.[75] At the beginning of the council when the members of the 'de fide deputation' responsible for dogmatic questions were selected on 14 December, Manning and his adherents drew up a list of candidates from the different nations including only those who were known to support the definition of infallibility.[76] As Bishop Adames noted in his diary, everything was agreed upon at a meeting of about twenty bishops in the villa Caserta on 6 December 1869: 'At the end it was agreed that within two days everyone was to hand his recommendation of candidates to Dr Manning.'[77] Another list was drafted by Cardinals de Angelis (archbishop of Fermo), Corsi (archbishop of Pisa) and Gonella (archbishop of Viterbo) which corresponded almost exactly to that drafted by Manning and his friends, although it is interesting to note that Bishop Senestréy of Regensburg, while appearing on de Angelis's list, was excluded from Manning's.[78] Having considered the wishes of the Neapolitan bishops a final list was drawn up,[79] lithographed and then circulated among the different national groups with the help of certain sympathetic bishops.[80] As the council had only just started the bishops had not yet had time to form their own opinions on the many bishops from the other countries, so the majority of them tended to elect candidates from Manning's list. This list was circulated in such a way as to give the impression that it had received the approval of the pope.[81] Manning was the chief orchestrator of the whole intrigue, as Archbishop Arrigoni of Lucca noted in his diary; Cardinal de Angelis (1792-1877) had merely allowed his name to be used.[82] Manning and his acolytes had thus hoped to prevent the election of even one opponent of infallibility. One opponent did, however, get elected — the Hungarian primate, Simor — and it was only because Manning and his group had mistaken him for a sympathiser (which he was not) that he got elected to the deputation.[83] Manning's view was a simplistic one: 'Heretics only come to a Council to be heard and then be condemned, not to participate in the formulation of Church teaching.'[85] The consequence of Manning's intrigues was that the minority (i.e. those who opposed the dogmatisation of papal infallibility) became an embittered opposition because of their fear that they were about to be crushed by the sheer strength of numbers of the majority, who had not even accorded them a proper hearing.[86]

The next target for Manning and his friends, among whom were included the bishops of Bombay and Gibraltar,[87] was to ensure that the question of infallibility was at least considered by the council, and for this purpose Manning and his closest ally, Senestréy, drew up a petition.[88] In their characteristically devious manner they attached to their list the names of bishops whom they thought would support a discussion of infallibility at the council without even asking the bishops themselves. Two names had to be dropped because of the opposition of the bishops concerned to the dogmatisation of infallibility.[89] In January 1870 450 of the 700 bishops at the council had signed the petition,[90] and on 6 March a chapter on papal infallibility was added to the *schema*.[91]

Their next objective, now that infallibility had been put on the agenda, was to have it raised up on the agenda so that it would be discussed at an early stage in the council; otherwise it would be many months before the matter was considered.[92] On 10 March 1870 Cardinal Cullen, a member of the 'de postulatis deputation', wrote to his secretary: 'Everything is so slow. I am urging those in power to bring on Infallibility before Easter.'[93] During holy week (10-6 April 1870) the infallibilist group prepared their strategy during meetings with Manning.[94] Yet Cardinal Bilio, chairman of the deputation on faith (*de fide*), prevaricated: he declared at the end on holy week to Senestréy, who wanted to have a discussion on infallibility as early as 18-19 April 1870: 'But Monsignore, this is a definition, binding the faithful to believe something. We may have a schism.'[95] Therefore on 19 April Manning, Senestréy and five other bishops begged the pope himself to have infallibility discussed at the council without delay and on 23 April the pope was given another petition bearing 150 signatures. On 27 April their efforts were rewarded when it was announced that infallibility would receive an early hearing.[96]

Manning and his friends now resolved to secure as extreme a definition of infallibility as possible. On 5 May, however, Cardinal Bilio proposed a very mild formula of infallibility to the deputation of faith.[97] Manning and Senestréy were alone in their opposition to it[98] so once again they resorted to private action. In May 1870 the *Civiltà cattolica* printed emendations of the formula for infallibility and these were drawn up by Manning's theologian at the council, Fr Liberatore, and submitted to the pope by Fr Piccirillo. The pope, who was initially not very well informed, gave his sanction to the venture and promised to talk to the president of the council on their behalf.[99] Also under Manning's influence was Fr Wilmers, SJ (1817-99), who was theologian to the vicar apostolic of Bombay-Puna, Bishop Méurin (the probable author of the words 'ex sese' in the eventual definition.)[100]

Having induced Cullen to attack Cardinals Schwarzenberg and Rauscher in a speech at a general sitting of the council on 19 May,[101]

Manning himself delivered a speech in favour of the dogmatisation of infallibility at a general sitting on 25 May.[102] During his speech Manning supported his argument by recalling that 'all English papers' believed that papal infallibility was a necessary consequence of the teaching of the infallibility of the church. Later he named *The Times,* the *Standard* and the *Pall Mall Gazette.*[103] Bishop Ketteler characterised Manning's method in his notebook:

> He cites the main English papers and takes what in their opinion is a damning accusation, namely that the consequence of all Catholic principles is the absolutism of the pope (in their opinion a shameful tyranny) as a) correct and b) a recognition of the church, and makes of this invention of the enemies of the church a proof that the infallibility of the church must in consequence lead to the infallibility of the pope and that whoever denies the latter also abandons the former.

Finally Ketteler summed up his opinion of Manning: 'Everything subjective; *one* favourite idea, with it stands or falls the whole church. ... No trace of any development.'[104] Dupanloup also noted in his diary that Manning's way of thinking was uncatholic, subjective and dominated by a single fixed idea.[105]

During the council Lord Acton exerted the same influence on the minority that Manning exerted on the majority. The interaction of the two extremes is evidenced by the fact that Acton and the fanatical ultramontane Ward were personally well acquainted. 'This good relationship between Acton and Ward continued in some form as late as 1871.'[106] Acton's concept of infallibility had been shaped by Ward. Relations between Manning and Acton had been so close at one time that in 1855 Acton had intended to appoint Manning as his private chaplain.[107] Since the publication of the *Syllabus* Acton harboured mixed feelings towards the catholic church; he was rather impulsive and in 1867 had this to say about the church state: 'I pray to God that I may live to see the whole fabric destroyed, and the Tiber flow with the blood of the massacred priests.'[108] In September 1869 he wrote to his wife: 'I confess I know of no bishop whose sincerity can be trusted.'[109] Acton was predestined to play a dominant role in the council proceedings for many reasons: his aristocratic ancestry and newly-acquired English peerage enabled him to establish contacts more easily with the European bishops, most of whom were descended from aristocratic families themselves; being a nephew of a cardinal facilitated his access to the Italian bishops and curia;[110] being the son of a Dalberg enhanced his status among German bishops and, with regard to France, he was a personal friend of Bishop Dupanloup, the central figure of French opposition at the council. In 1842-3 he had studied in France under Dupanloup's guidance (the latter was father confessor to Acton's mother). Through Dupanloup Acton became acquainted with the other French minority bishops, and his acquaintance with Bishop Darboy of Paris developed into a friendship during the council. Among the German bishops Acton was personally acquainted with Bishop Ketteler of Mainz and Archbishop Scherr of Munich. Acton's linguistic ability (he spoke German, French and Italian fluently) made it easy for him to contact the other bishops and discuss matters with them. He soon became mentor to the minority and co-ordinator of the different national groups. The minority included most of the German and French and a number of the American bishops. Of the American bishops, Archbishops Kenrick (born in Dublin) of St Louis, Connolly of Halifax, Purcell (born in Kinsale) of Cincinnati and Bishop Fitzgerald (born in County Limerick) of Little Rock were prominent. Acton had established contacts with the American hierarchy during a visit there in 1863. Acton's friend, Richard Simpson, had accompanied Archbishop Connolly to the council and introduced him to Acton in 1869.[111] Kenrick had met Manning in Paris on his way to Rome, and Manning's opinions on infallibility had so shocked him that he wrote some articles. Isaac Hecker, procurator of the bishop of Columbus, acted as mediator between Kenrick and Döllinger. Hecker was introduced to Acton by Simpson who stated that Hecker had 'great influence with the Episcopate of the U.S. and Canada'.[112] Gladstone commented in a letter to Acton: 'Of all the prelates at Rome ... to none is a more crucial test now applied, than to those of the United States. For if ... the propositions of the Syllabus are still to have the countenance of the episcopate, it becomes really a little difficult to maintain in argument the civil rights.'[113]

Seventeen eastern bishops, whose expenses were paid by the pope, nevertheless also signed a petition against the definition of infallibility.[114] The Irish primate Cullen wrote to his secretary on 13 June 1870: 'The Chaldaic bishops have, it is said, received notice [from home] that if they accepted any terms from the Pope, they need not return home.'[115]

Acton was behind the initiative of Archbishop Haynald, a member of the Hungarian house of lords, to found an international committee; the function of this committee was to co-ordinate the different groups in the minority.[116] Acton had great influence on the bishops of the minority, who came to him daily.[117] Russell observed: 'The Opposition could not have been organized without Lord Acton whose marvellous knowledge, honesty of purpose, clearness of mind and powers of organisation have rendered possible what appeared at first impossible. The party he has helped to create is filled with respect for him. On the other hand the Infallibilists think him the Devil.'[118]

Acton also had his contacts among the diplomats in Rome: the Bavarian attaché to the legation was his brother-in-law, Count Arco (1845-91), who furnished Acton with all the necessary information;

Acton also became friends with the Prussian ambassador, Count Arnim,[119] and on several occasions he met the Russian chargé d'affaires, Count Kapniste (1839-1904).[120] Through his cousin, Minghetti (1818-86), Acton had access to government circles in the kingdom of Italy.[121] Du Boys noted in his council diary: 'Acton passait pour l'agent secret de M. Gladstone.'[122]

Acton played a double role: not only was he mentor of the minority but he also acted as Döllinger's informer, passing on Russell's information.[123] He sent long reports on the deliberations of the council to Döllinger, even though these proceedings were held in the strictest secrecy. Döllinger used them for his 'Briefe vom Concil' (Letters from the Council) which were printed anonymously in the *Allgemeine Zeitung* from 17 December 1869 till 29 July 1870.[124]

On 12 May 1869 Clarendon informed the Prussian ambassador in London that the best means of counteracting council decisions 'was in influencing European public opinion through the press'.[125] In March 1870 Bishop Ketteler of Mainz began to suspect who was really behind the 'Letters from the Council'; he wrote of the *Allgemeine Zeitung:* 'It even seems to be connected with certain governments which use it to mislead the world about the true importance of the Council.' Ketteler then actually named Russell 'who is most intimately connected with all the anticatholic land mines that have been set up for such a long time by England and Italy'. Ketteler summed up: 'It is the great action of lies to mislead Germany on the Council.'[126]

In his anonymous reports on the council Döllinger merely regurgitated the same clichés and anti-Italian prejudices which were so readily propagated by the whigs (anti-Italian prejudice was a feature common to both Acton and Döllinger).[127] Döllinger then depicts the antagonism between supporters and opponents as being racial in origin, essentially between Germans and Mediterraneans.[128] Thus he asks: 'Can one make a new dogma just for the Spaniards, Italians and South-Americans? ... It would really be unsafe to show to the peoples of the Germanic race so pointedly the abyss which exists between their religious needs and thoughts and those of the Romance peoples and to make this abyss even wider.'[129] In his attack on the 'infallibilist army' he talks of the 'Romance South-Americans, whose ignorance is generally even greater than that of the Spaniards'.[130] With disparaging irony he writes: 'The more disputed the dogma the more necessary is the impressive consensus of five continents and of negroes, Malays, Chinese, Hottentotts, Italians, and Spaniards.'[131] German theology is praised as if it were the only one worthy of the name. This national chauvinism and pride was upset by the Italian character of the curia and so provided ample justification for the formation of a German national church outside the control of the Roman catholic fold — as proved by the foundation of the 'Old Catholic' church.[132]

Acton was unwilling to accept even a mild form of infallibility; on 28 November 1869 he asked Döllinger to prevent a compromise formula.[133] When Bishop Martin of Paderborn sought the adoption of such a compromise definition, based on the decree of the council of Florence, an article appeared in the *Allgemeine Zeitung* bearing the authority of Döllinger's name in which he asserted, without having consulted the manuscripts, that the decree of Florence had been tampered with and that the council of Florence had not been ecumenical.[134]

The reporting of council proceedings in the *Roman Letters* followed the same pattern of anti-papalism which had already characterised Döllinger's previous journalism. He wrote fifteen letters as manifesto-letters without using Roman sources to any noticeable extent.[135] He composed thirty-eight letters using information received from Acton and, after 10 June 1870, from Count Arco; he reprinted fifteen letters written by Acton without any change in their original form.[136] When reporting to Döllinger Acton could draw on his earlier experience in journalism: from 1859-62 he had edited the *Rambler,* from 1862-4 the *Home and Foreign Review;* from 1866-7 he wrote articles for the *Chronicle* and in 1869 for the *North British Review.* Acton received most of his information through conversations with minority bishops. Sometimes they allowed him to see the speeches they were about to make or had made at the council; the bishops did not suspect that Acton was using this confidential material. He instructed Döllinger to leave out names he had underlined in his reports, to paraphrase certain paragraphs and generally to be cautious not to divulge the sources of his information.[137] Apart from the bishops, his main source of information were the secretaries and theological advisers to the bishops, especially Dupanloup's secretary Lagrange, Friedrich (theological adviser to Cardinal Hohenlohe) and Vorsak (1833-80, canon of San Geronimo in Rome and theological adviser to Bishop Strossmayer of Diakovar in Croatia). Vorsak supplied Acton with all-important secret documents.[138] Acton's motives are described in a letter he wrote to Odo Russell: 'Il faut sacrificier la Papauté pour sauver l'Église.'[139] Acton's aims were three-fold: he wanted to influence public opinion, to bully the majority and to influence the minority bishops for his own ends. With regard to public opinion, Acton succeeded in creating a storm in the world's press and alarm among governments by publishing the text of the 'de ecclesia constitution'. People had already been influenced by the manner in which the letters were published in the *Allgemeine Zeitung;* there was a short précis on the front page in the news section and then the full text in the supplement. The *Letters from the Council* themselves had comment intermingled with reporting so that readers would find it difficult to form a different opinion.[140]

Acton did not, however, succeed in influencing the minority

bishops with his letters (Nos 12, 20, 21, 28, 32-4, 37, 39, 44, 48, 51-4). They were overwhelmed by Döllinger's own copious material which merely served to neutralise Acton's arguments, as the extremist stance taken by Döllinger was distasteful even to anti-infallibilists. The fact that the letters were printed anonymously did not help their cause.[141] The Irish primate Cullen reported to his secretary on the effects of Döllinger's journalism: 'Several bishops ashamed to be found in such bad company are coming over to the great majority; others are repudiating all connexion with Döllinger.'[142]

The oath of secrecy to which all bishops at the council were bound under threat of excommunication allowed Döllinger to control the monopoly for council reporting in the *Allgemeine Zeitung* and this gave him the opportunity to exert pressure on public opinion to prevent the acceptance of infallibility.[143] Döllinger also provided other papers with information on the council:[144] one of these was the *Münchener Neueste Nachrichten,* the leading Munich paper which was a member of that group of papers secretly subsidised by Bismarck; here Döllinger's and Acton's *Letters* were printed in an abbreviated form. This was not a quality paper and the *Letters* were therefore given a demogogic tone.[145] The liberal press in Bavaria embarked on a virtual campaign of anti-catholic agitation. Döllinger also attempted to persuade French papers to reprint the *Letters.*[146] Acton sent several reports to *The Times.*[147] The letter of protest by French bishops against the new standing orders for the council were published by Acton in the Florence paper *Perseveranza.*[148] A false impression was created in the minds of readers through the misrepresentation of the infallibility issue in the *Letters:*[149] the belief that the dogma of infallibility posed a threat to the state had already taken deep roots among liberals in the public.[150] The *Letters,* which were already published in book form in 1870, in German and in an English translation, provided ammunition for the anti-catholic onslaught of the Kulturkampf and the 'No Popery!' fanatics in England and the U.S.[151] Döllinger's misrepresentations must surely account for the general impression of catholicism and the papacy created in the minds of non-catholics right into the twentieth century; this is true with regard to not only journalism but also scholarly books.[152] Clarendon's avowed ambition to 'throw dirt on the Council' had been achieved.[153]

Lord Clarendon also continued his interest in schismatical inclinations within the catholic church; on 18 May 1870 he instructed the English minister in Munich, Sir Francis Howard:[154] 'Pray keep me as well informed as you can of the sayings and doings of Döllinger. We are all ... interested in them as possibly indicating what the policy of liberal Churchmen will be when infallibility is not only defined but acted upon.'[155]

However, the strategy to split the catholic church did not succeed. Russell reported disappointingly on 9 June 1870: 'To confess the honest truth I have failed to find among the Opposition Bishops that faith and courage that makes martyrs, and doubt whether more than a dozen, if so many, would face excommunication.'[156] Clarendon wrote in bitter disappointment of the 'opposition bishops': 'I never thought there would be energy enough in France for schism.'[157]

The bishops of the minority had departed from Rome before the final vote on infallibility. Papal infallibility was defined on 18 July 1870 in a moderate form; it had been drafted on 16 June by Cardinal Cullen[158] and the words 'ex cathedra' and (at the behest of the Spanish bishops) 'non autem ex consensu ecclesiae' were added:

> Romanum Pontificem, cum ex cathedra loquitur, id est, cum omnium Christianorum pastoris ac doctoris munere fungens pro suprema sua Apostolica auctoritate doctrinam de fide vel moribus ab universa Ecclesia tenendam definit, per asistentiam divinam ipsi in beato Petro promissam, ea infallibilitate pollere, qua divinus Redemptor Ecclesiam suam in definienda doctrina de fide vel moribus instructam esse voluit; ideoque eiusmodi Romani Pontificis definitiones ex sese, non autem ex consensu Ecclesiae, irreformabiles esse.
>
> (The Roman Pontiff, when he speaks ex cathedra — that is, when in the exercise of his office as pastor and teacher of all Christians he defines, by virtue of his supreme Apostolic authority, a doctrine of faith or morals to be held by the whole Church — is, by reason of the divine assistence promised to him in blessed Peter, possessed of that infallibility with which the divine Redeemer wished his Church to be endowed in defining doctrines of faith and morals; and consequently that such definitions of the Roman Pontiff are irreformable of their nature and not by reason of the Church's consent.)[159]

Papal infallibilty as defined in this document extended only to *ex cathedra* pronouncements by the pope on matters of faith and morals. Disraeli stressed this in *Lothair,* which was published on 2 May 1870 (i.e. months before the final vote), when in answer to a question on infallibility the following answer is given: '"In matters of faith and morals," said the Cardinal quickly. "There is no other infallibility."'[160]

2. THE AFTERMATH

The bishops of the minority submitted to the council's decision. Only a few catholics actually left the church because of it. In August 1870 nine German bishops met at Fulda and a joint pastoral, drafted by Ketteler, was agreed upon and later received the approval and signature of seventeen bishops. The pope expressed his praise and approval to the signatories and by so doing acknowledged the moderate interpretation of the dogma of papal infallibility contained in this pastoral, thereby distancing himself from Manning.[161]

Attempts by anglicans to make capital out of the situation did not succeed.[162] On 30 August 1870 Lord Acton issued a *Sendschreiben an einen deutschen Bischof des Vaticanischen Concils* (Open letter to a German bishop of the Vatican council),[163] of which Odo Russell was well aware.[164] In the *Sendschreiben* Acton appealed to the bishops of the minority:

> Priests and laymen rejecting the decrees is nothing but the consequence of their example, the echo of their episcopal words. The movement is following the way they have directed them to. They are the originators; they are the natural leaders. On them it will depend if the defence of the old Church organism will halt at barriers of [canon] law and will adhere to the aim of conservation [of unity] or if Catholic science will be forced to a fight which would then be directed against the bearers of Church authority themselves.

In other words he threatened that if the bishops failed to take the lead in the fight against infallibility the 'Old Catholic' movement would also fight against them. Acton also made it clear to the bishops that if they failed to act according to his wishes he would expose them to all the world as being characterless. His *Sendschreiben* culminated in the statement that 'one has to persevere to the end and give the world an example of courage and steadiness which it needed so much'.[165]

However, by persevering (i.e. by refusing to submit to the dogma) the bishops would have incurred the penalty of excommunication from the church. Manning repeatedly expressed his opinion that he regarded the anathematisation of reluctant bishops as the only solution for the church.[166] Early in September 1870, immediately after the Fulda bishops' conference[167] but before the publication of the joint pastoral of the German bishops accepting the dogma of papal infallibility in its mild form, Acton sent a copy of the *Sendschreiben,* together with a copy of the 'Old Catholic' declaration of Nuremberg *(Nürnberger Erklärung)* condemning infallibility, to every German bishop.[168] The Times propagated the *Sendschreiben* and published extensive extracts.[169] When a reader sent in Bishop Ketteler's reply to Acton's *Sendschreiben, The Times* published a defence of Acton's article under the pseudonym 'Vigorniensis'. The author was Malcolm MacColl (1831-1907), theologian and collaborator of Gladstone.[170]

Meanwhile the pope's temporal power had finally come to an end. France and Germany were engaged in a war against each other, and France was consequently forced to withdraw her troops from Rome on 4 August 1870. Odo Russell also left Rome to assume a new posting as British ambassador to Bismarck's new Reich. He was replaced in

Rome by Sir Henry Clarke Jervoise (1839-1920), a man of quite different talents to Odo Russell: where Russell was brilliant, cunning and impressive, Jervoise was faithful, honest and impressionable. In London too there was a change: Clarendon died; but he was succeeded by Granville who continued to pursue the same line as his predecessor.

De Leonardis has evaluated this period in great detail and all relevant documents have been published as British parliamentary papers;[171] it will therefore suffice here to give but a brief summary. On 8 September 1870 Visconti Venosta informed the British ambassador in Florence, Paget, of Italy's intention to occupy Rome. Manning asked his friend Gladstone to offer protection to the pope, but all the liberal government was willing to do was to send the H.M.S. *Defence* to the papal port, Civita Vecchia, in case of danger. Jervoise was sympathetic to the pope but unlike Russell he was a man without influence. In one of the last despatches from papal Rome he presented a moving picture of the final days before the Italian occupation:

A Triduum was ordered at St Peter's, to invoke 'the intercession of the Blessed Virgin for the protection of the Church from oppression, and for the deliverance of Christ's Vicar on earth from sacrilegious attack'. I attended two of these services for the purpose of seeing for myself how this appeal to the prayers of the people was answered, and I was greatly impressed by what I saw. Having witnessed the ceremonies at Easter, when the church is chiefly thronged with a crowd of sightseers, the Procession of the 'Corpus Domini' attended by all the peasantry within the reach of Rome, the Great Feast of the Apostles, St Peter and St Paul, and the crowds that attended the Public Sessions of the Oecumenical Council, I was indeed surprised by the sight of the multitude I found flocking over the Bridge of St Angelo in carriages and cabs as well as on foot — Roman Princes, middle class and artizans (with their families), ecclesiastics and students. The Pope attended each day without ostentation; and I could not but be struck by the devotion of the people there assembled, as their voices with one accord echoed through the building the responses in the Litany of the Saints, 'Ora pro nobis.' There is, it seemed to me, a large mass of people really loyal to their Government. In leaving the church the venerable Pontiff could scarcely make his way through the crowds who rushed forward to embrace his hand.[172]

Five days later Rome was invaded by the kingdom of Italy and the pope's temporal power was brought to an end.[173]

The cessation of temporal power in fact removed a great burden from the church. Pius IX's successor was able to direct his attention to the needs and problems of our time, as shown in *Rerum Novarum* or *Humanum genus*.

While the pope had lost his temporal power the catholic church had retained its unity. Even Lord Acton refrained from joining the 'old catholic' church when it split from the catholic church in 1871. He was disgusted by its leaders and furthermore saw no future for such a community.[174] On 7 February 1871 he reported to Döllinger with obvious displeasure Kenrick's submission to papal infallibility. Acton commented to Döllinger: 'If you were not alive, every Catholic in the world would give in this way.'[175] On 5 September 1871 Acton had to report a further blow — the submission of Archbishop Haynald: 'This means the loss of the total Hungarian Hierarchy.'[176] This hierarchy had been the last to withstand submission. As Acton informed Canon Meyrick (1827-1906), the chief mediator between anglicans and 'old catholics', he had taken on a chaplain who like himself did not accept infallibility and lived as if the dogma had never been defined.[177] The last bishop to persevere in his opposition to papal infallibility was Bishop Strossmayer (1815-1905) of Diakovar in Croatia. In 1875 he made his peace with Pius IX without, however, explicitly submitting. Gladstone corresponded with him on church government as late as 1879, yet in 1881, under Leo XIII, Strossmayer finally submitted to the dogma of papal infallibility.[178] Although anglican committees were formed in England and America to assist 'old catholic' theology students and although there were numerous other anglican endeavours such as those initiated by the second Lambeth conference of 1878, all these came to nothing. The 'old catholic' church remained a small and ineffectual group. Papal infallibility never did, and never has, posed a threat to the unity of the church.[179]

A Survey of Anglo-Papal Relations 1870-1982

J ERVOISE first concern after the Italian occupation of Rome was to protect the interests of British subjects in Rome, especially soldiers of the papal army which was dissolved, and the property of British ecclesiastical institutions, i.e. monasteries and colleges, which were in danger of being expropriated by the new Italian regime. The fact that the Church state had ceased to exist was seized as an opportunity by ultra-protestants to demand Jervoise's withdrawal from Rome. Repeatedly the Gladstone administration had to defend the existence of an agent dealing with the Holy See against the attacks of Mr Newdegate (1816-87) and his friends in Parliament. After Gladstone's defeat in the elections of 1874, the tories took over again, and Stanley, now Lord Derby, again became Foreign Secretary. He recalled Jervoise from Rome. There is evidence that Bismarck, engaged in his fight ('Kulturkampf') against the Catholic church in Germany, induced the conservative government to this measure. On 1 July 1875 even the act of 1848 allowing anglo-papal relations was repealed.

With the return of Gladstone to power in 1880, British contacts with the papacy were resumed. The situation in Ireland with hunger, agrarian crime and the new powerful Land League necessitated this. In January 1881 Leo XIII (pope 1878-1903) wrote to archbishop MacCabe of Dublin sympathizing with the Irish in their plight, but at the same time calling on them to abstain from revolutionary actions. Sir George Errington (1839-1920), a nephew of Archbishop Errington and M.P. from 1874 to 1885 for County Longford as a Home Ruler, was sent to Rome late in 1881 on an unofficial mission by Foreign Secretary Lord Granville. The Chief Irish Secretary W.E. Forster, at whose instigation the Habeas Corpus Act had been suspended for Ireland, sent Lord O'Hagan (till then Irish Lord Chancellor) to Rome in the last days of 1881. Also in December 1881 Gladstone in his turn tried to engage Cardinal Newman as yet another mediator between the government and the papacy. Newman, however, declined and tried to make Gladstone realize that the pope had only limited influence on Irish catholics in political matters. While O'Hagan soon returned home, Errington's missions to Rome lasted until 1885. His ecclesiastical opposite number in his dealings with the Holy See was Cardinal Howard. While Gladstone abandoned Forster's coercion policy in May 1882, Leo XIII issued two letters to the Irish bishops on 1 August 1882 and 1 January 1883 seconding just demands of the Irish people, but at the same time recommending to them quiet, order, and tolerance. Errington was, however, unable to prevent the appointment of Dr Walsh (1841-1921) as Archbishop of Dublin on 3 July 1885.

The new conservative government led by Lord Salisbury again ceased contact with the papacy. Yet, Anglo-French rivalry in the Mediterranean and Africa in the late nineteenth century soon brought them together again. The Archbishop of Malta, Scicluna (1800-88), was in ailing health and in April 1885 received an administrator in the person of Bishop Buhagiar (1846-91), who had been consecrated bishop by Cardinal Lavigerie of Algiers. Cardinal Lavigerie played an important political role for French imperialism, and the British Governor of Malta, Sir J. Linton A. Simmons (1821-1903) was rather alarmed at having a *protegé* of Lavigerie as Archbishop of Malta, especially as there was then a possibility of war with France. The Colonial Office urged the Foreign Office to contact the Holy See to prevent Buhagiar from becoming Scicluna's successor. Cardinal Howard was contacted and promised that the Holy See would not name him successor at the event of Scicluna's death. In March 1887 Howard issued a memorandum asking the British government to reestablish a permanent mission to the Holy See. Leo XIII was eager to end the isolation of the Holy See since 1870 when most states had diplomatic representatives to the Italian government in Rome, but none to the Holy See, while the Holy See would not deal with representatives to the Italian government. At the occasion of Queen Victoria's golden jubilee a papal delegation led by the nuncio in Munich, Mgr Ruffo Scilla, came to London to congratulate her. In return the Duke of Norfolk headed an official British delegation congratulating Pope Leo XIII on his golden episcopal jubilee later that year. The delegation used the opportunity to talk about Ireland and the Maltese bishopric. In 1888 Scicluna died, and Baron Strickland Count della Cantena (1861-1940), an Anglo-Maltese politician, twice came from Malta to Rome to negotiate with Cardinal Secretary of State Rampolla and Pope Leo XIII himself, who finally gave way regarding Buhagiar. Rampolla and Leo XIII both urged the necessity of a British diplomatic mission to the Holy See, which would in future prevent misunderstandings as in the case of Buhagiar. Even a right of veto in episcopal nominations seemed possible in return for the establishment of such a mission. In January 1889 the new archbishop was nominated in accordance with British wishes. In November 1889 Governor Simmons of Malta came to Rome to negotiate with Rome on a number of questions concerning the catholic church of Malta. As regards episcopal nominations the Holy See was willing to inform the British government before someone was nominated and then to nominate only those that were acceptable to the government. This, however, was always to be done in oral negotiations for which a special minister would have to come to Rome. This presence of a British minister was the reason why the Holy See made this concession. In 1890 permanent Anglo-papal diplomatic relations would undoubtedly have been established had it not been for the agitation of the Orange lodges, the Protestant Alliance, and other ultra-Protestants against them.

A point of the agreement between Simmons and the Holy See had been that a law setting down Catholic marriage ceremony and Catholic education of the children of mixed marriages was to be enacted for Malta. As the British government in view of the opposition of the just mentioned protestant pressure groups refrained from doing this, Cardinal Rampolla strongly protested through the nuncio in Paris in 1895 and through the Cardinal Archbishop of Westminster in 1897.[2]

In 1902 a papal delegation led by Mgr Merry del Val, who had already been part of Nuncio Ruffo Scilla's delegation to London in 1887, went to London for the coronation of Edward VII, while a British delegation led by the earl of Denbigh (1859-1939) came to Rome to congratulate Leo XIII on his silver jubilee as pope.

Cardinal Rampolla had a bad name with the British government as a Francophile and at the conclave of 1903 following Leo XIII's death they made the Austrian emperor Franz Joseph charge a cardinal (the Archbishop of Cracow) with issuing the Austrian veto against the election of Rampolla as pope, which he did. Thus St Pius X became pope, who selected as his secretary of state Cardinal Merry del Val. Thus the Francophile Rampolla was succeeded by a man who — although Irish and Spanish by blood — was born in London and had grown up in England and who wrote of himself in 1903 as 'English to all intents and purposes'.

In 1914 the first world war broke out and St Pius X died. His successor Benedict XV (pope 1914-22) was a pupil of the later Cardinal Rampolla. To counteract the influence of the enemy countries Austria-Hungary and Germany the British government again sent an agent to reside in Rome and represent British interests with the Holy See. He had the diplomatic rank of a minister plenipotentiary and was at first only to stay there for the time of the war. As first British minister to the Holy See Sir Henry Howard was nominated. In 1916 Sir John de Salis Count Soglio (1864-1939) became minister. When the war ended the British government decided to continue to have a minister accredited to the Holy See. Since then there has been an uninterrupted succession of British ministers to the Holy See.

In 1972 Hachey published their annual reports up to 1939.[3] It is noteworthy that one of these ministers was Sir Theo Odo Russell, a son of the Odo Russell mentioned above as British agent in Rome from 1858 to 1870. During Sir Theo's term of office (1923-28) King George V and Queen Mary paid Pope Pius XI (pope 1922-39) an official visit. In 1929 the Roman question was settled in the Lateran treaties between Italy and the Holy See, in which Italy recognized the Vatican as an independent sovereign state. Now the Vatican was in a much stronger and securer position regarding diplomatic relations.

One of the most interesting despatches of D'Arcy Godolphin Osborne (1881-1964), Minister to the Holy See from 1936 to 1947, is perhaps his account of his audience on 28 December 1938 with Pius XI. During this audience Pius XI, who had recently criticized the Hitler regime in his encyclical 'Mit brennender Sorge' (With ardent alarm) and had pointed out to the fact that Hitler did not keep treaties, was very outspoken in his criticism of the appeasement policy and the treaty of Munich. Osborne in his private report to Foreign Secretary Lord Halifax regarded Pius XI views as unfortunate.[4] Whose views and policies were in fact unfortunate was proved only too soon by Hitler's further actions and the war which followed.

In autumn 1938 a papal representative took up residence in London, if only an apostolic delegate, i.e. *de jure* a representative to the catholic church in Great Britain, not a diplomat representing the pope to the British government as a nuncio.

During the war papal peace and rescue operations were severely hampered as the Political Warfare Executive, the secret propaganda agency of the British government, thought it necessary to include the Vatican in their psychological warfare. All sorts of lies ('sib') concerning the pope were invented to mislead the Nazi regime, e.g. that Mussolini had asked the Vatican to mediate for a separate peace for Italy and Britain, or that Roosevelt's representative to the pope, Myron C. Taylor, was organising the pope's evacuation from Rome, etc.[5]

In January 1982 full diplomatic relations between Great Britain and the Vatican were at last established. The British minister to the Vatican has become an ambassador, while the apostolic delegate in London became a pro-nuncio. (For his becoming a nuncio it would be necessary for Great Britain to accept the rule set down by the Congress of Vienna in 1815 that a nuncio is automatically doyen of the diplomatic corps.)

DOCUMENTS

Documents

NO. 1

Leist, Counsellor of the Hanoverian Legation,
to Count Münster, Hanoverian Minister, London
Rome, 12 April 1817
N.H.A.H., Hann. 92, XXXIII, I, 15, 1a, ff.90–1

Allem Anscheine nach wird die Hannoversche Gesandtschaft in ihren Verhandlungen glücklicher als manche audere seyn, welches man fast allein dem Englischen Hofe zu verdanken hat, der hier in höchsten Ansehen steht und dessen Einfluß so gross ist, dass man zu sagen pflegt: um in Rom etwas durchzusetzen, sey es nur erforderlich, dass der Prinz Regent sich dafür verwende, da der Papst ihm nichts abschlagen könne.

NO. 2

Lord Burghersh, British Minister at Florence,
to Canning
Florence, (end of August 1823), priv., draft
West. Pps., Cuba, microfilm BM, M 511, section 4, f.27

My Dear Mr Canning,
I send you in my Dispatch of this day's date the little intelligence I am enabled to get from Rome. Mr Parke [the British consul in Rome] who, being placed under me is instructed to keep me informed of what is passing, and who has constantly received my directions to do so is either absent or refractory for I hear nothing of him nor can I get an answer to the Queries as desired in your late Dispatch I have put him upon the shipping regulations in the Papal States. Under these circumstances and a little moved by the curiosity of seeing the Coronation of the new Pope if he should be elected of the Cardinals in Conclave, I have determined to run down for a few days to Rome. ...

NO. 3

Canning to Burghersh
F.O., 15 September 1823
Introduction no. 5
West. Pps., Cuba, BM M 526, sect. 1, pp. 1–5

My Lord,
Although His Majesty feels no other concern in the approaching election of a Pope than that which naturally arises from a wish that the choise may fall on

a person most likely to promote and to preserve Peace, Ecclesiastical as well as Civil, in Catholic Europe; it may not be indifferent to your Government to be informed of events in that election. I have therefore received His Majesty's Commands to direct your Lordship to proceed to Rome; there to reside during the sitting of the Conclave; and to keep me regularly informed of such occurrences as may appear to your Lordship worthy of being brought to the knowledge of His Majesty.

It cannot be necessary to caution your Lordship that, so far from taking any active part, you are not ever to express a lively interest, on the part of your Court, in the success of either of the contending candidates.

It is obvious, however, that the object which I have stated as alone interesting to His Majesty in the Issue of the election, — that of peace, ecclesiastical and civil, throughout Europe, — is likely to be attained, in proportion as the choice is connected with Political Intrigue, or with the political Prepoderancy of any foreign Power; and that this consideration points out the choice of an Italian Cardinal as most desirable. — Among Candidates of that description, the moderate course of counsels which generally distinguished the late Pontiff's Reign, would perhaps be most likely to be maintained by that one, who should be understood to have the support of the Cardinal Consalvi. . . .

N O. 4

Burghersh to Canning
Rome, 2 October 1823
Despatch no. 42, draft
West. Pps., Cuba, BM, M526, sect.1, pp.25–8

. . . The day after the nomination of Cardinal della Somaglia as Secretary of State, as I had long been acquainted with him, having transacted with him at the business I was charged with at the period of the expedition against Naples in 1815 when he was at the Head of the Roman Government I waited upon him to say that I hoped he would allow me to continue the same correspondence with him whenever any circumstance should require it which I had been accustomed to do with his predecessor. His Eminence assured me of his anxious desire to cultivate the same harmony and good will which has so long existed between our respective Governments, and in the most flattering terms disclosed his readiness to communicate with me upon all subjects upon which I should think fit to address him. I stated to him that as I had on all former occasions had the honour of presenting my respects to the late Pope I should be happy, to do the same to his successor, he told me he would take the orders of the Pope upon the subject, and in the evening he announced to me that His Holiness would receive me the following day, I waited upon the Pope in consequence on Tuesday last, and was received by him in great kindness and condescencion, . . . He thanked me for the attention I had shewn in determining to wait upon him and he assured me he had no object more at heart than to maintain the terms of intimate friendship which had so long existed between the British Government and that of Rome, he begged me to recommend the Catholics of England to the protection of the Government and expressed the satisfaction he had felt at the many advantages which of late years had been granted to them.

Appendix

I explained to His Holiness that whatever restrictions existed with regard to the Catholics in Great Britain, they were purely of a political nature, since the existence of their religion was as much under the protection of the law as the established religion of the State. . . . (This last paragraph is crossed out in the draft).

N O. 5

Burghersh to Aberdeen
Rome, 14 April 1829
Despatch no. 16, draft
West. Pps., Cuba, BM, M526, sect.1, pp.295–302
(Part of this despatch was printed by Broderick, *Holy See and Repeal*, p.70)

My Lord,

The day after the election of the Pope I waited upon Cardinal Albani, with whom I had long been acquainted, to congratulate him upon his appointment as Secretary of State, and to express to him my hope that if any occasion should allow me to correspond with him as I had been accustomed to do with his predecessors. I conceived that it was fitting I should at the same time inform him that, as on the occasion of the last Conclave, I had now been instructed by his Majesty's Government to attend at Rome during the one which had just terminated, but merely in the capacity of an observer and for the purpose of reporting the result of the election. I took this opportunity of stating also to His Eminence that as on all former occasions of my being to Rome I had had the honour of paying my respects to the late and preceeding Popes I should be happy to have the honor of doing the same on the present occasion.

I was received by Cardinal Albani with the utmost civility, and with assurance of his anxiety to use his ministry with the view of cultivating and strengthening as far as it was in his power the relations of harmony and amity which for so long a period had existed between the Governments of England and of Rome. He begged me to be sure of the readiness with which he would take every opportunity of being of service to me and whenever any occasion should present itself, he requested that I would communicate with him without reserve and convince myself that his only desire would be to do that which would be agreeable to me. He thanked me for the communication of the purport of the instructions under which I was acting and assured me he would take the Pope's pleasure as to the time he would appoint to receive me.

The day after the coronation I received an intimation from the Cardinal that the Pope would receive me on the following day, I consequently waited upon his Holiness on Tuesday last and was received by him with every mark of urbanity and condescension. His Holiness after making use of expressions of great civility towards myself assured me of the regard and respect he had ever entertained for His Majesty and for the British Government and People, that no person more than himself had admired the great and magnanimous exertions of that great country during the revolutionary war, or the attitude it had maintained since the happy moment of peace. His attention had now been called to the great measure of the admission of the Roman Catholics to the equal enjoyment of civil rights with their Protestant fellow subjects. He stated that nothing would equal the gratitude he felt to the British Government for this mark of their confidence in his fellow Catholics, that his Majesty might rely on their gratitude and their devoted loyalty, that the happiest moment in his life would be when he should know, as he was convinced at no distant period would be the case, that His Majesty felt assured that in his dominions he had no subjects more entirely loyal and devoted to him, than those who professed the Catholic religion. That obedience to their Sovereign was the first duty of true Catholics, that the first authority on earth was that of the Sovereign, that it emanated from the Supreme Being, that even under Pagan Sovereigns the duty of Catholics was obedience, that it was due to a Nero, how much more so then to a Christian King, nay to a Most Christian King, such as the present Sovereign of the British Empire. It was true that there were some points of religious difference between His Majesty and himself, which he regretted, but that these were of no avail in the question he was treating. His Majesty might therefore rely upon it that there was no exertion in his power which he would not make (although he was convinced that none would be necessary) to render the great benefit he was conferring upon the Catholics a blessing to himself and a source of strength to his empire.

His Holiness then spoke to me of the nature of the present measure; he was delighted to find it was not dogged with any of those restrictions [veto and exequatur] which had been thought of on previous occasions some of which during Lord Castlereagh's administration he had been called upon to examine; with regard to the non-assumption of the titles which belonged to the clergy of the Established Church, he believed it was only a continuation of the law as it at present exists and altho' he was yet in ignorance upon the subject yet he was anxious for any measure which would prevent the great and respectable body of the clergy of the established Church from looking with any jealousy or hostility upon their Catholic brethren. Upon other subjects as he was not as yet entirely informed he begged me to state to him whether there was any religious point upon which the Roman Catholic clergy or laity either objected or made representations. I was happy in being able to reply that up to the time I was speaking, after the subject had for a considerable time been under discussion I was not aware of any. His Holiness expressed his utmost satisfaction at this circumstance and after informing me that he had announced his elevation to His Majesty he took leave of me with the expression of the mostfelt pleasure it had given him to have so early an opportunity of expressing to me the feelings of attachment and gratitude with which he was actuated towards his Majesty.

NO. 6

William IV
to Ludwig von Ompteda, Hanoverian Minister at the King's Person
Windsor Castle, 23 March 1833
N.H.A.H., Hann.92XLI 127h, f.2

The King has reason to believe that either Earl Grey or Viscount Palmerston will speak to Baron Ompteda about a Communication to be made through Mr de Kestner to the Papal Government on the Point of the Irish Catholic Clergy. His Majesty therefore is desirous the Baron should express the King's wishes that some *Compliment* or *Present* should be made to Mr de Kestner from the British Government.

William R.

Appendix

Ompteda to Kestner
London, 5 April 1833, in cipher
N.H.A.H., Hann. 92 XLI, 127h, ff.3–6

Monsieur,

C'est par ordre de Sa Majesté que je dois appeler, Monsieur, Votre attention et Vos soins aux circonstances suivantes.

Les troubles malheureux, qui déjá depuis quelque temps ont compromis la sûreté de l'intérieur de l'Irlande, eu exposant la vie et la propriété des fidèles subjets de Sa Majesté dans cette partie de ses vastes Royaumes aux plus grands dangers, n'ont pu échapper à Votre connaissance.

Les griefs réels de ce pays ont occupé depuis longtemps la sollicitude paternelle du Gouvernement Britannique; les reminds, qu'on pense y porter, ne sont pas restés inconnus, surtout depuis qu'ils sont devenus l'objet des soins d'une Législature, qui n'a rien plus à cour, que de rétablir l'ordre de ce pays sur des bases solides et bien faisantes.

Malgré tous ces soins assidus et bienveillants, les désordres insurrectionnels dans certains parties de l'Irlande n'ont pas seulement continué, mais ils ont été porté à un degré inconnu jusqu'alors, et incompatible avec tout gouvernement bien reglé.

Par la maniere dont ces troubles se manifestent, il n'est que trop évident, que leurs veritables causes ne sauraient être attribuées exclusivement à un certain malaise senti en Irlande, mais que c'est l'esprit de parti qui les excite, et que l'agitation insurrectionnelle mise en moment, est fomentée par des individus, qui en profitant de cette disposition des esprits, ont pris à tâche d'en organiser les excès, pour satisfaire leurs vues ambitieuses et révolutionnaires.

L'influence exercée par ces agitateurs politiques sur les esprits égarés d'une partie de la population Irlandaise ne s'est point bornée à des réunions et associations politiques, dont ils se sont servi pour exécuter leurs dessins pernicieux, mais cette agitation dangereuse a penetré jusque dans les scantuaires de la religion, destinée uniquement au service du culte divin. Quelque respectable que soit la majeure partie du Clergé catholique en Irelande, il n'est malheureusement que trop vrai, qu'il s'est trouvé des individus parmi le dit Clergé, qui, en abusant de l'influence spirituelle qu'ils exercent à juste titre sur les individus de leur culte, se sont permis d'employer le service confie à leurs soins dans les églises, pour le mêler en même temps avec des discussions politiques. Au lieu de prêcher le respect pour les préceptes divines, les égards aux authorités legitimement instituées, et l'obéissance aux lois, comme les seuls moyens pour assûrer l'ordre, la tranquillité, et le bonheure d'une nation, ils se sont permis, à ne pas pouvoir en douter, d'inspirer à leurs ouailles un esprit de désobéissance et des principes politiques, qui ne sauraient mener qu'à la dissolution de l'ordre social, à l'anarchie, et, par conséquent, au crime.

Cette conduite est d'autant plus incompréhensible, qu'il est connu de tout le monde, que les mesures, que le Gouvernement Britannique de Sa Majesté se propose d'adopter pour améliorer l'état des choses en Irlande, tendent principalement à améliorer le sort des sujets et du Clergé catholique en Irlande, en fixant l'existence temporelle de l'Église établie dans ce Royaume sur une base moins onéreuse pour la nation, et en mettant par là la portion catholique de la nation en état, de pourvoir avec d'autant plus de facilité aux besoins de leur propre clergé.

Il est évident, Monsieur, qu'aucun Gouvernement ne saurait tolérer des menées tellement subversives de tout ordre social, et ouvertement déstructives de la tranquillité, de la sureté et de la prospérité de la nation elle même. Le Gouvernement Britannique de Sa Majesté préférant cependant même à la rigueur de la loi les voies de la douceur, de la conciliation, et de la persuasion, désirerait employer les moyens les plus propres, pour ramener à leurs devoir de prêtres et de citoyens la partie du Clergé catholique en Irlande, qui, égarée peut-être elle-meme, s'est écartée de sa véritable destination, ou exercant une influence indue et préjudiciable sur des affairs politiques, qui ne sont ni de leur ressort, ni de leur compétance.

C'est à cet effet Sa Majesté le Roi, notre august Maître, Se repose avec une confiance illimitée sur les sentiments de justice, d'équité et de bonne amitié du St. Pére, pour que Sa Sainteté veuille employer tous les moyens, que Sa sagesse Lui suggérera, et que Son influence salutaire sur le Clergé catholique en général Lui administera, pour éclairer le Clergé catholique en Irlande sur ses veritables interêts, et pour lui rappeller ses devoirs, comme serviteurs de Dieu, et comme bons citoyens et sujets. En exercant une influence pareille, Sa Sainteté pourrait Se procurer la douce satisfaction, d'avoir contribué éfficacement et essentiellement au rétablissement de l'ordre et de la tranquillité en Irlande, ébranlés par l'esprit de parti et par toutes sortes d'agitations condamnables et d'être devenu par la même le bien-faiteur d'une partie de la nation Irlandaise, qui, même dans ses égaremens, n'a jamais cessé d'être l'objet des soins infatiguables et de la sollicitude paternelle de Sa Majesté et de Son Gouvernement Britannique.

En Vous exposant les observations contenues dans cette dépêche, Vous sentirez bien, Monsieur, qu'elles ne sauraient faire l'objet d'une communication ou d'une correspondance officielle avec le Gouvernement de Sa Sainteté. Il n'appartiendrait point à un Agent diplomatique Hanovrien de Sa Majesté, de se mêler officiellement d'interets politique, qui, comme tel, doivent lui être étrangers. Ce n'est donc que pour vous faire connaître les sentiments de Sa Majesté et de Son Gouvernement Britannique, que j'ai dû entrer dans les détails ci dessus, expirant que vous saurez en faire l'usage le plus convenable et le plus salutaire, d'apres les vues bienfaisantes de Sa Majesté. Ayant été accrédité depuis longtemps auprès du Gouvernement du St. Pere, Vous saurez le mieux juger, et de la marche à suivre à cet égard.

N O. 8

Kestner to Ompteda
Rome, 23 April 1833, in cipher
N.H.A.H., Hann.92 XLI, 127h, ff.7—8

Monsieur le Baron,

C'était Samedi dernier, 20. du courant, que j'avais l'honneur de recevoir la Dépeche de Votre Excellance du 5.; et après en avoir fini le déchiffrement Dimanche soir, je me suis hâté hier matin de me consulter sur son contenu important avec le Cardinal Bernetti; car cette communication, à laquelle Votre Excellance m'avait sagement autorisé, était la seule voie et la plus éfficace pour m'acquitter des ordres dont Sa Majesté a daigné m'honorer. La conduite séditieuse de quelques Prêtres Irlandais, partisans des agitateurs politiques,

Appendix

étant inconnue au Cardinal, il m'a représenté avec bien des regrets la difficulté de les frapper par quelque mesure, surtout en Angleterre où n'est admis ni Nonce ni Agent de Sa Sainteté, difficulté qui avait été, sous des circonstances semblables, fortement sêntie en Russie et en Prusse; Son Eminence ajouta malgré cela avec décision, que Sa Sainteté avec Son humanité et Sa loyalité ne suivrait jamais l'exemple de ces Papes qui par rancune ou ambition avaient pris le parti des Peuples contre les Souverains, et me permis de faire immédiatement ce Mardi matin un Rapport secret au Pape, et de recommender instamment à Sa Sainteté d'adresser immédiatement des admonitions aux Evêques les plus importants de l'Irlande. A mon observation que notre secret pourrait être compromis par quelque Secretaire, (car il y a bien lieu à se garder en cette affaire de l'indiscrétion et de la malveillance des fanatiques), le Cardinal s'offrit de se charger lui même de la rédaction. Capaccini, le confident sans tâche, doit être consulté: car il n'y a que lui qui connaisse les affaires de l'Angleterre; ainsi, quant à moi, je garantis que le secret ne passera à un cinquième individu. Le Cardinal m'adonne l'honneur de rapporter après demain, pendant qu'il m'a recommandé instamment de prier Votre Excellence de bien vouloir me remettre aussitôt que possible les noms et les résidences des Prêtres en question ainsi que les détails, autant que possible, sur leur conduite répréhensible.

N O. 9

Kestner to Ompteda
Rom, 27 April 1833, in cipher
N.H.A.H., Hann.92, XLI, 127h, ff.9–14

Monsieur le Baron,

...J'ai eu Mercredi mon rendez-vous avec le Cardinal, mais un resultat désiré m'y manquant, ... Ce mercredi le Cardinal me signifia de la part du Pape, que Sa Sainteté n'avait pas besoin de m'assurer combien Elle désapprouvait profondement l'opposition épuisée par le Souverain; mais Elle regrettait de ne pas savoir quelle démarche à faire dans le cas en question, vu que tout ce que S. Mᵉ. notre Auguste Maître désirait qu'Elle fasse fut éffectué dans Son Encyclique du mois d'Aout dernier. Sa Sainteté savait que cette lettre Pontificale était même traduite en langue Anglaise, et elle ne saurait donner meilleur conseil au Gouvernement Britannique que de faire usage de cette émanation du Chef de l'Église pour réduire à l'ordre ces Prêtres. Le Pape me fit observer en même temps, que des Admonitions Papales qui ne seraient pas fondées sur des faits précis et marquants auraient l'effet indubitable de trahir ma communication sècrète. Et Son Eminence ajouta confidentiellement que les dispositions du Pape n'étaient, comme je pouvais bien m'imaginer pas favorables à cette Négociation, comme Sa Sainteté ne pouvait pas encore oublier Son chagrin sensible sur la publication des pièces formant la négociation de Sir George Seymour. Sur celà je fis mon possible pour réclamer l'assistance du Cardinal qui, de son côté, ne garde pas longtemps une rancune, d'adoucir l'esprit de Sa Sainteté; pourtant Votre Excellence daignera Se rappeller que je manque d'autorisation pour combattre éfficacement le soupcon concu de la part du Cabinet Pontifical contre celui de Sa Majesté à cet égard, laquelle m'aiderait beaucoup dans ce moment. Quant à l'Encyclica, je fis rappeler au Cardinal qu'elle avait plusieurs passages atrocement offensans aux Protestans, et que particulièrement le Gouvernement Britannique ne pourrait en aucune manière faire l'usage proposé par le Pape, en considération des attaques injurieuses y contenues, nommément contre la liberté de la presse et même celle de la conscience. Le Cardinal, qui avait oublié ces particularités convenait a cette objection et se chargea de la montrer au Pape. Ensuite je lui fis observer que, si le St. Père voulait accorder les admonitions à des Prélats de marque en Irlande, que je sollicitais, on n'aurait point besoin de compromettre le Gouvernement Britannique; le grand nombre d'étrangers fournirait assez de prétext d'avoir des informations sur l'Irlande. Le Cardinal, d'accord avec mes argumens, me promit d'essayer de nouveau de disposer son Monarque en faveur de mes demandes.

Ce matin, suivant le Rendez-vous qu'il m'avait donné j'ai appris la résolution du Saint-Père: elle n'est pas refusante mais dilatoire. Le Pape me fait répondre, que la circonstance que le Gouvernement Britannique est satisfait de la conduite de la généralité du Clergé Irlandais, lui défend d'adresser des réproches ou bien des admonitions au Clergé en entier; surtout qu'il avait naguères dans Son Encyclica le plus instamment ordonner aux Prêtres de prêcher obéissance aux lois et aux Souverains. S'il y avait des individus qui n'avaient pas obéi à Ses préceptes, il ne pourrait S'en prendre qu'à eux seuls; mais ne sachant, en conscience, où s'adresser pour les trouver n'ayant recu aucune information en défaveur d'aucun Prêtre Irlandais, il devait m'engager de lui faire connaître les coupables et leurs actions blâmables afin de pouvoir les ramener à leur devoir. ...

Je ne pouvais pas disconvenir que la dite Encyclica ... rappelle dans plusieurs passages, nommément page 10, aux Prêtres, que la foi des fidèles enseigne une strict obéissance même aux Souverains infidèles; mais quant à cette objection du Pape, qu'il ne saurait écrire à des inconnus, je répliquai, que si le Pape comme je supposais, croyait au fait, c'est-à-dire qu'il y avait des Prêtres incertains en Irelande, Sa Sainteté pourrait cela me semblait, appeler contre eux l'autorité de ces Préposés qui jouissaient une éstime générale parmi le Clergé de ce Royaume. Pour appuyez cela avec plus d'énergie et d'empressement, je proposai de demander à Sa Sainteté une audience particulière pour moi. Le Cardinal comprit mon désir; mail il répéta que je ne devais point douter de l'empressement qu'il avait mis dans ses réprésentations, et il se déclara convaincu que le Saint Père, insistant sur des argumens si mûrement reflêchis, ne saurait les subordonner à l'estime qu'il me portait. Par cela j'ai abandonné cette idée, en demandant pourtant Son Eminence la faveur de prier le Pape de Se prévaloir du moins de chaque expédition que le Saint Siège adressait peut-être pendant l'époque actuelle à des Ecclésiastiques en Irlande, pour y exciter les Préposés de veiller sur les Prêtres et de les exhorter à appaiser le Peuple; et le Cardinal s'en est chargé. Bien que cette Négociation rencontre des préjugés et le défaut d'une bonne volonté parfaite, j'éspère pourtant de réussir aussitôt que Votre Excellence daignera me communiquer ces détails indiqués à la fin de mons très humble Rapport du 23., et j'en serai plus sur encore s'il y avait moyen adoucir l'aigreur du Pape sur la publication sus mentionnée.

Appendix

NO. 10

Ompteda to Kestner
London, July 1833, in cypher
N.H.A.H., Hann.92, XLI, 127h, ff.15-17

Monsieur,

J'ai eu l'honneur de recevoir en son temps les Depêches, que vous avez bien voulu m'adresse en date du 23 et du 27 Avril dernier, et je n'ai pas manqué de les mettre sous les yeux du Roi, et d'en communiquer avec les Ministres Britanniques de Sa Majesté. Le Roi m'a témoigné Sa grande satisfaction du zèle et de la prudence, avec laquelle vous avez tâché de Vous acquittez des ordres, que j'ai du Vous faire parvenir par rapport aux affaires de l'Irlande, et les Ministres Britanniques m'ont prié de Vous en exprimer toute leur reconnaissance.

L'on ne saurait que regretter vivement, que Vos éfforts n'ont point eu le succès que Sa Majesté en désirait, et auquel on croyait pouvoir s'attendre d'après les sentiments connus du Saint Père et de Son Ministre. Vous avez su Vous convaincre par la Depêche, que j'ai eu l'honneur de Vous adresser en date du 5 Avril qu'il n'était aucunement dans l'intention du Gouvernement Britannique, de persécuter ou de faire punir des individus du Clergé, qui se sont rendus coupables d'une conduite aussi imprudente que repréhensible. Les moyens n'en auraient pas manqué au Gouvernement du Roi, et il ne serait point difficile de nommer les coupables, et de fournir les preuves d'une conduite aussi peu convenables à l'état que ces individus professait qu'elle aurait été réprouvée sans doute par le Chef de l'église catholique. Ce que le Gouvernement Britannique désirait, c'était devoir ramener à leur devoir de prêtres et de bons sujets ceux du Clergé catholique en Irlande, qui s'en étaient manifestement écarté; de leur faire sentir par des admonitions sérieuses et convenables les torts aussi bien que les dangers qui resulteraient immanquablement d'une influence exercé sur l'esprit public, qui ne saurait qu'augmenter l'agitation actuelle excitée parmi une grande partie de la nation Irlandaise; de leur inculquer de nouveau les préceptes de Notre Seigneur, prêchant respect et obeissance aux authorités constituées et aux loix divines et temporelles; enfin de leur inspirer les mêmes principes et les mêmes sentimens qui distinguent si éminemment le caractère de Sa Sainteté, et dont Vous avez fait mention dans Vos Depêches.

Il semble, Monsieur, que les moyens n'auraient pas pu manquer au Gouvernement Pontifical pour inspirer un esprit pareil au Clergé catholique en général en Irlande, en montrant une confiance illimitée bien méritée à cette partie du dit Clergé qui se rendrait dirgne de leur état ecclésiastique, et en ne condamnant que ceux, qui se rendraient coupables d'une conduite opposée et réprouvée par Sa Sainteté Elle même et en se réservant l'animadversion infaillible contre les perturbateurs de l'ordre public.

Elle était proprement l'intention du Gouvernement Britannique, et Vous avez parfaitement bien indiqué à Son Eminence le Cardinal Bernetti, la marche à suivre a cet égard.

Il parait d'ailleurs, qu'une mesure pareille serait tout-à-fait conforme aux interêts de l'église catholique elle-même, ainsi qu'aux interêts du Clergé et du Gouvernement Pontifical. Car, l'experience du dernier temps n'a que trop prouvé, que partout où les mouvements insurrectionnels du peuple ont conduit à des révolutions politiques, le clergé catholique lui-meme en a été une des

Great Britain and the Holy See

prémières victimes. De tentatives pareilles Vous les avez eu sous Vos yeux et l'on ne saurait assez s'applaudir, de ce que les États du Pape ont été hereusement préservé des cultes funestes du mouvement des Libéraux et des Tachés.

Quant à la sensation fâcheuse produite auprès du Gouvernement Pontifical contre le Gouvernement par la publication des pièces formant le négociation de Sir George Seymour, je suis maintenant à même de Vous déclarer de la manière la plus positives, que les soupcons existans à cet égard sont absolument destitués de tout fondement. Les Ministres de Sa Majesté m'y ont authorisé, en donnant le démenti le plus formel à ces inculpations aussi frivoles qu'insidieuses. Les Ministres Anglais sont intimement persuadés, qu'il ne faut que s'en prendre à l'indscrétion, soit imprudent soit intentionelle, de quelque Office subalterne, et peut-être ne serait-il point difficile d'en tracer les sources, et d'en fourni des preuves.

Vous êtes libre, Monsieur, de confirmer Votre language aux déclaration ci-dessus, et il appartiens à Vous de juger, quel sera l'usage que Vous pourrez encore faire du contenu de cette dépêche. Quelqu'en soit le résultat, Sa Majesté ne doutera jamais des bonnes intentions de Sa Sainteté; mais en même temps Sa Majesté est intimement persuadée, qu'en donnant aux Trônes et à l'Église tout l'appui moral, que Son influence spirituelle Lui accorde, Sa Sainteté pourra acquerir la douce conviction d'être devenu un des plus grands bienfaiteurs de l'humanite.

NO. 11

Kestner to Ompteda
Rome, 13 August 1833, in cipher
N.H.A.H., Hann. 92 XLI, 127h, ff.19−25

Monsieur le Baron,

J'ai eu l'honneur de recevoir Jeudi passé la dépêche de Votre Excellence du 19 Juillet et je suis plein de réconnaissance de ce que Votre Excellence a daigné adoucir mes regrets sur le non-succès de mon négociation en me faisant part que notre auguste Maître a gracieusement agréé le zèle que m'anime mes devoirs sacrés appartenant à Son service. C'est à cette génereuse indulgence du Roi et à ma conscience que je fais tout mon possible pour m'en rendre digne que je tiens dans ce moment mon Coeur affligé; car le Cardinal Sécretaire d'État vient de me communiquer un nouveau refus du Pape. Vendredi passé j'ai communiqué au Cardenal le contenu de la Dépêche de Votre Excellence. Son Eminence y regretta les noms des Prêtres coupables et les détails sur leur conduite séditieuse ce que Sa Sainteté avait jugé nécessaire de connaître avant de les frapper comme agitateurs; mais il donna audience à mon objection que la discrétion délicate des Ministres de Sa Majesté cachant les noms des individus au Saint Siège, devait être agréable au chef de l'église et l'engager à être favorable aux désirs de Sa Majesté; ensuite il apprécia parfaitement l'importance de la considération contenue dans la Dépêche de Votre Excellence, que les Prêtres agitateurs ont été presque partout les prémières Victimes des crises révolutionnaires, ainsi que de l'assertion des Ministres de Sa Majesté à l'égard de la publication des pièces formant la négociation de Sir George Seymour; et à l'aide de Considérations semblables le Cardinal espérait avec moi d'inspirer des dispositions plus favorables au Saint Père. Comme Il

186

me promit de vouloir se concilier sur ma négociation avec Monseigneur Capaccini, je l'ai dévancé dans le Cabinet de cet ami et préparé les conseils que devait donner celui-ci. It était pénétré, comme toujours, de bonne volonté, ainsi que remplie d'idées ingénieuses pour disposer le Pape en ma faveur. Le Cardinal m'avait donné Rendez-vous hier pour me communiquer la résolution de Sa Saintété, et je partis en me flattant des meilleurs espérances.

Mais mon espoir m'a trompé: Les instances du Cardinal, appuyées par les considérations valables que nous avions concertées, ont été, me dit-il en confiance, énergiques de même que ses vues de Ministre d'Etat ont été en opposition avec celles du Souverain Prêtre et ont emporté le Cardinal à des expressions même un peu trop vives. Il se plaigna de l'obstination toujours croissante du Saint Père, dont l'esprit et les vues limitées le rendent si peu capable à gouverner dans une époque si grave, et si dangereuse que la présente. Le Pape prétend et soutient qu'il ne saurait faire aucune démarche contre les Prêtres Irlandais sans compromettre le Saint Siège, en fournissant des armes contre eux au Gouvernement de Sa Majesté. Il ne dois pas cacher qu'il y a réellement un obstacle d'un précedent très facheux et nuisible à ma négociation, auquel Sa Saintété se rapporte et qui rend le Saint Père si circonspect et même soupconneux; c'est que le Pape avait accordé à Sa Majesté l'Empereur de Russie un Breve contre des prêtres impliqués dans la Révolution Polonaise et lorsque ces Prêtres, malgré cela, continuaient à fomenter la Révolution, le Gouvernement employait le Breve Papal pour aggraver leur condition, en faisant valoir pour preuve irréfragable de leur perversité le témoignage du Chef de l'Eglise.

Le Saint Père, a dit le Pape, se vit donc à la fois dans le double danger et de rendre pire la cause des prêtres catholiques, et de voir par eux mêmes, c'est-à-dire par leur désobéissance, trahi l'autorité Papale.

A la vérité le Cardinal Bernetti ne croit pas beaucoup à l'influence de l'autorité du Pape en Irlande, je n'ai pas pu éclaircir ce que le Pape lui-même pense là-dessus. Et si l'on me demande, continua le Pape, que je me jette dans une position si embarrassante, je puis exiger de mon Coté, que l'on donne à juger à moi-même si les circonstances sont urgentes en effet jusqu'à m'engager à m'exposer si gravement, ou doit me faire connaître les individus et les faits qu'on leur réproche.

Le Cardinal, sans méconnaître le poids de ces objections, croyant avec moi que le Pape aurait moyen d'émettre des admonitions telles que le Roi, notre Maître, les désire sans compromettre si gravement le Saint Siège, prononca un chagrin semblable au mien sur ce qu'il devait me réfuser au nom du Pape une chose qu'il aurait, dit-il, certainement accordée se trouvant à sa place.

En voyant si bien disposé le Cardinal, je l'ai persuadé à repeter le lendemain, c'est-à-dire aujourd'hui, mes instances les plus empressées à Sa Sainteté; à quoi j'ai saisi l'opportunité, que le Cardinal devait réclamer du Pape un extrait de la Dépêche de Votre Excellence que je lui avais remis et qui resta hier dans les mains du Saint Père. J'engageais le Cardinal de combattre à cette occasion nommément l'analogie de la Pologne appliquée par Sa Saintété au cas present. Le Breve addressé a ces Prêtres en Pologne avait été remis par le Pape à l'Envoyé Russe près du Saint Siège. Par une indiscretion commise à Rome ou à Petersbourg cette Pièce est parvenue aux journaux et la publication est surtout ce que deteste le Saint Siège; c'est pourquoi j'ai démontré au Cardinal qu'un semblable n'a pas lieu lorsque le Pape émettra, ainsi que je le lui ai demandé, un breve directement aux Evêques principaux d'Irlande nommement à l'Archévèque de Dublin sans l'entremise de personne. Je n'ai pas manqué de faire aussi rappeller au Pape le mérite de l'Angleterre à la restitution du Siège Papal et de ses Provinces. Je reviens de mon Rendez-vous que le Cardinal m'avait donné ce matin; Son Eminence venait de descendre dans son cabinet après avoir eu une longue audience, et j'ai appris à ma douleur sensible que le Paper a été inflexible. Le Cardinal m'assura, et je suis sure qu'il a dit vrai, d'avoir employé tous ses moyens de persuasion imaginables, jusqu'à se servir pour aide de l'interêt personel, dont le Pape daigne m'honorer: J'avais fait observer au Cardinal qu'heureusement jamais une négociation ne m'avait échoué, et lui avec sa bonhommie a prié le Pape de m'épargner ce chagrin. Sur cela le Saint Père a chargé son ministre de m'expliquer que l'on ne saurait appeler une négociation échouée ce qui n'était qu'une divercité de vues; car il ne me refusait rien, mais il prétendait de l'avoir dejà donné par son Encyclicale. Une très longue discussion a eu lieu, tous les argumens exposés de part et d'autre ont été recommander au Gouvernement de Sa Majesté de faire usage de Son Encyclicale, en répêtant qu'il ne pouvait pas donner des admonitions nouvelles sans savoir si les premières n'avaient pas été respectées.

Je ferme ce tres humble rapport avec la conviction qu'aucune cause ne saurait être mieux recommandée que la présente l'a été dejà par le Cardinal Bernetti et qu'il n'y ait argument à atteindre par mes humbles lumières et celles du Cardinal qui n'ait été dit et redit plusieurs fois, et ces éfforts, manqués derechef, ont confirmé mon opinion, que le Pape me consentira à rien avant de connaître les noms des Prêtres en question et le détail de leur conduite coupable.

N O. 12

Mr Sheil to
the foreign office
No. 11, 18 March 1851
P.R.O., F.O.79/149

I think it may be advisable that Lord Normanby should impress upon the Nuncio Garibaldi that a decision in favour of the Irish Synod would greatly exasperate the English People. It is obviously the interest of the Court of Rome that the public feeling recently created in England should be allayed.

In a conversation with Mr Petre, Cardinal Antonelli expressed his approbation of Lord Clarendon's government of Ireland, when Mr Petre took occasion to observe that Lord Clarendon attached great importance to the Queen's Colleges, and that the majority of Bishops against them was only 13 to 12. "Still, said Cardinal Antonelli, it is a majority." Mr Petre adverted to the interference of the Synod with the rights of Property. Cardinal Antonelli expressed his surprise at any such intervention, and stated that he had not been aware of what he should strongly condemn.

In a subsequent occasion Cardinal Antonelli stated to Mr Petre that the majority of Bishops against the Colleges was larger than Mr Petre had supposed, as it was 14 to 11. ...He however appeared to Mr Petre to be hostile to the Colleges.

It appears to me that before an adverse judgement shall be pronounced, it would be profitable to make some further Prepositions to the Roman

Government. Their chief objection is founded, I am convinced, upon the alleged danger to the Catholic religion, arising from the Professorship of History being filled by a person inimical to the Church. The negotiation in reference to this subject would occupy a considerable time, and thus an advantage would be obtained. In the present state of excitement both in England and Ireland, a decision is not to be desired. I very much doubt whether a reversal of the resolutions of the Synod would not produce in Ireland a religious agitation which would assume a political character and produce exceeding injurious effects.

N O. 13

Lord Cowley, British ambassador in Paris,
to Lord Palmerston
Paris, 17 April 1851, no.101
P.R.O., F.O.27/900

My Lord,
    In consequence of the instructions in your Lordship's despatch No.134 of the 1st instant I took the opportunity of speaking to the Nuncio, Mgr Garibaldi, upon the subject of the decision of the Synod of Thurles upon the question of the Irish Colleges. The Nuncio listened to all I had to say in the way of narrative with much courtesy, but when it appeared to him that I wished to make through him any suggestion to Rome, His Excellency gave me to understand that he knew nothing whatever of the details of the question or as to the views taken of it by the Holy See. In short he left me confirmed in the impression which I mentioned to your Lordship privately in the course of the winter that in consequence of the Publication of conversations which had passed between me and the former Nuncio, Cardinal Fornari, which his Eminence conceived confidential, the means had been lost for the present of those indirect negociations with the Court of Rome upon these questions for which my former connexion with Irish affairs had previously given peculiar facilities.

N O. 14

The prime minister, Lord Derby,
to Sir Henry L. Bulwer, British minister at Florence,
St James's Square, 24 June 1852, private
Arundel Castle, MD 2388

My dear Sir,
    I have this morning received from Lord Naas a large collection of Papers illustrative of the Political Part which the Roman Catholic Clergy are playing in Ireland not only without rebuke from, but with the apparent sanction of their Ecclesiastical Superiors....They will shew the extreme activity of the Clergy in working as an organised body to control the approaching elections, and to direct every effort of an easily excitable People to the attainment of objects subversive of all the rights of Property....Such activity in Political matters would hardly in my mind be consistent, in any circumstances, with the sacred profession of the Clergy...least of all when they are such as invade the

rights of Property, sow dissension between Landlords and Tenants, and even tend to the encouragement of actual crime and violence, and to the palliation of the act of murder itself.

...I do hesitate to say that every Roman Catholic Member who enters the House of Commons with a fixed purpose to injure or destroy that Protestant Establishment (of the Church of Ireland), enters it with a fixed purpose to violate the very condition by which, under the Act of 1829, he obtains the right of sitting there, and every Priest who urges upon him such a course urges him to take a solemn oath with the distinct and avowed intention of violating it....
Now this is a subject well worthy of the attention of the Papal Goverment, in its own interests.

...We are not in a condition to propose a *Concordat* with Rome; but I should be very anxious to know confidentially what Rome would really desire, which she has not, in respect to her religion; and what amount of control she would be willing that we should exercise in return, to secure the loyalty and good conduct, in civil matters of her Priesthood.

N O. 15

Cowley
to the foreign secretary, Lord Malmesbury
Paris, 27 September 1852
P.R.O., F.O.27/937

M. Droyn de Lhuys read me this morning a despatch which he had received from the French Ambassador at Rome, in which Monsieur de Ragneval recounts a conversation which he had with Cardinal Antonelli on the subject of one of the objects of Sir Henry Bulwer's visit to Rome — M. de Ragneval had, in obedience to the instructions he had received, advised that the Pope should take steps for admonishing the Roman Catholics in Ireland to pay greater respect to the law. Cardinal Antonelli has replied that the Papal Government could not take the initiative in this matter...but he promised that if any one of the Roman Catholic bishops in Ireland would address himself to the Pope for instructions how to act, the Pope would with pleasure take the opportunity of inculcating by his spiritual authority a proper obedience on the part of the Irish Roman Catholics to the law of the land.

N O. 16

Bulwer to Malmesbury
Rome, 23 October 1852, confidential, No.69
P.R.O., F.O.79/160 and Arundel Castle, MD 2388

My Lord,
In different conversations I have had since my stay in Rome with Cardinal Antonelli he has more than once expressed to me his very strong disapprobation of the conduct of that portion of the Irish Clergy who have lately been making use of their religious influence for political ends; as well as of all such as have used violent and indecorous language in addressing themselves to the Authorities of the State. This day H. Eminence has authorised me to state thus much to Your Lordship in the most formal manner and with the wish that

his sentiments on this subject be generally known. I should add that he spoke at the time in terms of deep regret at, and severe reprehension, of a letter addressed by Dr MacHale on the 19th September last to the Earl of Derby.

I may observe that the Cardinal on the occasion to which I have alluded said repeatedly that the sentiments he expressed were those of the Church and of H.H. the Pope which entirely accords with everything said by the Pope himself to me in an interview which I had the honor of having with H. Holiness.

N O. 17

Bulwer to Malmesbury
Florence, November 1852, copy of draft (original sent 7 December 1852),
confidential, Arundel Castle, MD 2388
(original P.R.O., F.O.79/161)

My dear Lord.

As I had different conversations with Cardinal Antonelli in which the Tenant Leagues and also the attacks upon the Protestant Church..., I requested Mr Petre to call on Cardinal Antonelli and to ascertain clearly from His Eminence what I may state to Your Lordship as the options of His Holiness' Government with respect to the two questions referred to and Mr Petre informs me that upon this occasion the Cardinal said to him, and observed that he had said to me and had given me full authority to repeat, that He as His Holiness' Secretary of State disapproves in the strongest manner possible of the conduct of a Portion of the Catholic Clergy in Ireland during the late Elections and that His Holiness as well as the Cardinal himself look upon their conduct as detestable. (I quote His Eminence's own words) His Eminence likewise said that he held the same opinions in regard to the conduct of the portion of the Irish Clergy above mentioned in regard to joining the Tenants Rights Legue which he considered to be an attack upon property and civil rights and which could never receive any countenance from the Holy See.

N O. 18

Bulwer to Malmesbury
Florence, 3 November 1852
P.R.O., F.O.79/161

...(Antonelli stated that) although he might consider it a hardship that the Protestant Church representing the minority of the Irish people should be richly provided for whilst the Catholic Church representing the majority of the Irish population depended wholly on voluntary support nevertheless he should condemn the Catholic Clergy of Ireland if they took part in any scheme for altering this state of things as long as it was established by law...finally he repeated to me more than once that as far as the spiritual liberty and condition of the Catholics in Great Britain were concerned he had nothing to wish for except that things should remain as at present. He spoke also on one or two occasions of the Catholic Priests coming from the British Colonies and reporting most favourably of their treatment.

N O. 19

Bulwer to Malmesbury
Florence, 16 November 1852, secret and confidential,
Arundel Castle, MD 2388

My Lord,

I have thought it a duty to state to Your Lordship in my different communications relative to my recent visit to Rome that I met with great civility from Cardinal Antonelli in the different interviews I had with His Eminence and that his language on all those subjects on which we conversed was upon the whole conciliatory and satisfactory; but at the same time I am bound to observe that there is no doubt existing in the Roman Government and especially in that branch of it not under the Cardinal's control I mean the College of the Propaganda which has the special direction of ecclesiastical affairs, the most erroneous ideas concerning the regligious state of Great Britain and by no means a friendly feeling towards the British Government. In fact as nearly all the information which the Roman Government now obtains with respect to Great Britain and its Policy is from interested parties or bigoted individuals it is not astonishing that it is led to the belief that the People of Great Britain are becoming daily more and more reconciled to the Roman Catholic Church and that the British Government is in the greatest degree hostile and tyrannical to its Roman Catholic Subjects. And having said this much with respect to the opinions or feelings of the Roman Government towards Great Britain in particular I may add that if I undertook to paint the color or disposition of its general policy towards all nations at this moment, I should be compelled to say that there now appears at this time dominant at Rome in a more marked manner than at any period for the last century that Priestly ambition, that desire and determination to extend the power of the Church over the State, it matters not whether in Protestant or Catholic countries — which has ever in a greater or lesser degree been the striking characteristic of the Papacy.

N O. 20

Lyons, the British agent in Rome, to Scarlett, the British
minister in Florence
Rome, 23 April 1853, No. 2
P.R.O., F.O.79/164

...I said to the Cardinal that I was instructed to assure His Eminence of the friendly feelings entertained by Her Majesty's Government towards the Holy See, and of their desire that more intimate relations should exist between the two Governments. The Cardinal replied that I must be aware that in the present state of the English Law it was impossible to establish official relations: that friendly relations existed already, and would, he felt confident, continue to exist. He said that the Holy See was not, and did not desire to become, a Political Power; and that in Foreign Countries all its business and all its interests were ecclesiastical, and never had been, and never could be entrusted to lay hands. I answered that Her Majesty's Government...were quite willing to accredit a Minister to Rome without requiring that one should be sent to London in return....I observed to His Eminence that Ministers from Russia and Prussia were received at Rome, although a resident Nuncio was not admitted to either of these Courts...His Eminence did not in direct terms assert that either Russia or Prussia would receive a resident Nuncio, but he did not admit that they would not. I pointed out to His Eminence that the excitement and painful discussions which were the consequences of the appointment of Roman Catholic Bishops in England rendered the repeal of the Eglinton Clause [prohibiting the pope from having an ecclesiastic as his representative in London] now impossible....I begged His Eminence to consider maturely whether some practical means could not be devised for the establishment of those avowed and regular relations, the absence of which was so much to be regretted. The Cardinal said that the question had been already more than once most fully considered and discussed, — that similar overtures had been made by the Earl of Minto, by Sir William Temple when the Pope was in the Kingdom of Naples, and lately by Sir Henry Bulwer, as well as on several occasions by Mr Petre; ...that if our Law prevented our receiving an Ecclesiastic, the nature and Constitution of the Holy See rendered it impossible for the Pope to send a Layman; — that His Holiness might with equal reason declare that He would receive no Minister from England except a Catholic Bishop; and finally that a due regard for the dignity and independence of the Holy See precluded any approach to the establishment of Diplomatic Relations, except upon perfectly equal terms....I cannot recall any expression which seemed intended to lead me to think that he was desirous that a British Mission should be established at Rome: on the contrary he appeared to me rather to wish to leave the impression on my mind that he was indifferent on the subject.

The conversation on this matter being concluded, I said to the Cardinal that we were aware that rumours unfavourable to the Government and People of England were frequently spread at Rome, and that many of these originated with the Roman Catholic Clergy of Ireland. I begged His Eminence not lightly to credit such rumours, and engaged if he would do me the honour to refer to me on such occasions to furnish him with information the correctness of which would be guaranteed by the British Government. The Cardinal took occasion from this to speak at some length of the Irish Roman Catholic Clergy. He said ... that he was far from approving the language and conduct of some of the Irish Priests at the last Elections, but that he understood great licence was allowed by our laws during Elections ... he must suppose that so long as their conduct did not expose them to prosecution it was consistent with their legal rights ... I said ... that most unfavourable impressions had been made by the turbulence and violent language and conduct of a portion of the Irish Roman Catholic Clergy, that such conduct was peculiarly shocking in Ministers of Religion, and had been very injurious to the Religion itself which they professed ... Mr Petre afterwards introduced me at the Quirinal to Mons. Berardi, the Under Secretary of State, upon whom I endeavoured particularly to impress the importance of not attaching credit to the numerous unfounded assertions respecting England often current at Rome. I begged him to refer to me on such matters.

N O. 21

Lyons to Scarlett
Rome, 27 August 1853, No. 54
P.R.O., F.O.79/168

...I hear that Archbishop Cullen is likely to visit this place in the course of next October. [*Ad limina* visit] ... Archbishop Cullen appears to be highly esteemed here; his learning is much thought of; and his strong ultramontane and exclusive religious views are in themselves a strong recommendation to him, especially with the reigning Pope. The Archbishop is represented here as strongly disapproving the turbulent and factious conduct of many of the Irish Roman Catholic Clergy, and, although extremely uncompromising on religious points, still, is conscientiously desirous to promote loyalty and tranquility, and to confine his Clergy, as much as possible, to the peaceful discharge of their Ecclesiastical Duties.

N O. 22

Lyons to Scarlett
Rome, 15 October 1853, No. 70
P.R.O., F.O.79/169

...A few days ago Cardinal Antonelli, without my having in any way led to the subject, said to me that he had seen a Charge lately made by Dr Cullen to the Irish Roman Catholic Clergy, which appeared to him to be very ably and judiciously drawn up, and to be entirely in conformity with the sentiments which he himself expressed to Sir Henry Bulwer. — ...The Cardinal went on to say that Dr Cullen from his long residence here, was probably better acquainted with the principles and sentiments of the Holy See, and less influenced by local feelings than the generality of the Irish Roman Catholic Bishops. His Eminence appeared to entertain much the same opinion of the Prelate in question, as that which I had heard in other Quarters here, and to which I referred in ... No. 54 ... on 27 Aug.

N O. 23

Lyons to Scarlett
Rome, 28 January 1854, No. 5
P.R.O., F.O.43/58

...Cardinal Antonelli spoke (as he had done on more than one previous occasion) in praise of the tact and moderation of Dr Cullen. His Eminence deplored the violent language of many of the Roman Catholic Clergy in Ireland and instanced especially Dr MacHale: he said that he thought the Roman Catholic Church in that Country would derive considerable advantage from the influence of a Prelate like Dr Cullen, who, having resided so much at Rome, was free from Irish local passions and prejudice, and was imbued with a really Catholic spirit.

At the conclusion of the conversation, I observed in reply to a remark from the Cardinal, that I could not answer for the effects of a surprise, such as that which had been so unfortunately made by the erection of the Hierarchy in

1850: but that I had very little apprehension, either respecting friendly relations between Great Britain and Rome, or respecting the interests of Her Majesty's Roman Catholic Subjects in all parts of the world, provided precise and timely communications respecting its wishes and intentions were made by the Papal Court to Her Majesty's Government.

N O. 24

Lyons to Bulwer
Rome, 25 October 1854, No. 67
P.R.O., F.O.43/58

...The number [of bishops assembled to confer on the doctrine of the immaculate conception] being so large, it is not likely that much attention can be given by the Pope to the spiritual affairs of any particular Country or Diocese. As regards Ireland, I think that such advice as is given, will, in the main, be probably in accordance with the sentiments elicited by you from Cardinal Antonelli, when you visited Rome two years ago. The Irish Clergy will very likely be recommended to avoid violent language; to abstain from too active an interference in politics; to attend more exclusively to religious duties. These counsels will however be probably couched in general terms, and not very scrupulously followed if they are unacceptable to those who receive them. If I am correctly informed, Dr Cullen's own opinion is in accordance with such counsels, but I doubt whether he would recommend the See of Rome to take any public measures for enforcing attention to them. By Dr MacHale and his adherents, they will be presented as proceeding from an imperfect acquaintance, on the part of the Court of Rome, with the state of Ireland; and an argument which has always great weight here, will no doubt be brought forward. It will be urged that an active interference in political matters, and the use of strong language respecting them, are necessary to preserve the influence of the Irish Roman Catholic Clergy over the People: and it will perhaps be insinuated that the attachment and submission to the Holy See, both of Clergy and People, might be weakened by an attempt to interfere authoritatively with such conduct and language.

It is to be apprehended that strong encouragement will be given to the endeavours to set up a Roman Catholic University in Dublin. The recommendation to attempt to found such an establishment came from Rome, — the Pope has always expressed the greatest interest in it. ... I have constantly borne in mind the instruction given to me, by order of the Earl of Clarendon, in Mr Scarlett's Confidential Despatch No. 22 of the 1st October 1853 (to recommend Dr Grant).

...to me Cardinal Antonelli has more than once volunteered to express his astonishment at much of the language of Dr MacHale and the more violent Irish Roman Catholic Clergy [*vide* Lyons to Scarlett, No. 70 of 1853, 2 & 5 of 1854]. His Eminence has, on the other hand, several times spoken to me with approbation of Dr Cullen.

Great Britain and the Holy See

Lyons to Bulwer
Rome, 10 November 1854, No. 73
P.R.O., F.O.43/58

Sir,

I have observed in the Irish Article of the *Times* of the 1st instant (which reached Rome the day before yesterday) a report of a speech made by Mr Lucas, M.P. for Meath, and Editor of the *Tablet* Newspaper, at a Tenant Right Meeting held at Callan on the 29th ultimo. Mr Lucas is reported to have spoken as follows: 'I am sorry to say that Father Mathew Keefe of this Parish has been forbidden by Ecclesiastical Authority henceforward to take any part whatever in the Political Affairs of this Country ... We intend as soon as possible to bring the question before the Holy See, and to solicit its ultimate Decision, as to whether the Clergy, the honest Clergy, of this Country, are to be silenced, and their mouths closed forever. .... Before a month is over, some of us will cross the Channel and will find ourselves, with the Blessing of God, beneath the Shadows of the Vatican.' Considering that Dr Cullen, Dr MacHale, and other Irish Roman Catholic Bishops, are now at Rome, I thought, after some reflection, that it was desirable to lose no time in speaking to Cardinal Antonelli on the matter. I accordingly waited upon His Eminence this morning, and acquainted him with the substance of Mr Lucas' Speech. I said that I had received no instructions on the subject, and did not know that I was likely to receive any; that I had merely read the report of the Speech in a Newspaper, but that it had struck me as involving considerations of so much importance, that I was anxious to call his attention to it without delay. The Cardinal replied that he hardly thought that the matter would be brought before the Holy See by laymen in the manner proposed; — that if the Priest felt himself aggrieved, he might canonically appeal from the Bishop to the Metropolitan, and from the Metropolitan to the Holy See.

I said that I did not know that the particular case of the individual priest was of any importance in itself; and I added that the efforts of Mr Lucas and his adherents would be directed towards obtaining, if possible, a general decision of the Holy See that Priests in Ireland should not be restrained by their immediate Ecclesiastical Superiors from taking part in Politics.

The Cardinal said that it was not the custom of the Holy See to give any decisions whatever, on a mere application from private individuals; — that if it was consulted by the Bishops of any Country it was its duty to give them its advice; — that as to its emitting a decision declaring that it approved of the Clergy taking part in politics, that was absolutely impossible. "The Holy See," the Cardinal continued, "abstains entirely from interfering in political matters. We no doubt regret very much of the language and conduct of many Irish Clergy; we have not hesitated to express in general terms our disapprobation of such proceedings, and our desire that the Clergy should devote themselves to their spiritual duties. And this is all we can do. We have neither the means nor the right, to interfere with the conduct of the Clergy, as Citizens. Our Principle is to preach obedience to the existing Government and laws in all countries: but it appears that the law in Ireland permits the strong language and proceedings adopted by some of the Clergy in Ireland." I said that our laws certainly permitted the free expression of political opinions, but that many of the Irish Roman Catholic Clergy had done themselves and the

Church to which they belonged, the greatest injury, by the manner in which they abused this liberty. I added that it seemed to me to be particularly the interest of the Roman Catholic Church to restrain this violent interference in Politics, on account of the scandalous disputes to which it not unfrequently led among the Clergy themselves.

The Cardinal replied that these disputes were certainly very deplorable; and he went on to say that if a Deputation, such as Mr Lucas announced, really came to Rome, it was probable they would receive no answer at all. As to the Holy See giving a decision in favour of the Irish Priests engaging in Political Agitation, that, he repeated, was absolutely impossible.

I had not made any allusion to the Irish Roman Catholic Bishops now here, but the Cardinal said he had seen Dr Cullen and Dr MacHale. He told me that he had had great satisfaction in expressing to Dr Cullen approbation of the moderation and tact with which the conduct in Ireland of that Prelate had been marked. His Eminence said he had (though somewhat indirectly) spoken in favour of moderation to Dr MacHale, and had dwelt, in conversation with him, on the Blessing of the present tranquility in Ireland, and on the advantages of the conciliatory course adopted by Dr Cullen. His Eminence added that the Holy See would always counsel the Irish Clergy to be obedient to the Law, to be mild and decorous in their behaviour on all occasions, and to avoid engaging in political agitation, but that he had stated to you (when you were at Rome) it could only give these counsels vaguely; it had no power to enforce attention to them in special cases.

I proceeded to say to the Cardinal that I had been anxious to speak to him at once, on reading Mr Lucas' speech, because it had struck me that if such a Deputation as was announced came to Rome, it would produce a crisis, concerning not only the relations between the Courts of Great Britain and of Rome, but also the position of the Roman Catholic Body in the United Kingdom. I spoke to His Eminence of the difficulty which Her Majesty's Government had, during the last Session of Parliament in resisting legislative measures directed against Roman Catholics. I referred to proceedings which have taken place in England during the recess ... I pointed out the deplorable effect it could not but have, if the Holy See furnished arms to its own enemies, and those of the Roman Catholics, by appearing to approve and encourage agitation and disaffection in Ireland. I reminded His Eminence that the Roman Catholics in the United Kingdom were very inferior in number to the Protestants, and still more inferior to them in wealth and influence. I said that the only possibility of really effecting anything in favour of the Roman Catholics, was to endeavour to allay excitement, and to second the efforts of the numerous sincere and zealous Members of the Roman Catholic Church, who were labouring to ameliorate the Ecclesiastical and Civil condition of their Coreligionists by prudent and justifiable means ... I pointed out how fatal it would be to the interests of the Roman Catholics in the United Kingdom, if the Holy See should appear to take part with the Demagogues against the moderate and practical Party. I said that if a Deputation of the violent Party came to Rome, as was announced, the greatest caution would be requisite; for that the imagination of Irishmen was very lively, and a Word from the mouth of the Pope, which might proceed only from the habitual graciousness and kindness of His Holiness to all who approach Him, might be caught up and magnified into a Declaration of approval and sympathy.

The Cardinal thanked me very cordially for having spoken on the matter to him; ... he added that if I examined the entire conduct of the Holy See regarding Ireland, I should see that it had always most carefully abstained from taking any part in political Questions.

NO. 26

Lyons to Bulwer
Rome, 11 January 1855, No. 4
P.R.O., F.O.43/60

Sir,

I understand that Mr Lucas ... was admitted the day before yesterday to an Audience of the Pope. His Holiness is in the habit of receiving almost all persons who apply for an Audience; ... On the 5th instant the Cardinal [Antonelli] told me that he had not had any communication with Mr Lucas himself, but that he had sounded the Irish Bishops who are here about him and had found that in general they did not seem to have a very high opinion of him. ... Referring apparently to what I had said [Document no. 25 above] ... the Cardinal said that he had put the Pope on his guard.

The last time I saw Cardinal Antonelli (which was the day before yesterday) he observed that the question of restraining the Irish Priests from violent interference in Politics was a very delicate matter for the Holy See, and one which required to be treated with great caution. His Eminence expressed the same sentiments on the question which he has so often manifested, but it is unnecessary that I should again report them in detail. Indeed I could add nothing to the very clear statement of them contained in your Despatch to the Earl of Clarendon No. 54 of the 6th November last.

I believe that it is likely that in consequence of Mr Lucas' visit the whole question will be anew seriously examined and discussed at Propaganda. ... The views taken of the question by Roman Catholics appear to be two. The Party represented by Mr Lucas desire that every facility should be afforded to the Irish Priests to engage in political agitation, and that the authority of their Bishops to restrain them, should actually be limited by the See of Rome. The more moderate Party would wish that, while each Parish Priest should exercise discreetly his natural influence in his own Parish, the Clergy should be discouraged from travelling about to attend public meetings in all Parts of the Country, from making violent speeches, and writing violently in the Newspapers. Neither Party, I imagine, would willingly consent that the Parish Priest should be prohibited from taking part in politics in his own Parish; and both alike urge, that considering the subjects that came before the House of Commons, it cannot be said that the Elections are political matters, indifferent to the Roman Catholic Church.

I have been told that a Canon was enacted by a Synod held at Drogheda, prohibiting the Clergy from interfering in political matters in any Parish without the consent of the Parish Priest; and that the practical question before the Propaganda is, whether this Canon shall be sanctioned by the See of Rome, and consequently be published and acted upon. I have heard that it is against the sanction of this canon that Mr Lucas' exertions at Rome are chiefly directed ... The predominant influence at Rome in Irish matters is that of Dr Cullen, who does not support Mr Lucas' views. I have been informed also that sentiments expressed by Mr Lucas have made an unfavourable impression upon Mons. Barnabò (prefect of Propaganda Fide).

I am aware that nothing would more weaken the effect in Ireland of any measure adopted by the Pope on the subject than the supposition that it had been procured by the influence of Her Majesty's Government, and that nothing would be more likely to prevent the adoption of such a measure at Rome than the idea that the Pope would be considered to have acted under that influence. I have consequently thought it peculiarly necessary to avoid all appearance of extraordinary curiosity or activity respecting the matter. ...

N O. 27

Lyons to the marquis of Normanby
Rome, 16 June 1855, No. 35
P.R.O., F.O.43/60

...I have been unable to procure any definite information on the issue of the struggle respecting the interference of the Irish Priests in Politics, which these Representatives of the two Parties (Cullen and Lucas) in the Roman Catholic Church of Ireland, are supposed to have been carrying on with each other at Rome since December last. ... I believe that both Parties are disposed to include Elections of M.P.s, and of Guardians of the Poor among the objects on which the influence of the Clergy may be legitimately brought to bear. I understand that the efforts of Mr Lucas and of some of the Irish Bishops have been directed against the power conferred by the Pope on Dr Cullen personally as Apostolical Delegate in Ireland. The views of Dr Cullen are in themselves in accordance with those of the Court of Rome. He is much esteemed and has considerable influence here. He was in a very unusual manner made an Archbishop of Ireland by the Pope although not presented as a Candidate by the Irish Clergy, and he is consequently likely to be supported by His Holiness. I am however unable to say how far he may have been himself influenced by the clamour raised by Mr Lucas' Party.

Having accidently met Dr Cullen at dinner at Prince Doria's in December, I was introduced to him, and had a short conversation with him. He attributed a great part of the evils of Ireland to the influence of bad and low Newspapers. ... He laid great stress on the evils resulting from the violence of the Press in Ireland.

N O. 28

Odo Russell to Lord John Russell
Rome, 7 July 1860, copy, private,
P.R.O., F.O.918/10, pp. 73–4

...Lord Lyons limited his acquaintances to a very few houses of the aristocracy, but I have endeavoured to know interesting people in all classes of Society so as to be better informed on all things connected with Rome and I also know many influential Priests and Dignitaries of the Church who are not generally accessible to foreigners.

I have endeavoured to know as many English and Irish Priests as possible so as to conciliate them and learn what they want and what they complain of and I must say that everybody I know is so kind and good to me that I have every reason to feel grateful for the good will I meet with everywhere. ...

N O. 29

Odo Russell to Lord John Russell
Rome, 16 September 1859, draft, private
P.R.O., F.O.918/10, p.29 (crossed out)

...The more I see with my own eyes what this Papacy really is, the more grateful do I feel to those men (and to those events) who freed England from her unwholesome influence....

N O. 30

Odo Russell to his mother
Rome, 6 November 1859, copy, private
P.R.O., F.O.918/85, f.229

...Nine Pins [Pius the Ninth] eats his dinner, scratches his belly, thinks himself a Martyr whom posterity will canonize and sleeps every night in peace and security after worshipping the immaculate goddess he invented.

N O. 31

Odo Russell to his mother
Rome, Christmas 1860, copy, private
P.R.O., F.O.918/85, f.279

...I have just been with Atty [Arthur Russell, M.P., his brother] to St. Peter's to see the great Mumbo Jumbo Nine Pins carried about in State. ...

The Roman Catholic Church, once freed from the millstone of Temporality round her neck and able to turn all her attention once more and exclusively to her spiritual interests, would be regenerated to an extend no one can realise at present. A clever Pope, who will care more for the Spiritual than the temporal interests of the Church, will then find a great and a noble task to undertake and the Roman Church will gain in Strength and influence.

N O. 32

Odo Russell to his mother
Rome, 15 December 1860, copy, private
P.R.O., F.O.918/85, f.278

...Gladstone's good opinion is also a treasure. If God gives me life and health it will not be any fault of mine that I shall fail in making some sort of decent career and my name, please God, shall never be a blot in the annals of the House of Russell.

Appendix

NO. 33

Odo Russell to his mother
Rome, 20 April 1861, copy, private
P.R.O., F.O.918/85, ff.284—5

...You tell me in that letter [of 11 April] an interesting fact, namely, that the Laird of "Put Luckhausen" [Lord Palmerston] as you call it, wishes Nine Pins [Pius IX] "wo der Pfeffer wächst" [at the bottom of the Sea] and you ask whether I have influenced his feelings. I have not, my policy is always conciliation. ...

The misfortune of the Church, as far as the temporalities go, is simply this, that despotic and irresponsible power has been assumed by a Fool and by a Knave. The former being 'der Kegelkönig [nine pins king, Piux IX], the latter 'der Excellenz Toni' (Cardinal Antonelli)

The Pope has a good name in hand ... let him turn to his Spiritual Power which no one can upset and make the most of that, since he has lost his temporal independence.

NO. 34

Odo Russell to Earl Russell
Rome, 1 February 1864, No.13, confidential
received 24 February
P.R.O., F.O.43/91A

My Lord,

A Priest of High Standing, who does not wish to be named, tells me that he has reason to know that an extensive conspiracy against British Rule is being organized all over Ireland by Irish Agents sent from the U.S. who bring money and promise Arms to the People. He assures me that the Papal Government have strictly forbidden the Irish Clergy to take any part whatever in this conspiracy and have ordered them to warn against it in the Confessional. My informant could or would not give me any further details, but he seems most anxious to make the fact known to Her Majesty's Government.

NO. 35

Odo Russell to Earl Russell
Rome, 28 February 1865, private, draft
P.R.O., F.O.918/10, pp.139—46

...Your private letter of the 20th inst. respecting the Succession of Cardinal Wiseman by Messenger Ridgeway reached me on Sunday afternoon 26th inst. ... Early this morning I called at the Vatican and found His Eminence at home. I told Cardinal Antonelli that I wished to speak openly and frankly to him about the Succession to Cardinal Wiseman. ... I had reason to think that the Chapter had already sent three names to Rome. ... Of these three ... the third Dr Ullathorne was a very injudicious man capable of putting forward claims which would rouse resistance and indignation in every part of England. What I knew Her Majesty's Government most desired would be that Dr Grant should extend his spiritual influence over London and Westminster retaining Southwark as his peculiar district. ...

Of Dr Ullathorne he [Antonelli] pretended to know very little; and of Dr Manning whose name had been incidentally mentioned he spoke favourably as a man of learning and eloquence, but added that he would not be suited for a Post like that held by Cardinal Wiseman. He ... added that now Cardinal Wiseman was dead he must tell me in confidence that the Pope had been misled by the Cardinal's assurances that the Hierarchy would pass quietly and unobserved in England and would raise no opposition; had they known the result they would have followed another course. ...

N O. 36

Odo Russell to Earl Russell
Rome, 5 May 1865, private, draft
P.R.O., F.O.918/10, pp.155-8

...Some days ago I informed you that the Roman Catholic Chapter of Westminster had recommended Drs Errington, Grant, and Clifford. ... When the Pope heard what they had done he waxed with wrath and said it was an insult to him to recommend a Bishop he had censured and suspended and that he would make the chapter feel his displeasure by appointing a Bishop of his own choice and not one of the three they had recommended. A correspondence then ensued between Westminster and the Vatican. Dr Clifford wrote a private letter and the chapter signed an explanatory address to His Holiness. Indeed I am assured on excellent authority though not by Cardinal Antonelli that the Pope relented and offered the Bishopric of Westminster under certain conditions both to Dr Grant and to Dr Clifford which they had not been able to accept. This however requires confirmation. Since then His Holiness has been very irritable and the cardinals of Propaganda have not dared to touch upon the subject at all. Cardinal Antonelli now tells me that the Pope shut himself up and prayed to God to inspire him and that the result had been a strong inclination to appoint Monsignor Manning which he concluded to be an inspiration from Heaven.

N O. 37

Odo Russell to Clarendon
Rome, 6 April 1866, No. 30, Most Secret
P.R.O., F.O.43/96A, ff.132-6

...With reference to Your Lordship's telegram of the 16th February last, respecting the Fenian Stephens, supposed to be travelling in company with an American named Harris, — I have the honour to inform your Lordship that Cardinal Antonelli shewed me this morning a Police report in answer to the enquiries I had requested His Eminence on the subject, according to which an American called '*Harris*' and supposed to be a Fenian Agent had arrived in Rome from Naples on the 22nd of February, had taken rooms at No. 9 Via di Capo le Case and had been closely watched ever since. — The report ended by stating that nothing important had hitherto been discovered. I took this opportunity of thanking Cardinal Antonelli, — and of expressing regret that the Roman Catholic Clergy in Ireland had not during the last twenty years opposed the secret societies and revolutionary organisation of part of their

Flock, which has at last culminated in Fenianism, the complete dissolution of all the ties by which society is held together, including the Roman Church and her Priests, who unhappily had been the active Apostles of disaffection and had taught the people that all the misfortunes they had brought upon themselves by their own idle Celtic habits were attributable to the government. — Bad harvests, emigration, the exercise of their rights by Landlords etc. etc. . . . I said, had all been laid at the government door and the people had been brought to believe that every earthly good would be enjoyed by them if they could shake off the yoke of England. — The people now thought they could do it, but not intending to do things by halves they meant also to get rid of those who had preached disaffection to them, and in the end the Roman Catholic Clergy now shared the Dangers which threatened the very Government they had so long opposed.

Cardinal Antonelli said he could not quite admit the accuracy of my views, — which he thought were extreme. The Irish Clergy had not in reality been the Apostles of disaffection towards the English Government, — far from it, although they had many just causes of complaint, of which, no doubt, they had spoken with that freedom which the British Government allots to all her subjects. — The Established Church and the question of Education were real grievances in Ireland, which could not be supported by Protestant Englishmen as he had often had occasion to observe in conversation with the most distinguished Englishmen of all classes who visited Rome. — He had talked the matter over with Mr Layard last November and he felt sure that the removal of those and other grievances would above all benefit the English Government.

As to the Irish Clergy not opposing the Secret Societies etc. etc. in Ireland, he begged to refer me to the Pope's last Encyclical against Freemasonry in which His Holiness condemned once and for all every kind of secret society and revolutionary organisation, as his Predecessors had done before him, and obedience was one of the first principles the Roman Clergy had to observe. . . .

NO. 38

Odo Russell to Clarendon
Rome, 4 May 1866, No. 38, secret
P.R.O., F.O.43/96A, ff.166—8

. . . I called this morning on the Cardinal Secretary of State and told His Eminence that I had received reliable information according to which the Priests in many places in Ireland had joined the Fenian movement and were known to receive the confessions of Fenians and to sympathise generally with them.

Cardinal Antonelli appeared much annoyed and said my report was difficult to believe after the clearly expressed condemnation of the movement by the Pope, — . . . if I would name individuals or localities he would at once see what could be done to remedy the evil . . . I replied that I felt sure that he could obtain a full information of what I said from the Irish College or the Irish Priests in Rome . . . I should greatly prefer it if he would himself inquire into a matter which interested the Papal Government quite as much as it did Her Majesty's Government since the Pope's authority had been utterly disregarded by the very Priests whose mission it was to uphold it. — . . . If

Your Lordship will furnish me with a List of the Priests who have joined the Fenian Movement I will endeavour to get them called to order by the Pope.

NO. 39

Odo Russell to Clarendon
Rome, 15 May 1866, No.45, secret
P.R.O., F.O.43/96A, ff.188–9

... His Eminence then went on to say that ... after repeating our conversation to the Pope, His Holiness had confirmed my statements by private letters which had just reached him from Ireland. The Evil, however, was limited to one or two cases only of disobedience and the Pope had already caused the erring Priests to be reminded of their duties.

NO. 40

Odo Russell to Clarendon
Rome, 23 May 1866, private
Oxford University Library, Cl.Pps., C.98, f.134

Dear Lord Clarendon,

Thanks for your letter of the 7th. I was most careful not to mention or allude in any way to Dr Russell, the President of the Maynooth College, but Cardinal Antonelli having spoken of the Death of Dr. Dickinson, [*sic*! Dixon] I asked whom the Pope had appointed in his place? — Cardinal Antonelli then told me that the Pope had no particular favourite in this case and would proceed legally, that is, he would wait until the chapter had recommended three candidates to Propaganda and would then select and appoint one of the three ... I said no more and changed the conversation so as not to let him think I had any further interest in the matter, and shall now abide my time. — But, meanwhile, I questioned my Irish friends at the Propaganda, who told me the Pope would appoint whoever was most recommended by Dr. Cullen, — probably Dr. Kieran, Vicar General and Capitular.

Perhaps Lord Wodehouse could let you know who Dr. Cullen is most likely to recommend to His Holiness? — I could then, if necessary, bring various indirect influences to bear on the Pope without appearing myself in the matter at all, according to your instructions, — for I have many strings to my Bow at present in Rome.

NO. 41

Odo Russell to Foreign Secretary Lord Stanley
Rome, 7 January 1868, No. 4
P.R.O., F.O.43/101, f.89

Cardinal Antonelli told me this morning that about forty Fenians had been discovered among the Irish Catholics who had come to enlist in the Papal Army ... the Pontifical Authorities ... had sent them back to Ireland ... His Eminence also informed me that he had ordered the Propaganda to reprimand an Irish Bishop (MacHale?), whose name he did not tell me, for having encouraged Fenian demonstrations in his Diocese.

N O. 42

Stanley to Odo Russell
London, 16 January 1868, telegram, received 17 January, in cypher
P.R.O., F.O.43/191, f.7

A person named Herbert Glasston giving his address Poste Restante Rome has offered information about Fenian plots. He says that he can pass for an Italian, and so mix with Americans without suspicion. He is poor. Endeavour to find him out and ascertain what reliance can be placed on his professions, and whether he is worth spending money on. You might give him a little if you can get any good information out of him.

N O. 43

Stanley to Odo Russell
London 17 January, 1868, telegram, received 17 January, in cypher
P.R.O., F.O.43/101, f.12

Obtain if possible from Antonelli names of Fenians sent home and particulars as to further destination. Also of any known in Rome. McAuliffe who wrote to Mr Levern [offering information] is known and can, if he will, give useful information. He should not be neglected but urged to give it at once. If returning someone would be sent to meet him at Paris.

N O. 44

Odo Russell to Stanley
Rome, 21 January 1868, No.13
P.R.O., F.O. 43/101, ff.116–8

I have not yet been able to obtain any information respecting Herbert Glasston ... Macauliffe, who wrote to H.M.'s consul Mr Levern, has been sent away by the Roman Police and is supposed to have gone to Florence. I have advised Mr Levern to apply to Mons. Raudi, the Governor of Rome, to obtain all the information he can about Fenians, and I have made a similar application to Cardinal Antonelli. With respect to the 40 Fenians (sent back) Cardinal Antonelli told me that they were from Glasgow and had pretended to be Scotchmen [sic], but that they had proved to be Irishmen and so unruly and unmanageable that they had to be sent back to Glasgow. ... His Eminence promised to give me a List of their names.

N O. 45

Odo Russell to Arthur Russell
Rome, 28 January 1867
F.O. 918/84, pp.64f — Copy

Dear Atty,

...Acton is a man of great natural parts and extraordinary learning. The only knowledge in which he appears to me deficient, is the knowledge of humanity. While studing in Books he has not had time to study men. Filled with youthful enthusiasm for Virtue and Science, he vents his disappointment in humanity in cynism, which he fancies supplies the place of Experience of Life he is wanting in. Although he has from early education and a strongly developed 'sentiment religieuse' clung to the outward form of Catholicism, — he is no longer a Roman Catholic, — but he persuades himself that he is, just as he persuades himself that a Belief in the historical development of Dogmas, is a belief in the Dogmas themselves, and tantamount to the faith prescribed and required by the Roman Church. Like many other Reformers he fancies that while reforming himself he is reforming the Church. As long as he acts privately and in the dark the illusion will last, — but if like those, 'die thöricht g'nug ihr volles Herz nicht wahrten' he acts openly and publicly, he will be ejected by the Church and discover he was preaching Schism and not Reform as he fondly imagined . . .

N O. 46

Odo Russell to Arthur Russell
Rome, 12 March 1867
F.O. 918/84, pp.72f — Copy

Dear Atty,
... Acton complained in bitter words of me to Cartwright. [William Cornwallis Cartwright (1826–1915), M.P. for Oxford, a friend of Odo Russell's very often in Rome]. He said my views were so narrow and my tendencies so shortsighted that he must give me up. To my surprize Acton told me he could not conceive a man like me discussing, admitting the possibility of the continuance of Temporal Power. It was unworthy of me to admit such a contingency when the duty of every honest man was to upset it as soon and as completely as possible!!!

Astonished at his language I once more explained to him that if Antonelli withdrew and that a sensible Se[cre]t[ary] of State sought, collected, secured, assured himself of all the real and great sympathies which exist in foreign Gov[ernmen]ts for the Pope's Temporal Sovereignty he might *easily* obtain material guaranties from Fance and other Powers for the continuance of the present state of things, — and that the establishment of the Capital of Italy at Rome would, in my opinion, meet with decided resistance on the part of the active portion of the Faithful which was not to be despised — etc. etc.

Acton replied in a long and eloquent condemnation of, the Papal Gov[ernmen]t and ended with these remarkable words, which made Cartwright bound in his chair and Mrs Craven who was present fold her hands in prayer to supplicate him to stop.

'I pray to God that I may live to see the whole of this Fabric destroyed and the Tiber flow with the blood of the massacred Priests.'

On our all exclaiming, he repeated these words in a solemn voice and with great stress.

On my asking for explanations he said in a very long conversation, that the Church could not be reformed and become what it ought and what he wants it to be, unless it be destroyed and rebuilt. He wants the liberty of the Press to destroy the Inquisition, and control the morals of the Priests etc. etc. *en un mot*, he wants to tear from the Church all the useless Scandal that has been plastered on it since the 13th–14th Centuries, — and deprive the Pope of his infallibility, which is a heresy, and of the Power of making Saints and Dogmas which he declares to be sinful etc.

I said: 'You forget that the Roman Church is a human institution and that without Angels you cannot, with the human material before you, reform the Church as you desire etc., etc., etc.

Acton said I had fallen into the Cant of Diplomacy and that I forgot Divine interests for mere human patchwork, — my views were those of an ordinary man of the world.

I cannot report this long and exciting conversation, I have not time, — but after a sleepless night Cartwright came to me early this morning to say he agreed with me and thought I took a practical statesmenlike view, while Acton was falling into wild dreams and Fools Paradises.

This extraordinary state of mind of Acton is to me *wonderfully interesting!* In the heat of conversation he told me he had four Cardinals who agreed with him and many Monsignors!!!

Cet homme finira mal!!!

Thanks for your valuable letters. I write in hideous haste, — I must have at Acton soon again in presence of Cartwright, — c'est par trop amusant . . .

N O. 47

Odo Russell to Arthur Russell
Rome, 16 March 1867
F.O.918/84, p. 74 — Copy

Dear Atty,
. . .if Acton's plan of depriving it [the Roman Church] of its Ceremonies, its Dogmas, its infallibility, its Inquisition, its index etc. etc. were carried out, the Roman Church, *in my opinion*, would be destroyed and would become a Protestant Sect. This opinion of Mine Acton calls 'Narrow diplomatic Views'.

N O. 48

Odo Russell to Arthur Russell
Rome, Palm Sunday (14 April) 1867
F.O.918/84, p. 75 — Copy

Dear Atty,
. . .Acton is tout bonnement a Philosopher, who like the Snail cannot live out of the House he was born in and therefore carries the Church on his back, into which he creeps and draws in his horns when alarmed. Honestly and sincerely unable to stand alone, he wants to make the Roman Church fit into, and subservient to his Philosophy, and he forgets that the Church is as closely attached to her own development in History, which she carries, on her back, as he, the Philosopher, is attached to the Church which he carries on his back, like the Snail and its Shell . . .

NO. 49

Odo Russell to Arthur Russell
Rome, 6 June 1867
F.O.918/84, p. 79 — Copy

Dear Atty,

...Sorely pressed by me Sir John [Acton] confessed to me that he would rather *retract*, than run the risk of being on the Index. Why? said I. 'Because my usefulness would cease if I were condemned by the Church!!'...

NO. 50

Odo Russell to Arthur Russell
Rome, 27 June 1867
F.O.918/84, p.81 — Copy

Dear Atty,

...The Dogma of personal infallibility of the Pope in matters of religion put forward by the *Civiltà Cattolica* [(Liberatore), Un nuovo tributa a S. Pietro, in CivCatt ser. VI, vol. 10 (1.6.1867) 641–651;] is irritating the Roman Clergy very much, whilst the foreign Priests are in favour of it. The Believers in it are to form a 'Legion' and take their vow on the day of St. Peter in presence of his statue we are informed by the *Osservatore* of last night. Manning is preparing an address to the Pope to be signed by the bishops ... [*vide* p. 130 above].

NO. 51

Odo Russell to Foreign Secretary Lord Clarendon
Rome, 27 January 1869
F.O.918/4, pp.33ff, priv. — Draft No. 4
Last paragraph printed in Blakiston, Roman Question *p. 358 No. 396)*

My dear Father,

...You may however feel certain that no influence whatever can alter or modify the policy to the Vatican in regard to the Irish Church, but that of Archbishop Manning, or Cardinal Cullen. — Whatever they say or recommend, will be believed and adopted by the Pope and his gov[ernmen]t and backed by the Propaganda.

Only yesterday Cardinal Antonelli said to me that he was charmed with Dr. Manning's views and opinions and that if you would consult him when he has returned to London, you would learn from him what were the measures the Papal Gov[ernmen]t would be willing to support at the Archbishop's suggestion.

In the afternoon I took a walk in the Pincio with Dr Manning and found him personally and politically devoted to Mr Gladstone of whom he spoke with the *warmest* affection. He also said twice that he was 'sincerely glad' you had replaced Lord Stanley at the F.O. ...

Appendix

NO. 52

Odo Russell to Clarendon
Rome, 24 February 1869
F.O.918/84, pp. 55ff, priv. — Draft No.6

My dear Father,

I wonder whether the 'gentle hint' you desired me to convey in soft language to Antonelli, Manning and Co. has been the cause of the marked modification in Card. Cullen's language at the Lord Mayor's dinner on the 8th of February as compared with his letter to the National Association at Dublin a month before?

That speech is called a concession to Mr Gladstone by the Irish in Rome and has given great satisfaction. — Antonelli of course never read it, but Dr Manning having approved, he is quite satisfied. —

Dr Manning leaves Rome on Monday next and travels by Genoa, Nice and Paris to London. — (No. 8 York Place.)

I told him all Antonelli had said and told Antonelli I had done so and they have also talked it over together so Dr Manning desired me to tell you that he would be at your orders when you wanted him —, — but he would not indiscreetly trouble you unless you sent for him. —

He has again and again assured me that he agreed entirely with Mr Gladstone and I think you will find him all you wish in spiritual questions and by no means indifferent to the 'suaviter in modo' in temporal matters. — You will like him . . .

NO. 53

Odo Russell to Clarendon
Rome, 21 April 1869
F.O.918/4, pp. 125f, priv. — Draft No. 14

My dear Father,

I gave Cardinal Antonelli your message about Archbishop Leahy's pastoral, which he received with unbounded satisfaction and desired me to offer you his compliments and best wishes as well as to 'La Sua Signora'. It appears to me that you have reason to be satisfied with the influence you established at the Vatican during your visits to Rome.

After your first message to Antonelli, — Cardinal Cullen changed his tone and language, called on Lord Spencer [Irish Viceroy] and made that very satisfactory speech at the Lord Mayor's dinner at Dublin and after your second message to Antonelli Archbishop Leahy published that very satisfactory Pastoral for which I have just been thanking His Eminence.

Facts certainly now prove that your messages are attended to at the Vatican with a promptitude that would rouse the envy of the four Catholic Powers if it were known . . .

NO. 54

Odo Russell to Clarendon
Rome, 14 July 1869
F.O.918/4, p. 153, priv. — Draft No. 17

My dear Father,

...Cardinal Antonelli sends you his compliments and desires me to thank you for your message and to say that H.M. Gov[ernmen]t may count on the cordial support of the Irish Clergy in the maintenance of peace and moral order in doing justice to Ireland, that he has unbounded confidence in Archbishop Manning ... and that whatever the Archbishop tells you in London is sure to meet with the entire approbation of the Pope in Rome, — ...

NO. 55

Clarendon to Odo Russell
The Grove, 13 December 1869, priv.,
Cl.Pps. C.475(4) ff263–5

...I wrote some time ago to Spencer for accurate details respecting the conduct of the Roman Catholic Clergy but I have not yet received them and can only therefore tell you en gros that we are much dissatisfied with them and that we wish you to consider in what way authority can be brought to bear on them as the opportunity should not be lost while all the Irish Bishops are in a cap together at Rome ...

We wish you to put yourself in communication with Bishop Moriarty [of Kerry] as he is the only one of them on whom reliance can be placed. Acton could manage bringing you together. He must naturally wish that his Brethren should be brought to act in the same way as himself and if asked in entire confidence he might suggest the sort of advice or orders that should be given to them and by whom. We think Manning would be useless for such a purpose or perhaps hostile as he will be guided by Cardinal Cullen, and these two together will probably neutralise all attempts to put a check on the Clergy. The attempt however is worth making and if you were to succeed great would be your glory. So pray make it your special business. ...

NO. 56

Odo Russell to Clarendon
Rome, 7 January 1870
F.O.918/4, p. 195f, priv. — Draft No. 24

My dear Father,

I have been as active as possible in urging the practical measures against Fenianism, — I have called on those I know, and on the Irish Dominicans from Dublin and have told them all I had said to Card[inal] Antonelli and to Card[inal] Antonelli I have recounted all I said to the Irish priests ... To my great satisfaction Bishop Moriarty confided to me today that he and his Brother Bishops had met in consequence and had determined to appeal to the Pope for greater Powers than they have hitherto enjoyed to condemn Fenianism in his name ...

Appendix

N O. 57

Clarendon to Odo Russell
F.O. 8 January 1870
F.O.918/2, pp. 196f, priv. — Original

My dear Odo,
...Fenianism is the natural result of forty years of rebellious teaching of the
Clergy ... it is true that an episcopal letter is occasionally launched ... [but] it
is never followed up by any act of vigour, and is generally regarded as without
serious meaning — the R.C. Clergyman, do what he like, can always reckon
on impunity ...

N O. 58

Irish Viceroy Lord Spencer to Clarendon
Vice Regal Lodge, Dublin, 21 December 1869
F.O.918/2, pp. 201–6 — Copy (enclosed in No. 57)

My dear Lord Clarendon,
Since we have been in office many R.C. Clergy have given support to the
Gov[ernmen]t against Fenianism and agrarian outrage — Foremost among
these have been Cardinal Cullen and Archbishop Leahy of Cashel. They both
issued strong pastorals against Fenianism and agrarian crime. Other Bishops
have acted in the same spirit, Bishop Moriarty among them.
There have been however some very strong speeches and letters written by
Priests which have indirectly encouraged crime and sedition, though they have
not actually transgressed the law. I am happy to say that in the last week two
of those who made themselves conspicuous have been suspended — Father
Ryan ... and Father Mooney ...

N O. 59

Odo Russell to Clarendon
Rome, 21 January 1870
F.O.918/4, p. 200, priv. — Draft No. 25

My dear Father,
...Some progress has been made towards Pontifical intervention in Ireland
and now that I am in possession of L[or]d Spencer's Memo, I hope to do more.
The Bishops and Irish monks I spoke to fully admitted that they were at
present powerless to do good without Papal Support and that is why I
appealed to H[is] H[oliness Pius IX] as you will see when the message gets
home, before I had received your Letter of the 10th ...

N O. 60

Odo Russell to Clarendon
Rome, 20 February 1870
F.O. 918/4, pp 246ff, priv. — Draft No. 32

My dear Father,
...Theologians and Diplomatists in Rome agree that the Pope has done his

211

best [the pope had condemned the Fenians] and cannot do more for the present ...

The American Bishops are angry at the Decree because they prefer the Fenians to the Britishers, but the Irish Bishops generally with the exception of MacHale are well disposed and ready to write vigorous Pastorals ... Cardinal Cullen and Bishops Moriarty and Leahy appear to be the best disposed of any at this moment. I am also well satisfied with Cardinal Antonelli, notwithstanding his attempts to persuade me that Infallibility will be the destruction of Fenianism. I told him that if the Pope succeeded in eradicating Fenianism from Ireland and revolutionary priests, I should perhaps begin to think that there might, under certain conditions, be something in it ... He [Antonelli] promised me solemnly that he would not allow the American Bishops to resist or even tamper with the Pope's Decree. I shall now turn all my energies to pressing upon the Bishops the necessity of eradicating from the minds of the people distrust of the gov[ernment] ...

N O. 61

Odo Russell to Clarendon
Rome, 9 March 1870
F.O.918/4, p. 269, priv. — Draft No. 36

My dear Father,
... the American Bishops are furious at it [the papal decree condemning the Fenians] and want to get it cancelled. I spoke again about it to Card[inal] Antonelli yesterday and he promised not to listen to them. — Card[inal] Cullen is all in favour of its application. McHale is the only Irish Bishop who has spoke against the Decree, but he cannot refuse to publish it ...

N O. 62

Odo Russell to Arthur Russell
Rome, 1 March 1870
F.O.918/84, p. 122 — Copy

Dear Atty,
...Mons[eigneu]r Maret says that the Papacy having shewn its incapacity to govern the Church ... — Schismatizing Germany and half France, rendering the Church ridiculous and dividing East and West for ever ... — the Papacy — 'dis-je' — must be abolished to save the Church! (sic).

Darboy & Co share these views and Blenner[hasset] and Bec[delievre = Acton] enthusiastic at the prospect ...

Blenner[hasset] has been here just now with a message from Bec [Acton] 'The Opposition to throw out the new "regolamento" or protest and go — the Austrian Bishops recalled by Beust to leave middle of March, — 47 French Bishops prepared with 4 Archbishops to refuse obedience to the Pope, *all* the Germans ready if necessary for Schism, — the Council to be broken up and dissolved in a fortnight, without having done anything, — and a special French Ambassador (Baroche?) coming to take the administration of the Church in hand to save "l'Honneur".

'All this from Darboy, Maret, Dupanloup, Stroßmayer, Haynald, — these certain, not to be doubted, evviva! ...'

Appendix

N O. 63

Odo Russell to Arthur Russell
Rome, 1 March 1870
F.O.918/84, p. 131 — Copy

Dear Atty, .
...I read a great deal of All[gemeine] Zeit[ung] now, it is a most useful Paper just now. Bec's [Acton's] letters on the Council have become very sarcastic about the German and French Bishops. He pitches into the Clergy with vigour and truth. In paper of 23rd March he gives it to Ketteler without naming him in strong but deserved blows. ...

N O. 64

Odo Russell to Arthur Russell
Rome, 9 June 1870
F.O.918/84, p. 135 — Copy

Dear Atty,
... The day of what Acton calls '*Scientific Catholicism*' has not yet come for the masses, — it is still the privilege of a select few like Acton, Döllinger and Stroßmayer. I cannot find among the Opposition Bishops men ready to face martyrdom and excommunication for their Faith ...

Notes

INTRODUCTION

1. Sir Theo Odo Russell (his son, who was also British minister to the Holy See, 1923–8), *Contacts*, privately printed 1938, p.61. **2.** Available since 1968 in the P.R.O. as 'Ampthill Papers' F.O.918/84 & 85; Randall, 'Lord Odo Russell and his Roman Friends' in *History Today* 26 (1976), pp.368–9. **3.** N. Miko, 'Die diplomatischen Beziehungen zwischen England und dem heiligen Stuhl im 19. Jahrhundert' in *Zeitschrift für katholische Theologie* 78 (1956), pp.206–25. **4.** N. Blakiston (ed.), *The Roman Question. Extracts from the despatches of Odo Russell from Rome 1858–1870*, London 1962, p.ixl. **5.** *Ibid.* **6.** V. Conzemius (ed.), *Ignaz von Döllinger — Lord Acton, Briefwechsel 1850–1890*, 3 vols, Munich 1963–71. **7.** 2 vols., Rome 1970 (Fonti per la storia d'Italia, II serie, vol.107/8). **8.** Louvain 1971. **9.** *Recusant History* 14 (1978), pp.193–210. **10.** P. O'Donoghue, 'The Holy See and Ireland 1780–1803' in *Archivum Hibernicum* 34 (1977). pp.99–108; J.F. Broderick, *The Holy See and the Irish Movement for the Repeal of the Union with England 1829–1847*, Rome 1951 (Analectica Gregoriana, vol.55). **11.** M. Buschkühl, *Die Irische, Schottische und Römische Frage*, St Ottilien 1980 (Kirchengeschichtliche Quillen und Studien 11). **12.** M. de Leonardis, *L'Inghilterra e la Questione Romana 1859–1870*, Milan 1980 (Scienze storice 28). **13.** G. Albion, *Charles I and the Court of Rome*, London 1935; Mooney, *Relations with the Holy See*, pp.205–6 n.7.

CHAPTER I

1. This interpretation of the Jacobites' defeat in 1746 is already confirmed by Samuel Richardson, *Sir Charles Grandison* (1754 in 7 vols), here used ed. London: Chapman & Hall 1902, vol.III, p.20; L. Borinski, *Der englische Roman des 18. Jahrhunderts*. 2nd ed., Wiesbaden 1978, p.148; J. Curry, *An historical and critical review of the civil wars in Ireland ... with the State of the Irish Catholics*, Dublin 1810, pp.556–7. **2.** M.J. Brenan, *An Ecclesiastical History of Ireland*, New ed., Dublin 1864, p.563. **3.** R. Haynes, *Philosopher King. The Humanist Pope Benedict XIV*, London 1970, p.91. **4.** Benedict XIV Papa, *Bullarium*, Mechliniae 1826, vol.I, pp.127–31. **5.** *Ibid.*, vol.10, pp.197–222. **6.** *Le lettere di Benedetto XIV al cardinale de Tencin. Dai testi originali*, ed. E. Morelli, vol.I: 1740–7, Rome 1955 (Storia e letteratura, vol.55), Nr.260, p.444: Benedict XIV to Tencin, Rome, 19 July 1747. Cardinal York appears very often in this correspondence *vide* the index of this vol. and of vol.II 1748–52, Rome 1965 (Storia e letteratura, vol.101). **7.** *Ibid.*, vol.I, Nr.260, p.463. **8.** Borinski, *Englischer Roman*, p.147 n.21; *Dictionnaire de Théologie catholique*, ed. A. Vacant/E. Mangepot, E. Amarie, vol.15, Paris 1946, p.115. **9.** Haynes, *Philosopher*, pp.219–20. **11.** W. Baum, 'Luigi Maria Torrigiani (1697–1777) Kardinalstaatssekretär Papst Klemens XIII' in *Zeitschrift für katholische Theologie*, 94 (1972), pp.46–78. **12.** C. Giblin, 'The Stuart Nomination of Irish Bishops, 1687–1765', in *Irish Ecclesiastical Record*, 5th ser. 105 (1966) 35–47. **13.** *Lettres à Monsieur Caraccioli*, Paris 1776, p.65. **14.** K. Wöste, *Englands Staats-und Kirchenpolitik in Irland 1795–1869 dargestellt am Beispiel des irischen Nationalseminars Maynooth College*, Bern, Frankfurt, Cirencester 1979, p.42. **15.** Clement XIV. (Ganganelli), *Lettre ed altre opere*, vol.I, Milan 1831 (Biblioteca scelta di opere italiane antiche e moderne 271), p.19: Ganganelli to Mr Stuart; see also *ibid.*, pp. 219, 232; *Storia della vita, azioni, e virtu di Clemente XIV Pontefice ottimo*.

Di nuovo arricchita d'Iscrizioni, ed'altri Monumenti, 2nd ed., Naples 1784, vol.III, pp.266–71. L. Izilas, 'Konklave und Papstwahl Clemens XIV (1769). Vorspiel zur Aufhebung der Gesellschaft Jesu am 21. Juli 1773', *Zeitschrift für katholische Theologie* 96 (1974), pp.287–99; J.J. Sprenger von Eijck, *Ganganelli (paus Clemens XIV) in zijn leven en karakter*, Arnheim 1848, p.130; X. de Ravignan, *Clément XIII et Clément XIV*, Paris 1854; J. Crétineau-Joly, *Papa Clemente XIV. seconda ed ultima lettera al P. Agostino Theiner*, Ital. transl., Modena 1854, pp.29–30. The most objective biography of this pope is that of A. von Reumont, *Papst Clemens XIV. Seine Briefe und seine Zeit*, Berlin 1847. See also Ludwig von Pastor, *Geschichte der Päpste*, vol.16/2, Frieburg i.Br. 1932. **16.** *H.N.Z.*, 18 March 1772: Rome 25 February; A. Theiner, *Geschichte des Pontificats Clemens XIV. nach unedirten Staatsschriften aus dem geheimen Archive des Vaticans*, vol.II, Leipzig & Paris 1853, pp.150–1. On this biography see Pastor, *Geschichte der Päpste*, vol.16/2, pp.438–40. **17.** *H.N.Z.*, no.46, 20 March 1772: Rome 29 Feb.; *Hamburger Relations-Courier*, no.46, 20 March 1772: Rome 28 Feb.; *St.G.Z.*, no.46, 20 March 1772: Rome 28 Feb. **18.** Theiner, *Clemens XIV*, p.152. **19.** *H.N.Z.*, no.50, 27 March 1772: Rome 7 March; no.51, 28 March; *St.G.Z.*, no. 48, 24 March; no.52, 31 March: Rome 10 March. **20.** *St.G.Z.*, no. 55, 4 April: Rome 13 March; no.60, 14 April: Rome 25 March; no.64, 21 April: Rome 30 March; no.66, 24 April: Rome 4 April; no.68, 28 April: Rome 8 April; no.72, 5 May: Rome 4 April; no.78, 15 May; Rome 25 April; Nr.82. 22 May: Rome 2 May. **21.** *H.N.Z.*, no.85, 27 May: London 19 May; *St.G.Z.*, Nr.85, 27 May: London 19 May; no.87, 30 May: London 22 May; no.112, 14 July: Rome 24 June. **22.** J.H. Jesse, *Memoirs of the Pretenders and Their Adherents*, vol.II, London 1845, p.136. **23.** Theiner. *Clemens XIV*, p.153. **24.** Curry, *State of Catholics*, p.560. **25.** *Ibid.*, pp.566–7. **27.** Theiner, *Clemens XIV*, pp.155–6: Cardinal Bernis to the French court, 24 June 1772; Mols, 'Caprara', *D.H.G.E.*, vol.II, Paris 1949, pp.944–5. G. Pignatelli ('Caprara', *D.B.I.*, vol.19, Rome 1976, p.181), on the other hand, regards Caprara's stay in England as 'short holidays'. **28.** *St.G.Z.*, no.153. 23 Sept. 1772. **29.** Arch. Vat., 203 colonia, Dispacci di Mons. Nunzio, Segretario di Stato, Colonia 180 D 284–5; 208 Clemente XIV cifre di M. Caprara Nunzio in Colonia 1772–5, Segr. di Stato, Colonia 185, 22r–29r. The report is printed in Paolo Brezzi, *La diplomazia pontificia*, Milan 1942, pp.245–54. On Caprara see G. Moroni, *Dizionario di erudizione storico ecclesiastica*, vol.IX. Venice 1841, pp.217–8. **30.** Theiner, *Clemens XIV*. pp.167–9. **31.** B. Pacca, *Historische Denkwürdigkeiten über seinen Aufenthalt in Deutschland in den Jahren 1786–1794*, Augsburg 1832, pp.40, 194. **32.** Cf. M.R. O'Connell. *Irish politics and social conflict in the Age of the American Revolution*, Philadelphia 1965. pp.106–7. **33.** 11 & 12 George III, C.XXI in *Irish Statutes* X, 1786, pp.262–3. **34.** Jedin. *Handbuch der Kirchengeschichte*. vol.VI/1, Freiburg i.Br. 1971, p.216. **35.** 'Briefliche Unterhaltungen über Irland und O'Connell' in *H.P.Bl.* 13 (1844), p.570; Wöste, *Kirchenpolitik*. p.28; O'Connell, *Irish Politics*, pp.107–8. **36.** *D.N.B.*, vol.III. p.303. **37.** *Memoirs and Correspondence of Viscount Castlereagh*, vol.III, London 1849, p.400: The anglican bishop of Meath to Castlereagh, Nov. 1800; D'Donoghue. *Holy See*, p.102. **38.** W.J. Fitzpatrick, *Secret Service under Pitt*, London 1892, p.273. **39.** On O'Leary's work for the British government see *ibid.*, pp.211 et seq., 272 et seq. **40.** Brenan. *Ecclesiastical History*, pp.567,575. **41.** O'Donoghue, *Holy See*, p.100: D.D.A., Antonelli to Troy, 26 April 1788.

CHAPTER II

1. O'Donoghue, *Holy See*, pp.100–1: Antonelli to the archbishops of Ireland, 23 June 1791, D.D.A. **2.** *Ibid.*, Antonelli to Troy, 24 Dec. 1791; Antonelli to O'Conor, 24 Dec. 1791, D.D.A. **3.** A. Zimmermann, 'Zur Geschichte Irlands am Ende des vorigen Jahrhunderts' in *H.P.Bl.* 108 (1891), pp.500,406; Plowden, *History of Ireland*, vol.I, p.16; Dickson, *Narrative*, p.31; L. Borinski, *Die Anfänge des britischen Imperialismus*, Göttingen 1980, pp.21–6, 30. **4.** H to W, 24 Aug. 1793, secret, W.Pps. BM Add MS 37848, *f*.92. **5.** O'Connell, *Irish Politics and Social Conflict*, pp.349–51. **6.** Mgr.

Barberi (secetary to Cardinal Zelada) to H, 26 May 1793, copy in P.R.O., F.O.43/12. **7.** F.MSS, N., A.IV.3 (c), pp.2-3. **8.** H to W, 24 Aug. 1793, secret, BM Add MSS 37848, W.Pps., vol.VIII, *f*.86, *f*.69. On Campanelli see *D.B.I.*, vol.XVII, pp.401-3. **9.** *Ibid.* **10.** *Ibid.*, *f*.84. **11.** Prince Augustus to H. Bologna, 17 June 1793, *ibid.*, *f*.107; H. to Prince of Wales, Rome 7 Sept. 1793, F.MSS, N., A.IV.15 (a); Hippisley to Burke, 20 Nov. 1793. *ibid.* A.IV.3 (c), p.3; V.F. Somerset, 'Edmund Burke, England, and the Papacy' in *Dublin Review* 202 (1938), p.145. **12.** H. to Cardinal Zelada, 19 June 1793, copy, BM Add MSS 37848, W.Pps., vol.VIII, *ff*.108-10; Lord Hood to H, 5 Aug. 1793, copy, *ibid.* *ff*.113-4; H to Burke, 18 Sept. 1793, F.MSS, N., A.IV.14 (a), pp.3-4; see also Lord Hood to H, Victory, Toulon, 7 Oct. 1793, extract *ibid.* A.IV.4(a), p.1. **13.** H to W, Gensano, 24 Aug. 1793, secret, BM Add MSS 37848, W.Pps., vol.VIII, *f*.71r. **14.** *Ibid.*, *f*.85. **15.** Wöste, *Kirchenpolitik*, pp.30-3; see William D. Killen, *The Ecclesiastical History of Ireland*, London 1875, vol.II, p.347. H to the prince of Wales, 7 Sept. 1793, copy in H to Burke, 18 Sept. 1793, F.MSS,N.,A.IV.15(a). **16.** Printed in *The Correspondence of Edmund Burke*, vol.VIII. Cambridge/Chicago 1968, pp.420-1; *ibid.* n. 1 & 2: H to W, 24 Aug. 1793, BM Add MSS 7848, W.Pps., *ff*.99-100; H to Burke, 7 Sept. 1793, F.MSS.,N.,A.IV.14a, 17 Sept. 1793. **17.** Burke, *Correspondence*, vol.VII, p.443 n.3; H to Burke, 20 Nov. 1793, F.MSS,N.,A.IV.3(a); copy in BM Add MSS 37848, *ff*.303-10; Burke to H, 3 Oct. 1793, printed in *Correspondence of Edmund Burke and William Windham. With other illustrative letters from the Windham papers in the British Museum*, ed. by J.P. Gilson, Cambridge 1910 (The Roxburghe Club 157), pp.63-8. **18.** Burke, *Correspondence*, vol.VII, p.441 n.1 & 2, copy, F.MSS, N., A.IV.15(a); H to W, 24 Aug. 1793, W.Pps., BM Add MSS 37848, *f*.86. **19.** O'Donoghue, Holy See, p.101: Antonelli to Troy, 17 & 24 Aug. 1793, Dublin Dioc. Arch.; copies in F.MSS,N.,A.VII.5, in P.R.O., F.O.95/5/6, and in W.Pps., BM Add MSS 37848, *ff*.130v-131. **20.** Cardinal Zelada to H, 31 Aug. 1793, copies in P.R.O., F.O. 95/5/6, and in W.Pps., BM Add MSS 37848, *ff*.128-30. **21.** H to W, 24 Aug. 1793, secret, BM Add MSS 37848, W.Pps., vol.VII, *f*.71v **22.** O'Donoghue, *Holy See*. p.101. **23.** W to H, London, 28 March 1793, copy, BM Add MSS 37848, W.Pps. vol.VII, *f*.65. **24.** Mooney, *British relations*, pp.194-5; Somerset, *Burke*, p.143; H to Burke, 20 Nov. 1793, F.MSS. N.,A.IV.3(b). On W *vide D.N.B.*, vol.XXI, pp.644-6. On Grenville *ibid.* vol.VIII, pp.576-81. **25.** H to W, 12 Oct. 1793 BM Add MSS 37848, W.Pps., vol.VII, *f*.241v. **26.** H to W, 24 Aug. 1793. *ibid.* *ff*.88-9. **27.** F.MSS, N., A.IV.3(c), pp.2-3; see also H to W, 24 Aug. 1793, *f*.88. **28.** Fitzpatrick, *Secret Service,* pp.280,227-8,258,264. **29.** H to W, 24 Aug. 1793, BM Add MSS 37848, W.Pps., vol.VII, *ff*.92-3. **30.** Zelada to Erskine, copies in P.R.O., F.O. 43/10 and F.MSS.N., A.IV.3(c), p.4. **31.** H to W, 24 Aug. 1793, secret, BM Add MSS 37848, W.Pps., vol.VII, *f*.71v. **32.** H to prince of Wales, 7 Sept. 1793, copy in F.MSS,N.,A.IV.15(a); see also W. Trevor (British envoy at Turin) to H, 10 Oct. 1793, extract *ibid.* A.IV.4(a), p.2. **33.** *Ibid.*, A.IV.4(b), pp.1-2; 4(c), pp.1-2; H to Burke, 27 Nov. 1793, **34.** Propaganda Fide to Archbishop Troy, 4 Nov. 1793, copy in P.R.O., F.O.43/10. **35.** Erskine to Andrew Stuart, 7 Sept. 1793. BM Add. MSS 37848, W.Pps., vol.VII, *ff*.101-2. **36.** S. Gasilee, 'British Diplomatic Relations with the Holy See' in *Dublin Rev.* 204 (1939), pp.1-19, here 3; A. Bellesheim, 'Cardinal Charles Erskine' in *H.P.Bl.* 110 (1892), p.864. **37.** Burke, *Correspondence,* vol.VII, p.483n.1; Somerset, *Burke*, pp.147-8, H to Burke, 18 Sept. 1793, F.MSS,N.,A.IV.14a(1); Burke to H, 3 Oct. 1793, printed in *Burke-Windham Correspondence*, pp.63-8. **38.** F.MSS,N.,A.IV. 3a-4d, 20 Nov. 1793. **39.** *Burke-Windham Correspondence*, pp.68-9: W to Pitt, 11 Oct. 1793, BM Add.MSS 37848, *f*.11. **40.** H to W, 24 Aug. 1793, secret, *ibid.*, *f*.71v. **41.** W. Maziere Brady, 'Memoirs of Cardinal Erskine' in Brady, *Anglo-Roman Papers*, London 1890, pp.131-3; Bellesheim, *Erskine,* pp.864-5. **42.** Wöste, *Kirchenpolitik,* pp.34-56. **43.** *Ibid.*, p.35; see Francis Plowden, *An Historical Review of the State of Ireland from the invasion of that country under Henry II to its union with Great Britain on 1st January 1801, vol.II, part 1, pp.443-5.* **44.** *Ibid.*: P.R.O., H.O. 100/46, *f*.110; Burke, *Correspondence,* vol.VIII, p.508; see Fitzpatrick, *Secret Service,* pp.259-65,280,285,378-9; M.R. O'Connell, 'The Political Background to the

Establishment of Maynooth College' *I.E.R.* 85(1956). pp.325–34, 406–15; 86(1956),
pp.1–16. **45.** *Ibid.*, pp.36–7; Moran, *Specilegium Ossoriense*, vol.III, Dublin 1884,
pp.462–4; Castlereagh, *Correspondence*, vol.III, pp.72–5. **46.** Cited from Cardinal
Gasquet, *Great Britain and the Holy See*, Rome 1919, p.17. Erskine's correspondence,
Arch. Vat., Italia Append. Epoca Napoleon, vol.X, fasc,C; Francia, Append. Epoca
Nap., vol.XIII, fasc.E. **47.** *Ibid.*, pp.20. **48.** Cretineau-Joly, *L'église romaine en face de
la révolution*, 2nd ed., Paris 1860, vol.I, pp.186–7; J. Hergenröther, *Der Kirchenstaat
seit der französischen Revolution*, Freiburg i.Br. 1860, p.181. **49.** Cardinal Bernis to
Bishop Francois of Arras, 10 June 1794, Cretineau-Joly, *L'église romain*, vol.I, p.192.
50. Hergenröther, *Kirchenstaat*, p.182. **51.** Antonelli to the vicars apostolic of England,
27 Feb. 1794, J. Rinieri, *Il Congresso di Vienna e la Santa Sede (1813–1815)*, Rome
1904, p.144. **52.** O'Donoghue, *Holy See*, p.103: Antonelli to Troy, 13 Dec. 1794,
D.D.A. **53.** *Ibid.*, pp.105–6, Antonelli to Troy, 13 Dec. 1794, D.D.A. **54.** *Ibid.*, p.106:
Troy to Antonelli, 28 Feb. 1795, D.D.A. **55.** Bellesheim, *Irland*, vol.III, p.271; P.
Hughes, *The Catholic Question in English Politics, 1688–1829. A Study in Political
History*, London 1929, p.230; O'Donoghue, *Holy See*, p.101; Antonelli to the
archbishops and bishops of Ireland, 7 Feb. 1795, D.D.A.; Antonelli to the vicars
apostolic of Great Britain, 2 Feb. 1795, copy in P.R.O., F.O.43/12. **56.** O'Donoghue,
Holy See, p.106. **57.** H to W, Cusa Cicciaporei, 8 Feb. 1794, BM Add.MSS 37848,
W.Pps., vol.VIII, *f*.19. **58.** H to Pius VI, 24 Jan. 1795, copy in P.R.O., F.O.43/12. **59.**
Pius VI to H, 26 Feb. 1795, copy *ibid.* **60.** H to W, 7 March 1795, BM Add.MSS 37848,
W.Pps., vol.VIII, *f*.155. **61.** *Ibid.*, copy, *ff*.154–5. **62.** Bishop Hay to Macpherson,
Edinburgh, 10 March 1793, copy, H.Corr., BM EG 2401. *f*.46; Bishop Douglas to
Smaft, London, March 1795, copy *ibid.*, *f*.47. **63.** H to W, 12 Oct. 1793, BM Add.MSS
37848, W.Pps., vol.VII, *ff*.239–40. **64.** Grenville to Portland, 26 Jan. 1795, Hist. MSS
Comm., Dropmore Pps., vol.III, p.145; R. Noakes, 'Cardinal Erskine's Mission
1793–1801', *Dublin Rev.* 204 (1939), pp.340–1; Mooney, *Diplomatic Relations*,
p.206n.11. **65.** Grenville to North, draft, Downing St., 9 Feb. 1795, P.R.O., F.O.43/1.
66. North to Grenville, Rome, 29 April 1795, priv., *ibid.* no. 1. **67.** North to Grenville,
Rome, 2 May 1795, priv., *ibid.* no.2. **68.** North to Grenville, Rome, 7 May 1795, priv.,
ibid. no.3. **69.** Report, Gardiner, 21 Feb. 1796, extract *ibid.* **70.** Report, Graves, 15 Feb.
1796, *ibid.* **71.** J.T. Ellis, *Cardinal Consalvi and Anglo-Papal Relations*, Washington
DC 1942, p.9; Gasquet, *Britain*, p.51. **72.** Wöste, *Kirchenpolitik*, p.53: Camden Pps. II,
20. **73.** Portland to Camden, 7 Sept. 1796, *ibid.*, pp.293–4; Portland to Camden, 8
Sept. 1796, *ibid.*, pp.296–7; Wöste, p.54. **74.** Freeman's Journal, 4 July 1795, 11 Aug.
1796; *ibid.*, p.57; Fitzpatrick, *Secret Service*, p.284. **75.** T. Hussey, *A pastoral letter to
the Catholic Clergy of the United Dioceses of Waterford and Lismore*, Dublin 1797,
pp.3–8; Wöste, *ibid.*, Fitzpatrick, p.281. **76.** Wöste, *ibid.*; Camden Pps., II, 229. **77.** H
to W, 24 Aug. 1793, BM Add.MSS 37848, W.Pps., vol.VII, *f*.95. **78.** Heneage,
Memoirs, p.157. **79.** Borgia to H., Padua, 14 Sept. 1799, BM Add.MSS 37848, W.Pps.,
vol.VIII, *f*.229; Archbishop Antonio Tendadori of Siena to H, 18 Oct. 1799, H.Corr,
BM EG 2401, *ff*.122–3; H to Andrew Stuart, 29 Oct. 1799, Lord Braye's MSS, *f*.61,
10th Report, Appendix, part VI, *The MSS of the Marquis of Abergavenny, Lord Braye*,
London 1887, pp.242–3; H to W, London, 4 Nov. 1799, BM Add.MSS 37848, W.Pps,
vol.VIII, *f*.227; Andrew Stuart to Dundas, 30 Oct. 1799, Braye's MSS, *f*.64, *ibid.*;
Andrew Stuart to H, 3 Dec. 1799, H.Corr., BM EG 2401, *f*.128. **80.** Heneage,
Memoirs, p.159. **81.** *Ibid.*, pp.160–2; Cardinal York to H, Venice, 26 Feb. 1800; Pius
VII to H, 10 March 1800, BM Add.MSS 37848, W.Pps., vol.VIII, *f*.231; Thomas
Coutts (Banker) to York, London, 20 Jan. 1800, Braye MSS, *f*.67; Minto to York,
Vienna, 9 Feb. 1800, *ibid.*, *f*.74,79; York to Minto, *ibid.*, *f*.82; York to H, n.d., *f*.87;
H to York, 15 April 1800; see also Hist.MSS Comm., 10th Report, as cited in note 75
supra, pp.243 *et seq.* **82.** Noakes, 'Erskine's Mission', pp.348–9. **83.** O'Donoghue,
Holy See, pp.101–2; Erskine to Troy, 6 April 1798, D.D.A. **84.** *Ibid.*, p.102: P.R.O.,
H.O. 100/76, *ff*.95–6; 100/78, *ff*.114–5. **85.** Wöste, *Kirchenpolitik*, p.64; *Hibernian
Journal*, 28 May, 4 June, 13 July 1798; Plowden, *Review*, II, part 2, app., 110, 294–6.
86. *Ibid.*, *Hibernian Journal*, 27 June, 20 July 1798; Moran, *Spicilegium*, vol.III,

pp.579–96,602. **87.** Brady, *Memoirs,* p.155; Hughes, *Catholic Question,* p.230. **88.** Brenan, *Ecclesiastical History,* p.591. **89.** R. O'Reilly (Armagh), J.J. Troy (Armagh), E. Dillon (Tuam), Th. Bray (Cashel), P.J. Plunkett (Meath), F. Moylan (Cork), D. Delaney (Kildare), E. French (Elphin), J. Canfield (Ferns) and J. Cruise (Ardagh). **90.** Charles Butler, *Historical Memoirs respecting the English, Irish and Scottish Catholics,* vol.II, London 1819, p.154; Brenan, *Ecclesiastical History,* pp.591–2, *Dublin Chronicle;* H. Brück, *Das irische Veto,* Mainz 1879, p.4. **91.** Fitzpatrick, *Secret Service,* p.282: Pelham MSS. **92.** *Ibid.:* Castlereagh Pps.,III, 87. **93.** Castlereagh, *Correspondence,* III, 405–9; O'Donoghue, *Holy See,* pp.103–4: P.R.O., H.O.100/85, *ff.*81–2; 100/99, *ff.*63–109. **94.** *Ibid.,* pp.401–2: Meath to Castlereagh, Nov. 1800. **95.** Fitzpatrick, *Secret Service,* p.282. **96.** *Ibid.,* p.281; Castlereagh, *Correspondence,* I. 264. **97.** *Ibid.,* p.282. **98.** *Ibid.* **99.** Erskine to Borgia, 3 April 1799, Archivio della S. Congregazione de Propaganda Fide, Scritture riferite nei Congressi, Irlanda, III, 267; Brady, *Memoirs,* p.154. **100.** Borgia to Troy, 15 June 1799, D.D.A., O'Donoghue, *Holy See,* p.104. **101.** *Ibid.,* Erskine to Borgia, 7 & 8 Aug. 1799, Arch. Propag. Fide, Scritture Congressi, Irlanda 17, *ff.*550–3. **102.** Brady, *Memoirs,* p.155. **103.** Noakes, *Erskine's Mission,* p.349. **104.** Robert Fagan to Lord William Bentinck, Rome, 17 April 1814, B.Pps., Pw Id2274; Prince Macedonia to Fagan, Rome, 19 April 1814, *ibid.,* Pw Id2280. **105.** O'Donoghue, *Holy See,* p.104; Luke Concanen, O.P., to Troy, 12 July 1800, D.D.A. **106.** Borgia to H. 6 July 1800, copy in P.R.O., F.O.43/12; printed in Castlereagh, *Correspondence,* vol.III, pp.384–5. **107.** Fitzpatrick, *Secret Service,* pp.288–9. **108.** *Ibid.,* p.287. **109.** H to W, 4 Aug. 1800, BM Add.MSS 37848, W.Pps., vol.VIII, *ff.*234–6. **110.** *Ibid., f.*237, Bellesheim, *Irland,* vol.III, pp.271–2. **111.** Quoted from H to W, Weymouth, 31 Oct. 1801, BM Add.MSS 37848, W.Pps., vol.VIII, *f.*274. **112.** Art.V,3; Wöste, *Kirchenpolitik,* p.55. **113.** H to W, 4 Aug.1800, BM Add.MSS 37848, W.Pps., vol.VIII, *ff.*237–8. **114.** *Ibid., f.*239. **115** Castlereagh, *Correspondence,* vol.IV, p.21; H to Castlereagh, 25 Jan. 1801. **116.** Bellesheim, *Irland,* vol.III, pp.277–8. **117.** O'Donoghue, *Holy See,* p.105. **118.** H to Castlereagh, London, 24 Nov. 1800; Castlereagh, *Correspondence* vol.III, p.413. **119.** Borgia to Troy, 14 Oct. 1800, D.D.A., O'Donoghue, *Holy See,* p.104. **120.** Domenico Coppola to Luke Concanen, 7 Aug. 1800, D.D.A., *ibid.,* p.105. **121.** H to York, London, 10 Feb. 1801, Braye MSS, Hist. MSS Comm. Report, pp.245–6. **122.** Chr. Weber, *Kardinäle und Prälaten in den letzten Jahrzehnten des Kirchenstaats,* 2 vols. (Päpste und Papsttum 13), Stuttgart 1978, vol.I, p.152. **123.** Brady, *Memoirs,* p.163; Noakes, *Erskine's Mission,* p.352. **124.** See the summary of Bellesheim, *Erskine,* pp.868–9.

CHAPTER III.1

1. Hughes, *Catholic Question,* p.257. **2.** On Milner see F.C. Husenbeth, *The life of the right reverend John Milner,* Dublin 1862; J. Bossy, *The English Catholic Community 1570–1850,* London 1975, pp.334–7. **3.** Fitzpatrick, *Secret Service,* pp.143–4. **4.** J.M. Milner, *Supplementary Memoirs of English Catholics,* London 1820, p.120; Husenbeth, *Milner,* p.124; Brück, *Irisches Veto,* p.6. **5.** Brenan, *Ecclesiastical History,* p.549; Brück, *Irisches Veto,* p.7. **6.** *Ibid.,* p.11; on the catholic committee see Bossy, *English Catholic,* pp.333–4. **7.** Brenan, *Ecclesiastical History,* pp.595–9; Brück, *Irisches Veto,* pp.15–6. **8.** Rinieri, *Congresso di Vienna,* pp.124–5; H to Cardinal de Gregorio, Stone Easton, Somerset, 24 Feb. 1825. **9.** *Ibid.,* pp.21 et seq.; Milner, *Supplementary Memoirs,* pp.198 et seq. **10.** *Ibid.,* pp.215 et seq.; Brück, *Irisches Veto,* p.26. **11.** *Ibid.,* pp.31–3; Latin text *ibid.,* pp.71–3 & in *Der Katholik* (1879) II, pp.358–60; Milner, *Supplementary Memoirs,* pp.218–20; Brenan, *Ecclesiastical History,* Appendix III; Rinieri, *Congreso di Vienna,* pp.673–6; Bibliotheca Vallicelliana, *fondo Falsacappo,* vol.51, *ff.*76–81. **12.** Pius VII to the prince regent, 1 April 1814, P.R.O., F.O.881/65, no.1; Mooney, *Diplomatic Relations,* p.199. **14.** *Ibid.,* Memorandum, earl of Liverpool, 3 June 1814, P.R.O., F.O. 881/65, no.2. **15.** Rinieri, *Congresso di Vienna,* p.29; Testaferrata to Pius VII, Lucern, 13 April 1814. **16.** Pistolesi, *Pio VII,* vol.III, p.209; Fagan to Bentinck, Rome, 17 April 1814, B.Pps.,

Pw Id2274. **17.** Fagan to Macedonia, Rome, 17 April 1814, B.Pps., Pw Id2280. **18.** Fagan to Bentinck, Rome, 17 April 1814, received at Genoa 28 April 1814, B.Pps, Pw Id2274–5; D. Montoni, Dir. Gov. di Polizia to Fagan, Rome, 17 April 1814, acknowledging Fagan's letter of 15 April concerning the appointment of vice consuls and the acceptance of their appointments, Pw Id2278; Count Macedonia, president of the Consiglio di Stato, to Fagan, Rome, 18 April 1814, acknowledging the appointments, Pw Id2279. **19.** Fagan to Bentinck, Rome, 20 April 1814, received Genoa, 18 May, Pw Id2276–7. **20.** Pius VII to the prince regent, Cesena, 3 May 1814, P.R.O., F.O.881/65, no.3. **21.** Pius VII to the prince regent, Foligno, 20 May 1814, *ibid.*, no.4 & 5. **22.** Report by Fagan, enclosed in Fagan to Bentinck, 17 June 1814, B.Pps., Pw Id2283. **23** Fagan to Bentinck, 18 June 1814, B.Pps., Pw Id2282. **24.** Pistolesi, *Pio VII*, vol.III, p.209. **25.** In the draft (B.Pps., Pw Id6679) of Fagan's report: 'His Holiness' (crossed out and concealing text written above).**26.** Report by Fagan, enclosed in Fagan to Bentinck, 17 June 1815, Pw Id2284.**27.** Fagan to Bentinck, 17 June 1814, Pw Id2281.**28.** Brenan, *Ecclesiastical History,* p.601.**29.** Fagan to Bentinck, 17 June 1814, B.Pps., Pw Id2281.**30.** Milner, *Suppl. Memoris,* p.231; Brück, *Veto, pp.34–5.* **31.** *Ibid.;* Butler, *Memoirs, vol.IV, pp.523 et seq.* **32.** Report by Fagan, enclosed in Fagan to Bentinck, 17 June 1814, B.Pps., Pw Id2281. **33.** Fagan to Bentinck, 17 & 18 June, Pw Id2281–2. **34.** N. Wiseman, *Recollections of the Last Four Popes and of Rome in Their Times,* London 1859, pp.72–3. **35.** Consalvi to Castlereagh, London, 23 June 1814, P.R.O., F.O.881/65, no.6. **36.** Rinieri, *Congresso di Vienna,* pp.131–41. **37.** Consalvi to Pacca, London, 5 July 1814, Arch.Vat., Congresso di Vienna, ann.1814, printed *ibid.,* pp.151–63. **38.** Bellesheim, 'Cardinal Consalvi in Paris, London und Wien' in *H.P.Bl.* 135(1905), p.289. **39.** Rinieri, *Congresso di Vienna,* p.168 n.2. **40.** Castlereagh to Consalvi, London, 9 July 1814, P.R.O., F.O.881/65, no.7. **41.** Consalvi to Pacca, Paris, 17 Aug. 1814, printed in Rivieri, *Congresso,* pp.170–5. **42.** Consalvi to Pacca, Paris, 17 Aug. 1814, printed *ibid.,* pp.179–80. **43.** Pacca to Congregation of Cardinals, 13 Aug. 1814, printed *ibid.,* pp.180–2. **44.** Bentinck to Pius VII, draft, 14 July 1814, B.Pps., PW Id4672. **45.** Pistolesi, *Vita del Pio VII,* vol.III, p.209. **46.** Fagan to Bentinck, Naples, 7 Sept. 1814, received 13 Oct., B.Pps., PW Id2290. **47.** *Ibid.* **48.** Pacca to Fagan, Rome, 8 Oct. 1814, Engl. to transl. enclosed in Fagan to Bentinck, 15 Nov. 1814, *ibid.,* PW Id2291. **49.** Fagan to Bentinck, Turin, 9 Nov. 1814, *Ibid.,* Pw Id2292, received Lyons 14 Nov. 1814. **50** Fagan to Bentinck, Lyons, 15 Nov. 1814, *ibid.,* PW Id2294. **51.** Mooney, *Diplomatic relations,* p.200L Cooke to Castlereagh, 18 March 1815, F.O.881/65, no.8. **52.** Letter of thanks, Pius VII to Bentinck, Genoa, 9 April 1815, B.Pps., PW Id4673; D.C. Bougler, *Lord William Bentinck,* Oxford 1892, pp.48–9; J. Roselli, *Lord William Bentinck and the British occupation of Sicily, 1811–1814,* London 1956, pp.168–9; Bellesheim, *Consalvi,* p.285. **53.** Brenan, *Ecclesiastical History,* p.606; Milner, *Suppl. Memoirs,* p.234. **54.** MS papers of Rev. R. Hayes, cited from Brenan, *op. cit.,* p.60 **55.** *Ibid.,* p.602. **56.** *Ibid,.* p.604. **57.** *See* H.U. Feine, 'Persona grata, minus grata', in *Festschrift Alfred Schultze,* ed. W. Merk, Weimer 1934, pp.78–9. The text of the rescript printed in Brenan, *Ecclesiastical History,* appendix IV and in Brück, *Veto,* pp.74 et seq.

CHAPTER III.2

1. Cf. document no.4 in the Appendix. **2.** Cited from Brenan, *Ecclesiastical History,* p.606. **3.** See below p.146 et seq. **4.** Brenan, *Eccles. Hist.,* p.607; the resolutions printed in Husenbeth, *Milner,* p.296 et seq. **5.** Wiseman, *Recollections,* p.90. **6.** Pius VII to Castlereagh, 26 Oct. 1815, P.R.O., F.O.881/65, no.9; pius VII to the prince regent, 26 Oct. 1815, *ibid.,* no.10, **7.** The prince regent to Pius VII, transl., 4 Dec. 1815, *ibid.,* no.11. **8.** Pius VII to the prince regent, 19 Feb. 1816, *ibid.,* no.12. **9.** Brenan, *Eccles. Hist.,* p.613. **10.** English transl. of the rescript in Butler, *Memoirs,* vol.I, ch.IV, pp.536 et seq. **11.** Brenan, *Eccles. Hist.,* p.614, the sermon printed in *Dublin Chronicle,* 15 April 1816. **12.** *Ibid.,* p.615. **13.** The commission of Mr Parke as consul, 10 Nov. 1816, F.O.881/65, no.46, appendix 2; *cf.* below, document no.4 in the appendix. **14.** Pius VII to the prince regent, accompanying letter, Rome, 6 July 1816, P.R.O., F.O.881/65, no.13. **15.** L. von Ompteda, *Irrfahrten und Abenteuer eines mittelstaatlichen Diplomaten*, Leipzig 1889, pp.283−366. On Münster *vide A.D.B.*, vol.23, pp.157−85. **16.** H.G. Aschoff, *Das Verhältnis von Staat und katholischer Kirche im Königreich Hannover 1813−1866* (Quellen und Darstellungen zur Geschichte Niedersachsens, 86), Hildesheim 1976, p.59: N.H.A.H., Hann. 92, IV, H.41, *f*.262. **17.** *Ibid.*, p.60; Münster to Ompteda, *ibid.*, *f*.518; Hann.92, XXXIII, 1, 15, 1, 8 Nov. 1816, *f*.16, draft; O. Mejer, *Zur Geschichte der römisch-deutschen Frage*, vol.II, Rostock 1873, part 2, p.126. On Kestner see *N.D.B.*, vol.XI, no.553−4. **18.** Pius VII to the prince regent, Rome, 23 Sept. 1816, P.R.O., F.O.861/1, no.14; prince regent to Pius VII, 16 Dec. 1816, *ibid.*, no. 15. **19.** E. Hegel, *Die Kirchenpolitischen Beziehungen Hannovers und der norddetschen Kleinstaaten zur römischen Kurie 1800−1846*, Paderborn 1936, p.55; Hann.92, XXXIII, 1, no.15a; text printed in Hegel, *ibid.*, n.157. **20.** *Ibid.*, p.57; Hann.12III, Rome no.II, 1, destroyed like all papers of the Hanoverian legation in Rome by bombs in world war II. **21.** Kestner papers, K.M.H, box 10, II A2.62, p.3, Kestner to Charlotte Kestner, Rome, 22 March 1817. **22.** Aschoff, *Hannover*, p.65n.48; Leist to Münster, 12 April 1817, N.H.A.H., Hann.92, XXXIII, I, 15, 1a *ff*.90−1, German text below appendix no.1. **23.** M. Jorns, *August Kestner und seine Zeit 1777−1853*, Hanover 1964, pp.105, 107. **24.** *Orthodox Journal or Catholic Monthly Intelligencer*, July 1817; July 1818; Brenan, *Eccles. Hist.*, pp.616−20; Butler, *Historical Memoirs*, vol.IV, p.176; Brück, *Veto*, pp.52−3. **25.** Castlereagh to Consalvi, draft, St. James's Square, 22 Jan. 1817, P.R.O., F.O.43/10. **26.** Castlereagh to Consalvi, draft, F.O., 30 April 1817, *ibid.*; Consalvi to Castlereagh, priv., 6 Oct. 1817, *ibid.* **27.** Hegel, *Beziehungen*, p.58; N.H.A.H., Hann.12a, III, Rome, no.II, 1, destroyed in world war II. **28.** Pius VII to the prince regent, Rome 30 March 1817, P.R.O., F.O.881/65, no.16; the prince regent to Pius VII, Carlton House, 29 May 1817, *ibid.*, no. 17; the prince regent to Pius VII, 6 Sept. 1817, *ibid.*, no.18; Pius VII to the prince regent, Rome, 26 Nov. 1817, *ibid.*, no.19; prince regent to Pius VII, 31 Jan. 1818, *ibid.*, no.20, **29.** H to Castlereagh, Rome, April 1818, P.R.O., F.O.43/10. **30.** O. Mejer, *Das Veto deutscher protestantischer Staatsregierungen gegen katholische Bischofswahlen*, Rostock 1866, p.18; report, Ompteda to the prince regent, Rome, 4 Oct. 1818, document destroyed in world war II. **31.** J.H. Whyte, 'The Appointment of Catholic Bishops in 19th Century Ireland' in *C.H.R.* 48 (April 1962) pp.12−32, here 14n.3; Propaganda Fide, Scritture riferite nei Congressi Irlanda, vol.21, *f*.144; Consalvi to Propaganda, 15 April 1819. **32.** Fitzpatrick, *Secret Service,* p.378; Field Marshall Lord Combermere to Fitzpatrick, 1860; Wellington, *Despatches*, compiled by Lieutenant-Colonel Gurwood, vol.II, London 1835, p.538. **33.** Whyte, *Appointment*, p.14n.3; Propaganda Fide, Acta, *f*.836. **34.** N.H.A.H., Hann.110 A1 no.8, Burghersh to Castlereagh, Florence, 19 March 1819; O. Mejer, *Der römische Kestner*, Breslau 1883, pp.22 et seq.; Kestner papers, Kestner Museum, Hanover, II A2.69, Kestner to Charlotte Kestner, Rome, 30 Jan. 1819. **35.** Aschoff, *Staat*, p.68; On Reden see *A.D.B.*, vol.27, pp.507 etr seq.; On Cappacini see *D.Bl.*, vol.18, pp.372−4. **36.** Mooney, *Diplomatic Relations*, pp.201−2; H.A. Smith, 'Diplomatic Relations with the Holy See, 1815−1930' in *Law Quarterly Review* 48 (1932), p.375; Pius VII to George IV, Rome, 18 March 1820, P.R.O., F.O.881/65 no.21; Consalvi to George IV, 18 March 1820, *ibid.*, no.22; Pius VII to George IV, 5 April 1820, *ibid.*, no.23, George IV to Pius VII, Carlton Palace, 29 April 1820, *ibid.*, no.24; Castlereagh to Consalvi, 5 May 1820, *ibid.*, no.25; Consalvi to Castlereagh, 2 Aug. 1820, *ibid.* **37.** *Ibid.*, no. 29.

CHAPTER IV.1

1. P.R.O., F.O.881/65 no.26. **2.** Document no.2 in the Appendix. **3.** Document no.3 in the Appendix. **4.** West.Pps., Cuba, microfilm BM, M526, sect.1, pp.9−10, B to Canning, 28 Sept. 1823, no.41. **5.** *Ibid.*, pp.13−31, here cited pp.22−4, B to Canning, Rome, 2 Oct. 1823, no.42; on the conclave *vide* R. Colapietra, 'Il diario del Concalve del 1823', in *Archivio storico italiano* 120 (1962), pp.76−146, and M. Rossi 'Il conclave di Leone XII. Lo Stato pontificio e l'Italia all indomani del congresso di Vienna', in *Bolletino della regia deputazione di storia patria per l'Umbria* 33 (1935), pp.135–215. **6.** See extract printed below as document no.4 in the appendix. **7.** B to Canning, Rome, 4 Oct. 1823, no.43, West.Pps, BM, M526, sect.i, pp.33–5, queries concerning commerce etc., *ibid.*, pp.37–46. **9.** Wiseman, *Recollections*, p.252; P. Schweitzer, *Trauerrede auf Leo XII*, Cologne 1829. **10.** Leo XII to George IV, Rome, 28 Sept. 1823, P.R.O., F.O.881/65, no.28; Cardinal della Somaglia to Canning, 28 Sept. 1823, *ibid.*, no.27; Mr Planta to the law officers, confidential, F.O., 28 Oct. 1823, *ibid.*, no.32, printed by Mooney, *Diplomatic Relations*, p.208, n.56; Robert Lc ̄n (deputy keeper of the state papers) to Planta, state papers office, Great George St., 26 Nov. 1823, *ibid.*, no.36; *ibid.*, no.37 **11.** *Ibid.*, no.29, extract from a Roman letter to Planta, Oct. 1823; Canning to Consalvi, F.O., 25 Nov. 1823, *ibid.*, no.34; Canning to Somaglia, 25 Nov. 1823, *ibid.*, no.35, and West.Pps., Cuba, BM, M526, sect.1, pp.61–8. **12.** Kestner to Reden, 21 June 1826, K.M, H, Kestner Pps. II A20, no.9. **13.** Kestner to his sister Lotte, 12 March 1836, *ibid.*; Mejer, *Kestner*, p.40. **14.** Second report of the select committee on the state of Ireland, printed on command, London 1825, p.177; Brück, *Veto*, pp.59–63; Brenan, *Eccles. Hist.*, pp.626 et seq. **15.** B to Canning, Naples, 2 April 1825, private, draft, West. Pps., Cuba, BM, M511, sect.4, pp.31–5, from original in P.R.O., F.O.79/44 printed by H. Temperley, 'George Canning, the Catholics, and the Holy See' in *Dublin Review* 193 (1933), p.12, by J. Broderick, *The Holy See and the Irish Movement for the Repeal of the Union with England, 1829–1847*, Rome 1951, p.68, and by Mooney, *Diplomatic Relations,* p.209, n.63. **16.** West. Pps., M511, sect.4. **17.** Mooney, *Diplomatic Relations*, p.203; P.R.O., F.O.79/45–7. **18.** *Ibid.*: Canning to B, 20 April 1826, P.R.O., F.O.881/65; Lord Clanricarde to the law officers, 30 Aug. 1826, *ibid.*, no.37, **19.** West. Pps., M511, sect.4. **20.** *Ibid.*, pp.39–41, Dudley to B, F.O., 23 Oct. 1827. **21.** Aschoff, *Staat*, p.115; Mejer, *Kestner*, p.43; Kestner to his sister Lotte, Rome, 24 Jan. 1828: every year circa 800–1000 English visitors come to Rome. **22.** K to Münster, Rome, 24 April 1828; Münster to K, London, 13 May 1828; Münster to Dudley, draft; N.H.A.H., Hann.92 XLI 127cl, *ff*.3–5. **23.** P. Ugolini, 'La Politica estera di card. Tommaso Bernetti, Segretario di Stato di Leone XII (1828–1829)' in *Archivio della Societa romana di Storia patria* 92 (1969), p.229: Lambruschini to Bernetti, Paris, 29 July 1828, disp.no.314, Arch. Vat., Segr. di Stato, R.248 B.417 *f*.3, *f*.45261; partly printed by R. Colapietra, *La chiesa tra Lamennais e Metternich. Il Pontificato di Leone XII,* Brescia 1963, p.502. **24.** Bernetti to Lambruschini, Rome, 9 Aug. 1828, *ibid.* **25.** *Ibid.*, p.272. **26.** *The Times,* 22 Nov. 1828, p.4. **27.** Wellington to Münster, 12 Jan. 1829. Münster Pps., N.S.H., Dep.110, A56. **28.** K to Münster, 27 Dec. 1828, *ibid.* Münster to Wellington, 9 Jan. 1829, copy, *ibid.*: Münster to Wellington, Grosvenor Place, 15 Jan. 1829, copy, *ibid.* **30.** Wiseman, *Recollections,* p.327. **31.** L.M. Manzini, *Il cardinale Luigi Lambruschini*, Vatican city 1960 (Studi testi 203), p.149. **32.** Brück, *Veto,* pp.65–7; Hansard, *Parliamentary Debates*, vol.20, p.774; Wellington's speech, *ibid.*, vol.21, p.54. **33.** Aberdeen to B, No.2, F.O., 28 Feb. 1829, West. Pps., Cuba, microfilm, BM, M526, sect.1, pp.201–3; copy in P.R.O., F.O.79/53. **34.** B to Aberdeen, No.3, Rome, 21 March 1829, draft, *ibid.*, pp.213–8; other reports, B to Aberdeen, No.6, Rome, 29 March 1829, draft, *ibid.*, pp.239–49; B to Aberdeen, No.8, Rome, 29 March 1829, draft, *ibid.*, pp.251–3; No.9, 29 March, *ibid.*, pp.255–62; No.15, 14 April, *ibid.*, pp.291–3. **35.** *Ibid.*, pp.263–5. **36.** B to Aberdeen, No.11, Rome, 2 April 1823, draft, *ibid.*, pp.267–72. **37.** Document No. 5 in the appendix. **38.** B to Aberdeen, No.18, Rome, 23 April 1823, draft, *ibid.*, pp.307–10. **39.** B to Aberdeen, No.1, Siena, 17 March 1823, draft, *ibid.*, pp.205–6; No.2, Rome, 20 March 1823, pp.209–10. **40.** Albani to Aberdeen, Rome, 31 March 1829, P.R.O., F.O.881/65, no.39; Pius VIII to George IV, N.H.A.H., Hann.92XLI 127e, *f*.20 and F.O.881/65 no.40; Aberdeen to Münster, 20 April 1829, *ibid.*, and 881/65, no.41. **41.** Münster to Kestner, London, 21 April 1829; *ibid.*, *f*.13; Kestner to Albani, 4 May 1829, copy, *ibid.*, *f*.9. **42.** Münster to Aberdeen, private, Grosvenor Place, 21 April 1829, draft *ibid.*, *f*.17, orig. 881/65 no.42. **43.** Albani to Kestner, 6 May 1829, copy *ibid.*, *f*.15. **44.** Kestner to George IV, No.429, Rome, 9 May 1829, *ibid.*, *f*.5. **45.** George IV to

Pius VIII, London 24 May 1829, *ibid.*, *f*.4. **46.** Brenan, *Eccles. Hist.*, pp.632—3; Brück, *Veto*, pp.69—70; the decree printed by Brück, pp.76—9. **47.** Whyte, *Appointment*, p.13. **48.** Wellington to B, 19 Oct. 1829, printed by Broderick, *Holy See*, pp.71—2 and R. Weigall (ed.), *The correspondence of Lord Burghersh*, London 1912, pp.264—5. **49.** Albani to Burghersh, 31 Dec. 1829. P.R.O., F.O.170/23, printed by Broderick, *Holy See*, pp.73—4. **50.** Manzini, *Lambruschini*, pp.149—56; Wiseman, *Recollections*, p.385. **51.** E. Münch, *Römische Zustände und katholische Kirchenfragen der neuesten Zeit*, Stuttgart 1838, pp.84—5. E. Perniola, 'De Internuntius Mgr. Francesco Capaccini en de Belgische Omwenteling van 1830' in *Mededeelingen van het Nederlandsch Historisch Instituut te Rome* 3 ser., 4 (1947), pp.53—169, on his stay in London pp.122—58, on his audience with Palmerston pp.153—8; *D.B.I.*, vol.18, 1975, pp.372—4; Münch, *Zustände*, p.97.

CHAPTER IV.2

52. Wiseman, *Recollections*, p.416; J.G. Köberle, *Rom unter den letzen drei Päpsten*, vol.2, Leipzig 1846, pp.68—70. **53.** Münch, *Römische Zustände*, pp.48—50, 96, 119. **54.** Köberle, *Rom*, vol.2, pp.168—9, 196, 207. **55.** Seymour diary, 12 March 1832, BM Add.MSS 60299, *f*.11. **56.** *Ibid.*, 13 March 1832. **57.** *Ibid.*, 18 March. **58.** *Ibid.*, 29 April; 19 March, 11 April, 13 April, 18 April. **59.** *Ibid.*, 25 March, 9 July. **60.** Seymour to Palmerston, 16 Aug. 1832, private, draft, P.R.O., F.O.170/23; Broderick, *Holy See*, p.76. **61.** Bernetti to Seymour, 12 Aug. 1832, copy, *ibid.*, 170/24. **62.** Same letter as note 60; printed by Broderick, *Holy See*, p.77. **63.** Sir George Shee to the law officers, F.O., 17 Aug. 1832, P.R.O., F.O.881/65, no.43. **64.** T. Denman & W. Horne to Shee, Lincoln's Inn, 20 Aug. 1832, *ibid.*, no.44; in the same vein, the solicitor-general to Palmerston, New Street, 24 April 1833, *ibid.*, no.45. **65.** Robert A. Graham, *Vatican Diplomacy*, Princeton, N.J. 1959, p.72. **66.** Seymour diary, 6, 16 & 18 Sept. 1832, BM Add.MSS 60299. **67.** Broderick, *Holy See*, p.78. **68.** Seymour to Palmerston, 7 March 1833, private, draft, P.R.O., F.O.170/25. **69.** Bernetti to Seymour, 19 Feb.1833, copy, *ibid.*; Broderick, *Holy See*, p.79. **70.** Bernetti to Cardinal Pedicini, 19 Feb. 1833, copy, riservata, Arch. Vat., Rubrica 280; *ibid.* **71.** Capaccini to Seymour, 19 Feb. 1833, copy, P.R.O., F.O.170/25, *ibid.* **72.** Aubin to Seymour, 20 Feb. 1833, private, F.O.170/25; printed *ibid.* **73.** Aubin to Seymour, 23 Feb. 1833, private, *ibid.* **74.** Aubin to Seymour, 4 March 1833, private, F.O.170/25; printed *ibid.* **75.** Aubin to Seymour, 21 June 1834; private, F.O.170/25; printed *ibid.* **76.** *Vide* Köberle, *Rom*, vol.II, pp.302—4. **77.** Document no.6 in the Appendix; on Ludwig von Ompteda (a relation of the former minister in Rome, Friedrich vom Ompteda) see L. von Ompteda, *Notizen eines deutschen Diplomaten, 1804—1813*, ed. by his great-grandson, Roderick von Ompteda, Berlin 1935, introduction. **78.** Document no.7 in the Appendix. **79.** Document no.8 *ibid.* **80.** Document no.9 *ibid.* **81.** Document no.10 *ibid.* **82.** Document no.11 *ibid.* **83.** Broderick, *Holy See*, p.83; H.L. Bulwer, *Life of Henry J. Temple, Viscount Palmerston*, London 1870, vol.2, p.186. **84.** Seymour to Aubin, 20 May 1834, private, P.R.O., F.O.170/26; Broderick, *Holy See*, p.84. **85.** *Ibid.*, p.83; Arch. Propaganda Fide, Acta 1834, vol.197, *ff*.179—83. **86.** *Ibid.*, p.86; P.R.O., F.O.170/25, Aubin to Seymour, 27 May 1834, private, copy. **87.** *Ibid.*, p.87; *ibid.*, Aubin to Seymour, 21 June 1834, private, copy. **88.** *Ibid.*, p.88; F.O.170/26, Seymour to Palmerston, 23 June 1834, private. **89.** Same letter as in note 36; *ibid.*, pp.88—9. **90.** Seymour to Palmerston, 6 July 1834, private, P.R.O., F.O.170/26; *ibid.*, p.90. **91.** See Münch, *Zustände*, pp.84—90. **92.** Aubin to Seymour, 30 June 1834, private, copy, F.O.170/25; Broderick, *Holy See*, p.92. **93.** Aubin to Seymour, 21 June 1834, as in note 36. **94.** Seymour to Palmerston, 5 Aug. 1834, private; Seymour to Palmerston, 9 Aug. 1834, private, F.O.170/26; *ibid.* **96.** *Ibid.*, pp.94—5. **97.** See *Catholic Encyclopedia*, vol.9, pp.499—501; B. O'Reilly, *John MacHale*, New York 1890. **98.** Broderick, *Holy See*, p.97; Ompteda to Kestner, London, 16 Dec. 1834, N.H.A.H., Hann.92, XLI, 127h, *f*.27. **99.** Seymour to Palmerston, 30 May 1834, private, draft, P.R.O., F.O.170/26; Broderick, *Holy See*, p.86. **100.** N. Wiseman, *Words of Peace*, 1848, p.6. **101.**

Strangways to the law officers, foreign office, 3 July 1837, P.R.O., F.O.882/65, no.48; Dobson, Campbell, Roffe to Strangways, doctor's commons, 6 Aug. 1837, *ibid.*, no.49. **102.** Kestner to Karl Kestner, 20 March 1835, K.M.H., II A2, no.145. **103.** Aubin to Abercromby, Rome, 25 Feb. 1837, P.R.O., F.O.79/86. **104.** Fransoni to MacHale, 26 Feb. 1839, Arch. Propaganda Fide, Lettere e Decrete 1839, vol.321, *ff*.155–6, printed by Broderick, *Holy See,* p.101; Fransoni to Crolly, *ibid.*, vol.202, *ff*.220–1, printed *ibid.*, pp.102–3. On Fransoni see *D.H.G.E.,* vol.18, pp. 1023–6. **105.** Crolly to Fransoni, 27 April 1839, *ibid.*, *ff*.255–6; Broderick, *Holy See,* pp.106–7. **106.** C. Weber, *Kardinäle und Prälaten in den letzten Jahren des Kirchenstaates,* Stuttgart 1978 (Päpste und Papsttum, 13), vol.II, pp.475–6. **107.** Metternich to Wittgenstein, 28 Aug. 1837, in H. Bastgen, *Forschungen und Quellen zur Kirchenpolitik Gregors XVI, Paderborn 1929, vol.I, pp.407–9.* **108.** Altieri to Lambruschini, 23 Sept. 1837, *ibid.*, pp.418–9. **109.** Altieri to Lambruschini, 4 April 1839, Arch. Vat., Nunziatura di Vienna, vol.280B. **110.** Altieri to Lambruschini, 10 May 1839, *ibid.*, printed by Broderick, *Holy See,* p.166. **111.** Aubin to Henry Edward Fox, Rome, 7 Jan. 1840, private and confidential, P.R.O., F.O.79/98. **112.** Aubin to Spencer Cowper, Rome, 23 Jan. 1841, F.O.79/101. **113.** Von Ohms to Metternich, 1 July 1843, reported by Baron Neumann, Austrian ambassador to London, to the foreign office, 4 Aug. 1843; P.R.O., F.O.7/313; printed by Broderick, *Holy See,* p.170. **114.** Gordon to Aberdeen, Aberdeen Papers, BM Add.MSS 43221, *ff*.40–1; also P.R.O., F.O.7/311, no.58. **115.** Graham to Peel, 30 Oct. 1843, private, Peel Papers, BM Add.Mss 40449, *ff*.167–8; printed by C.S. Parker, *Life and Letters of Sir James Graham,* London 1907, vol.I, p.401; Peel to Graham, 1 Nov. 1843, BM Add.MSS 40449, *f*.177; printed by Broderick, *Holy See,* p.171; Graham to Peel, 2 Nov. 1843, *ibid.*, *f*.186. **116.** Gordon to Aberdeen, 15 Nov. 1843, draft, F.O.120/204, copy in BM Add.MSS 43222, *ff*.65–6; printed by Broderick, *Holy See,* p.172; Altieri to Lambruschini, 5 Nov. 1843, riservatissimo, Arch. Vat., Nunziatura di Vienna, vol.280F; *ibid.* **117.** Broderick *Holy See,* p.173; Altieri to Lambruschini, 15 Nov. 1843, *ibid.* **118.** Peel to Graham, 27 Nov. 1843, confidential, Peel Papers, BM Add. MSS 40449, *ff*.233–4; printed by Parker, *Life of Graham,* vol.I, pp.401–2, and Broderick, *Holy See,* p.174; Graham to Peel, 29 Nov. 1843, private, *ibid.*, *f*.241; printed by Parker, p.402. **119.** Aberdeen to Peel, 30 Dec. 1843, Peel Pps., BM Add.MSS 40454, *f*.78; Peel to Aberdeen, 31 Dec., *ibid.*, *f*.82. **120.** Aberdeen to Gordon, F.O., 30 Dec. 1843, P.R.O., F.O.120/206 and F.O.7/309. **121.** Aberdeen to Gordon, 1 Jan. 1844, BM Add.MSS 43211, *ff*.381–2; on the Carbonari *vide* A. Falcionelli, *Les Sociétes Secrètes Italiennes. Les Carbonari. La Camorra. La Mafia,* Paris 1936. **122.** Lambruschini to Fransoni, 10 Feb. 1844, Arch, Propaganda Fide, Scritti non riferiti nei Congressi. Irlanda 1843–1846, vol.28; Broderick, *Holy See,* pp.176–8. **123.** Lambruschini to Altieri, 10 Feb. 1844, Arch. Vat., Nunziatura di Vienna, vol.281Q; the Promemoria is printed by Broderick, *Holy See,* Appendix 1. **124.** Gordon to Aberdeen, Vienna, 19 Feb. 1844, draft in P.R.O., F.O.120/210; copy in F.O.7/316. **125.** H. Reeve (ed.), *The Greville Memoirs,* London 1888, vol.V, pp.221–2, 29 Dec. 1843; Broderick, *Holy See,* p.99. **126.** The text of Fransoni's rescript is printed by Broderick, appendix II. **127.** Aberdeen to Peel, 4 Jan. 1845, Peel Pps., BM Add.MSS 40454 *f*.388; printed *ibid.*, p.189. **128.** Canning to Petre, F.O., 1 Oct. 1844, P.R.O., F.O.43/38. **129.** Canning to Petre, two letters of 7 Oct. 1844, *ibid.*, and one of 22 Oct., and one of 28 Nov. 1844, *ibid.* **130.** Petre to Aberdeen, 21 Oct. 1844, *ibid.*, printed by Broderick, *Holy See,* p.188. **131.** Petre to Aberdeen, 21, 25 & 28 Oct. 1844, 11, 24 & 29 Nov. 1844, and 17 Dec. 1844, F.O.43/38; 2 Dec. 1844 (audience with Gregory XVI) F.O.79/111. **132.** Aberdeen to Petre, 28 Dec. 1844, F.O.43/38, copy in F.O.170/41, printed by Broderick, *Holy See,* p.190; Petre to Aberdeen, 29 Nov. 1844, F.O.43/38. **133.** Petre to Aberdeen, 21 Jan 1845, private, Aberdeen Pps., BM Add. MSS 43151, M210–1; printed *ibid.*, p.191.

CHAPTER V.1

1. The college of cardinals to Victoria, 2 June 1846, P.R.O., F.O.881/65 No.50; the cardinal secretary of state to Victoria, 17 June 1846, *ibid.*, No.51; Pius IX to Victoria, 17 June 1846, *ibid.*, No.52. **2.** Franz Xaver Kraus, *Cavour* (Weltgeschichte in Karakterbildern 5), Mainz 1902, p.35. **3.** F. Hitchman, *Pius the ninth, a biography,* London 1878, p.3. This is by far the best biography of Pius IX in English; (T. Trollope, *The story of the life of Pius the Ninth,* 2 vols., London 1877, betrays the author's hatred of the catholic church). **4.** A.J. Nürnberger, *Zur Kirchengeschichte des XIX Jahrhunderts, I. Papsttum und Kirchenstaat,* part 2, Mainz 1900, pp.57−8. **5.** G. Martina, *Pio IX 1846−1850* (MHP 38), Rome 1974, pp.145−6; S. Walpole, *A History of England from the conclusion of the great war in 1815,* vol.V, London 1866, p.3 n.4. **6.** Nürnberger, *Kirchengeschichte,* vol.I/2, p.58; Martina, *Pio IX,* pp.46,164,168; see also O Bariè, *L'Inghilterra e il problema italano. Dalle riforme alle constitutione,* Milan 1958. **7.** H. Stieglitz, *Erinnerungen an Rom und den Kirchenstaat im ersten Jahre seiner Verjüngung,* Leipzig 1848. **8.** W. Ward, *The life and times of Cardinal Wiseman,* vol.I, London 1890, p.479; de Leonardis, *Inghilterra,* p.11. **9.** L. De Ruggiero, 'Inghilterra e stato pontificio nel primo triennio del pontificato di Pio IX' in *Archivio della Società romana di Storia patria* 76 (1953), pp.51−172, here 168−70; E. Ashley, *The life and correspondence of Henry John Temple, viscount Palmerston,* vol.II, London 1879, p.44. **10.** Cited from Graham, *Vatican Diplomacy,* p.76. **11.** Curato, Frederico (ed.), *Gran Bretagna e Italia nei documenti della Missione Minto,* (Fonti per la storia d'Italia, II serie, vol.107/8), Rome 1970, vol.I, p.44, No.9: P to Victoria, Royal Arch., J 1/8, F.O. 31 Jan. 1847. **12.** *Ibid.,* vol.I, p.81; Cl. to R, 1 Oct. 1847, P.Pps., GC/CL/480/4−9. **13.** See C. Woodham-Smith, *The Great Hunger,* New York 1962. **14.** R. Stewart, *The politics of protection. Lord Derby and the Protectionist Party 1841−1852,* Cambridge 1971, p.117. **15.** Bellesheim, *Ireland,* vol.III, p.437. **16.** G. Villiers, *4th earl of Clarendon, 1800−1870,* London 1938, pp.163−4. **17.** Stewart, *Politics of Protection,* p.128. **18.** Curato, *Minto,* vol.I, p.84: Clarendon Memorandum (as n.12). **19.** *Ibid.,* pp.81−3. **20.** Martina, *Pio IX,* p.165. **21.** Curato, *Minto,* vol.I, p.196, No.105: Minto to R, Rome, 15 Nov. 1847, P.R.O. 30/22/6. **22.** *Ibid.,* p.192, No.103: Minto to P, Rome, 14 Nov. 1847, P.Pps., GC/MI/467/1−4. **23.** 3 Jan. 1848, Martina, *Pio IX,* p.511 n.52. **24.** 18 Feb. 1848, *ibid.* **25.** Curato, *Minto,* vol.II, p.77, no.277: Minto to Petre, Naples, 26 Feb. 1848, N.L.S., M.Pps.683. **26.** Petre to Minto, Rome, 5 March 1848, (communicated to P on 8 March), P.R.O., F.O.43/42. **27.** Curato, *Minto,* vol.I, pp.190−1, No.103: Minto to P, Rome, 14 Nov. 1847, P.Pps, GC/MI/467/1−4. As an example of English catholic reaction to R's design see the earl of Arundel & Surrey's 'Observations upon Diplomatic relations between Great Britain and the Roman States', 1848, Arundel Castle, MD 2080. **28.** Bellesheim, *Irland,* vol.III, p.473. **29.** *Ibid.,* p.472. **30.** Graham, *Vatican Diplomacy,* p.74. **31.** Martina, *Pio IX,* p.461. **32.** *Ibid.,* p.462; Bellesheim, *Irland,* vol.III, p.476. **33.** Curato, *Minto,* vol.I, p.183, no.98: Minto to P, private, Rome, 12 Nov. 1847, P.Pps. GC/MI/466; pp.191−2, no.103: Minto to P, private, Rome 14 Nov. 1847, P.Pps. GC/MI/467/1−4; p.195, no.105: Minto to R, Rome, 14 Nov. 1847, P.R.O. 30/22/6; pp.203−4, no.III: Minto to P, Rome 17 Nov. 1847, P.Pps. GC/MI/468; p.230, no.128: Minto to P, private, Rome, 27 Nov. 1847, P.Pps. GC/MI/471/1−2. **34.** *Ibid.,* p.105, no.45: R to Minto, Downing St., 15 Oct. 1847, N.L.S., M. Pps.699. **35.** Martina, *Pio IX,* p.462. **36.** Cited from *ibid.,* p.463. **37.** *Ibid.,* Bellesheim, *Irland,* vol.III, p.479. **38.** J. Prest, *Lord John Russell,* London 1972, p.292: Temple to P, 5 Dec. 1848, Royal Archives D 19/5. **39.** *Ibid.,* Broughton diary, 5 Dec. 1848, BM Add.MSS 43748−56. **40.** G.I.T. Machin, *Politics and the churches in Great Britain 1832−1868,* Oxford 1977, p.215; see also Petre to Conyngham, Rome, 28 Feb. 1850, P.R.O., F.O.43/57. **41.** E. Lucas, *The life of Frederick Lucas, M.P., by his brother,* vol.II, London 1886, p.329−31. **41.** *Ibid.,* p.355. **43.** *Lothair* (1870), chapter 9, p.33; Buschkühl, *Irische Frage,* p.69.

CHAPTER V.2

44. T. Burbage, 'Masonic Crime and Terrorism', in: *Catholic Bulletin,* 7 (1917), pp.431−4; E. Cahill, *Freemasonry and the Anti-Christian Movement,* Dublin 1929, p.15; *Die römische Revolution vor dem Urtheile der Unparteiischen*. Transl. from the Italian, Augsburg 1852, p.121 and *passim*. **45.** *Correspondence respecting the Affairs of Rome 1849*. Presented to the house of commons by command of Her Majesty, in pursuance of their address of 14 April, 1851. London 1851. **46.** J.M. Stepischnegg, *Papst Pius IX. und seine Zeit*, vol.II, Vienna 1879, pp.21–2; J.S. Pelczar, *Pius IX i jego pointificat*, vol.I, Cracow 1887, pp.48–9. **47.** Martina, *Pio IX*, p.463. **48.** *Ibid.*, p.463, no.43; Arch. Vat., Fondo Segr. di Stato 1848, 241, 237–49; see also Prest, *Russell*, p.271: Ponsonby to R, 29 March 1847, P.R.O., R.Pps., 5B. **50.** Martina, *Pio IX*, p.464. **F.** Hitchman, *The public life of the rt. hon. the earl of Beaconsfield*, vol.I, London 1879, p.309; see also S. Walpole, *A history of England from the conclusion of the great war in 1815*, vol.5, London 1886, p.3, n.4. **51.** Curato, *Minto*, vol.I, p.311: Minto to P, 16 Jan. 1848, N.L.S., M.Pps. 700. It is typical of Prest's style to create the impression that Minto was ignorant of the hierarchy despite the fact that Prest knows and uses the Minto papers. **52.** *Ibid.*, pp.232–3: Shrewsbury to Charles Hamilton, Alton Towers, 4 Nov. 1847, P.Pps: GC/MI/470/2; see also Greville, *The Greville Memoirs*, 2nd part, vol.3, 1837–1852, London 1885: 7 Dec. 1847 & 15 Dec. 1847. **53.** O. Chadwick, *The Victorian Church*, vol.I, London 1966, p.286. **54.** J.W. Croker, 'Ministerial measures' in *Q.R.*82 (1847), pp.261–308, here 302 & 306. **55.** See *D.N.B.*, vol.V, pp.123–32. **56.** G.I.T. Machin, 'Lord John Russell and the prelude to the Ecclesiastical Titles Bill' in *J.E.H.* 35 (1974), pp.277–95, here p.288 Hansard, vol.94, p.816; vol.96, pp.707, 719; vol.101, pp.212, 229, 512. **57.** Ullathorne, *History of the restoration of the Catholic hierarchy in England*, London 1871, p.74. **58.** D. Gwynn, *Lord Shrewsbury, Pugin, and the Catholic Revival*, London 1946: Shrewsbury to Philipps, Feb. 1851. **59.** Martina, *Pio IX*, p.464. **60.** E. Halevy, *The age of Peel and Cobden. A history of the English people 1841–1852*, transl. from the French by E.I. Watkin, London 1947, pp.319–20. **61.** Machin, *Russell*, p.289. This disproves W. Ralls, 'The Papal Aggression of 1850: A study in Victorian anti-Catholicism' in *Ch.H.* 43 (1974), pp.242–56. **62.** Machin, *Politics*, p.211. **63.** O.R.'s report of Cardinal Antonelli's observation, O.R. to R, Rome, 28 Feb. 1865, P.R.O., A.Pps., F.O.918/10, draft, private. **64.** *The Times*, 9 Oct. 1850, p.3: The New Cardinals, From a Roman Catholic Correspondent; L. Borinski, 'Dickens als Politiker' in *Die Neueren Sprachen* 72 (1973), pp.385–95, hier 592, n.7. **65.** Machin, *Politics*, p.209. **66.** *The Times*, 4 Nov. 1850, p.4. **67.** L.F. Stock (ed.), *United States Ministers to the Papal States. Instructions and Despatches 1848–1868*, Washington D.C. 1933 (American Catholic Historical Association Documents 2), p.78, n.74. **68.** Halévy, *Age of Peel*, pp.320–21. **69.** *Ibid.*, p.321; Machin, *Politics*, p.217. **70.** Machin, *Russell*, p.285; Borinski, *Dickens*, p.593. **71.** 'Neujahrsbetrachtungen' in *H.P.Bl.* 27 (1851), p.52. **72.** P to Her Majesty's Representatives Abroad, P.R.O., F.O.12, Dec. 1850. **73.** Document no.12 in the Appendix. **74.** P's note, 7 April 1851; P to Normanby, 8 April 1851, No.134; P.R.O., F.O.79/49; Normanby to Cowley, No.134, 8 April 1851, F.O. 27/893. **75.** Document no.13 in the Appendix. **76.** Conyngham to Petre, 16 April 1852; Petre to Conyngham, Rome, 7 May 1852, private, P.R.O., F.O.43/57. **77.** Document no.14 in the Appendix; Bulwer to Petre, Florence, 8 July 1852, private, Arundel Castle MD 2388. **78.** Document no. 15 in the Appendix. **79.** Cass to the foreign secretary, Daniel Webster, Rome, 26 Oct. 1852, printed by Stock, *U.S. Ministers*, p.93. **80.** Document no.16 in the Appendix. **81.** Document no. 17 *ibid.* **82.** Document no.18 *ibid.* On the religious policies of Britain in the empire see Borinski, *Anfänge*, pp.22–4. **83.** Document no.19 in the Appendix. **84.** See T.W. Legh Lord Newton, *Lord Lyons*, 2 vols., London 1913. **85.** Document no.20 in the Appendix. **86.** Scarlett, the British Minister at Florence, to Lyons, Florence, 5 Sept. 1853, P.R.O., F.O.79/168, No.17. **87.** Lyons to Scarlett, Rome, 7 Sept. 1853, P.R.O., F.O.79/168, No.58; Lyons to Scarlett, Rome, 10 Sept. 1853, *ibid.*, No.61. **88.** Lyons to Scarlett, Rome, 4 Oct. 1853, P.R.O., F.O.79/169, No.67. **89.** Document no.21 and 22 in the Appendix. **90.** 28 Oct. 1853, P.R.O., F.O.79/174. **91.** Document no.23 in the Appendix. **92.** Lyons to Scarlett, Rome, 28 March 1854, confidential, No.21, P.R.O., F.O.43/58. **93.** Document no.24 in the Appendix. **94.** Document no.25 *ibid.* **95.** Cl. to Bulwer, F.O., 23 Nov. 1854, No.40,

confidential, draft, P.R.O., F.O.79/175. **96.** Lyons to Bulwer, Rome, 2 Dec. 1854,
No.78, P.R.O., F.O.43/58; sent to Cl. by Bulwer, Florence, 10 Dec. 1854, F.O.79/179;
Document no.26 in the Appendix, sent to Cl. by Normanby, Florence, 16 Jan. 1855,
F.O.79/183; Normanby to Lyons, 23 Jan. 1855, No.5, F.O.79/182; Document no.27 in
the Appendix; Normanby to Lyons, 2 July 1855, No.43, F.O.79/182. **97.** *Copies or
Extracts of Despatches received from Mr Lyons in the years 1855, 1856, and 1857,
respecting the Conditions and Administration of the Papal States,* printed on command
of the house of commons, 26 June 1860.

CHAPTER VI.1

1. Randall, 'Lord Odo Russell and his Roman Friends' in *History Today* 26 (1976),
pp.365—76, here 369. **2.** *Ibid.*, p.371. **3.** Sir Odo Russell, *Contacts,* p.66. **4.** See Weber,
Kardinäle, vol.I, pp.271, 276; F.J. Coppa, 'Cardinal Antonelli, the Papal States, and
the Counter-Risorgimento' in *Journal of Church and State* 16 (1974), pp.453—71, is of
the opinion that policies of the church states were determined by Pius IX's
intransigence. **5.** Conzemius, *Döllinger Correspondence,* vol.I, p.562, no.562: A to D,
London, ... **6.** Document no.28 in the Appendix. **7.** See Weber, *Kardinäle,* vol.I,
pp.186—199, especially Tab.15, p.198. **8.** O. van der Heydt, 'Mgr Talbot de Malahide'
in *Wiseman Review* No.502 (1964), pp.290—308, here 290—2. **9.** Cuthbert Butler, *The
life and times of Bishop Ullathorne, 1860—1889,* vol.I, London 1926, p.227. **10.**
P.R.O., A.Pps., F.O.918/85, p.276, copy, O.R. to his mother Lady R, Rome, 14 Dec.
1860; Blakiston, *Roman Question,* p.178, no.184: P.R.O.30/22/75, private, O.R. to R,
Rome, 11 June 1861. **11.** E.E. Reynolds, *Three Cardinals. Newman — Wiseman —
Manning,* London 1958, p.105. **12.** P. Thureau-Dangin, *La Renaissance catholique en
Angleterre au XIXe siècle,* vol.2, Paris 1903, p.311. **13.** O.R. to the foreign secretary,
Lord Malmesbury, Rome, 5 March 1859, private, P.R.O., A.Pps., F.O.918/6, *f.*70. **14.**
Blakiston, *Roman Question,* p.38, no.34: O.R. to R, Rome, 17 July 1859, no.89, secret,
P.R.O., F.O.43/71. **15.** *Ibid.,* p.39. **16.** P.R.O., A.Pps., F.O.918/10, p.52, draft, O.R.
to R, private, Rome, 19 Nov. 1859. **17.** Blakiston, *Roman Question,* p.112, no.114:
F.O.43/77, no.90, O.R. to R. Rome, 26 June 1860. **18.** P.R.O., A.Pps., F.O.918/85,
*f.*205, copy, O.R. to Lady R, private, Rome, 10 Sept. 1859. **19.** P.R.O., A.Pps.,
F.O.918/10, pp.69—70, draft, O.R. to R, private, Rome, 21 Jan. 1860. **20.** Documents
no.32 & 33 in the Appendix. **21.** R to O.R., F.O., 25 Oct. 1862, P.R.O., F.O.43/85,
no.46, printed in house of commons, *Accounts and Papers,* 1863, vol.75. *cf.* also de
Leonardis *Inghilterra,* pp.123—4. **22.** Conzemius, *Döllinger Correspondence,* vol.I,
p.297, no.80: A to D, 3 March 1863.

CHAPTER VI.2

23. Stock, *U.S. Ministers to the Papal States,* pp.262—3; Blatchford to Seward, No.1,
Rome, 29 Nov. 1862. **24.** *Ibid.,* p.273; Blatchford to Seward, No.6, Rome, 7 March
1863. **25.** *Ibid.,* p.275; Blatchford to Seward, No.8, Rome, 4 April 1863. **26.** *Ibid.,*
p.XXXVI. **27.** Text: *Acta Pii IX, vol.3, Graz 1971, pp.687—700 (Quanta Cura)*
701—17, *(Syllabus).* **28.** G. Martina, 'Osservazioni sulle varie redazioni dei "Sillabo" in
Chiesa e stato nell' ottocento. Miscellanea in onore di Pietro Pirri, ed. Aubert/Ghisal-
berti/D'Entrèves, vol.2 (Italia Sacra 4), Padua 1962, pp.419—523; Martina, 'Nuovi
documenti sulla genesi del Sillabo' in *A.H.P.* 6 (1968), pp.319—69. **29.** Martina,
Osservazioni, pp.467—9; *Genesi,* pp.351—3. **30.** *Ibid.,* p.352. **31.** J. Strong, *Our
Country,* New York 1885, enlarged edition 1891; new edition by J. Herbst, Cambridge,
Mass. 1963, ch.5. **32.** *Ibid.,* Herbst, Introduction, pp.IX, XIV. **33.** *Ibid.,* p.61. **34.**
Ibid., p.60. **35.** *Ibid.,* p.68. **36.** *Ibid.,* p.71. **37.** *Ibid.* p.72. **38.** *Vide* Cardinal
Hergenröther, *Katholische Kirche und christlicher Staat* (1872), vol.2 repr. Aalen 1968,
pp.806—864. **39.** Strong, *Our Country,* new ed., p.74. **40** *Ibid.,* p.65, n.14. **41.**
Spalding, 'Catholicism and Apaism' in N.A.R. 159 (1894), pp.277—87, here 286. **42.**
N.A.R. 154 (1892), pp.385—400. **43.** 'Hostility to Roman Catholics' in *N.A.R.* 158

(1894), pp.563–8 here 570. **44.** See below p. 166 **45.** Strong, *Our Country*, new ed. p.61, n.3, the volume referred to was published in New York in 1875. **46.** *Op.cit.*, first ed., p.51 from Gladstone, *Vatican Decrees*, p.45. **47.** Stock *U.S. Ministers to the Holy See*, p.327; King to Seward, No.30, Rome, 7 Jan. 1865. **48.** O.R. to Lady R, Washington 1857; Blakiston, *Roman Question*, p.XI; see also O.R. to Arthur R, Rome, 10 Jan. 1863, P.R.O., F.O.918/84, *f*.38. **49.** Blakiston, *Roman Question*, pp.299–300, No. 306; O.R. to R. Rome, 21 Dec. 1864, No.86, P.R.O., F.O.43/91B. **50.** *Lothair*, (1870), ch.50, p.208; Buschkühl, *Irische Frage*, p.87. **51.** Blakiston, *Roman Question*, p.361, No.402; O.R. to Cl., Rome, 6 April 1869, No.18, secret, P.R.O., F.O.43/103B. **52.** Martina, *Genesi del Sillabo*, pp.357–8. **53.** Martina, *Osservazioni*, p.485. **54.** *Ibid.*, pp.495–99. **55.** Cited from *ibid.*, p.494. **56.** *Ibid.*, pp.484–5, 506; Martina, *Genesi del Sillabo*, pp.363–5. **57.** Martina, *Osservazioni*, p.506. **58.** *D.B.I.*, vol.10, p.46; Weber, *Kardinäle*, p.440. **59** Martina, *Genesi del Sillabo*, p.358. **60.** *Ibid.*, p.322; Martina, *Osservazioni*, p.440. **61.** *Ibid.*, p.457; Martina, *Genesi del Sillabo*, p.336, n.23. **62.** Purcell, *Life of Manning*, vol.II, p.722, n.1. **63.** *The Letters and Diaries of John Henry Newman*, ed. Dessain & Gornall, vol.23, Oxford 1973, p.209; Ambrose St. John to Newman, Rome, 2 May 1867. **64.** 'Notes and Comments', in: *C.H.R.*40 (1954), pp.94–5, here 94. **65.** Martina, *Osservazioni*, p.458n. **66.** H.C.G. Matthew (ed.), *The Gladstone Diaries*, vol.6, Oxford 1978, p.481. **67.** See K. Deufel, *Kirche und Tradition*, Munich 1976, p.246; Martina *Osservazioni*, pp.428,456; Blakiston, *Roman Question*, p.142, No.146. **68.** P.R.O., A.Pps., F.O.918/85, p.236, copy, O.R. to Lady R, Rome, 3 Dec. 1859; see also *ibid.* p.304, copy, O.R. to Lady R. Rome, 1 June 1861; F.O.918/84, p.48, copy, O.R. to Arthur R, Rome, 13 June 1863; *ibid.*, p.52, copy, O.R. to Arthur R. Rome, 2 July 1863; *ibid.*, p.83, copy, O.R. to Arthur R, Rome, 13 July 1863. **69.** *Ibid.*, p.55, copy, O.R. to Arthur R, Rome, 13 Feb. 1864. **70.** *Ibid.*, p.60, copy, O.R. to Arthur R, Rome, 28 July 1866. **71.** Document no.34 in the appendix. **72.** *Notes and Comments*, p.95. **73.** S. Leslie, *Life of Cardinal Manning*, 2nd ed., London 1921, p.138. **74.** X. de Montclos, *Lavigerie, le Saint-Siège et l'Église de l'avènement de Pie IX à l'avènement de Léon XIII, 1846–1878*, Diss. Paris 1965, p.186, n.3. **75.** *Ibid.*, p.300. **76.** *Ibid.*, p.185. **77.** Weber, *Cardinals*, vol.II, p.512. **78.** J.M. Pica, *Le cardinal Bilio, barnabite, un des présidents du concile du Vatican (1826–1884)*, Paris 1898, p.19. **79.** I. von Senestréy, *Wie es zur Definition der päpstlichen Unfehlbarkeit kam. Tagebuch vom I. Vatikanischen Konzil*, ed. & commentary by K. Schatz, Frankfurt 1977, p.11. **82.** Jedin (ed.), *Handbuch der Kirchengeschichte*, vol.VI/2, Frieburg i.Br. 1973, p.7. **83.** *D.I.B.*, vol.10, p.46. **85.** Norman, *The Catholic Church and Ireland in the age of rebellion 1859–1873*, (in future cited as *Ireland*), London 1965, p.91; Manning to Gl., 22 Sept. 1867, Gl.Pps., BM Add.MSS 44249, *f*.8. **86.** V.A. McClelland, *Cardinal Manning*, London 1962, p.167; Manning to Gl., 11 Feb. 1868, Gl.Pps., vol.164, BM Add.MSS 44249. **87.** *Ibid.*, p.168; Manning to Gl., 11 March 1868, Gl.Pps. *ibid.* **88.** G.W.E. Russell, *Collections and recollections by one who has kept a diary*, (in future cited as *Recollections*), seventh ed., London 1898, p.46. **89.** Strong, *Our Country*, first ed., p.54. **90.** *Ibid.*, p.53. **91.** New ed., p.60 cited from E. Sh. Purcell, 'On Church and State, in *Essays on religion & literature*, second ser. ed. Manning, London 1867.

CHAPTER VI.3

92. O.R. to Lady R, Rome, 16 Jan. 1864, A.Pps., P.R.O., F.O.918/85, *f*.351. **93.** Blakiston, *Roman Question*, p.308, No.313; P.R.O.30/22/111; private, R to O.R., F.O., 20 Feb. 1865. **94.** Cwiekowski, *Vatican*, p.34. **95.** Bellesheim, *Irland*, vol.III, p.437. **96.** Blakiston, *Roman Question*, p.308. **97.** Document no.35 in the Appendix. **98.** J.D. Holmes, 'Some unpublished passages from Cardinal Wiseman's correspondence' in *D.R.*90 (1972), pp.41–52, here 48; Leslie, *Manning*, pp.132–7. **99.** Document no.36 in the Appendix. **100.** R. Aubert, *Le pontificat de Pie IX (1846–1878)*, (Histoire de l'Église, vol.21), Paris 1952, p.159. **101.** P.R.O., A.Pps., F.O.918/10, pp.167–74, draft private, O.R. to R, Rome, 5 May 1865; printed by Cwiekowski,

Vatican, p.31, n.2 from copy in P.R.O.30/22/77. **102.** Blakiston, *Roman Question*, p.313, No.320; telegr. no.45, F.O.43/94 A, R to O.R., F.O., 6 May 1865. **103.** *Ibid.*, p.315, No.324; P.R.O. 30/22/77, private, O.R. to R, Rome, 17 May 1865; draft in F.O.918/10, pp.179–82. **104.** Russell, *Recollections*, p.46. **105.** *Merry England*, Cardinal Manning, No. ..., 1 May 1886, with notes by 'John Oldcastle' (i.e. W. Meynell), p.89. **106.** Cwiekowski, *Vatican*, p.56; see also A.W. Hutton, *Cardinal Manning*, London 1892, pp.219, 223. **107.** Russell, *Recollections*, p.55.

CHAPTER VII.1

1. W. Sichel, *Disraeli: A study in personality and ideas*, London 1904, p.248. **2.** *Ibid.* p.250. **3.** *Vide* Buschkühl, *Irische Frage*, pp.29–37; L. O'Brien, *Fenian Fever, An Anglo-American Dilemma*, London 1971; W.S. Neidhardt, *Fenianism in North America*, London 1975; T.W. Moody (ed.), *The Fenian Movement*, Cork 1968. **4.** King to Seward, No.46, Rome, 18 Nov. 1865; Stock, *U.S. Ministers to the Papal States*, pp.350–1; *Foreign Relations*, pp.164–5. **5.** Telegrams, O.R. to U., Rome, 5 March 1866, U. to O.R., Rome, 6 March 1866, P.R.O., F.O.43/96A. **6.** Document No.37 in the Appendix. **7.** O.R. to U., Rome, 10 April 1866, U. Pps., C.98, *f*.128. **8.** Document No.38 in the Appendix. **9.** O.R. to U., Rome, 9 May 1866, U. Pps., C.98, *f*.132. **10.** Document No.39 in the Appendix. **11.** Document No.40 *ibid.*

CHAPTER VII.2

12. Cited from J. Pope Hennessy, 'Lord Beaconsfield's Irish Policy', in *Nineteenth Century* 16 (1884) 663–80, here p.665; J.P. Hennessy to Pius IX, 'Notizie politiche', Jan. 1866, Arch. Vat., Segretaria di Stato 1866, n.39747; de Leonardis, *Inghilterra*, ρ.168. **13.** See Leonardis, *Inghilterra*, pp.34–45, 104–116; M. Tedeschi, 'Clarendon, Gladstone e la Questione Romana (1859–1861)' in *Studi in onore di Pietro Agostino d'Avack*, Milan 1976, vol.3, pp.953–75. **14.** Blakiston, *Roman Question*, p.67: No.62: P.R.O. 30/22/III, priv., R. to O.R., F.O. 12 Dec. 1859. **15.** *Ibid.*, p.328, No.348: P.R.O. 30/22/16, R. to O.R., Downing St. 4 June 1866. **16.** Borinski, *Dickens als Politiker*, pp.592–3. **17.** Buckle, *Life of Disraeli*, vol.IV, London 1916, pp.399, 415; n.3; Disraeli in a letter 1864. J. Vincent, *Disraeli, Derby, and the Conservative Party. Journals and Memoirs of Edward Henry Lord Stanley, 1849–1869*, Hassocks, Sussex 1978, p.167: Disraeli to Stanley, House of Commons, 18 Feb. 1861. **18.** De Leonardis, *Inghilterra*, pp.31–33; Disraeli to Bowyer cited in Ward, *Life and Times of Cardinal Wiseman*, vol.2, p.449. **19.** Blakiston, *Roman Question*, pp.80–81, No.73; P.R.O.30/22/75, priv., O.R. to R., Rome, 7 Jan. 1860; see also p.84 No.78: F.O. 43/76, No.19, secret, O.R. to R., Rome, 31 Jan. 1860. **20.** De Leonardis, *Inghilterra*, pp.73,89; Hansard, *Parliamentary Debates*, 3rd series, (1860), vol.157, 1330, 1493; vol.158, 679–90, 10B; vol.159, 147–62, 1842. **21.** Sichel, *Disraeli*, p.175. **22.** Kebbel, *Lord Beaconsfield and other Tory Memoirs*, London 1907, pp.28–9. **23.** Buschkühl, *Irische Frage*, p.42; Buckle, *Disraeli*, vol.IV, p.325; N. Miko, *Das Ende des Kirchenstaats*, vol.I, Vienna 1964, p.415 No.755: d'Azeglio to Prime Minister Menarea, London, 14 March 1868, politico No.380, MAE Rome, No. 1350, Ing. 1868; de Leonardis, *Inghilterra*, p.135. **24.** I. Hermann, *Disraelis Stellung zur katholischen Kirche*, Diss. Freiburg 1932, H. Somerville, 'Disraeli and Catholicism' in *The Month* 159 (1932) 114–24; D.E. Painting, 'Disraeli and the Roman Catholic Church' in *Q.R.*304 (1966) 17–25; Buschkühl, *Irische Frage*, 102–5; on Clausson's anti-catholic 'English Catholics and Roman Catholicism in Disraeli's Novels' in *Nineteenth Century Fiction* 34 (1979) 454–74 see Buschkühl, p.102n. **25.** *Ibid.; John O'London's Weekly*, 25 Nov. 1922, p.280. **26.** Disraeli, *Lothair*, ch.48, p.201; ch.30, p.117. **27.** *Saturday Review*, vol.29, No.758, 7 May 1870, p.612; *A.Z.*, 5 May 1870, p.197. **28.** Disraeli, *Lothair*, ch.9, pp.29–30. **29.** Russell, *Portraits of the Seventies*, 2nd ed., London 1916, p.315, See Buschkühl, *Irische Frage*, p.95. **30.** *M.E.* 10 (1888) p.747: 'Cardinal Howard'. **31.** 'The late Cardinal Howard' in *The Tablet*, 24 September 1892, p.481. **32.** F. Boase (Ed.), *Modern English Biography*, vol.V, London (1912) repr. 1965, *s.v.* Howard, Edward Henry. **33.** Ch. P. Isaacson, *The story of the English Cardinals*, London 1907, p.284. **34.** *The Oscotian*, n.s. No.22, July 1888, p.171: 'Cardinal Howard'; On Patrizi vide Weber, *Kardinäle*, vol.2, pp.500–501. **35.** Russell, *Portrait of the Seventies*. **36.** In Jedin (ed.), *Handbuch der Kirchengeschichte*, VI/I, ch.33: J. Beckmann, 'Die Missionen 1840–1870', pp.619–23 there is no mention of this. **37.** *Oscotian*, No.22, p.171. **38.** P.R.O., A.Pps., F.O.918/85, p.299, coyp, O.R. to Lady R., Rome 27 Apr. 1861. **39.** Blakiston, *Roman Question*, p.288, No.298: F.O.43/91 B No.59, confidential, O.R. to R., Ariccia near Rome, 30 July 1864. **40.** 'Death of Cardinal Howard', in: *Times*, 17 Sept. 1892, p.7. **41.** *M.E.* 10 (1888), p.747; see Vincent, *Stanley journals, passim*. **42.** *Times*, 17 Sept. 1892, p.7. **43.** *I.L.N.*, 24 Sept. 1892, p.390. **44.** *Times, loc. cit.* **45.** See C.J. Woods, 'Ireland and Anglo-Papal relations, 1880–85', in *I.H.S.* 18 (1972), pp.29–60. **46.** *Tablet*, 24 Sept. 1892, p.483. **47.** *I.L.N., loc. cit.* **48.** H. d'Ideville, *Journal d'un Diplomate en Italie. Notes intimes pour servir à l'histoire du Second Empire*, vol.2: Rome 1862–1866, Paris 1873, p.33; Montclos, *Lavigerie*, pp.167,188,196. **49.** *Lothair*, ch.50, p.207. **50.** Miko, *Kirchenstaatsende*, vol.I, p.259, No.341: Report Minister d'Azeglio, London, to Foreign Minister Campello, 25 Sept. 1867, M.A.E. Rome, No.1349, Ing. 1867. **51.** *Lothair*, ch.50, p.209. **52.** *Cf. Auswärtige Politik Preussens*, vol.9, pp.237–8, No.169, 269–70, 197; Katte to Bismarck, 18 Sept. resp. 5 Oct. 1867. **53.** *A.Z.*, No.268, 25 Sept. 1867, p.4289. **54.** P. Challemel-Lacour, 'Le romain politique en Angleterre, Lothaire par M. Disraeli' in *R.D.M.* 40 (1870), vol.88, p.435. **55.** *Lothair*, ch.50, p.210. **56.** Mori, *Il tramoute del potere temporale 1866–1870 (Politica e storia 15)*, Rome 1967, p.27: Count Apponyi, Austrian Ambassador Beust, 19 Nov. 1866, communicated to Hübner, Austrian Ambassador in Rome, H.H.St.A. Vienna, pol. Arch. fasc. 219. **57.** Blakiston, *Roman Question*, p.335, No.355; F.O.43/96B, No.81, O.R. to Stanley, Rome 19 Nov. 1866. **58.** Conzemius, *Döllinger Correspondence*, vol.I, p.455, No.127. A. to D., Rome 13 Dec. 1866. **59.** *Lothair*, ch.9, p.33. **60.** *Ibid.*, ch.50, p.210. **61.** Borinski, *Dickens*, p.593, n.1. **62.** Miko, *Kirchenstaatsende*, vol.I, p.259, No.341: d'Azeglio to Campello, London 15 Sept. 1867, ser. pol. No.308, M.A.E. Rome, No. 1349, Ing. 1867. Cf. de Leonardis, *Inghilterra*, p.169. **63.** See Buschkühl, *Irische Frage*, pp.38–49. **64.** Bastgen (ed.), *Die Römische Frage*, vol.II, Freiburg 1918, pp.552–4, No.300: d'Azeglio to Menabrea, London, 29 Oct. 1867. **65.** Miko, *Kirchenstaatsende*, vol.I, p.286, No.427: d'Azeglio to Menabrea, London 28 Oct. 1867, politico No.315, M.A.E. Rome, No.1349, Ing. 1867. **66.** *Ibid.*, p.297, No.463: d'Azeglio to Menabrea, London 4 Nov. 1867, priv., M.A.E. Rome, No.1349, Ing. 1868. **67.** *Ibid.*, p.445, No.821: Maffei to Menabrea, London 8 Sept. 1868, politico, No.458, M.A.E. Rome, No.1350, Ing. 1868. **68.** De Leonardis, *Inghilterra*, p.112. **69.** *Lothair*, ch.50, p.212. **70.** Vincent, *Stanley journals*, p.217: 22 May 1864; p.259: 7 July 1866. **71.** *Lothair*, ch.69, p.282. **72.** Hansard, *Debates*, vol.195, p.2001. **73.** *Ireland and the Holy See*, Rome May 1883, p.3. **74.** *Ibid.*, pp.4,8,9,10,12. **75.** *Ibid.*, p.13. **76.** *Ibid.*, pp.19–21. **77.** Cullen to Bishop Lynch of Toronto, 13 May 1864, Dublin Diocesan Archives cited from E.D. Steele, 'Cardinal Cullen and Irish nationality', *J.H.S.*19 (1975) 239–60, here 241. **78.** P.F. Moran (ed.), Cullen's nephew, the future Cardinal primate of Australia), *Pastoral and other writings of Cardinal Cullen*, vol.2, Dublin 1882, p.397. **79.** Steele, *Cardinal Cullen*, p.257. **80.** Norman, *Ireland*, p.95: Leaky to Barnabo. **81.** *Ibid.*, p.117. **82.** Cited from *ibid.*, p.96. **83.** D. McCartney, 'The Church and Fenianism' in *Fenians and Fenianism*, ed. M. Harmon, 2nd ed., Dublin 1970, p.17. **84.** Leslie, *Manning*, p.194. **85.** *Cf.* Norman, *Ireland*, pp.100–102; McCartney, *Church and Fenianism*, p.18; McCartney, 'The Churches and Secret Societies' in T.D. Williams (ed.) *Secret Societies in Ireland*, Dublin/New York 1973, p.72. T. O'Fiaich, 'The patriot priest of Patry, Patrick Lavelle 1825–1886, *Journal of the Galway Archaeological and Historical Society* 35 (1976) 129–48. **86.** Buckle, *Disraeli*, vol.V, p.5. **87.** Pope-Hennessy, *Beaconsfield's Irish Policy*, p.677. **88.** *Ibid.*, p.665. **89.** *Lothair*, ch.6, p.17. **90.** *Ibid.*, ch.9, p.31. **91.** H.J. Hanham, *Scottish Nationalism*, London 1969, p.20. **92.** V.A. McClelland, 'The Irish Clergy and Archbishop Manning's Visitation of the Western

District of Scotland' in *C.H.R.* 53 (1967) pp.1–27 & 229–50, here 2. **93.** *Ibid.*, p.6; *cf.* J.E. Handley, *The Irish in Modern Scotland*, Cork 1947. **94.** *Catholic Directory for Scotland 1978*, Glasgow 1978, p.37. **95.** P. Corish, 'Der Aufstieg des Katholizismus in der angelsächsischen Welt' in *Handbuch*, vol.VI/I, pp.551–6, here 556. **96.** McClelland, *Irish Clergy*, pp.15–6,26. **97.** A. Bellesheim, *History of the Catholic Church in Scotland*, vol.IV, Edinburgh 1890, pp.296–7. **98.** McClelland, *Irish Clergy*, pp.244–5. **99.** Blakiston, *Roman Question*, p.349, No.380: F.O.43/101, despatch No.14, Rome 21 Jan, 1868, O.R. to Stanley. **100.** P. MacSuibhne (ed.), *Paul Cullen and his contemporaries*, vol.V, Naas, Co. Kildare 1977, p.209. **101.** McClelland, 'A Hierarchy for Scotland, 1868–1878' in *C.H.R.* 56 (1970), pp.474–500, here 480. **102.** *Ibid.*, pp.485–6. **103.** P.R.O., A.Pps., F.O.918/1, priv., Cl. to O.R., F.O., 14 Dec. 1868; the draft printed by Blakiston, *Roman Question*, p.354, No.387. **104.** F.O.918/4, p.15, O.R. to Cl., draft No.1, Rome 16 Dec. 1868. **105.** Blakiston, *Roman Question*, p.356, No.391: F.O.43/101B, Rome 1 Jan. 1869, No.1, O.R. to Cl. **106.** McClelland, *A. Hierarchy*, pp.485–6. **107.** P.R.O., A.Pps., F.O.918/4, p.35, O.R. to Cl., draft No.4, Rome 27 Jan. 1869. **108.** Isaacson, *English Cardinals*, p.285. **109.** 'Death of Cardinal Howard' in *The Times* 17 Sept. 1892, p.7. **110.** L. Apjohn, *The Earl of Beaconsfield*, London, 1881, p.213. **111.** W.W. Hunter, *A life of the early of Mayo*, vol.1, London 1875, p.78. **112.** Borinski, *Phineas Finn*, pp.211–2. **113.** Purcell, *Manning*, p.511. **114.** Norman, *Ireland*, pp.242–74. **115.** Matthew, *Gladstone diaries*, vol.VI, p.18: 20 March 1861; see introduction vol.V, p.LIX, vol.VI, p.285: 26 June 1864; p.291: 23 July 1864; p.455, 30 July 1866; p.460: 27 Aug. 1866; p.461: 28 Aug. 1866. **116.** *Ibid.*, vol.V, p.LIV. **117.** Norman, *Ireland*, p.273: Woodlock Pps., Cullen to Woodlock, 25 March 1868. **118.** Vincent, *Stanley journals*, p.323: 20 Nov. 1867; 331: 2 March 1868. **119.** E. Clarke, *Benjamin Disraeli*, 2nd ed., London 1926, p.178; Buckle, *Disraeli*, vol.V, p.16. **120.** Norman, *Ireland*, p.273, Blakiston, *Roman Question*, p.351 No.383: F.O.43/101, No.32, secret, O.R. to Stanley, Rome 26 March 1868. **121.** *A.Z.*, 16 Jan. 1869, p.158. **122.** Hansard, *Debates*, vol.190, p.1729. **123.** Norman, *Ireland*, p.274. **124** *Ibid.* p.274. **125.** *Lothair*, ch.9, p.33. **126** Fenchtwanger, *Gladstone*, p.143. **127** Kebbell, *Life of Lord Beaconsfield*, London 1888, p.172; E. Herve, *La crise irlandaise depuis la fin du dix-huitième siècle à nos jours*, Paris 1885, p.244; Buckle, *Disraeli*, vol.V, p.16. **128.** J.C. Beckett (ed.) 'Select documents XII. Gladstone, Queen Victoria and the disestablishment of the Irish Church, 1868–69' in *I.H.S.* 12 (1962), pp.38–47, here 41. **129.** Shearman, *Church of Ireland*, p.19. **130.** *Ibid.*, p.34; Bellesheim, *Irland*, vol.3, pp.615–6. See also J.D. Fair, 'The disestablishment of the Irish Church 1869' in Fair, *British Interparty Conferences*, Oxford 1980, pp.15–34. **131** Norman, *Ireland*, p.88, n.4: Cullen to Gl., 14 July 1869, Gl. Pps., B.M.Add MS 44421, *f.*150; *cf.* also Macsuibhne, *Cullen*, vol.V, p.178, No.182: Bayswater Pps., Cullen to Manning, Dublin, 14 Feb. 1872. **132.** Schmitz, *Englands politisches Vermächtnis an Deutschland*, Munich 1916, p.270. **133.** Documents No.41–4 in the Appendix; P.R.O., F.O.43/102, Consul Severn to Stanley, Rome 8 Jan. 1868, No.4, copy of letter of Fenian informer John F. McAuliffe.

CHAPTER VIII

1. *Vide* K.J. Rivinius, *Bischof Wilhelm Emmanuel von Ketteler und die Infallibiltät des Papstes* (Europäische Hochschulschriften, series 23 theology, vol.48) Diss. Münster 1975, printed Frankfurt 1976, p.102; G. Martina, 'Il concilio Vaticano I e la fine del potere temporale' in *Rassegna storica toskana* 16 (1970) pp.131–50, here 132. **2.** N. Miko, 'Die Römische Frage und das Erste Vatikanische Konzil' in *Römische Historische Mitteilungen* 4 (1960/61), pp.254–71, here 260, 267. **3.** *Lothair*, ch.84, p.346. **4.** Miko, *Kirchenstaatsende*, vol.II, p.XIV. **5.** *Lothair*, ch.84, pp.347–8. **6.** *Cf.* Disraeli, 'The Present Position of the Church' (14 Nov. 1861) in *Church and Queen. Five speeches ... by ... Disraeli*, London 1865; *Church Policy, a speech delivered ... Nov. 25, 1864*, London 1864; *The Prime Minister on Church and State* (17 June 1868), London n.d. **7.** *Lothair*, ch.38, p.153.

CHAPTER VIII.1

8. *Lothair,* ch.87, p.361. **9.** R. Aubert, *Vaticanum I* (1964), German ed. Mayence 1965, p.47. **10.** *The Tablet* (1868). **11.** Leslie, *Manning,* p.142: Talbot to Wiseman, 11 May 1863. **12.** Van der Heydt, *Monsignor Talbot,* p.299. **13.** Blakiston, *Roman Question,* p.368, No.411: Cl. Pps. C.487, Rome 14 July 1869, priv., O.R. to Cl. **14.** W. Brandmüller, *Ignaz von Döllinger am Vorabend des I. Vatikanum. Hereausforderung und Antwort,* St. Ottilien 1977, pp.127–9. **15.** Cwiekowski, *Vatican I,* p.94. **16.** *M.E.,* 1 May 1886, p.78. **17.** J.J. Dwyer, 'The Catholic Press 1850–1950' in G.A. Beck (ed.), *The English Catholics 1850–1950,* London 1950, p.477. **18.** Brandmüller, *Döllinger,* p.127; *vide* Ward, *W.G. Ward and the Catholic Revival,* p.255. **19.** Brandmüller, *Döllinger,* p.218, No.19: F.X. Dieringer to D., Bonn 30 Nov. 1869. **20.** *Ibid.,* pp.128–9; *Theologisches Literaturblatt,* No.14, 8 July 1867. **21.** A Franzen, *Die katholische – theologische Fakultät Bonn im Streit um das Erste Vatikanische Konzil.* Zugleich ein Beitrag zur Entstehumgsgeschichte des Alkatholizismus am Niederrheim (Bonner Beiträge zur Kirchengeschichte 6) Cologne 1974, p.328. **23.** Brandmüller, *Döllinger,* p.128; 'Über eine theologische Kontroverse jenseits des Kanals' in *Katholik* 47 (1867) vol.2, pp.349–66, 'Der Bischof von Birmingham und die Störenfriede' unter deu englischen Katholiken' in *Katholik* 47 (1867) vol.2, pp.641–55. **24.** Russell, *Recollections,* p.55; Hutton, Manning, p.121. **25.** Newman, *Letters and Diaries,* vol.23, p.111: Ullathorne to Newman, Birmingham 18 March 1867. **26.** K. Schatz, *Kirchenbild und päpstliche Unfehlbarkeit bei den deutschsprachigen Minoritätsbischöfeu auf dem I. Vatikanum* (MPH 40) Rome 1975, pp.108–9; Liberatore, 'Un nuovo tributo a S. Pietro' in *Civ. Catt.,* ser. VI, vol.10 (1 June 1867), pp.641–51; 'L'infallibilità pontificia ed il Gallicanismo' in *Civ. Catt.,* ser.VI, vol.3 (1868), pp.513–31; 'Il Concilio ecumenico intimato dal Santo Padre Pio IX' in *Civ. Catt.,* ser. VII, vol.3 (18 July 1868), pp.259–61. **27.** Blakiston, *Roman Question,* p.345, No.370; F.O.43/99B, No.51, O.R. to Stanley, Rome 19 June 1867. **28.** See Document No.50 in the Appendix. **29.** Newman, *Letters and Diaries,* vol.23, index pp.422–3. **30.** G. Martina (ed.), and G.G. Franco, *Appunti storici sopra il Concilio Vaticano* (MPH 33) Rome 1972, p.90n. 38; pp.18–19; see *A History of the Third Plenary Council of Baltimore Nov.9th–Dec.7th, 1884,* Baltimore 1885; T.E. Sherman, 'Father Charles Piccirillo' in *Woodstock Letters* 7 (1888) 339–50; on the reasons for Piccirillo being transferred to the U.S. *vide* G. Martina, 'Review of: Weber, Kardinäle' in A.H.P. 16 (1978) 406–16, here 16. **31.** Schatz (ed.), Senestrey, *Unfehlbarkeit,* p.1; Purcell, *Manning,* vol.2, p.420. **32.** See Document No.50 in the Appendix. **33.** Butler/Lang, *Das erste Vatikanische Konzil,* 2nd ed., 1961, p.74. **34.** *The centenary of St. Peter's and the general council,* London 1867; *Il centenario di S. Pietro ed il Concilio Ecumenico,* Rome 1867; *Das Centenarium des hl. Petrus und das allegemeine Concilium,* Mayence 1867. **35.** See Granderath, *Geschichte des Vatikanischen Konzils,* vol.I, Freiburg i Br. 1903, pp.63–5. **36.** L. Lenhart (ed.), 'Moufangs Briefwechsel mit Bischof Ketteler und Domdekan Heinrich aus der Zeit seines römischen Aufenthalts zur Vorbereitung des Vaticanischen Councils' in *A.Mrh.KG.* 3(1951), pp.323–54, here 325 No.1: Moufans to Ketteler, Rome 6 Jan. 1869. **37.** Lenhart (ed.), 'Regens Moufang als Konsultor zur Vorbereitung des Vaticanums im Lichte seines römischen Jagebuchs' in *A.Mrh.KG.* 9(1957), pp.227–55, here 231, 233, 230–1, 233–8. **38.** Lenhart, 'Regens Moufang und das Vaticanum' in *Jahrbuch für das Bistum Mainz* 5 (1950), pp.400–441, here 417. **39.** Lenhart, *Moufangs Briefwechsel,* No.1: Moufang to Ketteler, Rome 6 Jan. 1869. **40.** Lenhart, *Moufang und das Vaticanum,* pp.327–8, No.2: Moufang to Ketteler, Rome 27 Jan. 1869. **41.** Lenhart, *Moufangs Jagebuch,* p.233, entry 20 Jan. 1869. **42.** Lenhart, *Moufangs Briefwechsel,* p.331 No.3: Moufang to Ketteler, Rome 10 Feb. 1869. **43.** Lenhart, *Moufang und das Vaticanum,* pp.423–5 Latin orig. **44.** Both Latin text printed together *ibid.,* pp.420–2. **45.** U. Reid, 'Studien zu Kettelers Stellung zum Infallibilitätsdogma bis zur Definition am 18 Juli 1870' in *H.J.*47 (1927) 657–726, here 661. **46.** Lenhart, *Moufangs Tagebuch,* p.238, entry 1 March 1869. **47.** French correspondence in *Civ. Catt.,* ser. VII, vol.V (1869), pp.345–52. **48.** Granderath,

Vatikanisches Konzil, vol.I, pp.215−6. **49.** *D.B.I.,* vol.24, Rome 1980, pp.751−4; Weber, *Kardinäle,* vol.I, pp.26−7, tab.2; Jedin, *Handbuch,* vol.VI/2, ch.1. **50.** E. Veuillot, *Louis Veuillot,* vol.III, Paris 1909, p.482; P.R.O. A.Pps., F.O.918/85, p.337, copy, O.R. to Lady R., Rome 20 March 1863; Letters of Mario Chigi to O.R.: F.O. 918/70, pp.122−53. Nunci Chigi invited O.R. to dinner in the nunciature in Paris, e.g. on 14 April 1868: Flavo Chigi to O.R., Paris 12 April 1868. **51.** Aubert, *Vaticanum I,* p.90. **52.** Lenhart, *Moufangs Briefwechsel,* p.355 No.5: Moufang to Ketteler, Rome 14 March 1869. **53.** Ollivier, *L'Eglise et l'Etat au Concile du Vatican,* vol.I, Paris 1879, p.437. **54.** Weber, *Kardinäle,* vol.1, pp.278−80. **55.** *Ibid.,* p.269; vol.II, pp.437−8. **56.** K. Schoeters, *P.-J. Beck S.J. (1795−1887) en de Jezuitenpolitiek van zijn tijd,* Antwerpe 1965, p.206, P.R.O., A.Pps., F.O.918/84, p.101, copy, O.R. to Arthur R., Rome 26 Apr. 1869. **57.** *D.B.I.,* vol.22, pp.383−5; A.G. Pecorari, 'Mons. Luigi Martini tra Mantova e la Santa Sede (Una vicenda complessa e contraditoria)' in *Civiltà Mantovana* 12 (1978), pp.105−58; Weber, *Kardinäle,* vol.I, p.269; vol.2, pp.449−50; 558 (Doc.2); 678 (Doc.7). **58.** Schoeters, *Beckx,* pp.206−7; Piccirillo to Le Grelle, 4 May 1869. **59.** G. Caprile, 'La Civiltà catholica al Concilio Vaticano I' in *Civ. Catt.* 120 (1969) vol.IV, pp.333−41 & 538−48, here 335; Franco, *Appunti,* pp.232−4. **60.** *Ibid.,* p.233n. 272; MacSuibhne, *Cullen,* vol.V, p.46 No.44: Cullen to his secretary Conroy, Rome 21 Jan 1870. **61** Schoeters, *Beckx,* pp.206−7. **62.** Brandmüller, *Döllinger,* p.12. **63.** L. Pfleger, 'Zur Beurteilung Louis Veuillots' in *H.P.Bl.* 153 (1914), pp.355−66, here 356−7; W. Gurian, *Die politischen und sozialen Ideen des französischen Katholizismus 1789−1914,* M. Gladbach 1929, p.234. See also M.L. Brown, *Louis Veuillot,* Durham NC 1977. **64.** Breve of 16 May 1872, cited in Pfleger, *Beurteilung,* p.358. **65.** J. Ward/B. Gezzi, 'Pius IX's Voltaire: Louis Veuillot and Vatican I' in *Thought* 45 (1970), pp.346−70, here 359; Manning Veuillot, 4 Dec. 1864, BN, N.A.F. 26434, *f.*108. Manning to Veuillot, 11 Jan. 1867, *ibid. f.*231. 'Sayings of Cardinal Manning' in M.E., March 1892 (no page numbers in this issue). **66.** *De la Dévotion au Pape,* Paris 1860. **67.** Conzemius, 'Warum wurde der päpstliche Primat gerade im Jahre 1870 definiert?' in *Concilium* 7(1971), pp.263−7, here 265. **68.** Here I cannot agree with K. Schatz, 'Totalrevision der I. Vatikanums? Zur Auseinandersetzung mit den Thesen von August B. Hasler' in *Theologie und Philosophie* 53 (1978), pp.248−76, here 248 n.3. **69.** 'Man will mir die Unfehlbarkeit beilegen. Ich brauche sie gar nicht.' Hasler, *Pius IX,* p.98: AA Bonn, P.A., I.A.B. e46, vol.2, *f.*105, report Limburg Stirum, Rome 27 June 1869. **70.** 'Man spricht über die Unfehlbarkeit des Papstes. Ich glaube daran; aber in meinen Vorschlagen findet sich darüber kein Wort. Ich weiss nicht, ob das auf uns zukommen wird.' *Ibid.:* H.H.St.A. Vienna, P.A., XI213, *f.*699−700, report No.493 von Trautmannsdorff, Rome 6 Nov. 1869.

CHAPTER VIII.2

71. Miko, *Römische Frage,* p.257. **72.** Brandmüller, *Döllinger,* p.138. **73.** Weber, *Kardinäle,* vol.I, pp.212 & 218. **74.** J. Friedrich, *Ignaz von Döllinger,* vol. I, Munich 1899, pp.473, 478. **75.** Morley, *Gladstone,* Everyman ed., vol.I, pp.235−6; A.T. Basset (ed.), *Gladstone to his wife,* London 1936, pp.58−9; Lösch, *Döllinger,* p.138; *Gladstone Diaries,* vol.3, p.485: Glynne — Gladstone MSS, St. Dieniol's Library, Hawarden, Deeside, Clwyd. I am most grateful to Sir William Gladstone, Bt., for his permission to quote from Gl.MSS. **76.** Conzemius, *Döllinger correspondence,* vol.3, p.411, No.527: D. to A., Munich 9 Jan. 1868. **77.** Basset, *Gladstone to his wife,* p.59; *Gladstone Diaries,* vol.III, p.458: 1 Oct. 1845; Glynne — Gl.MSS, St. Deiniol's Library; cf. also Gl. to Mrs. Gl., Munich 5 Oct. 1845 in Basset, *op. cit.,* p.63; M. Drew (Gl's daughter), *Acton, Gladstone and others,* London 1924, p.5. **78.** Basset, *op.cit.,* p.59; *Gladstone Diaries,* vol.III, p.485; Glynne — Gl. MSS, St. Deniol's Library. **79.** See GL's Memorandum on this conversation in Lathbury (ed.), *Correspondence on Church and Religion of W.E. Gladstone,* vol.II, London 1910, pp.383−9, Add MSS 44735, *f.*77. **80.** *Ibid.,* p.390, BM Add MSS 44735, *f.*83; Manning, *The Unity of the Church,* London 1842. **81.** (Döllinger), 'Die Kirche und die Kirchen:! England' in

H.P.Bl. 13 (1844), pp.383–96; 'Die Anglokatholischen', *ibid.* pp.690–703 & 785–809, here 795–6. **82.** Lösch, *Döllinger*, p.33. **83.** Ward White, 'Lord Acton and the Governments at Vatican Council I', in: McElrath, *Lord Acton*, Louvain 1970, pp.143–83, here 148; Matthew, *Gladstone Diaries*, vol.V, Introduction p.LXXI; vol.VI, 485 et seq. **84.** G. Himmelfarb, *Lord Acton. A Study in Conscience and Politics*, London 1952. **85.** E.D. Watt, 'Rome and Lord Acton: A Reinterpretation' in *Review of Politics* 28 (1966), pp.493–507, here 500. **86.** J. Bower, 'Freedom's Advocate: Lord Acton and the Liberal Catholic Movement in England' in *Dublin R.* No. 503 (1965), pp.90–9. **87.** Conzemius, *Döllinger correspondence*, vol.I, p.194: A. to D., London 10 Feb. 1861. **88.** *Ibid.*, p.269: A. to D., London 8 June 1862. **89.** St. Petersburg/Leipzig 1861. **90.** Himmelfarb, *Acton*, p.80; (Acton), *Home and Foreign Rev.*3 (1863), p.692. **91.** *Ibid.*; (Acton), *Home and Foreign Rev.* 3 (1863), p.692. **92.** Rambler n.s. 5(1861), pp.17–61; Gl. on this essay in his *Diaries* (VI, 29) on 2 May 1861: 'most satisfactory'. **93.** Himmelfarb, *Acton*, p.81. **94.** Acton, *Political causes*, p.57. **95.** *Ibid.*, p.60. **96.** Conzemius, *Döllinger correspondence*, vol.I, p.157, No.3 3: A. to D. Aldenham, 25 Nov. 1858. **97.** See H.J. Schoeps, *Das andere Preussen*, 4th Berlin 1974, p.137. **98.** K. von Rotteck (ed.), *Staatslexikon oder Encyclopaedie der Staatswissenschaften*, vol.XI, Altona 1841, *s.v.* 'Nordamerikanische Verfassung'. **99.** Cited from Schoeps, *Preussen*, p.169 n.88. **100.** *Lothair*, ch.31, p.121. **101.** W.G. Winkler, *Englische Demokratie und Reformbill von 1867*, Diss. Leipzig 1927, p.125. **101a.** See Buschkühl, *Irische Frage*, pp.140–42. **102.** Döllinger, *Papstfabeln des Mittelalters*, Munich 1863, p.135. See G. Kreutzer, *Die Honoriusfrage im Mittelalter und in der Neuzeit* (Päpste und Papsttum 8) Stuttgart 1975, p.57. **103.** Cf. his letter to Moufang in J. Götten, *Christof Moufang Theologe und Politiker 1817–1890*, Mainz 1969, p.123. **104.** *Ibid.*, pp.128–31; text of the speech printed in: Döllinger, *Kleinere Schriften*, ed. by F.H. Reusch, Stuttgart 1890, pp.161–96. **105.** W. Baum, 'Johannes Janssen und Ignaz von Döllinger' in *H.J.* 95 (1975), pp.408–17, here 411. **106.** Brandmüller, *Döllinger*, p.141, n.48. **107.** Conzemius, *Döllinger correspondence*, vol.I, p.276, No.75; A. to D., Aldenham 26 Aug. 1862; p.278. No.76: A. to D., Aldenham 10 Aug. 1862; p.283, No.77: A. to D., London 27 March 1864. **108.** *Ibid.*, p.341 No.96: A. to D., London 27 March 1864. **109.** Artz, *Newman — Lexikon*, p.795. **110.** Conzemius, *Döllinger correspondence*, vol.I, p.302: A. to D., London 21 April 1863. **111.** *Ibid.*, p.191, n.8: A. to D., London 20 Jan. 1864; Artz, *Newman — Lexikon*, p.795. **112.** Conzemius, *op. cit.*, vol.I, p.334, No.93: A. to D., London 23 Feb. 1864. **113.** *Further considered with reference to a criticism in the Rambler for May 1862*, London 1862. **114.** (Ward), 'Rome and the Munich Congress' in Dublin R. n.s.3 (July 1864), pp.63–96; Conzemius, *Döllinger correspondence*, vol.I, p.127, n.8. **115.** *Ibid.*, p.411, No.527: D. to A., Munich 9 May 1868; Conzemius, 'Die Verfasser der 'Römischen Briefe vom Konzil' des 'Quirinus'' in *Freiburger Geschichtsblätter* 52 (1963) pp.229–56, here 251. **116.** Conzemius, *Döllinger correspondence*, vol.I, p.306, n.3; p.307, n.5. **117.** *Ibid.*, p.313, No. 86: A. to D., London 30 June 1863. **118.** *Ibid.*, p.517 No. 155: D. to A., Tegernsee 1 Sept. 1868; Brandmüller, *Döllinger*, p.7. **119.** Conzemius, *op.cit.*, vol.III, p.413, No.528: D. to A., Munich 1 Oct. 1868. **120.** *Ibid.*, vol.I, p.539, No.164: D. to A, Munich, 8 Feb. 1869. **121.** J. Finsterhölzl, *Ignaz von Döllinger* (Wegbereiter heutiger Theologie 2), Graz/-Vienna/Cologne 1969, p.159. **122.** Franzen, *Fakultät*, p.25. **123.** *Ibid.*, p.3; Baum, *Janssen*, p.413; Conzemius, 'Die Römischen Briefe vom Konzil'. Eine entstehungsgeschichtliche Untersuchung zum Konzils journalismus Ignaz von Döllingers und Lord Actons', part I (in future cited as: 'Die 'Römischen Briefe') in *R.Q.*59 (1964), pp.186–229, here 187–8; R. Lill, Die deutschen Theologieprofeseren im Urteil des Münchener Nuntius' in *Reformata Reformanda*, Festgabe für Hubert Jedin, vol.II, Münster 1965, pp.483–507, here 493; *Coll. Lac.*, vol.VII, pp.1046–8; on Reisach see Weber, *Kardinäle*, vol.II, pp.511–2. **124.** A. Bellesheim, *Henry Edward Manning*, Mainz 1892, p.38. **125.** Matthew, *Gladstone diaries*, vol.VI, pp.455, 471: 17 & 19 Oct., 472: 22 Oct. 1866; Conzemius, *Döllinger correspondence*, vol.I, p.455, No.119: A. to D., London 8 July 1866. **126.** See Brandmüller, *Döllinger*, pp.6–10. **127.** Ibid., p.3 n.3: 'Zweifel und Wahrheit', a speech delivered 11 Jan. 1845. **128.** *Ibid.*, pp.5–6,

Notes to pages 140–145

Döllinger's speech at the Munich congress of 1863. **129.** *A.Z.,* 31 Jan. 1869, p.461. **130.** *A.D.E.,* vol.55, Leipzig 1910, pp.431–4. **131.** R. Welrich, 'Braun, Otto' in *Biographisches Jahrbuch und Deutscher Nekrolog* 6(1901) Berlin 1904, pp.483–91. **132.** Brandmüller, *Döllinger,* p.20. **133.** Conzemius, *Die 'Römischen Briefe',* p.205. **134.** *A.Z.,* 10 March 1869, pp.1043–4; 11 March, pp.1062–3; 12 March, pp.1077–8; 13 March, pp.1094–5; 14 March, pp.1115–6; 15 March, pp.1125–6; reprinted with notes by Brandmüller, *Döllinger,* pp.147–80; for interpretation *vide ibid.,* pp.23–30. **135.** *A.Z.,* 11 March 1869, p.1063; Brandmüller, *Döllinger,* pp.154–5. **136.** *Ibid.* n.15; L.V. Ranke, *Englische Geschichte,* 1st ed., vol.I, Berlin 1859, pp.66–71. **137.** 3rd ed., Leipzig 1870, vol.I, p.51. **138.** Conzemius, *Döllinger correspondence,* vol.III, p.413, No.528; D. to A., Munich 1 Oct. 1868; p.414. No. 529: D. to A., Munich 5 Oct, 1868; vol.1, p.465, No.131: D to A., Munich 22 Jan 1867. **139.** Hergenröther, *Staat und Kirche,* vol.I, pp.240–47. **140.** Borinski, *Englischer Geist in der Geschichte seiner Prosa,* Freiburg i. Br. 1951, pp.116–7; Borinski, *Englischer Roman,* pp.30, 60–61; E.J. Hobsbawm, *Industry and Empire* (Pelican Economic History of England 3) 3rd ed. 1971, pp.79–108, especially 104–5. **141.** Borinski, *Englischer Roman,* p.61; Weber, *Kardinäle,* vol.I, pp.217–8, 331, 378–85, especially 381. **142.** *A.Z.,* 11 March 1869, p.10 3; Brandmüller, *Döllinger,* p.155. **143.** *A.Z.,* 15 March 1869, p.1126; Brandmüller, *op.cit.,* pp.177–80. **144,** *A.Z.,* 13 March 1869, p.1094; Brandmüller, *op.cit.,* p.164; *A.Z.,* 11 June 1869, pp.2493–4; Brandmüller, *op.cit.,* p.39. **145.** *Ibid.,* pp.56–7. **146.** *Ibid.,* p.58; *Janus,* p.47. **147.** *Ibid.,* p.61. **148.** Conzemius, *Döllinger correspondence,* vol.II, p.3, No.180: D. to A., Munich 14 Oct. 1869. **149.** Brandmüller, *Döllinger,* pp.53–5. **150.** *A.Z.,* No.268, 25 Sept. 1869, pp.4143–4. **151.** 'Zeitläufe. Social-politische Betrachtungen zu der Schrift des Grafen Montalembert über die politische Zukunft Englands' in H.P.Bl.38 (1856), pp.1190–1228, here 1191. **152.** J. Godfrey, 'Montalembert e le modèle anglas' in *Cahirs d'histoire* (Clermont-Ferrand) 15 (1970) pp.335–53, here 336. **153.** *Ibid.,* p.337; *Zeitläufe,* p.1203. **154.** *Ibid.,* Montalembert, *Oeuvres,* vol.I, p.438. **155.** R.P. Lecanuet, Montalembert, vol.III, Paris 1902, pp.1413–4; *Zeitläufe,* p.1192; Conzemius, *Döllinger correspondence,* vol.I, pp.157–8. **156.** J. Becker, *Liberaler Staat und Kirche in der Ara von Reichsgründung und Kulturkampf. Geschichte und Strukturen ihres Verkältnisses in Baden 1860–1876,* Mainz 1973, pp.140–1; 306–7; Brandmüller, *Döllinger,* p.66–7. **157.** P. Volkmuth, *Petrus und Paulus auf dem Konzil von Jerusalem,* Leipzig 1869, p.18. **158.** Vide Becker, *Staat,* pp.18,137–41: W. Müller, 'Ignaz Heinrich von Wessenberg (1774–1860)' in *Katholische Theologen Deutschlands im 19. Jahrhundert,* vol.I, Munich 1975, pp.189–204. **159.** *A.Z.,* 6 Jan. 1869, p.78. **160.** *A.Z.,* 21 Aug. 1869, p.3601. **161.** *A.Z.,* No.277, 4 Oct. 1869, p.4275; on Frohschammer see R. Hansl, in: *Katholische Theologen,* vol.III, pp.169–88. **162.** Brandmüller, *Döllinger,* pp.21–2n. 84; *A.Z.* No.131, 11 May 1869, p.2007. **163.** *Ibid.; A.Z.,* No.242, 5 Aug. 1869, p.3338. **164.** *A.Z.,* No.69, 10 March 1869, pp.1043–4. **165.** (Döllinger), 'Aussichten vom Concil' in *A.Z.,* 20 May 1869, p.2050. **166.** (Döllinger), 'Zum künftigen Concil' in *A.Z.* 11 June 1869, pp.2493–4; Conzemius, *Die 'Römischen Briefe',* p.198. **167.** Brandmüller, 'Die Publikation des 1 Vatikanischen Konzils in Bayern' in *Zeitschrift für bayerische Landesgeschichte* 31 (1968), pp.197–258 & 575–634, here 254. **168.** Brandmüller, *Döllinger,* pp.50–56; Grisar, *Circulardepesche,* pp.216–40, here 224; D. Albrecht 'Döllinger, die bayerische Regierung und das 1. Vatikanische Konzil' in Repgen/-Skalweit (ed.), *Spiegel der Geschichte. Festgabe für Max Braubach,* Münster 1964, pp.795–815. **169.** Brandmüller, *Döllinger,* pp.41–2; Cwiekowski, *Vatican,* p.92 n.3. **170.** *A.Z.,* No.323, 19 Nov. 1869; No.324, 20 Nov. 1869, p.4990. **171.** See Brandmüller, *Döllinger,* pp.46–7. **172.** *Ibid.,* pp.48–49; Lösch, *Döllinger,* pp.268–9. **173.** Manning, *The Oecumenical Council and the Infallibility,* p.131; Hasler, *Pius IX,* p.343. **174.** Cited from Cwiekowski, *Vatican,* p.196. **175.** *Ibid.,* p.197. **176.** Rivinius, *Ketteler,* p.140; G. Thils, *L'Infaillibilité pontificale,* Gembloux 1969, pp.60–1,65. **177.** Brandmüller, *Döllinger,* p.50; Dupanloup, *Sendschreiben an den Klerus seiner Diozese über die Frage der Unfehlbarkeit,* Munich 1869, 2nd ed. 1870. **178.** Cwiekowski, *Vatican,* p.93 n.4. **179.** Schatz, *Kirchenbild,* pp.350–1. **180.** J. Hennessy, *The first Council of the Vatican.*

234

The American Experience, New York 1963, p.59. Hennessy, 'National Traditions and the First Vatican Council' in *A.H.P.* 7(1969), pp.491–512, here 511. **181.** Manning to Veuillot, no date Hotel Windsor, Paris: BN, N.A.F. 24634, *f.*550; letter No.23 in Buschkühl, *Irische Frage,* appendix. **182.** Orleans 1869, pp.3 & 22–3; Gurian, *Ideen,* p.236; Pfleger, *Beurteilung,* p.361. **183.** E. Veuillot, *Louis Veuillot,* vol.IV, p.79. **184.** *Ibid.,* p.82; letter No.24 in Buschkühl, *Irische Frage,* appendix. **185.** Ward/Ghezzi, *Veuillot,* p.359; L. Veuillot, *Correspondence,* vol.10, ed. by F. Veuillot (Oeuvres complètes, ser. 2, vol.24), Paris 1932, p.253 No.249: Louis Veuillot to Eugene V., Rome 10 Jan. 1870.

CHAPTER VIII.3

186. Borinski, *Phineas Finn,* p.210; Borinski, *Dickens,* pp.593–4. **187.** See E.R. Norman, *Anti-Catholicism in Victorian England,* London 1968, passim. **188.** Borinski, *Phineas Finn,* p.211. **189.** Ward, *Cardinal Wiseman,* vol.2, pp.522–3. **190.** Purcell, Manning, vol.II, p.395: Manning to Talbot December 1866; p.396: Manning to Talbot, Autumn 1866. **191.** *Times,* Sept. 1867. **192.** See Borinski, *Phineas Finn,* pp.211–2. **193.** See Buschkühl, *Irische Frage,* pp.159–61. **194.** Borinski, *Phineas Finn,* p.212. **195.** Arnold, *Culture and Anarchy,* Nelson ed., p.138. **196.** *Ibid.,* pp.142–3. **197.** *Ibid.,* pp.57, 18. **198.** *Ibid.,* pp.301–2. **199.** *Ibid.,* pp.303, 306, 18. **200.** (Stanley), 'The Oecumenical Council' in *Edinburgh Review* 130 (1869) 297–336, here 302. **216.** Stanley, *Oecumenical Council,* p.331. **218.** O.R. to Cl., Rome 24 Nov. 18686, confidential No.48, F.O.43/103, *f.*222; Cl. to O.R., F.O. 14 Dec. 1868, copy, Cl.Pps.C. 475(4), *f.*197; Cl. to O.R., F.O. 17 Dec. 1868, draft, P.R.O., F.O. 43/101, *f.*76; O.R. to Cl., Rome 12 Jan. 1869, P.R.O., F.O. 43/103B, No.40, *f.*8; O.R. to Cl., Rome 5 Feb. 1869, *ibid.,* No.8, *f.*63. **219.** 'The Position of Liberal Catholics', in *Pall Mall Gazette,* No.1456, 12 Oct. 1869, p.2. **220.** Bagehot, 'The Political Aspects of the Oecumenical Council' in *Economist,* 11 Dec. 1869, pp.1460–1; repr. *Collected Works,* vol. VIII, pp.169–72, here 169.

CHAPTER VIII.4

221. Blakiston, *Roman Question,* p.357 No.393: Cl.Pps., C.487, priv., O.R. to Cl., Rome 13 Jan. 1869; draft in A.Pps. F.O.918/4, p.28. **222.** See Document No.51 in the Appendix. **222.** Blakiston, *Roman Question,* p.359, No.398: Cl.Pps., C.487, priv., O.R. to Cl., Rome 10 Feb. 1869. **224.** Document No.51 in the Appendix, also Document 53 *ibid.* **225.** O.R. to Cl., Rome 10 March 1869, P.R.O., F.O. 918/4, p.69, priv., draft No.7. **226.** O.R. to Cl., Rome 24 March 1869, *ibid.,* p.76, draft No.8. **227.** Cl. to O.R., 19 April 1869, Cl.Pps., C.475(4), *f.*229; Norman, *Ireland,* p.129. **228.** Blakiston, *Roman Question,* p.363 No.405; Cl.Pps., C.487, *f.*43, priv., O.R. to Cl., Rome 5 May 1869. **229.** Document No.54 in the Appendix. **230** Norman, *Ireland,* p.129: Cl.Pps., C.475(4), *f.*237, Cl. to O.R., 17 May 1869, see Document 57 in the Appendix. **231.** J.H. Whyte (ed.), 'Select documents XVIII. Bishop Morairty on disestablishment and the Union, 1868' in *I.H.S.* 10 (1965), pp.198–9, here 195: Gl.Pps. Add MSS 44152, *ff.*98–113. **232.** Document No.55 in the Appendix. **233.** Norman, *Ireland,* p.130: Cl.Pps., C.487, *f.*108, O.R. to Cl., 1 Jan 1870. **234.** *Ibid.:* F.O.43/106, No.2, Rome 2 Jan. 1870; cf. also F.O.43/106, telegram on same matter, same date. **235.** MacSuibhne, *Cullen,* vol.V, p.28, No.34: Cullen to Conroy, Rome 7 Jan. 1870. **236.** Document No.56 in the Appendix. **237.** Documents No. 57 & 58 in the Appendix. **238.** Blakiston, *Roman Question,* pp.380–1, No.429: F.O.43/106, No.13, secret, O.R. to Cl., Rome 13 Jan. 1870, and telegram, same date, Cl.Pps., C.487, *f.*114. **239.** MacSuibhne, *Cullen,* vol.V, p.27, No.33: Cullen to Conroy, Rome before 7 Jan. 1870. **240.** *Ibid.,* pp.42–3, No.42: Cullen to Conroy, Rome 20 Jan. 1870. **241.** Norman, *Ireland,* p.132: F.O.43/106, No.23, 23 Jan. 1870. **242.** MacSuibhne, *Cullen,* vol.V, p.48, No.45: Cullen to Conroy, Rome 28 Jan. 1870; cf. also documents No. 60 & 61 in the Appendix. **243.** Cited from Norman, *Ireland,* p.132. **244.** Conzemius, *Döllinger correspondence,* vol.2, p.162 n.2: Cl. to O.R., Rome 1 March 1870, Cl.Pps. F.O.361/1

245. E.D. Steele, 'Gladstone and Ireland' in *I.H.S.* 17 (1970), pp.58–88, here 73.

CHAPTER IX.1

1. Cwiekowski, *Vatican*, p.90 n.2: BM Gl.Pps., vol.48, Add MSS 44134, *f*.282, Cl. to Gl., Wiesbaden 31 Aug. 1869. **2.** *Ibid.*; report Cl. to Gl., 17 Oct. 1869, BM Gl.Pps., vol.49, Add MSS 44134, *f*.67. **3.** Conzemius, 'Preussen und das Erste Vatikanische Konzil' in *A.H.C.* 2(1970), pp.353–419, here 359. **4.** Conzemius, *Döllinger correspondence*, vol.2, p.4n.2: Cl. to Gl., 18 Sept. 1869. **5.** *Lothair*, ch.84, p.347. **6.** Matthew, *Acton*, p.195. **7.** Himmelfarb, *Acton*, p.93. **8.** Conzemius, *Döllinger correspondence*, vol.2, p.25n.2: Cl.Pps., C.487, priv., Cl. to O.R., 13 Dec. 1869. **9.** White, *Acton and the Governments*, pp.149–50. **10.** Purcell, *Manning*, vol.2, pp.433–4. **11.** Lytton Strachey, *Eminent Victorians*, London 1916, pp.90–91. **12.** Borinksi, *Phineas Finn*, p.210; Purcell, *Manning*, vol.2, p.444. **13.** A. Duval/Y. Congar (ed.), 'Le journal de Mgr. Darboy au Concile du Vatican (1869–1870)' in *Revue des sciences philosophiques et théologiques* 54 (1970) 417–52, here 438; entry for 23 Feb. 1870. **14.** Documents No.29–31 in the Appendix; Blakiston, *Roman Question*, p.144 No.149; F.O.519/205, O.R. to Earl Cowley, British Ambassador in Paris, Rome 5 Dec. 1860. **15.** Randall, *British agent*, p.43. **16.** Ward, *Acton and the Governments*, p.160. **17.** See H. Michael, *Bismark, England und Europa vorwiegend 1866–1870* (Forschungen zur Mittelalterlichen und Neueren Geschichte 5) Munich 1930, p.22n.3. **18.** Cwiekowski, *Vatican*, p.177. **19.** Conzemius, *Döllinger correspondence*, vol.2, p.359, n.2: BM,Gl.Pps., Add MSS 44134, Cl. to Gl., 21 April 1870. **20.** *Ibid.*, p.161n.2: Gl.Pps., BM Add MSS 44134, *ff*.151–3, Cl. to Gl., 23 Feb. 1870. **21.** Blakiston, *Roman Question*, p.396 No.449: Cl.Pps, C.487, priv., O.R. to Cl., Rome 20 Feb. 1870; in the draft (document No.60 in the Appendix) there is no exclamation mark. **22.** *Ibid.*, p.400 No.454: F.O.361/1, F.O. 1 March 1870, priv., Cl. to O.R. **23.** Conzemius, *Döllinger correspondence*, vol.2, p.171 n.11: Gl.Pps., BM Add MSS 44134, *f*.161, Cl. to Gl., 2 March 1870. **24.** A. Ramm (ed.), *The political correspondence of Mr Gladstone and Lord Granville, 1868–1876*, vol.I (Camden 3rd ser.81) London 1952, p.88: Gl.Pps., BM Add MSS 44167, *f*.8, Granville to Gl., Colonial Office 19 Jan. 1870. **25.** Conzemius, *Döllinger correspondence*, vol.2, pp.98–9, n.16; Cwiekowski, *Vatican*, p.179: report Cl. to Gl., Gl.Pps., BM Add MSS 44134, *ff*.134–6, 16 Jan. 1870. **26.** *Ibid.*, vol.2, p.132 n.11; Cwiekowski, *Vatican*, p.179: announcement Cl. to Gl., 23 Jan. 1870, Gl.Pps., BM Add MSS 44134–5, *f*.140–2. **27.** Mansi, vol.LI, pp.539–636. **28.** Ollivier, *L'Eglise et l'Etat*, vol.2, pp.102–110; Cwiekowski, *Vatican*, p.175. **29.** Conzemius, *Döllinger correspondence*, vol.2, p.120 n.4; *Coll.Lac.*, pp.1553–5. **30.** Montclos, *Lavigerie*, p.460 n.5. **31.** Cwiekowski, *Vatican*, p.180: Cl. to O.R., 7 March 1870, P.R.O., Cl. Pps., F.O.361/1, *f*.341. **32.** White, *Acton and the governments*, p.154. **33.** Cwiekowski, *Vatican*, p.180: Cl. to Gl., 16 Feb. 1870. Gl.Pps., BM Add MSS 44134, *f*.148; cf. also *ibid.* & in Conzemius, *Döllinger correspondence*, vol.2, p.160 n.2: Cl. to Gl., 23 Feb. 1870, Gl.Pps., BM Add MSS 44134, *ff*.152–4. **34.** E. Weinzierl–Fischer, 'Bismarcks Haltung zum Vatikanum und der Beginn des Kulturkampfes nach den österreichischen diplomatischen Berichten aus Berlin 1869–1871' in *Mitteilungen des österreichischen Staatsarchivs* 10(1957), pp.301–21, here 312; Bismarck, *Gesammelte Werke*, Friedrichsruher ed., vol.VI b No.1534; see also Conzemius, *Preussen*, p.394 n.171. **35.** *Ibid.*, p.393 disagrees with this, but see Weinzierl-Fischer, *Bismarck*, p.312. **36.** Conzemius, *Döllinger correspondence*, vol.2, p.231 n.4. Conzemius, *Preussen*, pp.389–91. **38.** Cwiekowski, *Vatican*, p.181: P.R.O., Cl.Pps., F.O.361/1, *f*.197, 23 March 1870, Cl. to Lyons. **39.** *Ibid.*, n.2: *ibid.* *f*.344, Cl. to O.R., 28 March 1810. **40.** *Coll. Lac.*, pp.1563–6; *vide* J. Gadille, 'La Phase decisive de Vatican I: mars-avril 1870' in *A.H.C.* 1(1969), pp.336–47, here 339–41. **41.** Conzemius, *Döllinger correspondence*, vol.2, p.326 n.9; Cwiekowski, *Vatican*, pp.182–3: Cl. to Gl., 5 April 1870, Gl.Pps., vol.49, BM Add MSS 44134, *f*.174. **42.** *Ibid.*, p.183: Cl. to O.R., 7 April 1870, P.R.O., F.O.43/105, No.32. **43.** *Ibid.*, p.184: Cl. to O.R., 7 April 1870, priv., P.R.O., Cl.Pps., F.O.361/1, *f*.350. **44.**

Gadille, *Phase decisive*, p.344; Ch.G. Kinsella, *The diplomatic mission of archbishop Flavio Chigi, apostolic nuncio to Paris, 1870–71*, Diss. Loyola Univ of Chicago 1974, pp.40–41. **45.** Blakiston, *Roman Question*, pp.426–7, No.490: O.R. to Cl., Rome 26 April 1870, No.102, F.O.43/107. **46.** Conzemius, *Döllinger correspondence*, vol.2, p.335 n.14. **47.** *Ibid.*, p.356: Gl.Pps., BM Add MSS 44134, *ff*.196–8, 18 April 1870, Cl. to Gl.; a copy was forwarded to O.R. on 2 May: P.R.O., A.Pps., F.O.918/3, *ff*.407–9. **48.** P.R.O., A.Pps., F.O.918/4, p.166, draft, O.R. to Cl., Rome 8 Dec. 1869. **49.** 'The New Dogma' in *The Spectator*, 16 July 1870, p.857. **50.** German original text printed by Miko, *Kirchenstaatsende*, vol.I, p.512 No.951: copy 149, DZA Merseburg, Rep. 81, Rom II A 45, vol.1; on 21 Jan. 1870 reported to Arnim in Rome. **51.** German original text printed by Weinzierl-Fischer, *Bismarck*, p.309: Wimpfen, 12 March 1870, H.H. St.A. Vienna P.A. III, Kart. 101, No.27C, confidential. **52.** Conzemius, *Preussen*, p.391: Perglas to the Bavarian prime minister Bray, 25 March 1870, Munich Geh. St. A., M.A.I., No.638. **53.** See Becker, *Staat und Kirche*, pp.182, 266. **54.** Conzemius, *Döllinger correspondence*, vol.I, p.355 No.109: A. to D., Aldenham 28 April 1869. See K.H. Neufeld, 'Rom und die Ökumene. Victor de Buck S.J. (1817–1876) als Theologe auf dem Vaticanum' in *Catholica* 33 (1979), pp.63–80. **55.** Blakiston, *Roman Question*, p.371 No.414: F.O.43/103B Rome 11 Dec. 1869. No.59, O.R. to Cl. **56.** German original text in Gregorovius, *Römische Tagebücher*, Ed. Althaus, Stuttgart 1892, p.456: Rome 30 Jan. 1870. **57.** Ramm, *Gladstone – Granville correspondence*, vol.I, No.193: Granville to Gl., Gl.Pps., vol.82, BM Add MSS 44167, *f*.8, Colonial Office 19 Jan. 1870. **58.** Conzemius, *Döllinger correspondence*, vol.2, p.370. **59.** Blakiston, *Roman Question*, p.386 No.435: Cl.Pps., C.487, priv., O.R. to Cl., Rome 24 Jan. 1870. **60.** Aubert, *Vaticanum I*, p.214; Cwiekowski, *Vatican*, p.178. **61.** P.R.O., A.Pps., F.O.918/84, p.118, O.R. to Arthur R., copy, Rome 22 Feb. 1870. **62.** Conzemius, *Döllinger correspondence*, vol.II, p.270: Gl. to D., 25 March 1870, Gl.Pps., BM Add MSS 44426, *f*.15; Lathbury, *Correspondence*, vol.2, p.45–6. **63.** *Ibid.*, No.266: D. to A., Munich 30 March 1870; p.277 No.269: D. to A., Munich 31 March, 1870. **64.** W. Taffs, *Ambassador to Bismarck. Lord Odo Russell, first Baron Ampthill*, London 1938, p.11. **65.** P.R.O., A.Pps., F.O.918/84, p.99, copy, O.R. to Arthur R., Rome 24 April 1869. **66.** Leslie, *Manning*, p.222. **67.** Conzemius, *Döllinger correspondence*, vol.2, p.310n.8. **68.** The editor of the Civiltà Piccirillo also had access to the pope during the council, but when both were waiting for an audience in the antechamber, the pope asked Piccirillo in first because he thought that he would not have much to talk with him while he had much to talk about with Manning. Franco, *Appunti*, p.287 No.674, 4 May 1870. **69.** S. Katzmann, 'Acton and the Bishops of the Minority', in: McElrath (ed.), *Lord Acton*, pp.187–217, here 196. **70.** Richter, *Geschichte der Freiwilligen*, pp.407, 77–8, 86; Russell-Killough, *Service pontifical*, p.391; L. Besson, *Frédéric-Francois-Xavier de Mérode, Ministre e Aumonier de Pie IX. Sa vie et ses Oeuvres*, 4th ed., Paris 1888, p.193. **71.** Conzemius, *Döllinger correspondence*, vol.2, p.149 n.4: Cl.Pps., C. 487; Blakiston, *Roman Question*, p.375. **72.** Duval/Congar, *Journal Darboy*, p.438: entry for 23 Feb. 1870. **73.** Schatz (ed.), Senestréy, *Unfehlbarkeit*, p.29. **74.** *Ibid.*, p.37; see Purcell, *Manning*, vol.2, p.417. **75.** E. Donckel (ed.), *Reise nach Rom zum 1 Vatikanischen Konzil. Tagebuch von Bischof Nikolaus Adames*, Luxemburg 1963, p.10. **76.** P. Mai, 'Bischof Ignatius von Senestréy's Aufzeichnungen vom 1. Vatikamischen Konzil' in *A.H.L.* 1(1969), pp.399–411, here 407; cf. also Franco, *Appunti*, pp.89–90 No.22–3. **77.** German original text printed by Donckel, *Adames Tagebuch*, p.20, entry for Monday 6 Dec. 1869. **78.** Franco, *Appunti*, pp.93–4, No.25. **79.** *Ibid.*, pp.95–6, No.29. **80.** Mai, *Senestréys Aufzeichnungen*, p.407–8; Mai, 'Bischof Ignatius von Senestréy als Mitglied der Deputation für Glaubensfragen auf dem 1. Vatikanum' in *Verhandlungen des historischen Vereins für Oberpfalz und Regensburg* 109 (1969), pp.115–143, here 121–2. **81.** Aubert, *Vaticanum*, p.147. **82.** M. Maccarone (ed.), *Il Concilio Vaticano 1 e il 'Giornale' di Mons. Arrigoni*, Padua 1966, vol.1, p.169. **83.** Butler, *Das 1. Vatikanische Konzil*, p.153. **85.** Butler, *Das 1. Vatikanische Konzil*, p.152. **86.** *Ibid.*, p.151. **87.** Donkel, *Adames Tagebuch*, p.71, entry for 15 May 1870. **88.** Schatz (ed.),

Senestréy, *Unfehlbarkeit*, pp.17, 44n.27; MacSuibhne, *Cullen*, vol.V, pp.37–8 No.39: Cullen to Conroy, Rome 11 Jan. 1870. **89.** Schatz, Senestréy, *Unfehlbarkeit*, p.18. **90.** *Ibid.*, p.17; MacSuibhne, *Cullen*, vol.V, p.39 No.40: Cullen to Conroy, Rome 13 March 1870; p.46 No.44: Cullen to Conroy, Rome 11 Jan. 1870. **91.** *Ibid.*, p.30 No.35: Cullen to Conroy, Rome 7 March 1870. **92.** Schatz, Senestrey, *Unfehlbarkeit*, p.18; MacSuibhne, *Cullen*, vol.V, p.50 No.46: Cullen to Conroy, Rome 1 Feb. 1870. **93.** *Ibid.*, p.77 No.64; Cullen to Conroy, Rome 10 March 1870. **94.** Schatz, Senestrey, *Unfehlbarkeit*, p.77. **95.** *Ibid.*, p.17. **96.** *Ibid.*, p.20. **97.** *Ibid.*, p.99. **98.** *Ibid.*, p.22. **99.** *Ibid.*, pp.23, 28, 113. **100.** *Ibid.*, pp.40–41 n.22. **101.** MacSuibhne, *Cullen*, vol.V, p.109 No.92: Cullen to Conroy, Rome 28 May 1870. **102.** The content of the speech in Granderath, *Konzil*, vol.III, pp.248–50. **103.** Bishop Ketteler's note of Manning's speech in Ried, *Studien*, pp.695 n.88. **104.** German original text *ibid.*, p.696; Rivinius, *Ketteler*, pp.252–3: Diözesau-u. Domarchiv Main No.1, 201b, *ff* 2 & 4. **105.** Hasler, Pius IX, p.39 n.57: Arch. du Séminaire St. Sulplice, Journal Duplanloup, *f.*54, 26 May 1870. **106.** D. Matthew, 'New Facts About Lord Acton' in *D.R.* 90(1972) pp.15–19, here 16. **107.** Conzemius, *Döllinger correspondence*, vol.1, p.75, No.15: A. to D., Aldenham 3 July 1855. **108.** Document No.46 in the Appendix; cf. also No.s 45, 47–9. **109.** Mathew, *New Facts*, p.18. **110.** Cardinal Carlo Acton (1803–47), see *D.B.I.*, vol.1, p.204. He was in contact with the earl of Shrewsbury sent to Rome to influence Rome against the Repeal Movement. He wrote of the Irish College in Rome to O'Connell's dismay as 'British College'. See MacSuibhne, *Cullen*, vol.V, pp.305–6, App.7: Daniel O'Connell to Cullen, Liverpool 9 May 1842. See also Weber, *Kardinäle*, vol.2, p.425. **111.** Conzemius, *Döllinger correspondence*, vol.2, p.149, n.4. **112.** Hennessy, *First Council*, p.29; on the American Bishops see also MacSuibhne, *Cullen*, vol.V, p.52 No.47: Cullen to Conroy, Rome 3 Feb. 1870; p.53 No.48, 5 Feb. 1870; p.95 No.77, 1 Apr. 1870; p.100 No.86, 1 May 1870; pp.101–2 No.87, 11 May 1870; pp.130–1 No.111, 29 June 1870; p.131 No.112, 1 July 1870, p.136 No.115, 8 July 1870. **113.** Morley, *Gladstone*, vol.2, p.511; by Hennessy, *First Council*, p.131 dated Dec. 1869/Jan.1870; rather after the publication of the schema de ecclesia. **114.** MacSuibhne, *Cullen*, vol.V, p.52, No.47: Cullen to Conroy, Rome 3 Feb. 1870. **115.** *Ibid.*, p.118 No.100: Cullen to Conroy 13 June 1870; this shows from which side really there was put pressure on them and disproves Hasler, *Pius IX*, p.116. See also Martina, 'Review of Hasler' in *A.H.P.* 16 (1978), pp.341–69, here 351–2. On Hasler's source see O.R. in Conzemius, *Döllinger correspondence*, vol.2, pp.138–9 n.4. **116.** Jedin, *Handbuch*, vol.VI/I, p.786. **117.** Katzmann, *Acton and the minority*, p.195. **118.** Blakiston, Roman Question, p.385 No.435: Cl.Pps., C.487, Rome 24 Jan. 1870, priv., O.R. to Cl. **119.** Conzemius, *Preussen*; Conzemius, 'Lord Acton and the first Vatican Council' (in future cited as: Vatican) in *J.E.H.* 20 (1969), pp.267–94, here 271. **120.** *Ibid.*, p.272; see Conzemius, *Döllinger correspondence*, vol.2, p.135 n.7. **121.** White, *Acton and the Governments*, p.148. **122.** J. Gadille, *Albert du Boys. Ses 'Souvenirs du Concile du Vatican, 1869–1870, L'Intervention du gouvernement impérial à Vatican 1*, Louvain 1968, p.105. **123.** Document No.63 in the Appendix. **124.** See Conzemius, *Die Verfasser*, pp.229–56. **125.** German original text in Conzemius, *Preussen*, p.359; Bernstorff to Bismarck, London 12 May 1869, presented 21 May, AA Bonn, PA, Abt.IA, Italien, No.14 Be 46, Akten Konzil, *ff*.159–62. **126.** Ketteler, *Die Unwahrheiten der Römischen Briefe vom Concil in der Allegemeinen Zeitung*, dated Rome 5 March 1870, pp.3–4. **127.** Mathew, *Acton*, p.180. **128.** Conzemius, *Die 'Römischen Briefe'*, p.204. **129.** German text: 'Römische Briefe vom Concil XXIII, Rome 16 Feb. 1870' in *A.Z.*, No.61, 2 March 1870, p.925. **130.** German text: 'Römischer Briefe vom Concil XIII, Rome 30 Jan. 1870' in *A.Z.*, No.39, 8 Feb. 1870, p.578. **131.** German text: 'Römische Briefe über das Concil II, Rome 18 Dec. 1869' in *A.Z.*, No.361, 27 Dec. 1869, p.5573. **132.** Conzemius, *Die 'Römischen Briefe'*, p.205. **133.** Conzemius, *Döllinger correspondence*, vol.2, p.18, No.184: A. to D., Rome 28 Nov. 1869. **134.** H. Tüchle, In beiden Lagern. Deutsche Bischöfe auf dem Konzil' in: *Hundert Jahre nach dem Ersten Vatikanum*, ed. G. Schwaiger, Regensburg 1970, pp.31–49, here 36. **135.** Conzemius, *Die 'Römischen Briefe'*, p.186. **136.** See list in

Conzemius, *Die Verfasser*, pp.252–6. **137.** Conzemius, *Vatican*, p.171. **138.**
Conzemius, *Die 'Römischen Briefe'*, p.87 n.63. **139.** P.R.O., A.Pps., F.O.918/84,
p.118, copy, O.R. to Arthur R., Rome 22 Feb. 1870; cf. document No.62 in the
Appendix. **140.** Conzemius, *Vatican*, pp.274–5. **141.** Conzemius, Die 'Römischen
Briefe' II: 'Lord Acton als Mitarbeiter Döllingers' (in future cited as *Acton!*) in *R.Q.*
60(1965), pp.76–119, here 112. **142.** MacSuibhne, *Cullen*, vol.V, p.66 No.57: Cullen to
Conroy, Rome 23 March 1870. **143.** Conzemius, *Acton*, p.114. **144.** Conzemius, *Die
'Römischen Briefe'*, p.226 n.193. **145.** M Weber, *Das I. Vatikanische Konzil in Spiegel
der bayerischen Politik* (Miscellanea Bavarica Monacensia 28) Munich 1970, p.60.
146. Conzemius, *Acton*, p.114n. **147.** Gadille, *Albert du Boys*, p.71. **148.** Conzemius,
Döllinger correspondence, vol.2, p.200 No.244, A. to D., Rome, 8 March 1870;
MacSuibhne, *Cullen*, vol.V, p.88 No.72: Cullen to Conroy, Rome 19 March 1870. **149.**
Franzen, *Konzil*, pp.128, 175. **150.** Brandmüller, *Publikation*, p.203. **151.** Conzemius,
Acton, p.115. **152.** *Ibid.*, p.114; U. Nembach, *Die Stelling der Evangelischen Kirche
und ihner Presse zum I. Vatikanischen Konzil*, Diss. Basel 1961, printed Zurich 1962,
pp.27, 80. **153.** See above p.152. **154.** See *Men of the Time*, 8th ed., 1872, pp.508–9; H.
Rall, 'England und Bayern im Frühjahr 1870' in *Großbritannien und Deutschland.
Festschrift für John W. Bourke*, ed. O. Kuhn, Munich 1974, p.248. **155.** Conzemius,
Döllinger correspondence, vol.2, p.25 n.3: Cl. to Howard, draft, 18 May 1870, P.R.O.,
Cl.Pps., F.O.361/1, *f*.302. **156.** Blakiston, *Roman Question*, p.441 No.512: Cl.Pps.,
C.487, Rome 9 June 1870; priv., O.R. to Cl.; cf. document No.64 in the appendix. **157.**
Ibid., p.445 No.517: F.O.361/1, F.O.15 June 1870, Cl. to Lyons, Ambassador to Paris.
158. MacSuibhne, *Cullen*, vol.V, p.121 No.102: Cullen to Conroy, Rome, 18 June
1870; cf. also p.126 No.107: Cullen to Conroy, Rome 21 June 1870. **159.** *Ibid.*, p.142
No.119: Cullen to Conroy, Rome 16 July 1870. **160.** *Lothair*, ch.84, p.347.

CHAPTER IX.2

161. Tüchle, *In beiden Lagern*, p.46; J. Beumer, 'Das Erste Vatikanum und seine
Rezeption' in *Münchener Theologische Quartalschrift* 27(1976), pp.259–76, here 270.
162. Conzemius, *Döllinger correspondence*, vol.2, p.99n.18. *Ibid.*, vol.2, p.440 No.331,
A. to D., Tegernsee, late July 1870. **163.** Printed Nördlingen Sept. 1870. **164.**
Conzemius, *Acton, Döllinger and Ketteler*, p.235 n.205: O.R. to Gl., 8 Sept. 1870,
Gl.Pps., BM Add MSS 44428, *f*.91. **165.** German text: Acton, Sendschreiben, pp.18–9.
166. Conzemius, 'Römische Briefe vom Konzil' in *Theologische Quartalschrift* 140
(1960), pp.427–62, here 439: Arco to D., Rome 17 June 1870. See also Neuner,
Döllinger als Theologe der Ökumene (Beiträge zur ökumenischen Theologie 19)
Paderborn 1979, pp.86–95. **167.** Schatz, *Kirchenbild*, p.23. **168.** Rivinius, *Ketteler*,
p.315. **169.** Conzemius, *Döllinger correspondence*, vol.2, p.459 No.348: A. to D.,
Aldenham, 23 Dec. 1870. **170.** *Ibid.*, vol.2, p.459, n.3. **171.** See de Leonardis,
Inghilterra, pp.190 et seq.; House of Commons, *Accounts and Papers*, 1871, vol.72,
'Correspondence respecting the Affairs of Rome'. **172.** Jervoise to Granville, Rome 15
Sept. 1870, *ibid.*, p.267. **173.** See T. von Santifaller, *Römische Erinnerungen*, ed. L.
Santifaller, Vienna 1947, pp.135–6, 184–5. **174.** Conzemius, *Döllinger
correspondence*, vol.3, pp.24–5 No.356: A. to D., Herrnsheim 19 Aug. 1871; p.33
No.360: A. to D. Herrnsheim 15 Dec. 1871. **175.** *Ibid.*, p.12 No.352: A. to D.,
Aldenham, 7 Feb. 1871; see G.P. Fogarty 'Archbishop Peter Kenrick's Submission to
Papal Infallibility' in *A.H.P.* 16(1978), pp.205–22. **176.** Conzemius, *Döllinger
correspondence*, vol.3, p.28, No.358: A. to D., Herrnsheim 5 Sept. 1871. **177.** F.
Meyrick, *Memoirs at Oxford and Experiences in Italy, Turkey, Germany, Spain and
Elsewhere*, London 1905, pp.287–8; on Meyrick see *DNB 1901–1911*, pp.617–8;
Neuner, *Döllinger*, p.174 n.2. **178.** I. Sivric, *Bishop J.G. Strossmayer. New Light on
Vatican I*, Rome/Chicago 1975, p.245; Conzemius, *Döllinger correspondence*, vol.2,
p.59n.34: Strossmayer to Gl., 13 March 1879, Gl.Pps., BM Add MSS 44459,
ff.188–90; Hasler, *Pius IX*, p.415n. 53; A. Spiletak, *Strossmayer i Pape*, Dakovo
1925. **179.** See Buschkühl, *Irische Frage*, pp.193–7.

CONCLUSION

1. *The Letter and Diaries of John Henry Newman,* vol.30, Oxford 1976, p.36 n.2: Gl. to Newman, 17 Dec. 1881; pp.36–7 & n.3: Newman to Gl., 23 Dec. 1881; p.45 & n.1: Newman to Gl., 2 Jan. 1882; St Gwynn/G.M. Tuckwell, *The Life of Sir Charles Dilke,* London 1917, I, pp.375–6; E. Fitzmaurice, *The Life of Granville: George Leveson Gower Sec. Earl Granville,* London 1906, II, pp.286–8; C.J. Woods, "Ireland and Anglo-papal relations, 1880–85" in *Irish Historical Studies,* 18 (1972) 29–60. **2.** Miko, *England und der Heilige Stuhl,* pp.216–25. **3.** T.E. Hachey (ed.), *Anglo-Vatican Relations 1914–1939: Confidential Annual Reports of the British Ministers to the Holy See,* Boston, Mass. 1972. **4.** L. Volk S.J. 'Päpstliche Kritik an der Appeasement-Politik von 1938. Ein unveröffentlichter Bericht des britischen Vatikangesandten' in *Stimmen der Zeit,* 197 (1979) 532–8. **5.** R.A. Graham S.J. 'Il Vaticano nella guerra psicologica inglese 1939–1945. La storia dei 'sib', cioè delle "bugie autorizzate" in *Civiltà cattolica* 129 (1978) I, 113–33

ADDENDA

Note to pages 57–61: 'Papers of Richard Joachim Hayes, O.F.M. in Franciscan Library, Killiney: Part 2, Oct.–Dec. 1815' in *Collectanea Hibernica* 23 (1981).

Note to pages 104–5: C. Edie O.S.B., 'Letter from Rome on Abbot Smith Letters' in *The Scriptorium* (St. John's Abbey) XI (March 1951) 21–35. G. Loeber O.S.B., 'Report on Smith Letters' in *The Scriptorium* XIII (April 1953) 29–32. V. Tegeder O.S.B., 'The Abbot Smith Letters and the American Benedictines' in *American Benedictine Review* 6 (September 1955) 24–39.

Note to pages 144–5: V. Conzemius, *Ignaz von Döllinger – Lady Blennerhasset, Briefwechsel,* Munich 1982.

Note to page 174: A. Randall, *Vatican Assignment,* London 1956.

Bibliography

Manuscript Sources

VATICAN CITY
Archivio Segreto Vaticano
Segretaria di Stato, Colonia 180, *ff*.284–5: despatch of Nuncio Caprara to Cardinal Secretary of State, 3 May 1772; Colonia 185, *ff*.22–9: despatch Caprara to Cardinal Secretary of State, 12 July 1772.
FRANCE
Bibliothéque nationale, Paris
N.A.F. 24634: Lettres addressées à Louis Veuillot
GERMANY
Kestner Museum Hanover
Kestner Papers, Kestner's letters from Rome
Niedersächsisches Hauptstaatsarchiv Hanover
Hann.92: German Chancery London
XLI – 127c British Consul in Rome 1828,
– 127d Catholic Emancipation
– 127e Notification of Pius VIII's election
– 127h Ireland 1833
Dep. 110: Münster Papers
BRITAIN
Arundel Castle
MD 2080: Earl of Arundel, Observations upon Diplomatic Relations between Great Britain and Rome, ca. 1848. Copies of despatches to and from Sir H.L. Bulwer concerning Rome, 1852.
Bodleian Library, Oxford
C.475(4) Clarendon Papers
C.487
British Library, Department of Manuscripts, London
Add.MSS 37848–9: Windham Papers, Letters of J.C. Hippisley,
Add. MSS 60299: George Seymour's Diary
EG 2401: Correspondence of Sir J.C. Hippisley
M 511 & M 526: Westmoreland Papers, Letters to and from Lord Burghersh in Rome
Clwyd Record Office, Hawarden, Deeside, Clwyd
Gladstone MSS at St Deiniol's Library: W.E. Gladstone to his wife, Munich, 2 & 5 Oct. 1845.
Northamptonshire Record Office, Northampton
Fitzwilliam (Milton) Manuscripts A.IV.3a–d; 4a–d; 14; 15; A.VII. 15 & 18: Letters of J. C. Hippisley to Edmund Burke.
University of Nottingham Library, Manuscripts Department
Bentinck Papers
PW Je4671–3: Correspondence between Bentinck and Pius VII
PW Je2274–94 & 6079, Correspondence between Bentinck and Robert Fagan
Public Record Office, Kew
F.O.7: General Correspondence, Austria
F.O.27: General Correspondence, France

Great Britain and the Holy See

F.O.43: General Correspondence, Italian States & Rome
F.O.79: General Correspondence, Tuscany & Rome
F.O.95/5: Correspondence, J.C. Hippisley
F.O.361: Clarendon Papers
F.O.881/65: Correspondence respecting the relations of Great Britain with Rome
F.O.881/200: Correspondence respecting the relations existing between foreign governments and Rome
F.O.918: Ampthill Papers
30/22: Russell Papers.

Printed sources

PRIMARY

Acta et decreta sacrorum conciliorum recentiorum, Collectio Lacensis VII (usually abbr. 'Coll.Lac'), Freiburg i.Br. 1890.
Acta Pio IX, vol.III, Graz 1971
Acton, Lord John, Political Causes of the American Revolution in *The Rambler* 5 (1861) 17−61
—Sendschreiben an einen deutschen Bischof des Vaticanischen Concils, Nördlingen, September 1870
—Zur Geschichte des Vaticanischen Conciles, Munich 1871.
Allgemeine Zeitung, Augsburg, July−October 1867, 1869, January−July 1870
Arnold, Matthew, *Culture and Anarchy* (1869) Nelson ed. London
Bagehot, Walter, 'The Political Aspects of the Oecumenical Council' in *Economist* 11.12.1869, repr.: Collected Works VIII, 169−172
Basset, A. Tilney (ed.), *Gladstone to his wife*, London 1936
Bastgen, Hubert (ed.), *Die Römische Frage. Dokumente und Stimmen*, 3 vols., Freiburg i.Br. 1917−1920
Benedict XIV Papa, *Bullarium*, 13 vols, Mechlin 1826−7
Blakiston, Noel (ed.) *The Roman Question. Extracts from the despatches of Odo Russell from Rome 1858−1870*, London 1962
Brady, W. Maziere, 'Memoirs of Cardinal Erskine' in Brady., *Anglo-Roman Papers*, London 1890, 121−268
Brezzi, Paolo, *La diplomazia pontificia*, Milan 1942
Browning, Robert, *The Ring and the Book*, 1869
Burke, Edmund, *Correspondence of Edmund Burke and William Windham. With other illustrative letters from the Windham Papers in the British Museum,* ed. J.P. Gilson (The Roxburg Club 157), Cambridge 1910
—*Correspondence,* ed. Thomas W. Copeland, vol.7, Cambridge Chicago 1968
Clemens XIV Papa, *Lettre ed altre opere*, vol.I (Biblioteca scelte di opere italiane antiche e moderne 271), Milan 1831; vol.2, Florence 1834
Collectio Conciliorum Recentiorum Ecclesiae Universae, ed. Archbishop Petit of Athens/J.B. Martin (Mansi 49−53) Arnheim, Leipzig 1923−27
Conzemius, V. (ed.), *Ignaz von Döllinger−Lord Acton, Briefwechsel 1850−1890,* 3 vols., Munich 1963−71
Croker, J.W., 'Ministerial Measures' in *Quarterly Review* 82 (1847) 261−308
Cullen, Cardinal Paul, *Ireland and the Holy See. A Retrospect 1866 v. 1883. Illegal and Seditious Movements in Ireland contrasted with the principles of the Catholic Church as shown in the writings of . . .* Rome 1883
—*Pastoral and other writings*, ed. Patrick Francis Moran, Bishop of Ossory, Dublin 1882
Curato, Federico (ed.), *Gran Bretagna e Italia nei documenti della Missione Minto*, 2 vols. (Fonti per la storia d'Italia, II serie, vols. 107/8) Rome 1970
Deutscher Merkur 5 (1874), 7 (1876)

Bibliography

Disraeli, Benjamin, *Lord George Bentinck: A Political Biography*, London 1852
—*Church Policy, A Speech*, Oxford 25 Nov. 1864, London 1864
—*Church and Queen. Five Speeches 1860–64*, London 1865
—*The Prime Minister on Church and State. Speech ... 17 June 1868*, London n.d.
—*Speeches on the Conservative Policy of the last 30 years*, ed. J.F. Bulley, London 1870
—*Lothair*, (1870), ed. with introduction, textual, and explanatory notes by Vernon Bogdanor, London 1975 (Oxford English Novels ser.)
—*Selected Speeches*, ed. T.E. Kebbel, 2 vols, London 1882
Döllinger, Joh.Jos.Ign. von, 'Die Kirche und die Kirchen: England' in *Historisch-politische Blätter für das katholische Deutschland*, 13 (1844) 383–396, 449–466.
—'Die Anglokatholischen', *ibid.* 690–703 and 785–809
—*Christentum und Kirche in der Zeit der Grundlegung*, Regensburg 1860 and 1868
—*Papstfabeln des Mittelalters*, Munich 1863
Donckel, Emile (ed.), *Reise nach Rom zum 1. Vatikanischen Konzil: Tagbuch von Bischof Nikolaus Adames, 15 November 1869–15, Mai 1870*, Luxembourg 1963
Duval, André/Congar, Yves, 'Le Journal de Mgr. Darboy au Concile du Vatican (1869–1870)' in *Revue des Sciences philosophiques et théologiques* 54 (1970) 417–452
Figgis, J.N./Laurence, R.V. (ed.), *Selections from the correspondence of the first Lord Acton*, London 1917
Friedrich, Johann, *Tagebuch während des Vaticanischen Concils*, Nördlingen 1871
Gadille, Jacques, *Albert du Boys, Ses 'Souveniers du Concile du Vatican, 1869–1870' L'intervention du gouvernement impérial à Vatican I* (Bibliothèque de la Revue d'histoire ecclésiastique 46) Louvain 1968
Gooch, G.P. (ed.), *The Later Correspondence of Lord John Russell 1840–1878*, vol.II, London 1925
Gregorovius, Ferdinand, *Römische Tagebücher*, ed. F. Althaus, Stuttgart 1892
Greville, Charles C.F., *The Greville Memoirs*, Second Part, vol.III, A Journal of the Reign of Queen Victoria from 1837 to 1852. London 1885
Hachey, T.E. (ed.), *Anglo-Vatican Relations 1914–1939: Confidential Annual Reports of the British Ministers to the Holy See*, Boston 1972
Holmes, J. Derek, 'Some unpublished passages from Cardinal Wiseman's Correspondence' in *Downside Review* 90, (1972) 41–52
d'Ideville, Henry, *Journal d'un diplomate en Italie. Notes intimes pour servir à l'histoire du Second Empire II Rome 1862–1866*, Paris 1873
—*Les Piemontais à Rome. Lettres recueillies et editées. Mentata–La prise de Rome 1867–1870*, Paris 1874
—*Der Katholik* 49 n.s. 21 (1869)I, 732–759: 'Rathschläge für das Concil'
Ketteler, Wilhelm E, von. *Die Unwahrheiten der Römischen Briefe vom Concil in der Allgemeinen Zeitung*, Mainz 1870
Lathbury, D.C. (ed.), *Correspondence on Church and Religion of William Ewart Gladstone*, 2 vols., London 1910
Layard, Sir A. Henry, *Autobiography and Letters*, 2 vols. London 1913
Lenhart, Ludwig (ed.) 'Moufangs Briefwechsel mit Bischof Ketteler und Domdekan Heinrich aus der Zeit seines römischen Aufenthalts zur Vorbereitung des Vaticanischen Concils' in *Archiv für mittelrheinische Kirchengeschichte* 3 (1951) 323–354
—'Regens Moufang als Konsultor zur Vorbereitung des Vaticanums im Lichte seines römischen Tagebuchs', *ibid.* 9 (1957) 227–55
Lettres à Monsieur Caraccioli, Paris 1776
Londonderry, Charles Vane, Marquess of (ed.), Memoirs and Correspondence of Viscount Castlereagh, Second Marquess of Londonderry III, London 1849
Maccarone, Michele, *Il Concilio Vaticano I e il 'Giornale' di Mons. Arrigoni*, 2 vols. (Italia sacra 7/8) Padua 1966
MacSuibhne, Peadar (ed.), *Paul Cullen and his contemporaries, with their letters from 1820 to 1902*, 5 vols, Naas, Co. Kildare, Ireland 1961–77

Great Britain and the Holy See

Mai, Paul, 'Bischof Ignatius von Senestréy als Mitglied der Deputation für Glaubensfragen auf dem I. Vatikanum' in *Verhandlungen des Historischen Vereins für Oberpfalz und Regensburg* 109 (1969) 115–143

—'Bischof Ignatius von Senestréys Aufzeichnungen vom 1. Vatikanischen Konzil' in *Annuarium Historiae Conciliorum* 1. (1969) 399–411

Matthew, H.C.G. (ed.), *Gladstone Diaries*, III, V, VI, Oxford 1974/78 (to 1868)

Meyrick, Frederick, *Memoirs of Life at Oxford, and Experiences in Italy, Greece, Turkey, Germany, Spain, and Elsewhere*, London 1905

Michaelis, H. (ed.), *Die auswärtige Politik Preussens* IX: Mai 1867–April 1868, Oldenburg i.O. 1936

Miko, Norbert (ed.), *Das Ende des Kirchenstaates*, 4 vols. Vienna 1962–70

Minghetti, Marco, *Miei Ricordi* (to 1859), 3 vols., Turin/Rome/Naples 1888/89

Morelli, Emilia (ed.), *Le lettre di Benedetto XIV al cardinale de Tencin. Dai testi originali*, vol.I (Storia e letteratura 55), Rome 1955; vol.II (Storia e letteratura 101), Rome 1965

Newman, John Henry Cardinal, *Letters and Diaries*, ed. Dessain vols. 12, 21, 23–25, Oxford 1961–73

Pacca, Bartholomäus, *Historische Denkwürdigkeiten über seinen Aufenthalt in Deutschland 1786–1794 in der Eigenschaft eines apostolischen Nuntius . . . zu Köln*, Augsburg, 1832

Pall Mall Gazette, Jahrgang 1869

Paul, Herbert (ed.), *Letters of Lord Acton to Mary, Daughter of Rt. Hon. W.E. Gladstone*, London 1904

Punch, 7 January 1865

Ramm, Agatha (ed.), *The Political Correspondence of Mr Gladstone and Lord Granville 1868–1876*, 2 vols. Camden 3rd ser., vol. 81/82 London 1952

Richardson, Samuel, *Sir Charles Grandison*, London 1902

Richter, Friedrich Nobile von, *Geschichte der österreichisch-slavischen und deutschen Freiwilligen und ihrer Kämpfe im Kirchenstaat im Jahre 1860*, Mainz 1861

Russell, George William Erskine, *Collections and Recollections by One Who Has Kept a Diary*, London 1898

Russell, Sir Odo, *Contacts*, privately printed 1938

Russell-Killough, Frank, *Dix années au service pontifical, récits et souveniers*, Paris 1871

Schatz, Klaus (ed.), Senestrey, Ignatius von, *Wie es zur Definition der päpstlichen Unfehlbarkeit kam. Tagebuch vom 1. Vatikanischen Konzil*, (Frankfurther Theologische Studien, Bd. 24) Frankfurt/M. 1977

Sickel, Theodor von, *Römische Erinnerungen*, ed. L. Santivaller (Veröffentlichungen d.I.Ö.G. 3). Vienna 1947

Spectator, 16 July 1870: 'The New Dogma'

Stanley, Arthur Penrhyn. 'The Oecumenical Church' in *Edinburgh Review* 13 (1869) 297–336

Stock, Leo Francis (ed.), *U.S. Ministers to the Papal States. Instructions and Despatches 1848–1868* (American Catholic Historical Association Documents I), Washington DC 1933

—*Consular Relations between the U.S. and the Papal States* (American Catholic Historical Association Documents 2), Washington DC 1945

Strong, Josiah, *Our Country*, New York 1885 and 1891, new ed. by Jürgen Herbst, Cambridge, Mass. 1963

The Times, October–November 1850

Trollope, Anthony, *Phineas Finn. The Irish Member (1869)* O.U.P. ed. London 1973 (with an introduction by Shane Leslie)

Ullathorne, Bishop, *History of the Restoration of the Catholic Hierarchy in England*, London 1871

Veuillot, Louis, *Rome pendant le Concile*, 2 vols., Paris 1872

—*Correspondence* IX/X (Jan. 1866–Sept. 1871). ed. Francois Veuillot (*Oeuvres*

Bibliography

complètes, ser. 2, vol.23/4) Paris 1932

Vincent, John, *Disraeli, Derby, and the Conservative Party, Journals and Memoirs of Edward Henry, Lord Stanley, 1849–1869,* Hassocks, Sussex 1978

Volk, L., 'Päpstliche Kritik an der Appeasement Politik von 1938. Ein unveröffentlicher Bericht des britischen Vatikangesandten' in *Stimmen der Zeit* 197 (1979) 532–8

Weigall, Rachel, *Correspondence of Lord Burghersh, afterwards 11th earl of Westmoreland, 1808–1840,* London 1912

Wellesley, Frederick A. (ed.), *Secrets of the Second Empire. Private Letters From the Paris Embassy. Selections from the Papers of Henry Richard Charles Wellesley first Earl Cowley, Ambassador in Paris 1852–1867,* New York 1929

Whyte, J.H. (ed.), 'Select documents XVIII: Bishop Moriarty on Disestablishment and the Union, 1868' in *Irish Historical Studies* 10 (1965) 193–199

SECONDARY

Albrecht, D., 'Döllinger, die bayerische Regierung und das 1. Vatikanische Konzil' in Repgen/Skalweit, (ed.), *Spiegel der Geschichte. Festgabe für Max Braubach,* Münster 1964, 795–815

Artaud de Montor, Alexis Francois, *Storia del pontifice Pius VIII,* 2 vols, Milan 1844

Aschoff, Hans-Georg, *Das Verhältnis von Staat und katholischer Kirche im Königreich Hannover (1813–1866)* (Quellen und Darstellungen zur Geschichte Niedersachsens 86) Hildesheim 1976

Aspinwall, Bernard, 'Charles de Montalembert and England' in *Downside Review* 88 (1970) 132–149

Aubert, Roger, *Le pontificat de Pie IX (1846–1878)* (Histoire de l'Église, Vol.21) Paris 1952

—'Mgr. Dupanloup au début du Concile du Vatican' in *Miscellanea Historiae Ecclesiasticae,* I (Bibliotheque de la Revue d'histoire ecclésiastique 38) Louvrain 1961, 96–116

Bäumer, Remigius, 'Die Badische Regierung, die Freiburger Theologische Fakultät und das I. Vatikanische Konzil', in *Freiburger Diözesan-Archiv* 97 (1977) 237–278

Barie, Ottavio, *L'Inghilterra e il problema italiano. Dalle riforme alle costituzione,* Milan 1858

Bastgen, Hubert (Beda), *Forschungen und Quellen zur Kirchenpolitik Gregors XVI,* 2 vols, Paderborn 1929

Baum, W., 'Luigi Maria Torrigiani (1697–1777) Kardinalstaats-sekretär Papst Klemens XIII' in *Zeitschrift für katholische Theologie* 94(1972) 46–78

Beales, Derek, *England and Italy 1859–60,* London 1961

Beck, George A. (ed.). *The English Catholics 1850–1950,* London 1950

Becker, Josef, *Liberaler Staat und Kirche in der Ära von Reichsgründung und Kulturkampf. Geschichte und Strukturen ihres Verhältnisses in Baden 1860–1876* (Veröffentlichungen der Kommission für Zeitgeschichte, v.14) Mainz 1973

Bellesheim, Alphons, *History of the Catholic Church in Scotland,* 4 vols., transl with Notes and Additions by Hunter Blair, Edinburgh 1887–90

—*Geschichte der Katholischen Kirche in Irland,* III, Mainz 1891

—*Henry Edward Manning,* Mainz 1892

—'Zwei berühmte Schotten auf dem Festlande. II Cardinal Charles Erskine' in *H.P.Bl.* 110 (1892) 862–9

—'Cardinal Consalvi in Paris, London and Wien', in *H.P.Bl.* 135 (1905) 282–92

—'Cardinal Consalvi in Paris, London and Wien' (Review of Rinieri, II congresso di Vienna e la Santa Sede ...) in *H.P.Bl.* 135 (1905) 282–292

Besson, Louis, *Frédéric-Francois-Xavier de Merode, Ministre et Aumonier de Pie IX, Archevêque de Mélitène. Sa Vie et ses Oeuvres,* 4th ed., Paris 1888

Beumer, Johannes, Ein neu veröffentlichtes Tagebuch zum ersten Vatikanum. Anmerkungen zu: Appunti storici sopra il Concilio Vaticano, ed. Giacomo Martina

Great Britain and the Holy See

(Miscellanea Historiae Pontificiae 33), Rom 1972' in *Annuarium Historiae Conciliorum* 6 (1974) 399–423

—'Das Erste Vatikanum und seine Rezeption' in *Münchener Theologische Zeitschrift* 27 (1976) 259–276

Blair, Rt. Rev. Sir David Hunter, *John Patrick 3rd Marquess of Bute (1847–1900). A Memoir*, London 1921

Blake, Lord R., *Disraeli*, London 1966

Boero, J., *Osservazioni sopra l'istoria del pontificiato di Clemente XIV scritta dal P.A. Theiner*, 2nd ed., 2 vols, Monza 1854

Bonfanti, Giuseppe, *Roma capitale e la questione romana* (Documenti e testimonianzi di storia contemporanea 5) Brescia 1977

Borinski, Ludwig, *Englischer Geist in der Geschichte seiner Prosa*, Freiburg i. Br. 1951.

—*Der englische Roman des 18. Jahrhunderts*, 2nd ed., Wiesbaden 1978

—'Anthony Trollope: Phineas Finn, the Irish Member' in *Der englische Roman im 19. Jahrhundert, Oppel-Festschrift*, Berlin 1973, 199–213

—'Dickens als Politiker' in *Die Neueren Sprachen* n.s. 22 (1973) 385–395

—*Die Anfänge des britischen Imperialismus* (Veröffentlichumgen der Joachim-Jungius-Gesellschaft der Wissenschaften Hamburg No.42), Göttingen 1980

Bossy, John, *The English Catholic Community 1570–1850*, London 1975

Boulger, Demetrius C., *Lord William Bentinck* (Rulers of India ser.) Oxford 1892

Bower, Jean, 'Freedom's Advocate: Lord Acton and the Liberal Catholic Movement in England' in *Dublin Review*, no.503, Spring 1965, 90–99

Brandes, Georg, *Lord Beaconsfield, ein Charakterbild* (Danish original 1878) (Gesammelte Werke 5) Munich 1903

Brandmüller, Walter, 'Die Publikation des 1. Vatikanischen Konzils in Bayern' in *Zeitschrift für bayerische Landesgeschichte* 31 (1968) 197–258 and 575–634

—*Damals geschehen, heute diskutiert*, St Ottilien 1977, 7–56; 'Das 1. Vatikanische Konzil 1869/70'

—*Ignaz von Döllinger am Vorabend des I. Vatikanums. Herausforderung und Antwort* (Kirchengeschichtliche Quellen und Studien 9) St Ottilien 1977

Brenan, M.J., *An Ecclesiastical History of Ireland*, new ed., Dublin 1864

Brewster, R.C., *Disraeli in outline*, London 1890

Broderick, John F., *The Holy See and the Irish Movement for the Repeal of the Union with England. 1829–1847, (Analecta Gregoriana, vol. 55, ser. Fac.Hist.Eccl.Sect.B, n.9)* Rome 1951

Brown, Marvin Luther, *Louis Veuillot*, Durham NC 1977

Brück, Heinrich, *Das irische Veto*, Mainz 1879

—'Studien über die Katholiken-Emancipation in Großbritannien, besonders über das s.g. irische Veto' in *Der Katholik* 1879 II 1–36 and 337–366

Bulwer, Henry Lytton, *The Life of Henry John Temple, Viscount Palmerston: with Selections from his Diaries and Correspondence*, 3 vols., London 1870

Burbage, T.H., 'Masonic Crime and Terrorism' in *Catholic Bulletin* 7 (1917) 309–316, 276–284, 429–436

Buschkühl, Matthias, *Die Irische, Scottische und Römische Frage. Disraeli's Schlüsselroman 'Lothair' (1870)*, (Kirchengeschichtliche Quellen und Studien 11) St Ottilien/ Bavaria 1980

Butler, Charles, *Historical Memoirs respecting the English, Irish and Scottish Catholics, From the Reformation to the Present Time*, 4 Vols. London 1819–21

Butler, Cuthbert, *Das erste Vatikanische Konzil. Seine Geschichte von innen geschildert in Bischof Ullathornes Briefen*, ed. Hugo Lang, Munich 1961

—*The Life and Times of Bishop Ullathorne, 1806–1889*, I, London 1926

Butterfield, H., *Lord Acton* (Historical Association Gen. Ser. No. 9) 1968

Cahill, E., *Freemasonry and the Anti-Christian Movement*, Dublin 1929

Caprile, Giovanni, 'La Civiltà Cattolica al Concilio Vaticano I' in *Civiltà Cattolica* 120 (1969) IV pp.333–341, 538–548

Bibliography

Castelot, André, *Napoléon III, ou l'Aube des temps modernes*, Paris 1974

Catholic Historical Review 40 (1954) 94*ff*: Notes and Comments (on Bernard Smith O.S.B. 1812–92)

Chadwick, Owen, *The Victorian Church*, 2 vols. (An Ecclesiastical History of England V) London 1966/70

Chevallier, Pierre, *Histoire de la franc-marconnerie francaise* II: La Maconnerie: missionare du Libéralisme (1800–1877) (Les grandes études historiques) Paris 1974

Conzemius, Victor, 'Römische Briefe vom Konzil' in *Theologische Quartalschrift* 140 (1960) 427–462

—'Acton, Döllinger und Ketteler' in *Archiv für Mittelrheinische Kirchengeschichte* 14 (1962) 194–238

—'Die Verfasser der Römischen Briefe vom Konzil' des 'Quirinus' in *Freiburger Geschichtsblätter* 52 (1963/4) 229–256

—'Review: Blakiston, *The Roman Question*' in *Theologische Quartalschrift* 144 (1964) 102 *ff*

—'Die 'Römischen Briefe vom Konzil'. Eine entstehungsgeschichtliche Untersuchung zum Konzilsjournalismus Ignaz v. Döllingers und Lord Actons' in *Römische Quartalschrift für christliche Altertumskunde und Kirchengeschichte* 59 (1964) 186–229; 60 (1965) 76–119

—'Lord Acton and the First Vatican Council' in *Journal of Ecclesiastical History* 20 (1969) 267–294

—*Katholizismus ohne Rom*, Zürich/Einsiedeln/Köln 1969

—'Preussen und das Erste Vatikanische Konzil' in *Annuarium Historiae Conciliorum* 2 (1970) 353–419

—'Warum wurde der päpstliche Primat gerade im Jahre 1870 definiert?' in *Concilium* 7 (1971) 263–267

—*Propheten und Vorläufer, Wegbereiter des neuzeitlichen Katholizismus*, Cologne 1972, 79–102: Ignaz von Döllinger; 136–158: Lord Acton

Coppa, Frank J., 'Cardinal Antonelli, the Papal States, and the Counter-Risorgimento' in *Journal of Church and State* 16 (1974) 453–471

Corish, Patrick J., *Political Problems 1860–78* (A History of Irish Catholicism, vol. 3) Dublin 1967

Cretineau Joly, J., *L'Eglise romain en face de la revolution*. 2nd ed., Paris 1860

—*Papa Clemente XIV*, Modena 1854

Curry, J., *An historical account of the Civil Wars of Ireland from the reign of Queen Elizabeth to the settlement under King William. With the State of the Irish Catholics, from that settlement to the relaxation of the popery laws in the year 1778.* Extracts from parliamentary records, state acts, and other authentic materials, new, improved ed., Dublin 1810

Cwiekowski, Frederick, *The English Bishops and the First Vatican Council*, Louvain 1971

Degli Alberti, Mario, 'La Missione Vegezzi ed il gran concordato propasta al P. Luigi Tasti. Con lettere inedite' in *Nuova Antologia*, 1 Oct. 1916, pp.322–43

Della Rocca, Fernando, *I Papi della Questione Romana*, Rome 1981

Deufel, Konrad, *Kirche und Tradition. Ein Beitrag zur Geschichte der theologischen Wende im 19. Jh. am Beispiel des kirchlich-theologischen Kampfprogramms P. Josef Kleutgens S.J. Darstellung und neue Quellen* (Beiträge zur Katholizismusforschung Reihe B: Abhandlungen) München 1976

Dibelius, *England*, 2 vols., Berlin/Leipzig 1923

Döllinger, I. v. ('Quirinus'), *Römische Briefe vom Concil'*, Munich 1870

Drew, Mary, *Acton, Gladstone and others*, London 1924

Dwyer, J.J., 'The Catholic Press 1850–1950' in Beck (ed.)., *The English Catholics*, London 1950, 474–514

E., H.M., *Ganganelli: der Kampf gegen den Jesuitismus* (Die Vorkämpfer für Bildung einer Nationalkirche I), Karlsruhe 1845

Great Britain and the Holy See

Ellis, John Tracey, *Cardinal Consalvi and Anglo-Papal Relations,* Washington D.C. 1942

Falcionelli, Albert, *Les Sociétés Secrètes Italiennes. Les Carbonari. La Camorra. La Mafia,* Paris 1936

Fasnacht, G.E., *Acton's Political Philosophy,* London 1952

Feine, Hans Erich, 'Persona grata, minus grata. Zur Vorgeschichte des deutschen Bischofswahlrechts im 19. Jahrhundert' in *Festschrift Alfred Schultze,* ed. Walter Merk, Weimar 1934, pp.65–83

Feuchtwanger, E.J., *Gladstone,* London 1975

Finsterhölzi, Johann, *Ignaz von Döllinger* (Wegbereiter heutiger Theologie 2) Graz/Vienna/Cologne 1969

—*Die Kirche in der Theologie Ignaz von Döllingers bis zum ersten Vatikanum,* ed. Brosseder (Studien zur Theologie und Geistesgeschichte des 19. Jahrhunderts 9) Göttingen 1975

Fitzpatrick, William John, *Secret Service under Pitt,* London 1892

Fogarty, Gerald P., 'Archbishop Peter Kenrick's Submission to Papal Infallibility' in *Archivum Historiae Pontificiae* 16 (1978) 205–222

Franzen, August, *Die Katholisch-Theologische Fakultät Bonn im Streit um das Erste Vatikanische Konzil. Zugleich ein Beitrag zur Entstehungsgeschcihte des Altkatholizismus am Niederrhein* (Bonner Beiträge zur Kirchengeschichte 6) Cologne 1974

Friedrich, Johannes, *Ignaz von Döllinger. Sein Leben auf Grund seines schriftlichen Nachlasses,* 3 vol., München 1899–1901

Gadille, Jacques, 'La phase décisive de Vatican I: mars–avril 1870' in *Annuarium Historiae Conciliorum* 1 (1969) 336–347

Gaselee, Sir Stephen, 'British Diplomatic Relations with the Holy See' in *Dublin Review* 204 (1939) 1–19)

Gasquet, Cardinal, *Great Britain and the Holy See 1792–1806; A Chapter in the History of Diplomatic Relations between England and Rome,* Rome 1919

Godfrey, J., 'Montalembert et le modèle anglais' in *Cahiers d'histoire* (Clermont-Ferrand) 15 (1970) 335–353

Götten, Josef, *Christof Moufang. Theologe und Politiker 1817–1890,* Mainz 1969.

Gooch, G.P., 'Lord Acton: Apostle of Liberty' in *Foreign Affairs* 25 (July 1947) 629–642

Granderath, Theodor, *Geschichte des Vatikanischen Konzils,* 3 Vols., Freiburg i.Br. 1903/6

Graham, Robert, A., *Vatican Diplomacy,* Princton, N.J. 1959

—'Il Vaticano nella guerra psicologica inglese 1939–1945. La storia dei "sib", cioè delle "bugie autorizzate"' *Civilta cattolica* 192 (1978) I, 113–33

Grisar, Josef, 'Die Circulardepesche des Fürsten Hohenlohe vom 9. April 1869 über das bevorstehende Vatikanische Konzil' in *Bayern: Staat und Kirche, Land und Reich; Forschungen zur bayerischen Geschichte vornehmlich im 19. Jh., Festschrift Wilhelm Winkler,* Munich 1960, pp.216–240

Gruber, Hermann, *Mazzini, Freimaurerei und Weltrevolution,* Regensburg 1901

Guadet, *Esquisses historiques et politiques sur le pape Pie VII, suivis d'une notice sur l'élection de Léon XII,* Paris 1824

Gurian, Waldemar, *Die politischen und sozialen Ideen des französischen Katholizismus 1789–1914,* M. Gladbach 1929

Gwynn, Denis, *Lord Shrewsbury, Pugin, and the Catholic Revival,* London 1946

Hales, E.E.Y., *Pio Nono. A Study in European politics and religion in the 19th century,* London 1954

Halevy, Elie, *The Age of Peel and Cobden. A History of the English People 1841–1852,* London 1947

Halkin, Léon-E., 'Les Archives des Nonciatures. Rapport au Comité directeur de l'Institut historique belge de Rome' in *Bulletin de l'Institut historique belge de Rome* 33 (1961) 649–700

Bibliography

Hasler, August Bernhard, *Pius IX. (1846–1878). Päpstliche Unfehlbarkeit und 1. Vatikanisches Konzil. Dogmatisierung und Durchsetzung einer Ideologie,* 2 vols. (Päpste und Papsttum 12) Stuttgart 1977

Haynes, Renée, *Philosopher King. The Humanist Pope Benedict XIV,* London 1970

Hegel, Eduard, *Die kirchenpolitischen Beziehungen Hannovers, Sachsens und der norddeutschen Kleinstaaten zur römischen Kurie 1800–1846,* Paderborn 1936

Hennesey, James, *The First Council of the Vatican: The American Experience,* New York 1963

—'Nunc venio de America: The American Church and Vatican I' in *Annuarium Historiae Conciliorum* 1 (1969) 348–398

—'National Traditions and the First Vatican Council' in *Archivum Historiae Pontificiae* 1 (1969) 491–512

Hergenröther, J., *Der Kirchenstaat seit der französischen Revolution. Historisch-statistische Studien und Skizzen,* Freiburg i Br. 1860

—*Katholische Kirche und christlicher Staat in ihrer geschichtlichen Entwicklung und in Bezeihung auf die Fragen der Gegenwart,* 2 vols. (1872) repr. Aalen 1968

Heuss-Burckhardt, Ursula, *Gladstone und das Problem der Staatskirche,* Diss. Zurich 1957

Heydt, Odo van der, 'Monsignor Talbot de Malahide', in: *Wiseman Review* No. 502 (Winter 1864) 290–308

Himmelfarb, Gertrude, *Lord Acton. A Study in Conscience and Politics,* London 1952

Hitchman, Francis, *Pius the Ninth. A Biography,* London 1878

—*The Public Life of the Earl of Beaconsfield,* 2 vols., London 1879

—'Lothair and Endymion' in *The National Review* 9 (1887) 382–394

Holmes, J. Derek, 'Cardinal Newman and the First Vatican Council' in *Annuarium Historiae Conciliorum* 1 (1969) 399–411

Hughes, Philip, *The Catholic Question 1688–1829. A Study in Political History,* London 1929

Hunter, W.W., *A Life of the Earl of Mayo,* 2 vols., London 1875

Husenbeth, F.C., *The Life of the Rt. Rev. John Milner, D.D.,* Dublin 1862

Hutton, Arthur Wollaston, *Cardinal Manning. With a bibliography,* London 1892

Illustrated London News, 24 Sept. 1892, 'The Late Cardinal Howard'

Ibid., 29 Oct. 1892, p.567: 'Cardinal Howard's Will'

Ibid., 3 Jan. 1891, p.4: 'Sir John Pope Hennessy'

Ibid., 17 Nov. 1891, p.498: 'Sir John Pope Hennessy, Obituary'

Isaacson, Charles S., *The Story of the English Cardinals,* London 1907

Jedin, Hubert (ed.), *Handbuch der Kirchengeschichte* VI/1 and 2, Freiburg i.Br. 1971–73, Eng. trans.: *History of the Church,* vols. 7 & 8, New York, 1981.

Jesse, John Heneage, *Memoirs of the Pretenders and their Adherents,* 2 vols, London 1845

Just, Leo, 'Die Quellen zur Geschichte der Kölner Nuntiatur in Archiven und Bibliothek des Vatikans' in *Quellen und Forschungen aus italienischen Archiven und Bibliotheken* 29 (1938–39) 249–96

Kinsella, Christopher Gerard, 'The Diplomatic Mission of Archbishop Flavio Chigi, *Apostolic Nuncio to Paris, 1870–71',* phil. Diss. Loyola Univ. of Chicago 1974

Jorns, Marie, *August Kestner und seine Zeit 1777–1853. Das glückliche Leben des Diplomaten, Kunstsammlers und Mäzens in Hannover und Rom. Aus Briefen und Tagebüchern zusammengestellt,* Hanover 1964

Katzman, Sue, 'Acton and the Bishops of the Minority' in McElrath, *Lord Acton,* Louvain 1970, 187–217

Kebbel, T.E., *Life of Lord Beaconsfield,* London 1888

—*Lord Beaconsfield and other Tory Memoirs,* London 1907

Kraus, Franz Xaver, *Cavour,* (Weltgeschichte in Karakterbildern 5) Mainz 1902

Lecanuet, R.P., *Montalembert,* III, Paris 1902

Lenhart, Ludwig, 'Regens Moufang und das Vaticanum' in *Jahrbuch für das Bistum Mainz* 5 (1950) 400–441

Great Britain and the Holy See

Leonardis, Massimo de, *L'Inghilterra e la Questione Romana, 1859–1870* (Vita e Pensiero, Scienze storice 28), Milan 1980

Leslie, Shane, *Henry Edward Manning. His Life and Labours*, London 1921

Leti, Giuseppe, *Carbonaria e massoneria nel Risorgimento Italiano* (1925) Bologna 1966

Lias, John James, 'Anglican and continental Churches' in *Internationale kirchliche Zeitschrift* 1 (1911) 31–36

Lill, Rudolf, Die deutschen Theologieprofessoren vor dem Vatikanum 1 im Urteil des Münchener Nuntius in *Reformata Reformanda. Festgabe für Hubert Jedin, II*, Münster 1965, 483–507

Linker, R.W., 'The English Roman Catholics and Emancipation: The Politics of Persuasion' in *Journal of Ecclesiastical History* 27 (1976) 151–180

Lösch, Stefan, *Döllinger und Frankreich. Eine geistige Allianz 1823–1871*, Munich 1955

Longhena, Francesco, *Sulla storia del pontificato di Clemente XIV del ... Theiner Osservazioni; coll' agiunto di ... parole ... alle osservazioni ... di Boero ...*, Milan 1854

Lucas, Edward, *The Life of Frederick Lucas, M.P., by his brother*, 2 vols., London 1886

Lunadoro, Cav., *Relazione della Corte di Roma*, Rome 1830

Luzio, Alessandro, *La Massoneria e il Risorgimento Italiano*, 2 vols., (1925) Bologna 1966

McCartney, Donal, 'The Church and Fenianism' in M. Harmon (ed.). *Fenians and Fenianism*, Dublin 1970, 13–27

—'The Churches and Secret Societies' in *Secret Societies in Ireland*, ed. T. Williams, Dublin 1973, 68–78

McClelland, V.A., *Cardinal Manning*, London 1962

—'The Irish Clergy and Archbishop Manning's Visitation of the Western Districts of Scotland, 1867' in *Catholic Historical Review* 53 (1967) 1–27 and 229–250

—'A Hierarchy for Scotland, 1868–1878' in *Catholic Historical Review* 56 (1970) 474–500

MacDonagh, Oliver, 'The Politicization of the Irish Catholic Bishops 1800–1850' in *Historical Journal* 18 (1975) 37–53

MacDonald, Fergus, *The Catholic Church and the Secret Societies in the U.S.* (U.S. Catholic Historical Society Monograph 22) New York 1946

MacDougall, H.A., *Lord Acton on Papal Power*, London 1973

McElrath, Damian (ed.). *Lord Acton. The Decisive Decade 1864–1874*, Louvaine 1970. 'An Essay on Acton's Critical Decade', 3–118

Machin, G.I.T., *The Catholic Question in English Politics 1820–1830*, Oxford 1964

—'Lord John Russell and the Prelude to the Ecclesiastical Titles Bill, 1846–51' in *Journal of Ecclesiastical History* 35 (1974) 227–295

—*Politics and the Churches in Great Britain 1832 to 1868*, Oxford 1977

McLaughlin, P.J., 'Dr Russell and the Dublin Review' in *Studies* 41 (1952) 175–188

MacSuibhne, Peadar, 'Ireland at the Vatican Council' in *Irish Ecclesiastical Record* 93 (1960) 209–222 u. 295–307

Manzini, Luigi M., *Il cardinale Luigi Lambruschini* (Studi e testi 203) Vatican City 1960

Martina, Giacomo, 'Osservazioni sulle varie redazioni del 'Sillabo',' in *Chiesa e stato nell'ottocento, Miscellanea in onore di Pietro Pirri* II, Aubert/Ghisalberti/Passerin d'Entreves (ed.), (Italia sacra 4) Padua 1962, 419–523

—'Nuovi documenti sulla genese del Sillabo' in *Archivum Historiae Pontificiae* 6 (1968) 319–369

—'Il concilio Vaticano I e la fine del portere temporale' in *Rassegna storica toskana* 16 (1970) 131–150

—*Pio IX 1846–1850* (Miscellanean Historiae Pontificae 38) Rome 1974

—'Review: Hasler, Pius IX, 1977' in *Archivum Historiae Pontifiae* 16 (1978) 341–369

—'Review: Weber, *Kardinäle*, 1978', *ibid.* 406–416

Bibliography

Mathew, David, *Lord Acton and his times*, London 1968
—'New Facts About Lord Acton' in *Downside Review* 90 (1972) 15−19
Maurin, Jean, *La politique ecclésiastique du Second Empire de 1852 à 1869*, Paris 1930
Maxwell, Herbert, *Life and Letters of George William Frederick 4th Earl of Clarendon*, 2 vols., London 1913
Meagher, William, *Notices of the Life and Character of His Grace. Most Rev. Daniel Murray, Late Archbishop of Dublin*, Dublin 1853
Mejer, Otto, *Das Veto deutscher protestantischer Staatsregierungen gegen katholische Bischofswahlen*, Rostock 1866
—*Zur Geschichte der römisch-deutschen Frage*, 3 vols., Rostock 1871−74
—*Der römische Kestner* (Deutsche Bücherei 28) Breslau 1883
Mevius, David Ghislain Baron de, *Histoire de l'invasion des Etats pontificaux en 1867*, Paris 1875
Meynell, Wilfrid ('John Oldcastle'), *Cardinal Manning No.*, *Merry England* 1. May 1886
—*Memorials of Cardinal Manning, Feb. No.*, *Merry England* 1892
—*Benjamin Disraeli. An Unconventional Biography*, 2 vols., London 1903
Michael, Horst, *Bismarck, England und Europa (1866−1870)* (Forschungen zur Mittelalterlichen und Neuren Geschichte 5) München 1930
Miko, Norbert, 'Die diplomatischen Beziehungen zwischen England und dem heiligen Stuhl im 19. Jahrhundert' in *Zeitschrift für katholische Theologie* 78 (1956) 206−225
—'Die Römische Frage und das Erste Vatikanische Konzil' in *Römische Historische Mitteilungen* 4 (1960/1), 254−271
Milner, John M. *Supplementary Memoirs of the English Catholics*, London 1820
Moens, G., *La Légitmité, l'ordre et le progres, ou La lettre encyclique de Grégoire XVI*, Liége 1832
Mollat, G., *La Question Romaine de Pie VI à Pie XI* (Bibliothèque de l'enseignement de l'histoire eccl. 23) Paris 1932
Montclos, Xavier de, *Lavigerie, le Saint-Siège et L'Église de l'avènement de Pie IX à l'avènement de Léon XIII, 1846−1878*, Diss. Paris 1965
Monypenny/Buckle, *Life of Benjamin Disraeli*, 6 vols. London 1910−20
Mooney, Gary, 'British Diplomatic Relations with the Holy See, 1783−1830', in *Recusant History* 14 (1978) 193−210
Moran, Patrick Francis, *Spicilegium Ossoriense*, vol.III, Dublin 1884
Mori, Renato, *Il tramonte del potere temporale 1866−1870* (Politica e storia 15) Rome 1967
Morley, John, *The Life of William Ewart Gladstone*, 3 vols. London 1912
Nembach, Ulrich, *Die Stellung der Evangeglischen Kirche und ihrer Presse zum 1. Vatikanischen Konzil*, Diss. Basel 1961, printed Zurich 1962
Neufeld, K.H., 'Rom und die Ökumene. Victor de Buck S.J. (1817−1876) als Theologe auf dem 1. Vatikanum' in *Catholica* 33 (1979) 63−80
Neuner, Peter, *Döllinger als Theologe der Ökumene* (Beiträge zur ökumenischen Theologie 19) Paderborn 1979
Newton, T.W. Legh Lord, *Lord Lyons, a record of British diplomacy*, 2 vols., London 1913
Noakes, Robert, 'Cardinal Erskines's Mission, 1793−1801' in *Dublin Review* 204 (1939) 388−353
Nolli, Robert Di, *Mentana*, Rome 1965
Norman, Edward Robert, *The Catholic Church and Ireland in the age of rebellion 1859−1873*, London 1965
—*Anti-Catholicism in Victorian England*, London 1968
Nurnberger, August Josef, *Zur Kirchengeschichte des XIX. Jahrhunderts, I. Papsttum und Kirchenstaat* 2 and 3, Mainz 1898/1900
O'Connell, Maurice Rickard, 'The Political Background to the Establishment of Maynooth College' in *Irish Ecclesiastical Record* 85(1956) 325−34; 406−15; 86(1956)1−16

Great Britain and the Holy See

—*Irish Politics and Social conflict in the Age of the American Revolution,* Philadelphia 1965

O'Donoghue, Patrick, 'The Holy See and Ireland 1780–1803' *Archivium Hibernicum* 34 (1977) 99–108

Ollivier, Emile, *L'Église et l'État au Concile du Vatican,* 2 vols., Paris 1879

Ompteda, Ludwig Freiherr von, *Irrfahrten und Abenteuer eines mittelstaatlichen Diplomaten. Ein Lebens- und Kulturbild aus der Zeit um 1800,* Leipzig 1894 *The Oscotian* NS No.22, July 1888

Ottmann, Johann Friedrich, *De Episcoporum in Hibernia nominatione quam vocant domesticam,* Diss. Königsberg 1850

Painting, David E., 'Disraeli and the Roman Catholic Church' in *Quarterly Review* 304 (1966) 17–25

Parker, Charles Stuart, *Life and Letters of Sir James Graham, Sec. Bart. of Netherby. 1792–1861,* 2 vols. London 1907

Pastor, Ludwig von, *Geschichte der Päpste,* vol.16, Freiburg i. Br. 1932

Pecorari, Anselmo G., 'Mons. Luigi Martini tra Mantova e la Santa Sede' in *Civiltà Mantovana* 12 (1978) 105–58

Pelczar, Jósef Sebastyan, *Pius IX i jego pontificat,* I, Cracow 1887

Pfleger, Luzian, 'Zur Beurteilung Louis Veuillots' in *Historisch-politische Blätter für das katholische Deutschland* 153 (1914) 355–366

Pfülf, Otto, *Bischof von Ketteler,* 3 vols., Mainz 1899

Pica, Ignatius M., *Le cardinal Bilio, barnabite, un des présidents du concile du Vatican, (1826–1884),* Paris 1898

Pistolesi, Erasmo, *Vita del sommo pontifice Pio VII,* 3 vols. (Guiseppe de Novaes, *Vite de' pontifici,* vols. 18–20) Rome 1824–5

Plowden, Francis, *An Historical Review of the State of Ireland from the invasion of that country under Henry II to its Union with Great Britain,* 2 vols, London 1803

Pope-Hennessy, J. 'Lord Beaconsfield's Irish Policy' in *Nineteenth Century* 16 (1884) 663–680

Prest, John, *Lord John Russell,* London 1972

Prothero, R.E./Bradley, G.C., *The Life and Correspondence of Arthur Penrhyn Stanley, Late Dean of Westminster,* 2 vols., London 1893

Purcell, Edmund Sheridan, *Life of Cardinal Manning,* London 1896

Rall, Hans, 'England und Bayern im Frühjahr 1870' in *Großbritannien und Deutschland, Festschrift J.W.P. Bourke,* Munich 1974, 247–256

Ralls, Walter, 'The Papal Aggression of 1850: A Study in Victorian Anti-Catholicism' in *Church History* 43 (1974) 242–256

Randall, Alec, 'British Diplomatic Representation at the Holy See' in *Blackfriars* 37 (1956) 356–363

—'A British Agent at the Vatican. The Mission of Odo Russell' in *Dublin Review,* no. 479, Spring 1959, 37–57

—'Lord Odo Russell and his Roman Friends' in *History Today* 26 (1976) 368–376

Ranke, Leopold von, *Englische Geschichte vornehmlich im 17. Jahrhundert,* I Leipzig 1870

Ravignan, Xavier de, *Clément XII et Clément XIV,* 2 vols., Paris 1854

Remond, Réne, *L'anticléricalisme en France, de 1815 à nos jours,* Paris 1976

Reumont, A. von, *Ganganelli-Papst Clemens XIV,* Berlin 1847

Ried, U., 'Studien zu Kettelers Stellung zum Infallibilitätsdogma bis zur Definition am 18 Juli 1870' in *Historisches Jahrbuch* 47 (1927) 657–726

Rinieri, Ilario, *Il Congresso di Vienna e la Santa Sede* (1813–1815) (Diplomazia pontificia nel secolo XIX, vol.4), Rome 1904

—*Die römische Revolution vor dem Urtheile eines Unpartheischen,* transl. from the Italian, Augsburg 1852

Rivinius, Karl Josef, *Bischof Wilhelm Emmanuel von Ketteler und die Infallibilität des Papstes* (Europäische Hochschulschriften, Reihe 23 Theologie 48) theol. Diss. Münster 1975, printed Frankfurt/M. 1976

Bibliography

Roselli, John, *Lord William Bentinck and the British Occupation of Sicily, 1811–1814,* London 1956

Ruggiero, Livia de, 'Inghilterra e Stato Pontificio nel prima triennio del pontificato di Pio IX', in *Archivio della Società romana di Storia patria* 76 (1953) 51–172

Russell, George William Erskine, *Portraits of the Seventies,* London 1916

Saturday Review 29, (7 May 1870), 612: 'Lothair'.

Saturday Review 29 (14 May 1870) 625: 'Cullen and the Fenians'

Schatz, Klaus, *Kirchenbild und päpstliche Unfehlbarkeit bei den deutschsprachigen Minoritätsbischöfen auf den I. Vatikanum* (Miscellanea Historiae Pontificiae 40) Rom 1975

—'Totalrevision der Geschichte des I. Vatikanums? Zur Auseinandersetzung mit den Thesen von August B. Hasler,' in *Theologie und Philosophie* 53 (1978) 248–276

Schmidlin, Josef, *Papstgeschichte der neuesten Zeit, II: Pius IX. and Leo XIII. (1846–1903),* Munich 1934

Schnütgen, Alexander, 'Ein Kölner Nuntius der Aufklärungszeit und die rheinischen Kurfürsten und Bischöfe. Nach vatikanischen Nuntiaturakten von 1770' in *Ehrengabe deutscher Wissenschaft für Prinz Johann Georg Herzog zu Sachsen,* ed. Franz Tessler, Freiburg 1920, pp.743–66

Schoeters, Karel, *P.-J. Beckx S.J. (1795–1887) en de 'Jezuiten Politiek' van zijn tijd* Antwerp 1965

Schuettinger, Robert L., *Lord Acton, Historian of Liberty,* La Salle, III. 1976

Schwaiger, Georg, *Hundert Jahre nach dem Ersten Vatikanum,* Regensburg 1970

—ed. *Konzil und Papst. Historische Beiträge zur Frage der höchsten Gewalt in der Kirche. Festgabe für Hermann Tüchle,* Munich Paderborn 1975

—'Ignaz von Döllinger', in Schweiger/Fries (ed.), *Katholische Theologen Deutschlands im 19. Jahrhundert,* III, Munich 1975, 9–38, Bibliography 38–43

Scott, Ivan, *The Roman Question and the Powers 1848–1865,* The Hague 1969

Sicehl, Walter, *Disraeli: A Study in Personality and Ideas,* London 1904

Sivric, Ivo, *Bishop J.G. Strossmayer. New Light on Vatican I,* Rome/Chicago 1975

Smith, H.A., 'Diplomatic Relations with the Holy See, 1815–1930' in *Law Quarterly Review* 48 (1932), 374–393

Somerset, H.V.F., 'Edmund Burke, England and the Papacy' in *Dublin Review* 202 (1938) 138–48

Somerville, H., 'Disraeli and Catholicism' in *The Month* 159 (1932) 114–124

Sparrow Simpson, W.J., *Roman Catholic Opposition to Papal Infallibility,* London 1909

Spectator, 31 Dec. 1864, 43(1870) 636: 'Mr Disraeli on Secret Societies'

Sprenger, van Eijck, Jacob Johannes, *Ganganelli (Paus Clemens XIV),* Arnheim 1848

Stanley, Arthur Penrhyn (Dean of Westminster), *Essays on Church and State. From 1850–1870,* (London 1870), Repr. 1969

Steinwachs, Otto, 'Die Unionsbestrebungen im Altkatholizismus' in *Internationale kirchliche Zeitschrift* 1 (1911) 169–186, 471–499

Steele, E.D., 'Gladstone and Ireland' in *Irish Historical Studies* 17 (1970) 58–88

—'Cardinal Cullen and Irish nationality' in *Irish Historical Studies* 19 (1975) 239–260

Stepischnegg, J.M., *Papst Pius IX und seine Zeit,* 2 vols., Vienna 1879

Stewart, Robert, *The Politics of Protection. Lord Derby and the Protectionist Party 1841–1852,* Cambridge 1971

Stieglitz, Hans, *Erinnerungen an Rom und an den Kirchenstaat im ersten Jahre seiner Verjüngung,* Leipzig 1848

Storia della vita, azione e virtu di Clemente XIV, 2nd ed., 2 vols, Naples 1784

Szilas, L., 'Konklave und Papstwahl Clemens XIV (1769). Vorspiel zur Aufhebung der Gesellschaft Jesu am 21 Juli 1773' in *Zeitschrift für katholische Theologie* 96 (1974) 287–99

The Tablet NS 48 (24 Sept. 1892): 'The Late Cardinal Howard'

Taffs, Winifred, *Ambassador to Bismarck. Lord Odo Russell, first Baron Ampthill* London 1938.

Great Britain and the Holy See

—'The General Election of 1868' in *Contemporary Review* 188 (1955) 178–182

Tansill, Charles Callan, *America and the Fight for Irish Freedom 1866–1922*, New York 1957

Temperley, Harold, 'George Canning, the Catholics, and the Holy See' in *Dublin Review* 193 (1933) 1–12

Theiner, Augustin, *Geschichte des Pontificats Clemens IX. nach unedirten Staatsschriften ans dem geheimen Archive des Vaticans*, 2 vols, Leipzig, Paris 1853

Thils, Gustave, *L'Infallibilité pontificale. Source – Conditions – Limites*, Gembloux 1969

Thureau-Daugin, Paul, *La Renaissance Catholique en Angleterre au XIXe siècle*, II & III (1845–1892), Paris 1903–10

Times, 16 Sept. 1892: 'International Old Catholic Congress;' 'Death of Cardinal Howard'

Tournon, Comte de, *Études statistiques sur Rome*, 2 vols, Paris 1831

Treitschke, *Deutsche Geschichte im 19. Jahrhundert*, 5 vols., Berlin 1879–96

Tüchle, Hermann, 'In beiden Lagern. Deutsche Bischöfe auf dem Konzil', in *Hundert Jahre nach dem Ersten Vatikanum,* ed. Schwaiger, Regensburg 1970, 31–49

Ugolini, Patrizia, 'La politica estera del card. Tomasso Bernetti, Segretario di Stato di Leone XII (1828–1829)' in *Archivio della Società romana di Storia patria* 92 (1629) 213–320

Valsecchi, Franco 'L'Inghilterra e la questione italiana nel 1859. La missione Cowlèy (27 Feb.–10 Mar. 1859)' in *Archivio storico Italiano* 1968, 479–494

Veuillot, Eugène & Francois, *Louis Veuillot*, 4 Vols., Paris 1901–13

Villiers, George, *A Vanished Victorian. Being the Life of George Villiers, Fourth Earl of Clarendon, 1800–70*, London 1938

Wallace, Lillian Parker, *The Papacy and European Diplomacy 1869–1878,* Chapel Hill, North Carolina, 1948

Wappmannsperger, Leopold, *Leben und Wirken des Papstes Pius IX,* Regensburg 1878

Ward, Bernhard, *The Eve of Catholic Emancipation*, 3 vols., London 1911–13

Ward, James/Ghezzi, Bertil, 'Pius IX's Voltaire: Louis Veuillot and Vatican 1' in *Thought* 45 (1970) 346–370.

Ward, Wilfrid, *William George Ward and the Catholic Revival*, London 1893

—*The Life and Times of Cardinal Wiseman,* 2 vols., London 1900

—'Disraeli' in: *Dublin Review* 152 (1913) 1–20 and 217–231

Watt, E.D., 'Rome and Lord Acton: A Reinterpretation' in *Review of Politics* 28 (1966) 493–507

Weber, Christoph, *Kardinäle und Prälaten in den letzten Jahrzehnten des Kirchenstaates. Elite-Rekrutierung, Karriere-Muster und soziale Zusammensetzung der kurialen Fürungsschicht zur Zeit Pius IX. (1846–1878).* 2 vols. (Päpste und Papsttum 13) Stuttgart 1978

Weber, Margot, *Das I. Vatikanische Konzil im Spiegel der bayerischen Politik* (Miscellanea Bavarica Monacensia 28) Munich 1970

Weill, Georges, *Histoire de l'idée laique en France au XIXe siècle*, Paris 1925

Weinzierl-Fischer, Erika, 'Bismarcks Haltung zum Vatikanum und der Beginn des Kulturkampfes nach den österreichischen diplomatischen Berichten aus Berlin 1869–1871' in *Mitteilungen des Österreichischen Staatsarchivs* 10 (1957) 301–321

White, Ward W., 'Lord Acton and the Governments at Vatican Council I' in McElrath, *Lord Acton*, Louvain, 143–183

Whyte, John H., 'The Influence of the Catholic Clergy on Elections in 19th century Ireland' in *English Historical Review* 75 (1960) 239–259

—'The Appointment of Catholic Bishops in 19th century Ireland' in *Catholic Historical Review* 48 (April 1962), 12–32

Wiseman, Nicolas, *Recollections of the Last Four Popes and of Rome in their Times,* London 1859

Bibliography

Wöste, Karl, *Englands Staats-und Kirchenpolitik in Irland 1795–1869 dargestellt an der Entwicklung des irischen Nationalseminars Maynooth College* (Europäische Hochschulschriften, ser. 23 Theology) Bern/Frankfurt/Cirencester 1979

Woods, C.J., 'Ireland and Anglo-papal relations, 1880–85' in *Irish Historical Studies* 18 (1972) 29–60

Index

Aberdeen, George Hamilton Gordon 4th Earl of 68–70, 80–81, 142
Abraham, William, Bishop of Waterford 70–71
Acton, Charles Cardinal 81, 107
Acton, John 1st Baron 15, 134–40, 148, 150, 152–3, 159, 162–6, 168, 170
Adames, Nicolas, Bishop of Luxemburg 160
Albani, Alessandro Cardinal 20
Albani, Giovanni Cardinal 26
Albani, Giuseppe Cardinal 69–71
Altenhöfer, August 140
Altieri, Giambattista Cardinal 78–9
Antonelli, Giacomo Cardinal 92–4, 96–7, 99, 103, 108, 112, 122, 131, 149–50, 154–6
Antonelli, Leonardo Cardinal 24–5, 32, 34–5, 38, 44
Arco, Count Emmerich 163, 165
Arezzo, Tommaso 52
Arnim, Count Harry 156, 164
Arnold, Matthew 146–7
Arrigoni, Giuglio, Archbishop of Lucca 160
Aubin, Thomas 72–9, 81
Augustus, Prince, Duke of Sussex 26–7, 32, 34, 36, 59
Azara, José Nicolas de 30

Baader, Franz von 143
Bagehot, Walter 148
Baines, Peter Augustus, Bishop (Western district of England) 68
Banneville, Gaston Robert Marquis de 156–7
Bannon, John 99
Bartram, Richard 47
Beck, Franz August 142–3
Benedict XIV 17–9, 25, 29
Benedict XV 173
Bentinck, Lord George 84
Bentinck, Lord William 46–8, 50, 53–5
Berardi, Giuseppe Cardinal 131
Bernetti, Tommaso Cardinal 67, 71–6, 78, 80
Bernis, Francois de, Cardinal 21, 28, 34
Bernstroff, Count Albrecht 116, 155
Bilio, Luigi Cardinal 104, 106, 161
Bismark, Otto Prince 152, 155, 157–8, 166, 168, 171

Blake, Michael, Bishop of Dromore 57
Blatchford, Richard 99
Blennerhasset, Charlotte Lady 144–5
Borghese, Adelaide Princess 170
Borghese, Don Paolo 20
Borgia, Stefano Cardinal 37–8, 40–41, 44
Bowyer, George, M.P. 113
Brancadoro, Caesar Cardinal 38
Braun, Otto 140
Browne, Jacob, Bishop of Kilmore 76
Browning, Robert 146
Brownslow North, Bishop of Winchester 28
Buck, Victor de, S.J. 158
Bulwer, Sir Henry Lytton 92–3
Burke, Edmund, Bishop (Nova Scotia) 62
Burke, Edmund 28–30, 32–3
Burke, Richard 33
Bute, John Patrick Marquis of 122
Butler, Charles 46
Butler, George, Bishop of Limerick 150

Camden, John Marquis of 33, 36
Campanelli, Filippo Cardinal 25–6, 31
Campbell, John 1st Baron 146
Canning, George 26, 38, 46, 63–6, 69
Capaccini, Francesso Cardinal 63, 65, 71–7, 79–80
Caprara, Giovanni Cardinal 21
Cardella, Valerian, S.J. 129
Caroline, Princess of Wales 59
Cartwright, William Cornwallis 157
Casoni, Filippo Cardinal 38
Cass, Lewis 92–3
Castlereagh Robert Stewart Lord, Marquis of Londonderry 39–49, 42, 47, 51–2, 54, 58, 62–4
Caterini, Prospero Cardinal 131–2
Chateaubriand, Francois Vicomte de 69
Chigi, Flavio Cardinal 131
Chigi, Prince Mario 96
Clarendon, George Villiers 4th Earl of 54–5, 87, 93, 95, 111–2, 122, 143, 146, 149–59, 164, 166–7, 169
Clement XIII 19
Clement XIV 19–22
Clifford, Joseph, Bishop of Clifton 107–8

Index

Clinch, Bernard 40
Coffin, Robert Aston, Bishop of Southwark 108
Concanen, Luke 41
Conn, George 16
Connolly, John, Archbishop of New York 163
Consalvi, Ercole Cardinal 34, 50–3, 55, 57–63, 69
Cooke, Edward 55
Corsi, Cosimo Cardinal 160
Cornwallis, Charles Lord 39
Croker, John Wilson 89
Crolly, William, Archbishop of Armagh 78, 81, 85–6
Crotty, Bartholomew, Bishop of Cloyne 74
Cullen, Paul Cardinal, Archbishop of Dublin 87–8, 94–5, 111, 118–21, 123–5, 132, 138, 149–51, 161, 163, 166–7
Cumberland, Richard 30
Curtis, Patrick, Archbishop of Armagh 62–3, 73

Darboy, Georges, Archbishop of Paris 153, 158, 163
Daru, Napoleon Count 154–6
D'Azegilo, Cesare Taparelli Marchese 143–4
De Angelis, Filippo Cardinal, Archbishop of Fermo 160
Derby, Edward 13th Earl of 92–3, 98, 113–4
Derby, Edward 15th Earl of 114, 117–8, 149, 171
Derry, John Bishop of Clonfert 150
Dillon, Charles 12th Viscount 28
Disraeli, Benjamin 83–4, 87–7, 98, 103, 111–4, 116–8, 120, 122–7, 167
Dodwell, Edward 48, 54
Döllinger, Ignaz von 15, 128, 133–45, 148, 153, 159, 163–6, 170
Doergens, Heinrich 143
Douglas, John Bishop (London district) 29–30, 35, 39
Douglas, Sir Robert 16
Doyle, James, Bishop of Kildare 65–6, 73
Dromgoole, Thomas 61
Du Boys, Albert 164
Dundas, Henry 37
Dupanloup, Felix, Bishop of Oreléans, 130, 144–5, 148, 158, 162, 165

Edward VII 105, 173
Errington, George, Archbishop 108, 122
Errington, Sir George 116, 171–2
Erskine, Charles Cardinal 26, 30–34, 37–41, 44, 50, 71
Esmonde, Sir Thomas 57

Eyre, Charles, Archbishop of Glasgow 122

Faber, Frederick William 132
Faber, George Stanley 132
Fagan, Robert 41, 47–50, 53–4
Ferra, Luigi 50, 53
Feretti, Joseph Cardinal 98
Fitzgerald, Edward, Bishop of Little Rock 163
Fitzgerald, Edward Lord 45
Fitzgerald, Michael, Archdeacon, Rathkeale 135–6
Fitzherbert, Maria Anne 41
Flood, Peter 37, 39
Fontana, Francesco Cardinal 55, 60–61
Foran, Nicolas, Bishop of Waterford 70
Forbes, Alexander, Bishop of Dundee 138
Fornari, Raphael Cardinal 84, 92
Forster, W.E. 171
Francis I 57
Francis Josephus 173
Fransoni, Jacopo 78, 80–81, 86
Friedrich, Johannes 165
Frohschammer, Jakob 143

Garibaldi, Pietro, Mgr. 92
Garibaldi, Giuseppe 113, 116–8, 146
George II 17
George III 19–21, 25, 28, 30, 32–4, 38, 43
George IV 31, 47–8, 51, 58–60, 62–5, 69–71
George V 174
Gibbons, James Cardinal, Archbishop of Baltimore 101
Giustiniani, Jacopo Cardinal 71
Gladstone, William E. 103, 105, 107, 123–5, 134–5, 137, 139 142, 147, 149, 152–6, 158–9, 163–4, 166, 169–71
Gloucester, William, Duke of 19–22
Gonella, Eustace Cardinal, Archbishop of Viterbo 160
Gordon, Sir Robert 79–80
Gorham, George 90
Gormanston, Edward 1st Baron 39
Graham, Sir Robert 79
Grant, Ulysses, President 103
Grant, Thomas, Bishop of Southwark 107–8
Granville, William George 2nd Earl 152, 158–9, 169, 171
Grattan, Henry 45–6
Gray, John, Bishop (Western district of Scotland) 121–2
Gregorio, Emmanuele Cardinal de 69, 71–2, 74
Gregorovius, Ferdinand 158
Gregory, VII 144

Gregory XVI 69, 71–83, 103
Grenville, William Baron 29, 35, 42–3, 46
Grey, Charles 2nd Earl 46, 79–80
Guizot, Francois 147

Hamilton, Sir William 41
Hay, George, Bishop (Lowland district of Scotland) 35,
Hayes, Richard 55, 57–61
Haynald, Lajos Cardinal, Archbishop of Kalocsa-Bacs 163, 170
Hecker, Isaac 163
Hennessy, Sir John Pope 112–3, 120
Hippisley, Sir John Cox 22, 26–31, 34–9, 41–6, 57, 62
Hobart, Lord 42–3
Hohenlohe, Chlodwig Prince 142, 144
Honorius I 170
Howard, Edward Henry Cardinal 114–7, 120, 122, 171–2
Howard, Sir Francis 166
Howard, Sir Henry 173
Huber, Johann Nepomuk 141
Hussey, Thomas, Bishop of Waterford 30, 33–4, 36–7, 40–41

Inglis, Robert 86, 80
Innocent XII 146

James III 19, 26
Janssen, Johannes 137
Jervoise, Sir Harry Clarke 169, 171

Kain, John, Bishop of Wheeling 101
Kelly, Thomas, Archbishop of Armagh 173
Kenrick, Peter, Archbishop of St Louis 163, 170
Kestner, August 60, 63, 65, 67–9, 74–5, 77
Ketteler, Wilhelm Baron von, Bishop of Mainz 130, 162–4, 167–8
King, Rufus 99, 111

Lagrange, Francois 165
LaMarche, Jean, Bishop of St Pol de Leon 28, 31
Lambruschini, Luigi Cardinal 67, 78–82, 127
LaTour d'Auvergne, Henri Prince 116–7
Lavelle, Patrick 120–21, 150
Lavigerie, Charles Cardinal, Archbishop of Algiers 154, 172
Leahy, Patrick, Archbishop of Cashel 119, 149
Leist, Justus 60, 63
Leo XII 38, 48, 52, 64, 68
Leo XIII 116–6, 123, 131, 169–73
Liberatore, Matteo, S.J. 129–30, 161
Lipp, Joseph von, Bishop of Rottenburg 143
Litta, Lorenzo Cardinal 50, 55, 57, 60

Liverpool, Robert 2nd Earl of 66
Louis Philippe 83
Lowe, John 91
Lucas, Frederick, M.P. 87–8, 94–5
Ludwig I 49
Lynch, James, Bishop of Kildare 121–2
Lynch, Patrick, Bishop of Charleston 99
Lyons, Richard Viscount 93–6, 154

Macaulay, Thomas baron 142
MacCabe, Edward Cardinal, Archbishop of Dublin 171
MacClosky, John Cardinal, Archbishop New York 150
MacDonell, Alexander Bishop of Kingston, Ont. 62
MacEachern, Angus, Bishop of Charlottetown, P.E.I. 62
MacEvilly, John Bishop of Galway 150
MacHale, John, Archbishop of Tuam 76–9, 81, 86–7, 93–4, 113, 120, 150
MacMaster, James 145
Macpherson, James 35, 46
Magauly Cerati, Francesco Felippe 47
Mangan, Francis 45
Manners, Lord John 86
Manning, Edward Henry Cardinal, Archbishop of Westminster 90, 105–110, 115–6, 120–24, 127–32, 134–5, 137–9, 141, 143–6, 148–50, 152–3, 159–63, 168–9
Maret, Henri, Bishop 144
Markey, James 23
Martin, Konrad, Bishop of Paderborn 165
Mattei, Alessandro Cardinal 53
Maury, Jean Cardinal 28
Mayo, Richard 6th Earl of 123–4
Mazio, Raphael Cardinal 52, 58, 62
Merry del Val, Raphael Cardinal 173
Metternich, Klemens Prince 60, 78–80
Meurin, Gabriel, Bishop of Bombay 161
Meyrick, Frederick, 170
Milner, John Bishop (Midland district of England) 45–6, 49–50, 52–3, 55–6
Minghetti, Marco 164
Minto, Gilbert 1st Earl of 38, 42
Minto, Gilbert 6th Earl of 83--7, 89, 112
Molyneux, Sir Henry 116
Montalembert, Charles count 136, 142
Moriarty, David, Bishop of Kerry 119, 149–50
Moufang, Franz 130–31
Moylan, Francis, Bishop of Cork 39, 41–3, 52
Münster, Ernst Count 27, 34, 59, 67–70
Murat 47, 50, 54–6
Murdoch, John, Bishop (Western district of Scotland) 121
Murhard, W.H. 136
Murphy, John, Bishop of Cork 57

Index

Murphy, William 146
Murray, Daniel, Archbishop of Dublin 49, 57, 79, 82, 85−7

Napoleon 37, 46, 48−50, 54, 56
Napolen III 96, 98, 117−8, 132, 135, 152, 155
Nelson, Horatio Lord 41
Newman, John Henry Cardinal 105, 110, 128, 137, 171
Nicholson, Francis, Archbishop of Corfu 87
Norfolk, Henry 13th Duke of 68
Norfolk, Henry 15th Duke 172
North, Frederick 35−6

O'Connell, Daniel 46, 65, 67−8, 78−7, 82, 86
O'Conor, Charles 25
O'Conor, Owen 57
O'Hagan, Thomas Baron 138, 171
O'Leary, Arthur 23
Ollivier, Emile 155−6
Ompteda, Frederick Baron von 59−63,
Ompteda, Ludwig Baron von 74−5
Osbourne, d'Arcy Godolphin 174
O'Toole, Peter 92
Oxenham, Henry Nutcombe 137, 142

Pacca, Bartholomaeus Cardinal 38, 50−55
Palmerston, Henry 3rd Viscount 71, 73, 76, 83−5, 89, 97
Panzani, Gregorio 16
Parsons Lathrop, George 101
Patrizi, Constantin Cardinal 115
Peel, Sir Robert 66, 68, 79−81, 86
Pelham, Thomas, Earl of Chichester 44
Petre, William 12th Baron 81−2, 85, 88, 91−3
Piccirillo, Carlo, S.J. 131−3, 161
Pierce, Franklin K., President 105
Pitt, William 29−30, 32, 37−9, 41−44
Pius VI 22, 26−8, 31−2, 34−6, 41
Pius VII 38, 41, 43, 46−65
Pius VIII 69−76
Pius IX 15, 83−9, 91, 95−102, 104, 106, 108−9, 111−2, 116, 118, 124, 126, 128, 131−3, 134, 140, 144, 150, 161 163, 167−70
Pius X 70, 173
Pius XI 173
Plessis, Joseph, Bishop of Quebec 62
Ponsonby, John 1st Viscount 88
Portarlington, John Dawson 1st Earl of 28
Portland, 3rd Duke of 23, 33, 35−7 41−2, 46
Poynter, Bishop 55−6

Quarantotti, Giovanni 46, 49−51

Rampolla, Mariano Cardinal 173

Ranke, Loepold von 140
Rauscher, Joseph Cardinal, Archbishop of Vienna 145, 161
Reden, Franz von 63−5
Reisach, Karl Cardinal 108, 130, 139, 141
Riario-Sforza, Sisto, Archbishop of Naples 106
Richardson, Samuel 18
Rigg, J., Bishop of Dunkeld
Rotteck, Carl von 136
Ruffo, Fabrizio, Cardinal 38
Russell, John 1st Earl 83, 86−7, 89−91, 96−7, 99, 102−3, 107−9, 112−3, 139
Russell, Odo 1st Baron Ampthill 15, 96−99, 102, 105, 107−9, 112, 117−8, 122, 125, 129−31, 149−59, 163−6, 168−9, 173
Russell, Sir Theo Odo 173−4
Ryan, Patrick 150
Ryder, Henry Ignatius Dudley 129

Scherr, Gregor von, Archbishop of Munich 163
Scheeben, Matthias 129
Schwarzenberg, Friedrich Prince von, Archbishop of Prague, 145, 161
Senestréy, Ignatius von, Bishop of Regensburg 129, 159−61
Seward, William Henry 99
Seymour, George 72−4, 77
Sheil, Richard Lalor 90−92
Shrewsbury, John Earl of 89
Simmons, J. Linton A. 172−3
Simor, Johann Cardinal Archbishop of Gran 160
Simpson, Richard 163
Smith, Bernard 104−6
Somaglia, Giugio M. della, Cardinal 56, 64−5
Spalding, Martin John, Archbishop of Baltimore 101, 151
Stanley, Arthur P., Dean of Westminster 147−8
Strong, Josiah 102−4, 106−7
Strossmayer, Joseph, Bishop of Diakovar 170
Stuart, Andrew 31, 37, 165
Stuart, Charles Edward 17, 19−21
Stuart, Henry Benedict Cardinal, Duke of York 17−9, 21, 37−8 44, 71

Talbot, George, Mgr. 97, 105, 108−9, 128, 146
Taylor, Sir Brook 172
Temple, Sir William 85, 87
Tencin, Pierre Cardinal 18
Torrigiani, Luigi Maria Cardinal 19
Trollope, Anthony 146
Troy, John, Archbishop of Dublin 23−5, 31−4, 38−9, 41−2, 55, 58, 61
Trullet, Angelo 105

Ullathorne, William, Archbishop of Birmingham 108−9, 129, 144

259

Vaughan, William Cardinal, Archbishop of Westminster 129
Ventura, Goacchino 86
Veuillot, Louis 131–3, 145
Viale Prelá, Michele Cardinal 88
Victoria 83–4, 117, 124, 152, 172
Visconti Venosta 169
Volkmuth, Peter 143
Vorsak, Nicolas 165

Walpole, Sir Horace 18
Ward, William George 105, 128–30, 133–5, 137, 139, 142, 154–6, 148, 162

Weld Thomas Cardinal, 68, 70–72, 76, 78
Wellington, Arthur 1st Duke of 63, 66–8, 71, 115
Westmoreland, Henry 10th Earl 33, 66
Westmoreland, Henry 11th Earl 56, 59 62–4, 66, 68–70
Wilmers, Wilhelm, S.J. 161
Windham, William 26–7, 29–30, 32, 35, 37, 41–3
Wiseman, Nicholas Cardinal, Archbishop of Westminster 68, 71 84, 88–91, 97–8. 106, 108, 113, 115, 121, 137, 146

Zelada, Cardinal 26, 28–9, 31, 36